The Poems and Songs of Henry Hall of Hereford
A Jacobite Poet of the 1690s

LEGENDA

LEGENDA is the Modern Humanities Research Association's book imprint for new research in the Humanities. Founded in 1995 by Malcolm Bowie and others within the University of Oxford, Legenda has always been a collaborative publishing enterprise, directly governed by scholars. The Modern Humanities Research Association (MHRA) joined this collaboration in 1998, became half-owner in 2004, in partnership with Maney Publishing and then Routledge, and has since 2016 been sole owner. Titles range from medieval texts to contemporary cinema and form a widely comparative view of the modern humanities, including works on Arabic, Catalan, English, French, German, Greek, Italian, Portuguese, Russian, Spanish, and Yiddish literature. Editorial boards and committees of more than 60 leading academic specialists work in collaboration with bodies such as the Society for French Studies, the British Comparative Literature Association and the Association of Hispanists of Great Britain & Ireland.

The MHRA encourages and promotes advanced study and research in the field of the modern humanities, especially modern European languages and literature, including English, and also cinema. It aims to break down the barriers between scholars working in different disciplines and to maintain the unity of humanistic scholarship. The Association fulfils this purpose through the publication of journals, bibliographies, monographs, critical editions, and the MHRA Style Guide, and by making grants in support of research. Membership is open to all who work in the Humanities, whether independent or in a University post, and the participation of younger colleagues entering the field is especially welcomed.

ALSO PUBLISHED BY THE ASSOCIATION

Critical Texts
Tudor and Stuart Translations • *New Translations* • *European Translations*
MHRA Library of Medieval Welsh Literature

MHRA Bibliographies
Publications of the Modern Humanities Research Association

The Annual Bibliography of English Language & Literature
Austrian Studies
Modern Language Review
Portuguese Studies
The Slavonic and East European Review
Working Papers in the Humanities
The Yearbook of English Studies

www.mhra.org.uk
www.legendabooks.com

Litany

From a Peace with new Taxes, and yet w:th out Trade
For the Good of Old England by a Forreigner made
From building his House till his Debts be first paid
Libera

From an Act lately made (y:t there ne're was (y:t Peer on't
To free us from Danger, w:n there was no fear on't
That hangs up poor Mortalls before they can hear on't

From a Senate (y:t whilst they're w:th one hand a giving
In (y:t space of a Creed, are w:th t'other receiving
Whilst by (y:t fine Trade half (y:t house get their living
From Times that are harder by much than (y:t Weather
From a Czar that's a Strolling (y:t knows yet whither
And has with himself too, his Climate brought hither

From Generous Claret brought o're from (y:t Rhine
From making a Peace with a wicked Design
Since wee're freinds w:th (y:t French, but at warrs w:th
theirdine

Libera nos

Hall's autograph text of his satirical song 'From a peace with new taxes and yet without trade' (with verses 3–4 run together), reproduced, with permission, from the National Library of Wales manuscript designated O1d in the present study.

The Poems and Songs of
Henry Hall of Hereford

A Jacobite Poet of the 1690s

❖

OLIVER PICKERING

l

LEGENDA

Modern Humanities Research Association

2022

Published by Legenda
an imprint of the Modern Humanities Research Association
Salisbury House, Station Road, Cambridge CB1 2LA

ISBN 978-1-83954-139-1

First published 2022

Copy-Editor: Charlotte Wathey

CONTENTS

❖

To the memory of
Chris Sheppard, 1947–2014,
librarian and friend

PREFACE AND ACKNOWLEDGEMENTS

❖

I first encountered Henry Hall more than thirty years ago when Chris Sheppard, then Sub-Librarian in the Brotherton Collection at the University of Leeds, suggested I catalogue, individually, the English poems to be found in the Collection's substantial holdings of seventeenth- and eighteenth-century verse manuscripts. Thus began the project known as BCMSV (Brotherton Collection Manuscript Verse), which developed into a freestanding online database of some 5,500 records until in due course it became part of the amalgamated web-based catalogue of Special Collections holdings at Leeds. The BCMSV records themselves had, by that time, been added (by invitation) to the *Union First Line Index of English Verse* established by the Folger Shakespeare Library.

Two of the Brotherton Collection manuscripts in question, Lt 6 and Lt q 5, were wholly devoted to Henry Hall's poems, while some of his political satires cropped up in other, miscellaneous manuscripts. I became intrigued, as also by the evidence for Hall's fondness for revising his poems. In particular it became clear that he had drawn on two earlier tributes to his friend Henry Purcell (both contained in MS Lt q 5) when composing the public tribute to Purcell published in 1698 in *Orpheus Britannicus*. I wrote up this finding for *The Library* in 1994 and — already alerted by the kindness of Peter Beal to the existence of autograph manuscripts of Hall's verse in the National Library of Wales — said in a footnote that I was preparing a checklist of all the poems and songs attributed to Henry Hall. I allowed myself a further confident statement in 2004, when I claimed in my short account of Hall for the *Oxford Dictionary of National Biography* that a study entitled 'The Poems and Songs Attributed to Henry Hall of Hereford' was 'forthcoming'.

The length of time taken to bring the present work to a conclusion has at least enabled me to take advantage of the continuing expansion of the *Union First Line Index,* and of other developing online finding aids, to trace many other occurrences of poems and songs attributed to Hall. The checklist that forms Appendix A of this study records as many as 152 separate items, while Appendix C lists a total of ninety-nine manuscript sources (additional to Lt 6, Lt q 5, and the manuscripts in Aberystwyth), and Appendix D, sixty-three printed sources (often with music) stretching from 1685 to my cut-off date of 1721. Many of these manuscript and printed sources contain multiple items attributable to Henry Hall.

This count of manuscript and printed sources, and indeed of poems and songs, is not of course final. Other witnesses will certainly come to light, and this is both desirable and inevitable in a study of this kind, which has sought to track the mainly anonymous circulation of the output of a relatively minor but prolific provincial poet, many of whose verses were clearly found attractive by his contemporaries.

Whether an edition of Hall's complete output is justifiable is a different matter, and the present study restricts itself to presenting an edited selection of twenty-five poems.

I am indebted to the Arts and Humanities Research Board (as it then was) for a Research Exchange Award, which allowed me to spend the first three months of 2001 based in the School of English at Leeds. This period of time was invaluable in allowing me to engage thoroughly with the material for the first time, assisted by the expert guidance of Paul Hammond. Since then I have received much help and encouragement from other colleagues, near and far, including John Barnard, Peter Beal, Roger Davis, Andrew Hadfield, Elizabeth Hageman, Harold Love, Peter Holman, Martin Holmes, Hilton Kelliher, Tom Lockwood, Michael Londry, Bill Mitchell, Carolyn Nelson, and Bryan White. For permission to quote extensively from manuscripts in their care I am grateful to the National Library of Wales and to the Brotherton Collection, Leeds University Library, as I am also to the Governing Body of Christ Church, Oxford, and the National Library of Wales for permission to reproduce manuscripts in Henry Hall's hand. And I am of course greatly indebted to the staff of numerous other British, Irish, and American libraries for patiently answering research queries about their manuscript holdings, especially where I was unable to visit in person. I should like to record special thanks for much help provided by Hereford Cathedral Library and Archives (where I always received a warm welcome), and as ever to Janet Pickering.

When quoting from manuscript sources I generally follow scribal spelling but apply modern capitalization and punctuation practice. The main exception is that when citing individual Henry Hall poems by first line (my usual mode of reference) I use the regularized form adopted in Appendix A if a particular manuscript is not at issue. When quoting from printed sources of the period I again apply modern capitalization practice.

Oliver Pickering
Menston, West Yorkshire, June 2022

LIST OF ABBREVIATIONS

❖

Manuscript sigla

B1	Leeds University Library, Brotherton Collection, MS Lt q 5
B2	Leeds University Library, Brotherton Collection, MS Lt 6
C	Manuscript copies of Hall's poems within 'Cooke', below
M	University of Minnesota, MS 690235f
O1, O2 etc.	The Ottley manuscripts of Hall's verse, held within the National Library of Wales, Pitchford Hall (Ottley) English Literary MSS (uncatalogued)

Other abbreviations

BL	British Library, London
Bodleian	Bodleian Library, Oxford
Cameron	*Poems on Affairs of State: Augustan Satirical Verse, 1660–1714.* V: *1688–1697,* ed. by William J. Cameron (New Haven, CT: Yale University Press, 1971)
CCED	*Clergy of the Church of England Database,* <https://theclergydatabase.org.uk>
CELM	*Catalogue of English Literary Manuscripts, 1450–1700,* <https://celm-ms.org.uk>
Cooke	William Cooke, 'Biographical Memoirs of the Custos and Vicars Admitted into the College of Hereford from 1660 to 1823', mid-19th century (Hereford Cathedral Library, HCA 7003/4/3, unpaginated)
CUL	Cambridge University Library
DM	Cyrus Lawrence Day and Eleanore Boswell Murrie, *English Song-Books, 1651–1702: A Bibliography with a First-Line Index of Songs* (London: Bibliographical Society, 1940)
Ellis, VI	*Poems on Affairs of State: Augustan Satirical Verse, 1660–1714.* VI: *1697–1704,* ed. by Frank H. Ellis (New Haven, CT: Yale University Press, 1970)
Ellis, VII	*Poems on Affairs of State: Augustan Satirical Verse, 1660–1714.* VII: *1704–1714,* ed. by Frank H. Ellis (New Haven, CT: Yale University Press, 1975)
ESTC	*English Short-Title Catalogue* <estc.bl.uk>.
Foxon	David F. Foxon, *English Verse, 1701–1750: A Catalogue of Separately Published Poems, with Notes on Contemporary Collected Editions,* 2 vols (London: Cambridge University Press, 1975)

HCA	Hereford Cathedral Archives
Hunter	David Hunter, *Opera and Song Books Published in England, 1703–1726: A Descriptive Bibliography* (London: Bibliographical Society, 1997)
New Grove Dictionary	*The New Grove Dictionary of Music and Musicians*, 2nd edn, ed. by Stanley Sadie and John Tyrrell, 29 vols (London: Macmillan, 2001)
ODNB	*Oxford Dictionary of National Biography* <https://www.oxforddnb.com>
Pickering 1994	Oliver Pickering, 'Henry Hall of Hereford's Poetical Tributes to Henry Purcell', *The Library*, 6th series, 16 (1994), 18–29
POAS, II–IV	The original volumes II–IV of *Poems on Affairs of State / State Poems*, issued in 1703, 1704, and 1707, respectively
RISM	*Répertoire international des sources musicales* <https://rism.info>
UL	University Library
Union First Line Index	*Union First Line Index of English Verse* <https://firstlines.folger.edu/>

CHRONOLOGY

❖

1656	Likely year of Henry Hall's birth, in New Windsor, Berkshire.
1660	Restoration of the monarchy; Charles II becomes king.
Mid-1660s	Hall a chorister at the Chapel Royal, Whitehall.
1672	Hall leaves the Chapel Royal.
1674–79	Organist and Lay Vicar Choral at Exeter Cathedral.
1679	Appointed Assistant Organist and Vicar Choral at Hereford Cathedral.
Mid-1680s	Likely period of Hall's first marriage, to Catherine Woolmer, and of the birth of his son, Henry.
1685	Death of Charles II; James II becomes king.
1685	Hall's first published song, 'Haste Charon haste', vilifying Oliver Cromwell.
1688	James II flees to France.
1688	Hall succeeds to the position of Organist at Hereford.
1689	Accession of William III and Mary II, as joint monarchs.
1689–97	Nine Years' War against France, the stimulus for many of Hall's political songs and satires.
1690	Death of Catherine Hall, 19 January.
1694	Death of Mary II.
1694	Hall contributes poems to the *Gentleman's Journal*.
1695	Death of Henry Purcell.
1696	Hall marries Anne Gower, 28 October.
1698–1702	Hall publishes poems paying tribute to Henry Purcell, John Blow, John Dryden, and Henry Playford.
1700	Death of John Dryden.
1700	Birth and death of Hall's daughter, Anne.
1702	England again declares war on France (the War of the Spanish Succession); death of William III; Queen Anne succeeds to the throne; Hall's poems become more celebratory.
1703–07	Certain of Hall's political satires included in volumes of *Poems on Affairs of State*.
1704–06	Hall contributes poems to Henry Playford's *Diverting Post*.
1707	Hall dies, 30 March.

INTRODUCTION

❖

Henry Hall (*c.* 1656–1707), Organist of Hereford Cathedral from 1688 until his death, is a largely unknown writer. He is far better documented in modern scholarship as a composer of serious, mainly liturgical music. He has an entry in the *New Grove Dictionary* — where he is described as 'undoubtedly the most distinguished among the lesser composers of Purcell's generation' — and he is treated at some length in Ian Spink's *Restoration Cathedral Music.*[1] His ode on the death of Henry Purcell, 'Yes, my Aminta, 'tis too true', was recorded by the Parley of Instruments in 1992.[2]

In contrast, most of Hall's verse, comprising songs, satires, epistles, and many occasional poems, has either long been forgotten or, remaining largely in manuscript, never entered circulation. A miscellaneous portion of it appeared in print during his lifetime or shortly afterwards, sometimes with accompanying music. Sir John Hawkins included brief examples when discussing Hall's place in musical history in 1776.[3] Thereafter his verse generally disappeared from view until some of the satires were published by William J. Cameron in 1971 as part of the Yale edition of *Poems on Affairs of State.* A single, four-line squib by Hall ('Rejoice ye fops your idol's come again') was included in *The New Oxford Book of Seventeenth Century Verse* of 1991.[4]

One problem that has complicated previous discussion and assessment of Hall has been that of correct attribution, a problem that affects much late seventeenth-century English verse, particularly satires, at the highest levels of poetic activity; it is only natural that the difficulty should be greater where minor writers are concerned. In Hall's case his rather nebulous literary identity has been exacerbated by a long-standing scholarly tendency to attribute much of his verse-writing to his son and successor as Organist, Henry Hall the younger (*d.* 1714).[5] I have discussed this matter elsewhere, showing that there is no contemporary evidence for the poet widely referred to as 'Henry Hall of Hereford' being other than a single author, no evidence for Hall's son having composed poetry — he would in any case have been too young to have written most of it — and no reason to argue that bodies of 'serious' and 'light' verse, or of 'serious' and 'light' music, must each be the work of a different writer or composer (as was Hawkins's belief).[6] Nevertheless, even with the son put to one side, the problem of establishing the output of such a versatile writer as Henry Hall is considerable. Much of the verse attributed to him is concentrated in a group of interrelated manuscripts in the National Library of Wales (the Ottley manuscripts) and in two manuscript compilations held in Leeds University Library's Brotherton Collection. A minority of these poems are, however, found widely distributed in contemporary manuscript and printed sources where they are usually not attributed to Hall and are occasionally attached to the names of other writers. Conversely, there are numerous poems attributed to Hall in such sources that do not occur in the abovementioned collections of his verse. There are particular problems with the songs set to music, where it is often unclear if the attribution to Hall refers only to the music or also to the words.

Establishing Henry Hall's poetic identity is, nevertheless, a worthwhile activity, as he is a lively and accomplished writer of great interest. He was a disenchanted Jacobite and crypto-Catholic, educated at the Chapel Royal but earning his living in the provinces as Organist of Hereford Cathedral. Evidently a highly sociable man, used to performing, it is likely that he began turning out verses for convivial social occasions, probably initially to entertain Hereford's College of Vicars Choral, of which he was a central member. A number of his poems show that such activity extended to the Black Lion Club in the city, and it is clear that he was one of a like-minded circle of friends opposed to the overthrow of James II and to what he portrays as the puritanical local civic establishment. Numerous poems make fun of these opponents and their families, while others make very clear his distaste for the Oath of Allegiance to William and Mary, which he appears to have taken through gritted teeth. One verse epistle, 'Dunned by the bells I rose from bed', shows that his social circle, at least for gambling purposes, extended to the local land-owner James Brydges, Lord Chandos, but Hall's rakish depiction of himself as an inveterate wencher — more skilled at love-making than at cards — may be a deliberate exaggeration, for effect, when addressing a social superior. Given Hall's great poetic facility and no little literary skill, it is not impossible that aspects of the personality exhibited in poems addressed to other members of his circle were similarly constructed, but the eight epistles sent to his close friend Dr Broughton, though high-spirited, appear to show him writing candidly about matters of mutual interest and concern.

The surviving manuscript collections of his verse demonstrate that Hall built up a considerable local reputation, and it appears that certain of his poems — or poems attributable to him — began to circulate at an early stage, with or without his involvement. He clearly had no difficulty turning out verses; he was prolific, and his range was wide. Not only epistles and social satires, but also drinking songs, love songs, riddles, celebratory poems, personal tributes, political satires, miscellaneous poems on contemporary events and personalities, local and otherwise: his corpus encompasses all these genres, and others. The range of his verse forms is also very wide, encompassing four- and five-stress couplets, stanzas exhibiting many varieties of rhyme scheme and metre, and irregular odes.

Writing (as it seems) primarily for social purposes and from within a manuscript culture, Hall may often have been relaxed about the fate of his verse, particularly the occasional poems, but he was not altogether indifferent. As will be seen, he relied on Dr Broughton to keep copies of some of his output, and another friend, Archdeacon Adam Ottley, appears to have enlisted him in an effort to assemble a compilation of his work. Moreover, at various times in his life he sent poems to London to be printed, and he may well have played a part in the public circulation of his numerous political satires, a body of material of which any assessment of his literary achievement has to take account.

The political satires, however, return us to questions surrounding Hall's poetic identity, because W. J. Cameron, when editing several for the Yale *Poems on Affairs of State*, found it hard to believe that 'the organist of Hereford' could really have been responsible for them; and it is indeed the case that, with a single exception, the contemporary (non-Hereford) manuscript miscellanies into which some of them were widely copied never name Hall as author. Given that most of the satires in question appear in one or other of the deliberate compilations of his poetry, and generally match his other work stylistically, Cameron's position is contested in what follows, as would be expected. But it has to be acknowledged that Hall is accused in a contemporary literary satire (*A Tryal of Skill; or, A New Session of the Poets*, 1704) of passing off another writer's work as his own, and there are occasional suspicions elsewhere that he may at times have taken a casual attitude to what was or was not 'his' verse. Collaboration with or borrowing from others — not so unexpected if verse writing is a social activity — may be one explanation.

The approach adopted in this study is that (lacking other evidence) the occurrence of a poem within one ore other of the main manuscript collections equates to a high degree of presumption of Hall's authorship. Appendix A lists 152 poems or songs attributed or attributable to him. The selected edition that follows the main discussion of his work comprises annotated texts of twenty-five poems, grouped as follows: Epistles to Dr Broughton, Epistles to other friends, Political satires, and Love poems. These will, I hope, serve as a lively and varied introduction to his work.

Notes to the Introduction

1. Bruce Wood, 'Hall, Henry (i)', in *New Grove Dictionary*, X, 699–700; Ian Spink, *Restoration Cathedral Music* (Oxford: Clarendon Press, 1995), pp. 267–71.
2. It is included in *Odes on the Death of Henry Purcell*, The Parley of Instruments, dir. by Roy Goodman and Peter Holman (Hyperion Records, CDA66578, 1992).
3. Sir John Hawkins, *A General History of the Science and Practice of Music*, 5 vols (London: for T. Payne & Son, 1776), V, 19–22.
4. *The New Oxford Book of Seventeenth Century Verse*, ed. by Alastair Fowler (Oxford: Oxford University Press, 1991), p. 792 (beginning 'Rejoice you sots, your idol's come again').
5. The main culprit has been the old *Dictionary of National Biography*, which had separate entries for the two men, but the tradition was established in the later eighteenth century by Hawkins. Both Cameron, in his volume of *Poems on Affairs of State*, and Fowler, in *The New Oxford Book of Seventeenth Century Verse*, regard the author whose work they are printing as Henry Hall the younger.
6. Pickering 1994, pp. 18–22. The *New Grove Dictionary* continues to describe Hall the younger as also a poet, as does the entry for Hall senior in Philip H. Highfill Jnr, Kalman A. Burnim, and Edward A. Langhans, *A Biographical Dictionary of Actors, Actresses, Musicians, Dancers, Managers, and Other Stage Personnel in London, 1660–1800*, 16 vols (Carbondale: Southern Illinois University Press, 1973–93), VII, 22–23.

CHAPTER 1

❖

Hall's Life and Milieu

Henry Hall, born *c.* 1656, is said by the antiquarian Anthony Wood (1632–95) to have been the son of Captain Hall of New Windsor, Berkshire, but documentary evidence for his parentage is lacking.[1] The Captain Hall in question (1616–72, 'Captain' apparently being his given name) was a member of the borough council at New Windsor from 1662, and served two terms as Bailiff.[2] When young, presumably in the mid-1660s, Henry Hall became a chorister at the Chapel Royal in Whitehall under the tutelage first of Henry Cooke and then of Pelham Humfrey, who were successively (1660–72 and 1672–74) Masters of the Children of the Chapel.[3] One of Captain Hall's known sons, also called 'Captain' (b. February 1651/52), is recorded as a chorister at St George's Chapel, Windsor, in 1668–69.[4]

Hall made friends at the Chapel Royal with Henry Purcell (1659–95), a fellow-chorister, and he may, like him, have studied composition with Pelham Humfrey. He retained a deep affection and respect for Purcell in later life, and wrote poetical and musical tributes to him after his death.[5] Hall, who would have received a good general education while attached to the Chapel Royal — as is clear from the wide range of classical, literary, and historical allusion in his poems — remained there until his voice broke, probably in the later part of 1672.[6] On 17 January 1673 Humfrey was granted 'the usual clothing [...] for the use of Henry Hall, late child of the Chapel, whose voice is changed and is gone from the Chapel', together with the customary sum of £30 (with effect from 25 December 1672) for his former pupil's maintenance.[7] At some point, with Purcell as fellow-pupil (and so perhaps in 1673–74), Hall studied composition with John Blow, whom he refers to as his teacher in his tribute to Purcell prefaced to Book 1 of *Orpheus Britannicus* (1698):[8]

> *Apollo's* harp at once our souls did strike,
> We learnt together, but not learnt alike:
> Though equal care our master might bestow,
> Yet only *Purcell* e'er shall equal *Blow*:
> For thou, by Heaven for wondrous things design'd,
> Left'st thy companion lagging far behind.

In 1700 Hall wrote commendatory prefatory verses to Blow's own collection of songs, *Amphion Anglicus* (beginning 'A public good, does public thanks require'), where he describes him as 'his esteemed friend'.

Hall was very likely the 'Mr Hall' who was temporarily Organist of Wells Cathedral in the early summer of 1674.[9] In August of that year, at the age of approximately eighteen, he was appointed Organist and Lay Vicar Choral at Exeter Cathedral, but he remained there fewer than five years, leaving in the earlier part of 1679 with an undischarged debt.[10] On 27 June 1679, however, he was appointed to Hereford Cathedral, where he was granted £20 a year ('till the Chapter shall further provide for him) to carry out duties specified as 'assisting the Organist, instructing the choristers thrice a week, and assisting in the Chore'.[11] On the same day, at the special request of the Dean and Chapter, the College of Vicars Choral agreed to allow him board and lodging, and on 27 December 1679, by which time he was described as 'clericus' — he had evidently quickly obtained holy orders — he was elected a Vicar Choral for the usual probationary period of one year.[12] The post was perpetuated in January 1681,[13] and he remained a Vicar Choral until his death. On 30 December 1679 Hall was also elected to the vicarage ('in the choir') of St Mary, as was the custom for each new Vicar Choral, and the records show that in subsequent years he was installed in the similar vicarages of Holme Lacy, St Agnes, and Cawkbridge.[14]

The speed of Hall's acceptance at Hereford, following his seemingly unhappy experience at Exeter, may be linked to the fact that Herbert Croft, Bishop of Hereford 1661–91, had been Dean of the Chapel Royal from 1668 to 1670.[15] Hall, however, had to be content with the position of Assistant Organist until 15 September 1688, when he was elected Organist following the death of John Badham.[16] Both before and after this date he played his part in the running of the Vicars' College, serving as Auditor (i.e. of accounts) in 1682–84, 1688–90, 1692–94, 1702–03, and 1706–07, and as Chapter Clerk in 1686–88 and 1703–04.[17] In 1694, in common with the other Vicars Choral, he responded to a series of questions about the current state of the College put by the Dean and Chapter as part of an official visitation, seemingly admitting some responsibility for shortcomings in the teaching of the choristers.[18]

Hall was evidently married by the mid-1680s, as his son Henry, who succeeded him as Organist and held the post until his own death in January 1714, is said to have been twenty-seven or twenty-eight when he died, which would place his birth in the period 1685–87.[19] Hall's wife, Catherine, presumably Henry's mother, died on 19 February 1690 at the age of twenty-one, and was buried the following day.[20] On 28 October 1696 Hall subsequently married, by licence, Anne Gower, 'singlewoman'; their infant daughter, Anne, baptised on 1 August 1700, was buried on 5 October of the same year.[21] Dean and Chapter records of 1699 and 1700 show Hall occupying a house 'built by James Jacket' behind the cathedral just to the south of Castle Street, where he presumably lived with his family.[22] He died on 30 March 1707, and was buried in the cloisters of the Vicars College.[23]

Hall composed a considerable amount of music to be sung in Hereford Cathedral. Ian Spink, discussing his sacred music, notes the survival of at least twenty-eight anthems, five services, and a *Benedicite*, figures that the *New Grove Dictionary* increases to at least thirty-five anthems and eight services (in whole or in part), adding also three chants and a number of instrumental works.[24] Many manuscript copies survive, and there is no doubt that Hall's work was widely admired.[25]

'In Henry Hall,' writes Spink, 'Hereford acquired a real composer — the most distinguished between John Bull and S. S. Wesley'.[26] Spink shows that Hall's first anthems date from his time in Exeter, supporting the view that he was already well known as a composer by the time he joined the staff at Hereford.[27] According to Spink, 'By the waters of Babylon was the one that circulated most widely, and one of the earliest. The text was a poignant reminder of Charles II's exile, as also of the Church's during the Interregnum.'[28]

Particularly famous was Hall's Te Deum in E flat which from early in the eighteenth century was paired with a Jubilate by William Hine, Organist of Gloucester.[29] Anthony Boden, historian of the Three Choirs Festival which in its original form linked Gloucester, Hereford, and Worcester from c. 1715, wrongly attributes this Te Deum to Hall the younger, and from this builds the notion that Hall the younger and Hine were the first beginners of these joint music meetings, c. 1709.[30] Further, he suggests that the forerunner of the festival may have been a Hereford Vicars Choral music club that possibly dated back to the 1670s: 'The College Hall and Library were finished by 1 September 1676, and soon, perhaps immediately, the hall became the focus for a college musical club — a venue for the performance and enjoyment of secular music'.[31] Paul Iles develops the theme: '[Hall] took a full part in the social life of the college and wrote secular music for the evening concerts of the vicars which were popular and held regularly in the college hall after it had been refurbished.'[32] The story of the College music club appears to derive from William Cooke's nineteenth-century memoir of one of Hall's fellow-Vicars Choral, Peter Senhouse (who resigned his position in 1705), whose 'name [is] recorded as a regular performer in the musical club, at that time existing in the College'.[33] Cooke, however, makes no mention of a college musical club in the course of his memoir of Hall himself.[34]

One of Hall's songs certainly refers to a monthly club where music was sung, but the toast is to a secular patron, Lord Chandos, who is likely to have been present.[35] The social club that Hall mentions by name is the Black Lion Club, evidently held in the Black Lion inn that still stands near Wye Bridge in Hereford.[36] It is this club with which Cooke, seemingly drawing on local tradition, links Hall when censuring him for failing to concentrate on his 'greater duties':

> Since among his poems several songs are inserted, it is presumed, that in his twofold capacity of poet & musician, he had no difficulty in giving proof of this combination of talent, by carolling those ditties in the Black Lion Club Room, where frequent carousals are spoken of, among his jovial & political associates; compeers of those nightly revelries, which most likely diverted his thoughts from the greater duties of his professions, for which education & genius had so abundantly qualified him.[37]

Cooke, nevertheless, admits that Hall had talent as a poet, even if much of the interest of his poems 'has long since passed away':

> But exclusive of musical talents, Mr Hall had a great turn for poetry, & making allowance for the depraved taste & ribaldry, in those days so prevalent, there is considerable point & humour in his verses; a portion of which, collected

in a M.S. volume, is at this time in possession of the Revd. Wm Cooke of Bromyard. Much however of the interest, connected with these poems, has long since passed away; local, personal & political allusions are at best, but ephemeral: as a rank Jacobite the denunciations against Wm the 3rd, as Prince of Orange, can at this time only raise a smile; if we consider the earnestness & acerbity, which crowd his rhymes, on the ingratitude of the nation towards James the 2nd and his family.[38]

And he takes the trouble to copy out, at the end of his memoir, portions of Hall's poetic tributes to Henry Purcell and his publisher Henry Playford (as published in volumes 1 and 2, respectively, of *Orpheus Britannicus*) as well as five poems from the manuscript then in his own possession, to be discussed in Chapter 3.2 below.[39]

Hall seems to have started writing secular poems and songs in the mid-1680s, and many of them leave no doubt that he was indeed 'a rank Jacobite', as well as a High Churchman tending strongly to Catholicism, despite his employment in a Protestant cathedral. His earliest known secular composition is 'Haste Charon haste 'tis Nol commands thy speed', a song vilifying Oliver Cromwell, which was published in 1685 and achieved wide circulation. More overtly political poems begin to appear in the later 1680s; thus a poem celebrating 'the birth of the Chevalier', i.e. James Stuart, son of James II and Mary of Modena, can be dated to 1688. The crucial year of 1689 sees a barely disguised Jacobite catch ('Let disputes of the law and religion alone'), along with Hall's first datable anti-Williamite song ('The clergy and the laymen'), satirizing the establishment for replacing James II with William III. The 1690s then see Hall fully in opposition to both the monarchy and government, as detailed in the discussion of his political satires in Chapter 7 below. His witty drinking song 'To our monarch's return', dated in one manuscript to 1691, provides a light-hearted foretaste of what is to come:

> To our monarch's returne we our glasses advance,
> Whilst one is in Flanders and t'other in France.
> In this Catholick circle I'm sure there are none
> But wishes to kings and to each man his owne.
> Here here's to that king, let him come, let him come,
> Send one into England and both are at home. (B1, p. 11)[40]

Hall's many local poems also mark him out as an oppositional figure, but — as Cooke's memoir indicates — a decidedly convivial one. He was certainly no recluse, and his verse epistles to friends are explicit about his drinking, gambling, and, it would appear, womanizing. While it is of course possible that Hall deliberately exaggerated the rakish and scandalous sides of his life for his friends' benefit, the detail is such that a sense of a real urban locality comes through to the modern reader. The earliest datable poem relating to Hereford life (1686) is a light-hearted satire on a clergyman turned local politician John Abrahall (Chapter 3.2 (a) below), and a good many of these local poems are addressed to, or treat of, named Herefordshire people, including other members of the cathedral clergy.

Hall's own intimates are unsurprisingly of a like-minded political and religious persuasion, in particular his close friend Dr Broughton, to whom he addresses eight outspoken epistles, which are among Hall's most striking and successful poems. They show him speaking freely and confidentially to a fellow-Jacobite in a markedly informal, conversational style, and their contents and manner of expression (sometimes bawdy or obscene, often satirical) make it certain that they were not for public consumption. Hall's themes in these poems may be summarized as drinking and Hereford nightlife, sickness and the problems of advancing age, the business of writing, and Jacobitism and other oppositional political stances. One of the poems, however, makes it clear that Hall's beliefs did not necessarily stretch to rigid principles, as it describes how he and Broughton swore the oath of allegiance but avoided signing it:

> Clean and unclean, like beasts i'th Ark,
> Some sett their hand and some their mark,
> Tho' this wee wisely both forbore,
> And wou'd not sign, altho' we swore;
> For words will soon blow off again,
> Whilst letters oft too long remain. (B1, p. 71)

'Dr Broughton' is very likely the Dr Edward Broughton of 'Kingstone', i.e. Kington, some fifteen miles north-west of Hereford, who married Lucy Jones, granddaughter of Sir Philip Jones, royalist commander in Monmouthshire during the Civil War.[41] Her brother Edward, an army officer, is very likely the 'Captain Jones' who is co-recipient with Broughton of the epistle 'From college hall where thirsty vicar', in which Hall arranges to meet them for lunch in Kington.[42] Broughton himself is mentioned in two other of Hall's local poems, including 'The Black Lion Club in 1690'.[43] As will be seen, he is central to Hall's verse-making in that he apparently maintains a copy of all the poems Hall sends him.

Others within Hall's circle included the Revd Dr Adam Ottley (1655–1723), from a landed royalist family, who was a prebendary of Hereford Cathedral and Archdeacon of Shropshire.[44] His apparent part in assembling the Ottley manuscripts of Hall's verse is discussed in Chapter 2.3. Another intimate was James Brydges, eighth Baron Chandos (1642–1714), mentioned above as honoured by a toast at a musical club, who was the recipient of one of Hall's most memorable and scurrilous epistles, 'To your Lordship after being ruin'd at play' ('Dunned by the bells I rose from bed'). Brydges had a seat at Wilton Castle, ten miles to the south of Hereford; his son James Brydges, later first Duke of Chandos, who became an MP for Hereford in 1698, was credited with helping Ottley become Bishop of St David's in 1713.[45] Similar conversational epistles are addressed to a fellow-Jacobite Edmund Addis, one of them requesting a gift of cider with which to drink the health of the exiled James II, the other (which survives in two versions) reminding him of a promise to send wood for his fire.[46] Other light-hearted poems reveal his friendship with particular members of the cathedral clergy. Thus he warmly congratulates Dr Richard Bulkley on becoming a canon, and sends a witty apology to Dr Ottley for missing a dinner invitation because of the previous night's overindulgence.[47] Tom Broad, a fellow Vicar Choral, is affectionately characterized as 'changeable' in the little poem 'For missing thee how canst thou Burren blame'.

Hall's social and ideological adversaries, in contrast, are the members of the local Low Church and Puritan-inclined Hereford establishment, who are mocked without restraint. Two such poems take a panoramic satirical view of the city's various professions,[48] but three others are directed at members of the Mathews family, against whom Hall clearly has a recurring animus.[49] 'Old' Mathews, a Williamite apothecary and receiver of taxes, also features in one of the epistles to Dr Broughton.[50] But Hall does not hold back from attacking, or lampooning, his own clerical colleagues. One poem is a short, sharp indictment of a Mr Lewis for committing 'a spirituall sort of fornication' by accepting 'of Mr Bensons prebendary', while a Mr Page is castigated twice, once in a light-hearted satire in which he is depicted as torn between marrying for love or money, once more bitterly ('But fools are marked for all mankind to know') as the main target in a poem about undeserved promotion.[51] The subject of the fiercest of these attacks on fellow-clergy is no less than the serving Bishop of Hereford, Gilbert Ironside (1632–1701), a strong supporter of William III, whom Hall accuses of hypocrisy in glorifying the memory of the executed Charles I while siding against his son, the exiled James II.[52] There is, it should be said, no evidence that Hall was ever in trouble with the authorities for his beliefs or behaviour.

Other poems reveal friendships with people in the wider region. The Charles Hoskins to whom Hall writes in praise of Edmund Waller ('Not Waller read and yet so well to write') is no doubt the man recorded as Vicar of Longhope, Gloucestershire, in 1700–03.[53] The humorous poem 'If rhyme for rhino could atone' (wishing that verse could be a substitute for money), addressed to a friend and creditor, Robin Clayton, suggests that Hall may possibly have visited Bristol for the annual St Paul's fair. A definite excursion was to the hill known as the Skerrit (Skirrid-Fawr), some seventeen miles south-south-west of Hereford, near Abergavenny ('Whether those hills that round you spread'). The resulting lengthy poem, describing the climb and his ensuing reflections, is addressed to Hall's host, Captain Nicholas Arnold of Llanthony (b. 1669, son of the Whig politician John Arnold), who sold his inherited estates to the Harleys of Brampton Bryan.[54]

That Hall habitually travelled in Wales is suggested by a reference in his one known letter, written to a younger Adam Ottley (nephew of Dr Ottley) in July 1704. Hall writes here that he 'was unluckily making the Welch tour' when Ottley's own letter reached Hereford. Ottley was a student at Balliol College, Oxford, at the time, and there are indications from manuscript sources (noted in Chapter 4) that Hall's work had some circulation in the Oxford area.[55] Two other poems, relating to Brecknock and Ludlow, respectively, attest to Hall's interest in local political matters (the latter is a lively account of the breaking up of a Presbyterian meeting).[56] Rather different is a good-natured, bawdy satire 'On Jane Mayo the Fatt Woman of Newant' (i.e. Newent in Gloucestershire), but Hall also takes the opportunity to allude to the cost of William III's war with France.[57]

Less clear are his friendships in London. In his tribute to John Blow contributed to *Amphion Anglicus* in 1700, Hall describes himself as cut off physically from the capital, making out he never visited:

> Thus while you spread your fame, at home I sit,
> Amov'd by fate, from melody and wit,
> Whe[re] British bard on harp a treban plays,
> With grated ears I saunter out my days.
> Shore's most harmonious tube, ne'er strikes my ear,
> Nought of the Bard, besides his fame, I hear:
> No chaunting at St. Paul's, regales my senses,
> I'm only vers'd in Usum Herefordensis.[58]

This self-portrait of isolation is, however, almost certainly a conceit. Hall, as Organist of Hereford Cathedral, is likely to have needed to visit London periodically in a professional capacity, to keep up to date with developments in church music, and if so he no doubt took advantage of being in the capital in other ways. His poem 'The progress of the stage', dated 1699 in two manuscripts, reveals detailed knowledge of the London theatre, suggesting personal experience, and it is very likely that Hall maintained links with Purcell and Blow.[59] He clearly established a lasting friendship with the music publisher Henry Playford, as will be seen. The 1690s also saw verses by him published in London, and there is no doubt at all, from references in many of his poems, that he kept himself well informed about the political and cultural scene in the capital during William and Mary's reign ('the Bard', in l. 6 of the above quotation, is almost certainly John Dryden, even though he died in May 1700).[60]

The accession of Queen Anne in 1702 markedly changed Hall's attitudes — opposition to the Crown is at once replaced by adulatory loyalty — and evidently strengthened his links with London. He published numerous poems in Playford's journal *The Diverting Post* (see Chapter 5.3 below), and his inclusion in *A Tryal of Skill; or, A New Session of the Poets* (London, 1704) as a highly unsuitable candidate for 'the poetical crown' (see Chapter 9.1) shows that he became a known member of London's literary scene. The poem 'We heard indeed of glorious actions done', describing the celebrations in the capital following Marlborough's victory at Blenheim in August 1704, suggests that Hall himself was present,[61] and he wrote songs celebrating the success of English arms abroad, some of which were successfully sung in the theatres.[62] In addition, suggests Ian Spink, 'the belligerent text [of 'Blessed be the Lord my strength'] suggests that this may have been a thanksgiving anthem for one of Marlborough's victories'.[63] Hall wrote fulsomely in praise of the new queen. The ode 'Bless Albion bless thy stars above' is a full-scale panegyric, with vocal and instrumental parts, which survives in his autograph in the library of Christ Church, Oxford (see Chapter 6.1). And on the evidence of the singers named in the surviving manuscript score of his church service in G minor, Spink judges that it 'must have been sung in the Chapel Royal early in the eighteenth century', which suggests that Hall may even have re-established links with the court.[64] It would seem that Hall, politically, was at last content.[65]

Notes to Chapter 1

1. For Wood's assertion, see Bodleian, MS Wood D. 19(4), f. 65r: 'Hall Henry was borne at New Windsore in Berks. brid up in the Kings Chappell & was afterwards organist of Hereford — now living 1695 aged 40 or thereabouts', with, above this entry, 'son of Captane Hall or Tayla' and 'his xtian name', with a line indicating that this phrase refers to 'Captane'. Hawkins, *A General History of the Science and Practice of Music*, v, 19–22, possibly drawing on Wood, similarly begins his account of Hall: 'Henry Hall, born about the year 1655, the son of Capt. Henry Hall, of New Windsor'. An important manuscript source for Hall's life is Cooke, Memoir 10, 'Henry Hall', which records that Hall died in 1707 'in his 51st year'. A somewhat different version of the memoir, kept with B1 (the major manuscript collection of Hall's poems), gives the date of his death as 1706, and adds 'He was about 50 years of age'. For the Rev. William Cooke (1785–1854), see his obituary in the *Gentleman's Magazine* for December 1854, pp. 631–32.

2. See *The First Hall Book of the Borough of New Windsor*, ed. by Shelagh Bond, Windsor Borough Historical Records Publications, 1 (Windsor: The Royal Borough of New Windsor, 1968), p. 169. The original *DNB* entry for Hall states that Captain Henry Hall [*sic*] 'was connected with Windsor between 1657 and 1675', referring to R. R. Tighe and J. E. Davis, *Annals of Windsor, Being a History of the Castle and Town*, 2 vols (London: Longman, 1868); that work refers first to 'Captaine Hall' (pp. 281, 284, 303) and then (for the year 1673) to 'Captain Samuell Hall' (p. 362), possibly a different man.

3. For an account of the Chapel Royal, its masters and choristers, including mention of Hall, see Spink, *Restoration Cathedral Music*, especially the introductory pp. 101–05.

4. See *The First Hall Book of the Borough of New Windsor*, ed. by Bond, p. 169. I am grateful to St George's Chapel Archives for confirming the references to Captain Hall junior in the Chapter Acts at Windsor, and to Berkshire Record Office for providing me with references to the baptisms of Captain Hall senior's four known children from the parish registers of New Windsor (St John the Baptist).

5. Pickering 1994, and Oliver Pickering, 'Henry Hall of Hereford and Henry Purcell: A Postscript', *The Library*, 7th series, 3 (2002), 194–98.

6. See Spink, *Restoration Cathedral Music*, p. 104.

7. Quoted from *Records of English Court Music*, ed. by Andrew Ashbee, 9 vols (Snodland, Kent: Andrew Ashbee, 1986–96), I: *1660–1685*, 121. See also Spink, *Restoration Cathedral Music*, p. 104: 'For the period up to about 1685 the normal procedure was for a lad to be given a suit of clothes and maintenance for a year or two until a suitable job could be found.'

8. *Orpheus Britannicus: A Collection of All the Choicest Songs for One, Two and Three Voices, Compos'd by Mr. Henry Purcell* (London: for Henry Playford, 1698), p. vi ('Musick the chiefest good the gods have giv'n'). Blow did not succeed Humfrey as Master of the Children until the latter's death in July 1674, but he was clearly associated with the Chapel in the preceding years; see Spink, *Restoration Cathedral Music*, p. 121.

9. See Watkins Shaw, *The Succession of Organists of the Chapel Royal and the Cathedrals of England and Wales from c. 1538* (Oxford: Clarendon Press, 1991), p. 288, quoting from Wells Cathedral accounts ('£5 to Mr Hall, late organist, for two months allowed him in the accounts for 1674'). Shaw provides a valuable and well-documented summary of Hall's career as a cathedral organist.

10. Ibid., p. 111, citing Exeter Cathedral Library, Chapter Acts 7 (1667–77) and Chapter Acts 8 (1677–86). I am grateful to the Cathedral Library and Archives for providing me with specific references to entries for 8 August and 29 August 1674, relating to Hall's appointments (D&C 3560), and for 15 February and 14 June 1679 relating to his resignation ('upon Mr Henry Hall's deserting his Place of Organist') and the discharge of his debt (D&C 3561). Hall had been formally admitted as a Lay Vicar at Exeter on 31 August 1674 (Vicars Choral, VC 1, f. 39v).

11. HCA 7031/3, Chapter Act Books, 20 Jan 1600/01–10 Feb 1712/13, p. 372.

12. The College granted Hall 'the benefitt of Diett in their Comon hall or dineing roome, & beere as themselues have at meale times, with a Convenient Chamber of the Vacant ones to be repaired & furnished at his owne charge, & this to continue untill he be settled & better provided for [...] & that he shall pay for his beere at other buttry hours' (HCA 7003/1/3, Act Books of the Vicars Choral, Act Book 'B', 1 Sept 1660–20 Sept 1717, p. 83).

13. HCA 7003/1/3, pp. 85 and 90; HCA 7031/3, pp. 379–80. A note in the Dean and Chapter Acts for 3 December 1680 (HCA 7031/3, p. 388) records 'that Mr Dean will allow to Mr Henry Hall organist five pounds and that the Canons will allow him three pounds'.

14. HCA, 7003/1/3, pp. 85, 98, 144, and 182. Cf. the entries for Hall in *CCED*. Hall was present when the Bishop of Hereford made an official Visitation of the Cathedral in 1680 and again in 1703; on the first occasion he is described as 'curatus' and Vicar of St Mary's, on the second as 'clericus' and Vicar of St Agnes's (Herefordshire Archive Service, Hereford Diocesan Call Books, HD5/2 and HD5/4). The entry for Hall in the *New Grove Dictionary* says that he 'took deacon's orders in 1698 to qualify himself, it is said, for some preferment in the gift of the Dean and Chapter of Hereford', a statement duplicated in the entry for Hall in Andrew Ashbee and others, *A Biographical Dictionary of English Court Musicians, 1485–1714*, 2 vols (Aldershot: Ashgate, 1998), I, 534, but the surviving documentary evidence does not appear to support this assertion. However, the poem 'A Tryal of Skill', published in 1704 and discussed in Chapter 9 below, does refer to Hall as a (scandalous) deacon.

15. However, Cooke, 'Henry Hall', p. [1], asserts that Hall's original introduction to Hereford 'originated in an engagement made with Mr John Badham, Organist & Vicar Choral, "to officiate as assistant Organist at a salary agreed upon"'. He comments also that Hall's position at Exeter was, 'it may be supposed, very superior to that which he ultimately accepted at Hereford'.

16. HCA 7031/3, p. 470. During this period, seemingly in the early 1680s, he got to know the amateur musician Ambrose Warren (born *c.* 1656), who, writing about his early life in the preface to his *The Tonometer* ([Westminster], 1725), records that 'After some time more, I was called into Herefordshire, about 9 miles from that city, where I frequently convers'd with Mr Henry Hall the Organist etc. to my farther improvement of skill' (p. 7). I owe this reference to Peter Hoare.

17. HCA 7003/1/3, pp. 102, 107, 120, 129, 134, 139, 153, 187–88, and 194. However, his name does not appear in the College act book as frequently as that of some of his colleagues. A recent account of the College in this period, highlighting the 'convivial and worldly reputation' enjoyed by the vicars, is provided by Philip Barrett, 'The College of Vicars Choral', in *Hereford Cathedral: A History*, ed. by Gerald Aylmer and John Tiller (London: Hambledon, 2000), pp. 441–60 (pp. 452–54), and see also Paul Iles, 'Music and Liturgy since 1600', in *Hereford Cathedral*, ed. by Aylmer and Tiller, pp. 398–440 (pp. 405–06).

18. 'They have heretofore bin neglected, but of Late I'm sure they are taught as they ought to be, I mean to sing only' (HCA 3396, Vicars Choral, Visitations. Answers of the Vicars Choral to the questions of the Dean and Chapter at a visitation, 30 Oct 1694, which includes Hall's autograph written response). The answers given by Hall's fellow vicars to the same question are not entirely complimentary; cf. Iles, 'Music and Liturgy since 1600', p. 406.

19. No record of the birth of the younger Henry Hall is known; the relevant registers for the parish of St John the Baptist, the parish applicable to residents within the Cathedral precincts (cf. the next footnote), do not survive for the period before 1687, nor do records of Cathedral baptisms during the 1680s. The authority for the younger Hall's age at death appears to be Cooke, 'Henry Hall', p. [5]. The original *DNB* entry for Henry Hall the elder states that Hall had another son in the person of the court violinist William Hall (d. 1700), but this speculation has been discounted by modern musicological research; see Ashbee and others, *A Biographical Dictionary of English Court Musicians, 1485–1714*, I, 536–37, which shows that William Hall was active professionally from as early as 1671. The story that William was Henry Hall's son is perpetuated in Iles, 'Music and Liturgy since 1600', p. 407.

20. For the inscription on her memorial stone, formerly in the north aisle of the cathedral, see F. T. Havergal, *Monumental Inscriptions in the Cathedral Church of Hereford* (Hereford: Simpkin, Marshall, 1881), p. 37; for her burial, HCA D858/1/2, Baptisms, Marriages and Burials in the Parish of St John the Baptist, 1687–1727, p. 3. Catherine Hall was the daughter of Robert Woolmer, gentleman, of Worcestershire, and his wife Cecilia, who was the daughter of Fitzwilliam Coningsby of Hampton Court and his wife Cecilia, daughter of Henry Neville, Lord Bergavenny. For the memorial inscription to Cecilia Woolmer, who died shortly before her daughter in October 1689, see Havergal, p. 26. No record of the marriage of Henry and

Catherine Hall has been discovered, but it very likely took place in 1685 in Hereford Cathedral, the marriage registers for which survive only from 1686.

21. The marriage licence bond, signed by Hall, is dated two days previously and survives as HCA 7002/2/7, Dean's Peculiar Marriage Bonds, 1683–1699, f. 95. The bond states that the marriage will be solemnized in the church of St Peter's, but it took place in Hereford Cathedral: see HCA D859/1/1, Registers of Marriages in the Cathedral, 1686–1727, p. 30. For the baptism and burial of the infant Anne Hall see HCA D858/1/2, p. 15.

22. See HCA 3934/5 and 3936/3, Dean and Chapter property leases that define the property in question in relation to Hall's house. Vicars College records show that in 1687 he took over the room formerly used by the Custos of the College, agreeing to 'paying 10s to common rents, etc.' (HCA 7003/1/3, p. 126); this may have been in addition to a family home.

23. Richard Rawlinson, *The History and Antiquities of the City and Cathedral-Church of Hereford* (London: for R. Gosling, 1717), p. 60, records the wording of a memorial stone, which is no longer present: 'At the West End of the Cloisters, belonging to the College of Vicars, on a Gravestone, is this Inscription: Mr. Henry Hall, | Organist, died | March the 30th' (cf. Havergal, *Monumental Inscriptions in the Cathedral Church of Hereford*, p. 37). His burial the following day is recorded in HCA D858/1/2, p. 37. For his son's appointment as Organist in his place, see HCA 7031/3, p. 572 (25 June 1707); he is described as 'nunc vel nuper opidi de Ludlow', suggesting he may have been Organist there. For the inscription on Henry Hall the younger's tombstone, also no longer extant, see Rawlinson, p. 105, and Havergal, p. 37.

24. Spink, *Restoration Cathedral Music*, pp. 267–71; *New Grove Dictionary*, x, 699–700. Iles, 'Music and Liturgy since 1600', p. 407, attributes two of the services to Henry Hall the younger, but this is implicitly discounted by Spink and the *New Grove*. The latter two authorities, however, admit that he may have been responsible for a small number of the anthems.

25. The online catalogue *RISM* (<https://rism.info> [accessed 11 October 2021]) currently lists over 280 sources for compositions attributed to Hall (overwhelmingly in manuscript), including 156 instances of anthems, 74 of services, and 21 of sacred songs.

26. Spink, *Restoration Cathedral Music*, p. 267.

27. Ibid., pp. 255, 268; Iles, 'Music and Liturgy since 1600', p. 405.

28. Spink, *Restoration Cathedral Music*, p. 268. Musical examples, including an extract from *By the Waters of Babylon*, are given on pp. 269–70. For a briefer discussion of Hall's church music, including another musical example, see Ian Spink, 'Church Music II: From 1660', in *The Seventeenth Century*, ed. by Ian Spink, Blackwell History of Music in Britain, 3 (Oxford: Blackwell, 1992), pp. 97–137 (pp. 108–09). For Hall's secular vocal music, see Chapter 6 below. *The New Grove Dictionary* lists a number of pieces of surviving secular instrumental music by Hall, including airs, a chaconne, a hornpipe, and an overture.

29. Spink, *Restoration Cathedral Music*, p. 267, and also p. 26: 'The pairing [...] took [Hall's] work to almost every English cathedral in the eighteenth century.' Cooke, 'Henry Hall', pp. [3–4], summarizing Hall's church music, records that Hine and his pupil William Hayes added the *Jubilate* (Hine) and a *Cantate Domino* and *Deus misereatur* (Hayes) to Hall's *Te Deum* in the mistaken belief that he had not completed the service. The version of Cooke's memoir kept with B1 (see n. 1 above), goes into more detail, stating 'while they generally lamented the *socordia* [i.e. sloth or laziness] which habitually influenced him from finishing his original design', they added their own compositions 'as an earnest of their high opinion of the Te Deum' (p. [2]). It may be noted that the two versions of the memoir differ considerably in their accounts of the state of Hall's then surviving manuscripts and the work done to try to recover his music.

30. Anthony Boden and Paul Hedley, *The Three Choirs Festival: A History*, 2nd edn (Woodbridge: Boydell Press, 2017), pp. 7–8, and also Anthony Boden, 'The Three Choirs Festival', in *Hereford Cathedral*, ed. by Aylmer and Tiller, pp. 461–69 (pp. 461–62). Cf. Iles, 'Music and Liturgy since 1600', p. 407.

31. Boden and Hedley, *The Three Choirs Festival*, p. 4.

32. Iles, 'Music and Liturgy since 1600', p. 407.

33. Cooke, 'Biographical memoirs', no. 17. Hall supplied the musical setting for Senhouse's song 'Beauty the painfull mother's prayer', published in *Deliciae Musicae* [...] *The Second Book* (London: Henry Playford, 1695), pp. 9–12.

34. Cf. Elizabeth Chevill, 'Clergy, Music Societies and the Development of a Musical Tradition: A Study of Music Societies in Hereford, 1690–1760', in *Concert Life in Eighteenth-Century Britain*, ed. by Susan Wollenberg and Simon McVeigh (Aldershot: Ashgate, 2004), pp. 35–54, where Hall is mentioned (p. 40) merely as one of a number of distinguished musicians among the Hereford Vicars Choral. Ron Shoesmith, '"A Brave and Ancient Priviledg'd Place": The Hereford Vicars Choral College', in *Vicars Choral at English Cathedrals: 'Cantate Domino' — History, Architecture and Archaeology*, ed. by Richard Hall and David Stocker (Oxford: Oxbow, 2005), pp. 44–60, is devoted almost entirely to architectural history.

35. 'Where still once a month we all merrily meet', from the song 'How happy is this day'.

36. The poem in question is the longer of the two poems beginning 'Whilst Clio rehearses' (= 'Whilst Clio rehearses' [i]), entitled 'The Black Lion Club in 1690'.

37. Cooke, 'Henry Hall', pp. [4–5].

38. Ibid., p. [4]. He also remarks, apparently appreciatively, on 'Mr Hall's peculiar antithetical style of writing' (p. [7]).

39. It may be noted that Cooke, 'Henry Hall' (pp. [9–10]), takes issue with Sir John Hawkins's allocation of some of Hall's verse to his son (cf. the Introduction, above).

40. For B1, see Chapter 3.1 below.

41. John Burke, *A Genealogical and Heraldic History of the Commoners of Great Britain and Ireland*, 4 vols (London: Bentley, 1836–38), IV, 732. The Broughton family was well established in the town, and produced a succession of doctors; see [Richard Parry], *The History of Kington, by a Member of the Mechanics' Institute of Kington* (Kington: Humphreys, 1845), esp. pp. 229–30.

42. Burke, *A Genealogical and Heraldic History*, IV, 732.

43. 'Whilst Clio rehearses' [i]. The other is 'Poor Pug had loosed or broke his chain'.

44. J. D. Davies, 'Ottley, Adam (bap. 1655, d. 1723), Bishop of St David's', in *ODNB*.

45. Noted in Davies's *ODNB* entry for Dr Ottley. Hall may have known another local MP, Paul Foley, to whom he addresses a short, more formal poem on his election as Speaker of the House of Commons in 1695 ('The vacant chair the House no sooner view'). Cf. also the humorous dialogue 'Here have I lain Lord knows how many years', which alludes to Foley and his fellow MP, James Morgan.

46. 'Although to petition has been out of fashion' and 'Though rhyme of late's no more my talent', the latter reworked into 'This Sir's to you the second time'.

47. 'Though now in station to adjust us', to Bulkley, and 'Ye gods what gulfs are set between', to Ottley.

48. 'All you who delight and take pleasure in painting' and 'Whilst Clio rehearses' [i].

49. 'Poor Pug had loosed or broke his chain', 'Since coat of arms your race ne'er wore', and 'Whilst Clio rehearses' [ii].

50. 'As in a pump we water put'. Mathews is also a named target in 'Whilst Clio rehearses' [i] and an implicit one (as an apothecary) in 'All you who delight'.

51. The poems in question are 'If Reverend Sir', 'Sylvia and Leah were of widows a pair', and 'The sly designing patriot in convention'. Named in this last poem as 'John', he must be the John Page who was appointed to a prebend in Hereford Cathedral in 1692. According to *CCED* it was he, rather than Mr Lewis, who succeeded George Benson.

52. 'How durst thou thus disturb that surly shade'. The poem takes the form of an argumentative dialogue between Ironside and the ghost of the Parliamentarian soldier Colonel John Birch, who led the successful attack on Hereford during the Civil War.

53. See *CCED*.

54. See the entry in the online *Dictionary of Welsh Biography* <https://biography.wales/article/s-ARNO-LLA-1500> [accessed 22 October 2021].

55. For the younger Adam Ottley, see Joseph Foster, *Alumni Oxonienses: The Members of the University of Oxford, 1500–1714*, 4 vols (Oxford: Parker, 1891–92), III, 1096. For both the Ottleys, see further E. D. Jones, 'The Ottley Papers', *National Library of Wales Journal*, 4 (1945–46), 61–74.

56. ''Tis odd indeed indeed 'tis wondrous odd' and 'On the borders of Salop still stands a find town'.

57. The poem begins 'Whilst thus I sing the largest creature'.

58. John Blow, *Amphion Anglicus: A Work of Many Compositions for One, Two, Three and Four Voices* (London: printed by William Pearson for the author, 1700), p. ii.

59. The poem begins 'Your primitive players first acted in a cart'; see Chapter 4.2 below.
60. 'Shore', in l. 5, is a reference to a member of the trumpet-playing Shore family.
61. The poem is entitled 'On the Standards taken at Bleinheim; being carried to Westminster-Hall, and there Hung Up', and includes the line 'But when we saw the triumphs stream from far'.
62. 'Hark to the war the trumpet sounds' and 'To our arms on earth and seas'.
63. Spink, *Restoration Cathedral Music*, p. 271. It should be noted that such public praise did not preclude Hall writing light-hearted satires of Marlborough for the enjoyment of his friends; see the discussion in Chapter 8 of the three poems contained in his 1704 letter to Adam Ottley.
64. Ibid., p. 268.
65. Taken at face value, the six-line poem 'When I at Rome the Jubilee shall see', comparing an unnamed nobleman's glory to that of the Catholic Church's Jubilee of 1700, suggests that Hall hoped to travel to Rome, but the possibility, given his situation in Hereford, would seem to be remote. Cf. his ballad 'Come beaus virtuosos rich heirs and musicians' (Chapter 6), in which he imagines the tumultuous social scene in Rome at the time of the Jubilee.

CHAPTER 2

❖

The Nature of
Hall's Verse-Making

Hall fits well the category of 'social poet' as discussed in 1999 by Margaret Ezell, except that many of her late seventeenth-century examples relate to manuscripts compiled for friends or family of gentry status (or above) living well away from urban areas.[1] Hall fits the category because he writes verse to give pleasure to himself and his social circle, and because he is writing, for the most part, from within a manuscript culture, with little or no thought of print publication.

Verse-making evidently came naturally to Hall. As a result, many of his poems are short, 'occasional', and textually unstable. Apparently lacking literary ambition — there is no sign that he ever wished to see his collected verse in print — he would seem to have been unconcerned about the textual fate of his poems once he had given copies to friends. There is nothing in the way of autograph remains save for the few copies existing within the Ottley papers. From the evidence of the two posthumous manuscript collections of his verse held in Leeds (to be discussed in Chapter 3 below) it is likely that 'user publication' may often have occurred as recipients made further copies for private circulation, with resulting changes and corruptions.[2] In some cases it is clear that authorial revision has taken place, with the result that more than one version gets into circulation, with no apparent authorial concern. There is also no sign that those friends or admirers who made collections of his poems ever tried to achieve posthumous print publication for him. To quote Ezell, 'There was no need to go to the expense of having a printer produce one's texts in order to secure an audience as long as there was a social literary environment.'[3] Hall undoubtedly had his social readership, during his life and after his death.

Of course one factor that would have prevented print publication of a significant number of Hall's poems was their outspokenly satirical content, which was no doubt a determining factor in what appears to have been the overwhelmingly anonymous circulation of much of his poetic output.[4] This applies both to the merciless local satires, in which Hall's targets are usually explicitly named, and the 'national' ones, which mock and/or castigate the monarchy and government from an undisguised Jacobite viewpoint. As will be seen, many of the latter group of poems — which had a far wider manuscript circulation than the former — use established literary forms and are altogether more serious in their style of writing. Harold Love, discussing scribal publication, posits that manuscript poems that possess the 'required state of finish' to be seen in public might be regarded as having a published status; that is to say, 'when the text in question has adopted a polished public style or employs a recognizably public form of discourse, such as the political satire, the pedagogical treatise or the formal epistle'. The means by which the satires in question were put into circulation are quite unknown, but it may be that Hall himself was (or indeed was not) involved in what Love calls an 'initiatory' act of (manuscript) publication: 'when a private possessor of a text (who [...] will not necessarily be the author or even acting in accordance with the author's wishes) facilitates its first going forth into the world'. Love remarks also that 'the survival of a text in a large number of manuscript copies is certainly evidence for its having been published', even though not in printed form.[5] Here as elsewhere the extent of Hall's agency in publishing his work in this way can only be a matter of speculation; and not only in this way, because a total of ten 'national' satires attributable to Hall, all of them surviving within the main manuscript collections, were printed in volumes of *Poems on Affairs of State* between 1703 and 1707, the year of his death.[6]

It is not impossible that Hall had a hand in circulating the satires because the above characterization of his writing as belonging within a manuscript culture is not the whole truth of the matter. The majority of his poems remained in manuscript, and many of these stayed private, but Hall was certainly involved in the print publication of others. Later chapters will discuss these cases, but an outline can be given here.

In the eyes of the world (and perhaps himself), Hall was principally a professional musician, and it is with songs that his work first gets into print, usually accompanied by music and often with his name attached. The earliest occurrence is in 1685, when his royalist song 'Haste Charon haste' was included in Henry Playford's anthology, *The Theater of Music*, presumably as the result of musical contacts. Playford was subsequently an agent in the publication not only of other songs by Hall but of 'tribute' poems that Hall contributed to both volumes of *Orpheus Britannicus* (honouring first Purcell and then Playford himself) and to a collection in memory of John Dryden; the poem on Purcell was based on two earlier manuscript tributes to his former fellow-chorister. And in the early years of the eighteenth century Hall sent a sequence of short, often topical poems up to London to be printed in issues of the *Diverting Post*, in which Playford had a large hand. This might have been on Hall's own initiative or at Playford's instigation. A decade earlier, in 1694, and quite differently, Hall had had verse riddles published in Peter Motteux's *Gentleman's Journal*, as well as certain other short poems. In this case the initiative would certainly seem to have been his alone — on the reasonable assumption that he would have seen the *Journal* on sale in Hereford — but his name was generally disguised by the witty pseudonym 'Mr De la Sale', copying the common practice of many of the contributors, rather than representing an attempt by Hall to suppress knowledge of his authorship. Ezell remarks on how, from the 1690s, periodicals 'were promising venues for writers who were in search of a publisher for short pieces — such as single poems, essays, and epistles — but were expecting little or no payment', and discusses the *Gentleman's Journal* in particular.[7]

The above summary provides a useful indication of the range of Hall's writing, and may indicate a growing confidence in his use of print, though apparently stopping far short of any ambition to publish a collection. It also characterizes the essentially 'occasional' character of his verse, lacking any sense of a programme of work, and this may be because he was busy professionally, as organist and composer. Even though William Cooke, in his nineteenth-century memoir, blames Hall's frequent carousals and 'carolling' at the Black Lion Club for having 'divested his thoughts from the greater duties of his Professions', it is likely that his musical responsibilities occupied the greater part of his time.

2.1. Verse Style: Hall's Epistles to Friends

As for Hall's writing style (not the main focus of this study) the sheer variety of his verse forms will become apparent in what follows, particularly during discussion of the political satires. The present excursus is mainly limited to remarks about the private epistles he addressed to friends, especially Dr Broughton (all eight of the latter are edited below). These show Hall at his most distinctive, mingling narrative, debate, and reflection in a highly informal, conversational way. His chosen verse form for these poems is, unsurprisingly, couplets, varying between Hudibrastic four-stress lines for light-hearted subjects and slower pentameters for more serious material.

It is clear from Hall's verse in general that he is both well read and up to date with literary developments, and indeed he explicitly praises Samuel Butler and John Dryden, the two major poets whom one would suspect to have acted as inspirations or models for him. Butler is singled out in Hall's 'Of all the bards that e're were bent on fame' (addressed to the humorous balladeer John Grubb): 'Butler himselfe who taught us first the way | To marry rhyme and make burlesque obey' (ll. 27–28),[8] while Dryden, in the poem 'Not Waller read and yet so well to write', is held up as the natural successor to Edmund Waller and as one who will eventually be seen to have surpassed him:

> Dryden, who now our great example is,
> Rose to that height by makeing Waller his [...]
> Dryden alone can equallize his witt,
> But Dryden, well you know, is liveing yett.
> We to the quick are sparing of that praise
> Whome dead it crowns with everlasting bays.
> But when that poett shall i'mortall be
> And gett, what oft he gave here, imortallity;
> With how much wonder will his work be read!
> And then of Wallers selfe it will be sayd,
> He equal'd liveing and surpasses dead.[9]

Hall is writing here in the style of pentameter verse epistle commonly adopted when the purpose is also to praise the addressee, as in numerous poems by Dryden, although the praise in this case (rather awkwardly expressed) is principally bestowed on Waller and Dryden rather than the literary efforts of his friend. The poem in question is noticed further in Chapter 5.2 below in the context of Hall's explicit 'praise' poems, which include tributes to the composers Henry Purcell and John Blow, as well as a lengthy poem lamenting Dryden's death. As will be seen, his published poem on Purcell contains a clear verbal reminiscence of Dryden's 'To the Memory of Mr Oldham'.

Hall is likely to have felt a particular bond with Dryden given the latter's conversion to Catholicism and refusal to sign the Oaths of Allegiance. It is possible that he knew the older poet's only venture into octosyllabics, his verse epistle to Sir George Etherege beginning 'To you who live in chill degree | (As map informs) of fifty-three', which was published in 1691 along with the two epistles from Etherege to the Earl of Middleton that Dryden was imitating.[10] Hall's four-stress epistles are, however, closer in style to the Hudibrastic epistles of the young Matthew Prior, namely 'To Dr F. ...' ('To clear the Brain or purge the thought'), the 'Letter to J...' ('My little Wid. to you I send'), and the two epistles to Fleetwood Sheppard, all to be dated 1689–90.[11] These are in a lower register than the showy epistles linked to Etherege, and are characterized, like Hall's compositions, by their attention to narrative detail:

> When Crowding Folks, with strange ill Faces,
> Were making Legs, and begging Places;
> And some with Patents, some with Merit,
> Tired out my good Lord D — t's Spirit:
> Sneaking, I stood, among the Crew,
> Desiring much to Speak with You,
> I waited, while the Clock struck Thrice,
> And Footman brought out fifty Lies;
> Till Patience vext, and Legs grown weary,
> I thought it was in vain to tarry:
> But did Opine it might be better,
> By Penny-post to send a Letter.
> Now, if you miss of this Epistle,
> I'm balkt again, and may go Whistle.[12]

Compare Hall's account of a somewhat similar situation in one of the epistles he addresses to Dr Broughton, entertainingly complicated (in what is no more than arranging to meet for lunch) by a typical sequence of asides, including a swipe at the country's treatment of Charles I and James II:

> From colledge hall, where thirsty vicar
> To cool his draught letts down much liquor,
> I, namesake to't, doe send you greeting
> With greasy fists, just come from eating,
> And if the rimes prove something dull,
> It is because my belly's full.
> At one precisely at th'Kings Head
> Who was by's subjects murdered
> (And not content when they had don
> Have lately sent away his son)
> I'le meet both you and Captain Jones,

> I'le meet you, tho' I build a sconce [...]
> The time is short or more I'de send,
> But what (and that 'tis makes me end)
> I gett in rime I loose in friend. (ll. 1–12, 28–30)[13]

Hall also shares Prior's witty resort to artificial or outlandish rhymes. The same epistle to Fleetwood Sheppard has 'Or sent me with Ten Pounds to *Furney-* | *Vall's*-Inn, to some good Rogue Attorney' (ll. 44–45), with which can be compared a couplet from Hall's epistle to Broughton beginning 'Calling at Fountain's late last night': 'At length with tears (which eyes much sore- | rer made appear than were before)' (ll. 14–15). Hall also quite often forms a rhyme by pairing two single-syllable words with one of more than one syllable (as, again, is frequent in Prior's epistles), for example in the opening couplet of another epistle to Broughton, 'From place where long to lie does tyre one, | Where pillow does my head inviron'.[14] And Hall's epistles, characterized by similar high spirits and verbal dexterity, overall contain frequent verbal echoes of Prior's, occasioned by common themes and subject-matter, including petitioning for favours, verse- and letter-writing, drinking, dicing, and having to take medicinal pills.[15] He may therefore have been influenced by the younger poet, perhaps as the result of access to manuscript copies, as not all of Prior's epistles were available in print during the 1690s.[16]

Dryden's influence was very likely greater (as would be expected) in the case of Hall's epistles written in pentameters, and it seems certain in the satiric exaggeration of ll. 35–36 of that entitled 'To Dr Broughton after a fitt of sickness', a couplet in which Hall's target is another Hereford physician: 'Dunstan, whose useless care is cruelty, | Who ne'er kills one but let's whole hundreds dye' (B1, p. 73). This poem, beginning 'These grateful lines are doubly Sir your due' and paying tribute to Broughton's medical skill, is a good example of why Hall is worth reading, not just for his freedom of expression but for the rapidly changing arguments and the wide range of both contemporary and historical reference. In this respect another stylistic model may have been Abraham Cowley, whose 'On the Death of Mr Crashaw', a posthumous tribute poem in pentameter couplets published in 1656, ranges widely, like Hall's epistle, over matters of religion and belief in a discursive and extravagant manner. The possibility of Cowley's influence is strengthened by a clear echo of lines from his 'An Answer to a Copy of Verses Sent me to Jersey' (also from his 1656 *Poems*) in a letter sent by Hall to the younger Adam Ottley, where Hall writes:

> Sir, If the Muses don't dwell in Oxford, I'm sure you must not expect 'em in Herefordshire:
> > Since witt no more will in our country live
> > Than will our redstreaks when they're out on't thrive.[17]

Compare with this Cowley's:

> > > for you must know,
> > Sir, that Verse does not in this Island grow
> > No more than Sack; One lately did not fear
> > (Without the Muses leave) to plant it here.[18]

Hall, in 'These grateful lines are doubly Sir your due', begins by thanking Dr

Broughton for curing him, and for steadying his 'trembling hand' so that he can express his gratitude in writing. The next sentence, ending with an effectively delayed main clause and a light-hearted biblical reference, conjures up his now removed mental torments with typical exaggeration:

> Phantomes and sprites, those melancholly theams
> We wakeing think but clearly see in dreams,
> Hobgoblings, ghosts, and all the sooty train
> Disorder'd spiritts stamp upon the brain
> You've utterly dispell'd, and I'm agen
> As free from fayries as a Magdalen. (ll. 5–10)

Hall then moves on to extravagant praise of Broughton's medical abilities: tales of marvellous cures by ancient physicians are likely to have been much exaggerated (ll. 11–20); Broughton has a 'diviner art' (l. 20), and would have been more effective than the angel at the biblical pool of Bethesda (ll. 23–27, including a monetary pun on the word 'angell'). He needs 'no apochryphall recorded proof', having 'upright liveing witnesses enough' (ll. 30–31); if ever one of his patients dies it is because of treatment previously received from the doctor referred to as 'Dunstan' (ll. 32–36).[19]

But already the theme of Broughton's difficult political and religious position in Hereford society has come in (ll. 21–22), and Hall, with incisive wit, pictures how his friend's bitter enemies, who would like to see him dead, are forced in the end to seek his services:

> A Whig, when well, crys out he'l ne're employ
> A man that wou'd the government destroy.
> No sooner had he say'd it but the sott
> A surfett at the last election gott;
> Urg'd on by pungent pains and pittying friends,
> In far more haste then once he shun'd thee, sends,
> Where with thy noble remedies divine
> Thou gav'st him life that wou'd have taken thine. (ll. 39–46)

Some of them, Hall continues, are so opposed that they even make out they would rather die than call for Broughton's assistance, at which point — the satirical triplet followed by two assertive couplets — Hall changes tack to address the subject of his friend's atheism, the theme of the rest of the 70-line poem:

> Says Bigott, full of Dutch divinity,
> 'I'de rather then thy heathenish prescripts try
> Be sent by quack to him thou dost deny',
> Not knowing those who oft our insides see
> Can never atheist and physitian be.
> The deity does sure nowhere appear
> So evident, so wonderfull as there. (ll. 47–53)

No one 'who oft our insides' sees, maintains Hall, can deny the existence of God, and he reminds Broughton that kings, who are like gods, acknowledge a higher power when curing their subjects by touching for the king's evil (ll. 60–65). The king invoked by Hall is, not unexpectedly, 'Our banisht prince who did his subjects cure | Of lesser evills then he does endure' (ll. 60–61). His final clinching argument (with an exaggerated Old Testament metaphor) is that Broughton, as a doctor with much wider curative powers than a king, should make a sacrificial offering to God greater than any other:

> Higher than any should thy incense rise,
> Fatter and fairer be thy sacrifice,
> Since Heaven almost a miracle has shown
> In giveing mighty thee a power alone
> To cure all maledyes, to kings but one. (ll. 66–70)

As will next be seen, Broughton, who was such a friend (and, in effect, Muse, in inspiring such a remarkable epistle), also played a significant part in helping to preserve Hall's poetry, at least potentially — important evidence that Hall was not as unconcerned about the fate of his verses as might at first be suspected.

2.2. 'The book that me'll imortall make'

One of Margaret Ezell's social poets is a mid-seventeenth-century versifier, Herbert Aston, from Tixall in Staffordshire, whose wife assembled a fair copy of his poems. Aston, in this connection, wrote and asked his sister whether she had copies of any other of his poems, not represented on a list he is enclosing. From this it is clear that he, the author, had not kept copies of everything he had sent out.[20]

One of the eight familiar epistles that Henry Hall sent to Dr Broughton reveals a rather similar situation. The poem in question ('As in a pump we water put') is headed 'To Dr. Broughton desireing him to send me some verses of mine which I had forgott' (B1).[21] As the following extract shows, Hall is explicit about his wish for a copy to be made — by a third party ('m'amanuensis') who, it appears, will convey the present verse epistle to Broughton and then, presumably, bring back a fresh copy of the missing poem. This is interesting enough, but even more to the point, it becomes apparent that Broughton made a habit of keeping copies of Hall's poems in a book set aside for the purpose. I quote the opening nineteen lines of the epistle:

> As in a pump wee water put
> Only that more we may gett out,
> So I, my friend, by way of letter
> In rime petition you for meeter,
> And that you'l let m'amanuensis   5
> Transcribe what's quite forsook my sences.
> To me the stanzas and their theams
> Are all like Neb'cadnezars dreams,
> Yet you, who joak at prophecy,
> Shall Belteshazer be to me   10
> If in your hand a book you take,
> The book that makes Old Mathews quake,
> The book that me'll imortall make,
> Not for the loyalty or witt
> But, Sir, because by you 'tis writ,   15

> Altho' I fear the world will say
> Friendship your judgement did o'resway.
> I ask not, Sir, for all you've wrott;
> Some better much were quite forgott.[22]

Soon after this point Hall changes direction, imagining a law that would prevent works being written that no one wanted to read ('Nor had we seen Tom Shadwells rimes', l. 27, 'And Phillis freed from *billett doux*', l. 33), and ending with an attack on the oath of allegiance, so that the poem of which he wants a copy is (sadly) never specified. But Broughton's importance as a preserver of Hall's verse is made vividly clear (ll. 15 and 18 show that the volume is in Broughton's own hand), as is Hall's apparent desire to be a poet of lasting memory ('The book that me'll imortall make', l. 13), despite the way in which the ambitions of that line are immediately qualified by self-deprecation and irony (ll. 14–19). We may reasonably suppose that Broughton's manuscript contained not only the epistles addressed to him personally, but other of the satires in which Hall makes fun of the local Hereford establishment. There is no doubt from l. 12 that these included the various attacks on the Mathews family alluded to in Chapter 1, and there is even a suggestion in this line that 'Old' Mathews himself was aware of the volume's existence.

Whether Broughton made copies of Hall's poems for the benefit of other people (with or without their author's permission) is another question, as is the number of epistles Hall sent him. One of the eight now extant begins 'Once in a week a letter's due', suggesting a regular, frequent correspondence. All eight are preserved only in B1, which appears to have been assembled from a variety of sources. Five of the eight are also preserved among the Ottley manuscripts (for which see the next section), but are not amongst the poems there copied in Hall's own hand. These five may represent a selection with relatively respectable content; two of the three not in Ottley have a strong sexual element,[23] and one of those found in both collections ('Once in a week a letter's due') lacks, in Ottley, ten lines of obvious sexual innuendo.[24]

This same poem, intriguingly, ends with the revelation that verse-making was not an activity of Hall's alone but was meant to be reciprocal; Broughton, too, was supposed to produce verse epistles:

> This is to you the second time
> Without return I've wrot in rime.
> As I am yours, so you're my debtor:
> I owe you visits, you me meter,
> And so, dear Doc, here ends my letter. (B1, p. 85)

2.3. The Ottley Manuscripts: Autograph Evidence

The other major piece of evidence showing that Hall had some regard for the longer-term preservation of his verse is his participation in an effort apparently by Dr Ottley and others to make a collection of his poetry. What are here referred to as the Ottley manuscripts of Hall's verse comprise a small part of the papers of the Ottley family of Pitchford Hall in Shropshire, now in the care of the National Library of Wales, Aberystwyth, where they await cataloguing.[25]

With Dr Ottley, Archdeacon of Shropshire, being a cathedral colleague of Hall, there was every opportunity for the two men to meet and socialize. As noted in Chapter 1, Hall sent Ottley an apology in verse for missing a dinner appointment ('Ye gods what gulfs are set between'), and its easy familiar tone testifies to their close friendship. I quote the final eight lines:

> From dinner then excuse my missing,
> Tho' not at tennis, or a-fishing.
> Let me obtain your wonted pardon
> And all the blame lay on Carmarthen.
> Forgive this morning's little flights
> Which Muse invents and Harry writes,
> And the so maukish, sleepy sinner
> Invite another day to dinner.[26]

Surviving only in the Ottley manuscripts, the lines are in neither the author's nor the recipient's hand, but Ottley must have made sure they were preserved. He himself wrote out another little poem in the collection, 'For missing thee how canst thou Burren blame', in which Hall makes fun of a fellow Vicar Choral, Tom Broad. But Ottley's nephew Adam may have been at least as much involved in the overall enterprise, as it is with him that the literary manuscripts in the Ottley archive are particularly associated.[27]

For the present study (and given their uncatalogued status) the Ottley manuscripts of Hall's verse can conveniently be divided into three parts, as follows: O1, five 'source' manuscripts together containing twenty-seven poems, very likely assembled for copying purposes; O2, a fair-copy manuscript of thirty-four poems (twenty-nine of them attributed to Hall), mostly copied from O1; and O3, two manuscripts each containing three poems by Hall not represented in the fair copy. The manuscripts will be described in this order, with the source manuscripts arranged in the order in which their poems occur in O2.

O1a. A scrap of paper (93 × 150 mm) written on one side only in a slanting cursive hand. It contains a single 8-line poem, without title, 'For missing thee how canst thou Burren blame'. Copied into O2.

O1b. A bifolio (page size 313 × 193 mm), with text in a rounded hand on f. 1r-v and the upper part of f. 2r. It contains ll. 135–221 (the end) of the poem 'The paradox' ('Why towering tides submit to constant laws'), copied in full in O2. There are corrections in the second hand of O1d. The first part of the poem would have filled a preceding bifolio, now missing.

O1c. A document, folded twice (when unfolded 212 × 170 mm), endorsed 'To the Reverend Dr Oatly' in the form of a letter; a following word, presumably a place-name, is indecipherable. Within, written across the folds by the first hand of O1d (different from that on the dorse), is a single 22-line poem, without title, 'Ye gods what gulfs are set between'. Copied into O2.

O1d. An assemblage of quarto bifolios comprising paper of more than one stock and size, stitched together without a cover and paginated [1], 2–38. The page size is predominantly 215 × 165 mm, rising to 240 × 170 mm. All pages are written on, with the exception of unpaginated versos to pp. 35 and 38. In two informal hands, of which the second, noticeably bolder and less tidy, also supplies titles to all but one of the poems that have them, is the sole provider of marginal notes, and makes corrections throughout. O1d contains twenty poems, as listed in detail in Appendix B, below. The first hand is responsible for writing items 1–11, 20, and the second for items 12–19. I have judged two of the twenty poems not to be by Hall, namely item 13, 'Curse on those representatives', an adaptation of an earlier anonymous poem ('Curse on such representatives') that often occurs in manuscript as an 'Answer' to a poem known as 'The Chequer Inn';[28] and item 17, 'The great good man whom fortune does displace', which is by Hall's associate, Daniel Kenrick.[29] All twenty poems are copied into O2.

O1e. A squarish piece of paper (182 × 192 mm) bearing on one side, in the second hand of O1d, a 22-line poem 'A Fable' ('An honest good farmer by providence blest'), copied into O2. On the other side, in a cursive hand (which has also written 'Henry Hall' at the foot), there are two poems, the 12-line 'The healths' ('To our arms on Earth and seas') and the 7-line 'Landau took Nov. 1704' ('Since the town is our own what it cost us no matter'). These poems are also copied into O2. Written sideways to these last two poems in a different, smaller hand is an 8-line poem 'The great Sir George Tholouse did beat', which is not copied into O2.

O2. A quarto booklet of 40 leaves (195 × 152 mm) sewn into brown paper wrappers, and now foliated i, 1–39. The eleven pages beginning with f. 1r also bear contemporary pagination. Ff. i, 38v-39 are blank. Written in a single practised hand, probably of the early eighteenth century, with attributions to Hall supplied by a second hand, as follows: on the front wrapper and at the end of item 1, 'Henry Hall'; in the title of item 3, 'Henry Hall's plea for Burren, to Mr T. Broad'; and on f. 30v, after item 30, 'Henry Hall from the 11th page', i.e. f. 6r. O2 contains twenty-nine poems ascribed to Hall, including the non-Hall items 'Curse on those representatives' (its item 20) and 'The great good man whom fortune does displace' (item 23), as in O1d. One poem is copied from each of O1a, O1b, and O1c, twenty from O1d, and three from O1e, while three poems (items 1, 4, and 5) do not have corresponding source manuscripts. The other contents of the manuscript are item 2, 'Mr John Grubbs ballad', to which Hall's item 1 acts as a preface, and, at the end, two poems in Latin by Anthony Alsop that were published in 1706, and two anonymous verse satires in English, published in 1709 and 1713.[30] The full contents of O2 are listed in detail in Appendix B.

O3a. A single folio leaf (304 × 202 mm), written on one side only by the second hand of O1d, containing three poems, respectively of 17, 10, and 4 lines, namely: 'On the two monstrous fish lately taken at Greenwich' ('Once in a reign t'encrease our causeless fears'); 'On the late alterations at court' ('Two noble earls long since the court forsook'); and 'When church was mother, Ann was then her daughter'. The third of these is written sideways in the margin, and immediately below, also written sideways and in the hand that makes the attributions in O2, is the annotation 'H. Hall in a letter 1703'.

O3b. A letter, folded once (each page 205 × 162 mm), endorsed 'To Mr Adam Ottley at his Chambers in Balioll College in Oxon, by Abington'. Within, the text of the letter begins on the right-hand side of the opening, and ends, now written sideways, on the left-hand side. The whole document is again in the second hand of O1d. It is dated 'July 26th' and is signed 'I am Sir your most obedient and humble servant, Henry Hall'. The first paragraph of the letter includes an offset couplet (not treated in this study as a separate poem), as follows:

> Sir, If the Muses don't dwell in Oxford, I'm sure you must not expect 'em in
> Herefordshire:
> > Since witt no more will in our country live
> > Than will our redstreaks when they're out on't thrive.[31]
> You know Sir, 'tis the juce of the grape, and not of the apple inspires the poet,
> and to justify the assertion, read these epigrams.

Three poems then follow, each of them comprising six lines: 'On the Arch Duke's presenting his picture and sword set with diamonds to the Duke of Marlborough' ('Accept my Lord this humble glitt'ring thing'); 'His Graces answer' ('Your awkward Austrian phiz with joy I take'); and (now on the left-hand side of the opening), 'To my Lord G[odolphin], who struck the medal for the D[uk]e of M[arlborough] last year' ('Strike you new medals to your heros fame').[32] The letter concludes, before the subscription: 'I was unluckily making the Welch tour when your letter came to Hereford, so receivd it not till last Saturday'.

The foregoing descriptions set out the extent of the overlap between the Ottley manuscripts in terms of hands and contents, and the apparently organized nature of the enterprise is confirmed not only by the identification of Dr Ottley's hand as responsible for O1a (and possibly that of his nephew in the case of the second and third poems in O1e), but by the close involvement of Henry Hall himself.[33] Comparison with the hand of the signed letter, O3b, with that of Hall's written answers to questions put by the Dean and Chapter to the Vicars Choral in 1694 (Chapter 1 above), and with the hand that signs and supplies words to manuscript songs by Hall in the library of Christ Church, Oxford (Chapter 6.1 below), leaves no doubt at all that his is the boldly written second hand of O1d, the hand responsible also for the first poem in O1e, for O3a, and for corrections in O1b and the earlier part of O1d. As indicated above, the second hand of O1d is very much the dominant partner. As well as supplying titles, notes, and corrections, it is this hand that numbered the pages of O1d, thereby imposing order on the three stints of copying (item 20, in the first hand, was clearly written separately and was probably a later addition). It is apparent, too, that after an initial insertion of page numbers and titles, Hall returned subsequently to add further titles, in these cases writing them around existing page numbers (items 1, 2, 4, 9).

Of the other five hands in the Ottley manuscripts, three, responsible respectively for O1b, O2, and a minor item in O1e, occur only once, but the first hand of O1d also writes O1c, and the annotator of O2 also annotates O3a.

There can therefore be small doubt that the component parts of O1 represent a co-operative project to assemble poems by Henry Hall, with his active participation, and that O2 is a resulting fair copy. O1 and O2 are consistently very close, textually, and the latter takes over all of the corrections and marginal annotations in the source manuscripts, and unfailingly has titles only where they have titles. In the case of O1d it also preserves mistakes in the layout of certain poems, noticeably the reversal of two stanzas of their respective items 3 and 10 ('Whilst Clio rehearses' [ii]) and the running together of the final two stanzas of their respective items 9 and 16 ('O John O John O John Abrahall'). With this weight of evidence, O2's failure to follow the exact order of poems in O1d is likely to be of no significance, and the absence of source manuscripts for items 1, 4–5 in O2 is no doubt to be explained by accidental loss, in the same way that the first part of O1b is missing (cf. O2, item 6).[34]

The fair copying does not, however, appear to have taken place for some years. The assembling of the O1 materials is likely to have occurred between 1704, the date of the three copied topical poems in O1e, and Hall's death in March 1707. O2, however, which gives every appearance of having been written as a single task, has seemingly to be dated to 1713 or later on the basis of the publication date of the anonymous satire 'On the fall of a pis-pot', its item 34, unless that had prior manuscript circulation. Furthermore, O2 was not given over exclusively to poems by Hall, suggesting that an earlier intention may have changed, although the later annotator was at pains to point out which compositions were his and to put Hall's name on the front cover.

Why, in particular, were the three poems in O3a, written out by Hall in 1705 or later, not included in the fair copy?[35] Presumably they were not part of the plan as first conceived and were taken into the Ottley papers on a separate occasion. More broadly, what effort was made to find poems by Hall when the copying enterprise was planned, which poems were available, and what selection of material took place? The central source manuscript is O1d, which supplies twenty of the twenty-nine poems ascribed to Hall in O2. As was said, an unknown hand wrote out the first eleven items and (on larger paper) the final item, while Hall himself wrote items 12–19.[36] It is of great interest that this unknown hand predominantly copied local poems, comprising five epistles to Dr Broughton, a ballad making fun of 'Young' Mathews and his friends, the poem satirizing John Abrahall, the long reflective poem about climbing the Skerrit, and one of the poems to Edmund Addis. In contrast, Hall concentrated on his 'national' satires, the exceptions being the poem congratulating Dr Bulkley on becoming a canon and the diatribe against the cathedral clergyman John Page. The exceptions in the case of the first hand are Hall's lament for the death of Henry Purcell, a poem beginning 'Now love and war the self-same art is grown' (developing this conceit), and a song about a storm at sea during which a shipwreck is averted only by Venus's intervention.[37]

As was said, Hall paginates the manuscript and adds titles, notes, and corrections to the work of the first scribe, who also wrote out the poem sent separately to Dr Ottley (O1c). Given that this person clearly had access to Hall's private epistles, along with other local satires, it is possible that he is the trusted 'amanuensis' mentioned in 'As in a pump we water put', here working alongside Hall to compile material for the Ottleys. But the limited nature of the offering is strange, given how many other poems Hall had written. It is conceivable that O1d represents a deliberate selection of material, a plausible theory in the case of the epistles to Dr Broughton given the sexual content of two of the three not copied here (see section 2.2 above), and the exclusion of a third ('And art thou faith a true recluse become') possibly because Hall there makes light of Broughton's scruples about swearing the Oath of Allegiance. But the miscellaneous nature of the other poems included raises the possibility that these were all that Hall and his assistant had to hand at the time, unless they were poems with which the author was especially pleased. Four are unique to the Ottley manuscripts, namely one of the political satires ('Since we're undone the matter is not much'), the poem to Dr Bulkley, the attack on John Page, and the 46-line song, 'The storme', the chorus of which, naming both Venus and the Doge (of Venice), is likely to be related to the lost opera on the latter's marriage with the Adriatic Sea attributed to Hall by the eighteenth-century topographer Thomas Cox (see Chapter 6.2 below).

The apparent oddity of selection extends to the non-O1d poems copied into O2, except that some of these are datable to after 1700, notably a long abusive attack on the Dutch, found nowhere else, clearly written at the time of the War of the Spanish Succession ('Why towering tides submit to constant laws'); the tribute to Henry Playford published in 1702; the three poems copied from O1e, all datable to 1704; and possibly the unique tribute to the balladeer John Grubb, which may date to as late as 1707.[38] Given also the three poems in O3a, datable to 1703–05 and in Hall's own hand, that were not taken into O2, the evidence suggests that materials were prepared (by Hall and others) and received (by the Ottleys) at different times, perhaps over a span of years. Whatever the truth of the matter, Hall's co-operation with the enterprise represented by the Ottley manuscripts appears to be the closest he got to a planned collection of his verse.

Notes to Chapter 2

1. Margaret J. M. Ezell, *Social Authorship and the Advent of Print* (Baltimore, MD: John Hopkins University Press, 1999), Introduction and Chapter 1. See also Dustin Griffin, 'The Social World of Authorship, 1660–1714', in *The Cambridge History of English Literature, 1660–1780*, ed. by John Richetti (Cambridge: Cambridge University Press, 2005), pp. 37–60.
2. For the term 'user publication', see Harold Love, *Scribal Publication in Seventeenth-Century England* (Oxford: Clarendon Press, 1993), p. 47.
3. Ezell, *Social Authorship and the Advent of Print*, p. 111. She also draws attention (p. 106) to the small perceived market for literary writers on the part of provincial presses. *ESTC*'s first recorded example of printing of any kind in Hereford itself is dated '1717?' (N64677).
4. See Paul Hammond, 'Anonymity in Restoration Poetry', in his *The Making of Restoration Poetry* (Cambridge: Brewer, 2006), pp. 49–72, for a valuable discussion of the different contemporary aspects and uses of anonymity.
5. Love, *Scribal Publication in Seventeenth-Century England*, pp. 42, 44, 38.
6. For a discussion of the interlinked issues of agency, genre, and textuality (including issues surrounding the reworking of manuscript material for print), see Gillian Wright, *Producing Women's Poetry, 1600–1730: Text and Paratext, Manuscript and Print* (Cambridge: Cambridge University Press, 2013), esp. pp. 14–20.
7. Ezell, *Social Authorship and the Advent of Print*, pp. 87–88. She notes how the journal 'urged

readers to submit their short pieces — and even those by their friends — by leaving them at a coffeehouse and then reading about their acceptance or rejection in a future issue'. See Chapter 5.1 below for discussion of Hall's contributions to the *Gentleman's Journal*.

8. I quote from O2 (f. 1v), for which see section 2.3 below.

9. 'To Mr Charles Hoskins upon my lending him Mr Wallers Poems', ll. 13–14, 18–26, quoted from B1 (p. 51). The meaning of the final line is apparently 'He (Dryden) equalled Waller while he (Dryden) was alive and will surpass him once he (Dryden) is dead'.

10. See *The Poems of Sir George Etherege*, ed. by James Thorpe (Princeton, NJ: Princeton University Press, 1963), pp. 46–53, where the three poems are similarly printed together.

11. See *The Literary Works of Matthew Prior*, ed. by H. Bunker Wright and Monroe K. Spears, 2nd edn, 2 vols (Oxford: Clarendon Press, 1971), I, 83–91, 93, 103–04.

12. 'To Mr. Fleetwood Shepherd', ll. 1–14, quoted from *The Literary Works of Matthew Prior*, I, 83–84.

13. B1, p. 79. The poem is edited below. Line 2, 'draught', i.e. *OED*, *drought*, n., 4, 'thirst'. Line 3, 'namesake', i.e. to the college hall. Line 12, 'build a sconce', i.e. run into serious debt (*OED*, *sconce*, n.³, 1c).

14. B1, pp. 66, 83. See the editions, below.

15. For this last, see again Hall's 'From place where long to lie does tire one'.

16. The two epistles to Fleetwood Sheppard were not published until 1692 ('Epistle to Mr. Fleetwood Shepherd', the second of the pair) and 1697 ('To Mr. Fleetwood Shepherd', the first), while the other two poems appear to have remained in manuscript until modern times. See *The Literary Works of Matthew Prior*, II, 852–55, 856–57, 860.

17. See section 2.3 below ('redstreaks' are cider apples). Hall, in addition, will be seen to have set two of Cowley's lyrics to music.

18. Abraham Cowley, *Poems: Miscellanies, the Mistress, Pindarique Odes, Davideis, Poems Written on Several Occasions*, ed. by A. R. Waller (Cambridge: Cambridge University Press, 1905), p. 43.

19. He is identified in the edition of the poem, below, as Dr Bridstock Harford.

20. Ezell, *Social Authorship and the Advent of Print*, pp. 27–28.

21. As stated in the Preface (and demonstrated here and in the following offset quotation), when referencing poems by their first line I use the modern form of spelling found in Appendix A, but follow manuscript spelling when quoting from particular manuscripts.

22. B1, p. 70. A later corrector has filled in the 'the' of 'Mathews' in l. 12.

23. 'Calling at Fountain's late last night' and 'Coming from place where you have seen'.

24. It is noticeable that the same lines in B1 have been marked with a cross at beginning and end, possibly for excision when copying.

25. For an account of this collection, see Jones, 'The Ottley Papers'.

26. O1c. The poem is edited below. 'Carmarthen' refers to the acquaintance mentioned in disparaging terms earlier in the poem (clearly known to Ottley as well), with whom Hall had spent time the previous evening ('a rich queere Carmarthen tupp').

27. See Peter Beal, 'Poems by Sir Philip Sidney: The Ottley Manuscript', *The Library*, 5th series, 33 (1978), 284–95. I am grateful to Dr Beal for first drawing the Ottley manuscripts to my attention.

28. For further discussion, see Chapter 7.6 below.

29. For a discussion of this poem's authorship, see Chapter 9.2 below.

30. 'Mr John Grubbs ballad' was printed in 1707 as John Grubb, *The British Heroes: or, A New Ballad in Honour of St George* (Foxon G303–04; three editions in *ESTC*).

31. i.e. 'than will our red-streaked cider apples thrive when they're not in Herefordshire'. Cf. *OED*, *redstreak*, n.

32. See Chapter 8.1, below for a discussion of these poems. In the first case the words 'Duke' (twice) and 'Marlborough', initially written in abbreviated form, have been filled out by a later hand. In the third case, however, the abbreviated words have not been filled in.

33. These identifications are based on comparison with signed, non-literary documents within the overall Ottley papers. The hand of O1a was compared in particular with Ottley papers 1698, an account by Dr Ottley of the landing of the Prince of Orange on 10 December 1688.

34. Its item 24, 'The Czarr's health' ('Dragoons have a care'), is two items later than expected.

35. For their date, see Chapter 8.1 below.

36. It may be significant that the two poems in Hall's hand judged not to be his own compositions do not begin on fresh pages, alone of all the items in O1d.

37. For all the poems in question (some of which are referred to in Chapter 1), see the O1d items listed in Appendix B. The ballad satirizing Young Mathews, beginning 'Whilst Clio rehearses', is listed as 'Whilst Clio rehearses' [ii] because this first line is shared by two of Hall's local poems.

38. For the poems in question, see the O2 items listed in Appendix B. The date of Hall's tribute to Grubb is discussed in the Conclusion to this study. Another poem unique to O2 is 'How happy is this day', a drinking song sung at a meeting of a local club in honour of Lord Chandos.

CHAPTER 3

❖

Posthumous Manuscript Collections
of Hall's Verse

The two extant manuscript collections made after Hall's death are both held in Leeds University Library's Brotherton Collection, which contains a large number of seventeenth- and eighteenth-century English poetical manuscripts.[1] Two of these, designated MS Lt q 5 and MS Lt 6, are explicitly collections of Hall's poems. In the following descriptions (and throughout) they are referred to as B1 and B2. The chapter then passes to discussion of collections no longer extant.

3.1. The Brotherton Collection Manuscripts

B1 is a folio manuscript book of 116 pages (the pagination is contemporary), written in the earlier part of the eighteenth century.[2] The pages measure 325 × 198 mm. The manuscript has an inner covering of soft marbled card, and an outer binding of stiff marbled card; there are front and rear flyleaves between the two coverings. Within an envelope now attached to the front of the inner cover is another version of William Cooke's manuscript memoir of the poet, referred to in Chapter 1.

All except the last of B1's eighty-nine items are formally written in a single ornamental hand, almost certainly professional. There are flourished headings, and the poems are laid out with some spaciousness. The less elegant hand responsible for the final poem also provides an informal attribution to Hall ('Harry Hall's Poems') on the verso of the soft card cover. There is no list of contents, and pp. 114–16 are blank.[3]

A third hand, using a dark italic script, makes a large number of corrections, comments, and local identifications, scattered throughout the manuscript, beginning with a note also on the verso of the soft cover but referring to a poem on p. 35: 'This Saunders was a Presbyterian Ironmonger, whose Sister was Michael Brampton's Mother.' The work of this correcting hand, who appears to have had access to a more accurate copy of Hall's poems, is discussed below in section 3.2.

A fourth hand, probably also eighteenth-century, has numbered twenty-two poems in the first half of the manuscript in pencil, as if making a selection. It is very likely the same hand that adds some pencilled identifications to item 30 ('Whilst Clio rehearses' [-]) and which expands partially written words into 'House of Commons' in the title of item 70.

Even though it lacks the Ottley manuscripts' intimate association with Hall, B1 is the major assemblage of his poetry, its importance deriving partly from the huge quantity of material; partly from the high proportion of local, Hereford poems; and partly from the seemingly privileged knowledge of its corrector, although the sheer number of corrections also draws attention to the manuscript's comparative lack of textual authority. B1 is likely to have been commissioned by friends or associates of Hall after his death. In contrast to the Ottley manuscripts, however, only four poems (items 82 and 86–88) can be dated later than 1698.

Out of B1's eighty-nine poems one is explicitly not by Hall, being an extract from a song from Katherine Philips's play *Pompey*, transcribed on p. 50 for the sake of Hall's 'Answer'. Also included, as in O1d and O2, are the non-Hall poems 'Curse on those representatives' (item 77) and 'The great good man whom fortune does displace' (item 62). For a full list of contents, see Appendix B, below. Thirty-seven of the eighty-six poems by Hall are not known elsewhere, including a dozen relating to Hereford and another dozen or so on 'national' topics. Many in both these categories are satirical.

The contents of B1 range across the whole gamut of Hall's verse in terms of both content and genre. Local, political, and occasional poems abound, as do many kinds of stanzaic verse, especially for songs and ballads, and plentiful examples of rhyming couplets, especially for epistles and satires. There are even two 'pindarick ballads' (items 13 and 14, found nowhere else). There is, however, a concentration of poems on national topics at the beginning of the manuscript (items 1–15) and at the end (broadly from item 66 onwards). In between comes a great variety of local and occasional poems, including love songs, drinking songs, a tribute to and a lament for the death of Henry Purcell, poems addressed to women and to male friends, a 'Progress of the stage by way of epilogue', and many of the verse epistles and local satires referred to earlier in this study. The perceptible division between the two outer blocks of poems on national topics separated by the large central block of more miscellaneous material recalls the division in O1d between the more local compositions copied by the first scribe and the mainly political material transcribed by Hall. (It is noticeable that the hand that adds pencilled numbers to poems in the first half of B1 almost entirely avoids the 'national' items.) This suggests that the large corpus of poems assembled in B1 may derive, at least ultimately, from exemplars in which the two types of material were separated.

As indicated above, the final poem in the manuscript ('When of half a score lasses ten harlots you see'), a political satire headed 'A prophecy found in Ragland Castle in the year 1630', was added by a later hand. It is probably not coincidental that Sir Philip Jones, grandfather of Dr Broughton's wife Lucy, held Ragland (Raglan) Castle for the Crown during the Civil War.[4]

B2, measuring 180 × 108 mm, is not a physically separate manuscript but forms the final section of a composite octavo volume (in calf binding) that otherwise contains thirteen printed pamphlets. The first two of these, dated 1712 and 1713, were issued by the bookseller Edmund Curll (the first is *The Life and Character of Mr John Philips*); all the others, which predominantly contain poetry, were issued in 1709 by Henry

Hills. It is likely that B2 also dates from early in the eighteenth century, and that it was bound up with the printed pamphlets fairly soon after their publication. The hand responsible for Hall's poems also wrote a manuscript inscription into the blank front face of a monument to John Philips depicted in the hand-coloured frontispiece to the first printed item, suggesting that the scribe of the poems and the book's assembler were one and the same.

B2 contains no more than eighteen items on fifteen leaves, one of them being the same Katherine Philips lines as found in B1, with Hall's 'Answer' in this case directly run on, in effect creating a single poem (there is no mention of Philips).[5] The foliation is modern. The scribal hand is small and cramped, and is amateur work with some aberrant spellings and textual corruptions, but the poems, sometimes written on ruled lines, are provided with frames and titles. There is also a quasi-title-page, in the same hand, reading 'The Remains of Mr Henry Hall late organist of Hereford', below which is a boxed motto, 'Morte carebit opus'. After Hall's poems the final, unfoliated leaf is blank, save for an illegible Latin line on the recto and names of later owners on the verso (the names of mid-eighteenth-century owners occur also on the inside front cover and first flyleaf of the complete book).

The poems by Hall included in B2 comprise an almost equal number of national political satires and local or miscellaneous items, the different kinds of item interspersed rather than grouped. Two short poems are unique to B2: 'The vacant chair the House no sooner view', addressed to the local MP Paul Foley on his election as Speaker of the House of Commons in 1695, and 'Those tokens which avenging Heaven sent', fiercely asserting that Queen Mary's death from smallpox in December 1694 represents divine punishment. There are, in addition, three political satires not in B1 but known from elsewhere. The other twelve Hall poems in B2 are, however, all in B1, and include two of the satires on the Mathews family (copied sequentially) though none of the epistles to Dr Broughton. In contrast, no more than three of B2's poems (all also in B1) occur in the Ottley manuscripts.

B2 is explicitly a memorial collection of Hall's verse, presumably made locally. The title 'The Remains of Mr Henry Hall late organist of Hereford' may suggest that its creator, copying from another manuscript with the same contents, believed the eighteen poems in question (this count including the merged Katherine Philips item) to be the total of Hall's output. But it is perhaps more likely that the compiler — clearly a person of Hall's political persuasion — selected poems that appealed to him from an exemplar or exemplars not identical in content to those available to B1's scribe.

In this connection it is striking that the degree of textual overlap between B1, B2, and the Ottley manuscripts is not as great as might have been expected, given the undoubted local connections of Ottley and B1, and the presumption that B2 was also compiled in the Hereford area. Of the thirty-three poems attributable to Hall in Ottley, only fourteen occur in B1, while of the eighty-six in B1, no more than fifteen occur in Ottley. The inclusion in B1 of twelve of B2's seventeen Hall items shows these two manuscripts to be more closely aligned. A reasonable inference is that such was Hall's fecundity, and such the fluidity of his 'canon' and the methods of its circulation, that those intent on making compilations of his verse had a large and changing body of material from which to work.

3.2. Collections No Longer Extant

For the purposes of discussion it is assumed that the two manuscripts in question here were produced after the death of Henry Hall, i.e. without any input from him.

(a) The Cooke manuscript

This untraced manuscript was once owned by the Reverend William Cooke, the nineteenth-century Vicar of Bromyard, who copied extracts from it into his handwritten memoirs of the Hereford Vicars Choral referred to in Chapter 1 above. It is evident from Cooke's description of the manuscript as a 'volume of miscellaneous poems' containing 'Epistles, Songs, Catches, etc, satyrical & political' that it is likely to have been a sizeable compilation, and seeing that B1 alone contains all of the eight poems from which Cooke quotes (and the ninth to which he alludes) it may have been a parallel volume of some kind.[6]

Cooke transcribes, in whole or part, eight of the poems in his Hall manuscript, five of them in the section of his memoir of Hall headed 'Selections from the poems of H. Hall Senior' (p. [5]). His transcriptions (here referenced as 'C') are important because in the majority of cases they exhibit substantive textual differences from the versions found in other manuscripts, evidence, it would seem, of textual instability in Hall's canon. Leaving aside as unlikely the possibility that Cooke himself altered the wording or that another writer had intervened in what was evidently another deliberate collection of Hall's poems, it is probable, because of the nature of the differences, that they are authorial — that in these cases Hall had produced another version of what he had first written.

The poems within Cooke's memoir of Hall are as follows:[7]

· 'On the public fast — January 30th 1691' ('Cease hypocrites to trouble Heav'n'). 6 lines, p. [7]. Also in B1.[8] No significant differences.
· 'Catch on the absentees, K. James 2nd — and Pr. William' ('While one is in Flanders the other in France'). 6 lines, p. [7]. Also in B1. The line that normally begins the poem ('To our monarch's return let our glasses advance') is here placed second.
· 'On King William's return from Flanders' ('Rejoice ye fools your idol's come again'). 4 lines, p. [7]. Also in B1, where it begins 'Rejoice yee fops your idoll's come agen'.[9]
· 'On the marriage of the Revd Mr Page, one of the prebendaries of Hereford Cathedral — 1690' ('Belinda & Leah of widows a pair'). 40 lines, pp. [8–9]. Also in B1, where it begins 'Silvia and Leah were of widows a paire', has only 39 lines, and is headed merely 'On Mr Page's marriage'.
· 'On John Abrahall being elected into the common council of the Corporation of Hereford 1686 — He being then a priest of the Church of England' ('Amphibious John! O John Abr'all'). 24 lines, pp. [10–11]. In B1, as also in O1d/O2, it begins 'O John O John O John Abrahall', and has 32 lines.

C's text lacks the other manuscripts' final three quatrains, but earlier in the poem it has a quatrain that they do not have; and C alone has the detail, in the poem's title, that Abrahall was elected into the 'common council' of the corporation.[10]

The other three poems occur in Cooke's memoirs of two of Hall's contemporaries as Vicars Choral, Thomas Broad and Barnabas Alderson. In the case of Broad, Cooke states that Hall 'in his M.S. Poems has made many satyrical allusions to Mr Broade's peculiar temper and manners', in support of which he transcribes:

· 'On Tom Broade's Portrait by H.H.' ('For missing thee, the painter wilt thou blame'). 6 lines. B1 and O1a/O2 begin the poem more personally, by naming the artist in question ('For missing thee how canst thou Burren blame', 'For missing thee how canst thou Burring blame').[11]
· 'Lines to Lesbia, Miss .... of Hereford by H.H.' (''Twas in the temple first I saw'). 12 lines. C's text comprises no more than stanzas 1, 4, and 5 of the 28-line poem preserved in B1 (which is there entitled 'To Mrs Robins'), but this is very likely because Cooke is mainly concerned to quote the reference to Tom Broad, which is not in B1. See further section (b) below.

As for Alderson, Cooke writes: 'One of Mr Hall's M.S. poems describes the effects of the card parties then so numerously attended at the coffee house in Milk Lane (now St John Street), where much money & time were recklessly squandered. [...] Mr Alderson, as a member of the club, is mentioned in the following extract of the poem which is supposed to describe the complainings of an unlucky card player.' He then quotes a version of ll. 12–20 of the poem that begins 'Dunned by the bells I rose from bed', as found in B1, but with four lines replacing ll. 12–13, resulting in a total of 11 lines. One particularly striking variant reading is again discussed in section (b), below.

A general observation is that whereas C's versions of the above poems tend to have more explicit titles, seemingly preserving local detail, at other points of textual difference it often has blander, more expansive forms of expression where B1 and the Ottley manuscripts are tighter, more outspoken, and more allusive.[12] Overall it is difficult to decide the direction of revision (though some evidence for priority is presented in section (b)), and it may well be that Hall rewrote poems for different occasions or purposes, and was happy to have alternative versions in circulation.

William Cooke, it should be said, does not restrict his copying of Hall's poems to the collection in his possession. He precedes his selection with extracts (pp. [5–6]) firstly from Hall's poem in praise of Henry Purcell as printed in volume 1 of *Orpheus Britannicus* ('Music the chiefest good the gods have given') and then from that praising both Purcell and the publisher Henry Playford printed in the second volume ('Next to the man who so divinely sung').

(b) The manuscript used by B1's corrector

As noted earlier, the person who corrected and annotated B1 in a distinctive italic hand evidently had access to another copy of many of the poems contained in it. This copy may have been a similar collection of Hall's poems, again in volume form, although it is possible that it comprised loose materials in the manner of the Ottley manuscripts. Over half the poems in B1, of all kinds, attracted the corrector's attention, the interventions ranging from many small verbal changes, without comment, to a number of explicit marginal notes. Epistles to Dr Broughton are among the poems involved. It is valuable, given the importance of B1 for Hall's canon, that the corrector's work draws attention to the extant manuscript's sometimes dubious textual authority.

It is the marginal notes that reveal the status of the correcting hand most clearly. Some of the comments provide identifications of people satirized in the poems, as in the example found on B1's inside front cover: 'This Saunders was a Presbyterian Ironmonger, whose Sister was Michael Brampton's Mother', which refers to a line in 'Dunned by the bells I rose from bed', where Hall, in a mock will, leaves 'Scurrillity to Samuell Saunders' (p. 35).

Another example occurs on p. 82 during the poem 'Mathews's Coate of Arms' ('Since coat of arms your race ne'er wore'), where the annotator gives expression to Hall's habitual antipathy to the Mathews family. At the head of the poem he or she has inserted merely 'An Apothecary of Hereford and Receiver of Land-Tax', but towards the end, against the phrase 'poor Moll', there is the fiercely specific marginal note, 'Mathews's Daughter Mary, debauch'd by Henry Gorges of Eye, and afterwards married to Nicholas Philpott'.

These comments testify to precise local knowledge, as do cases where names left largely blank have been filled in, as with 'Alderson' (p. 34) in the passage from 'Dunned by the bells I rose from bed' referred to above in connection with the Cooke manuscript. But other annotations (as with many of the small textual changes) are explicit in revealing that the corrector was comparing B1 with a more accurate copy of Hall's poems, which is referred to as the 'orig.', presumably 'the original'. Thus, at the foot of p. 58, during the poem 'The progress of the stage' ('Your primitive players first acted in a cart'), the corrector notices that the scribe has omitted a word from a line given as 'When Barry now will be a maid' (referring to the actress Elizabeth Barry, 1658–1713). Unsure of the missing word, he or she inserts a dash (' — ') before 'maid', and adds in the margin: 'in orig. yielding, but eras'd for something like coming'. Similarly, on p. 91, against a line containing the word 'jerk' in the poem ''Twas in the temple first I saw', the corrector writes 'In orig. it seems to be yerk' (cf. *OED, yark, v²*, 6b, and the edition of this poem, below).

The annotations to this poem and 'Dunned by the bells' are especially important, because they suggest that in these cases readings transmitted by the lost Cooke manuscript are also more original than those in B1. In the reference to card-playing in l. 20 of 'Dunned by the bells', where B1's scribe has the apparently nonsensical 'Where Banc. Fillett so much in fashion' (p. 34), the corrector has the marginal note 'Lansquenet' (a game of cards of German origin), which matches exactly the reading in Cooke's extract, 'Where Lansquenet so much in fashion'. In the case of ''Twas in the temple', the line containing the word 'jerk' is, in B1, part of a stanza reading:

> Who preaches next is not my care,
> Or if they jerk or loll at ease,
> Provided I but see my fair,
> Wilcox, or duller Price will please. (p. 91)

This last line attracts the corrector's comment, 'Tom Broad & Page stood originally in this poem but were afterwards eraz'd'. C, in contrast, not only reads 'yerk' instead of 'jerk', confirming the corrector's note, but ends the stanza, 'Provided I see Lesbia there | Tom Broade may in the pulpit please'. These correspondences suggest that C may also preserve earlier versions of the poems that there begin 'Belinda & Leah' (in B1, 'Silvia and Leah') and 'Amphibious John!' (in B1 'O John O John').

The corrector's most outspoken remark, however, criticizes not so much the corrupt state of the B1's scribe's readings as his overall competence. On p. 90 the scribe has run together, under a single heading ('La Coquette'), a poem beginning 'To Phillis fools and men of witt resort' with another that begins 'The great good man whom fortune does displace', attributing the combined result to 'D. Kendrick'. The marginal annotation is uncompromising: 'The ignorance of the transcriber has clapp'd these two pieces of poetry of Hall and Kendrick, though of so different a nature, into one. Which I have sever'd with a line.' The matter is not, however, straightforward. As was noted, 'The great good man' occurs in O1d in Hall's own hand, and is copied as his in O2. There is further discussion of this problem of authorship in Chapter 9.2 below.

Notes to Chapter 3

1. The Brotherton Collection forms part of Special Collections. The great majority of the individual poems contained in these manuscripts are catalogued in the Brotherton Collection Manuscript Verse database (BCMSV), available at <https://library.leeds.ac.uk/special-collections-manuscript-verse> [accessed 16 February 2022]. Most of the records in question are also included in the *Union First Line Index*. Digital facsimiles of all the BCMSV manuscripts, thus including B1 and B2, are available through *Literary Manuscripts: 17th and 18th Century Poetry from the Brotherton Library, University of Leeds* <www.literarymanuscriptsleeds.amdigital.co.uk> [accessed 16 February 2022].
2. *CELM* [accessed 11 October 2021] dates the manuscript 'c. 1710–20?'.
3. The contents of B1 are listed in detail in Appendix B.
4. Burke, *A Genealogical and Heraldic History*, IV, 732.
5. As with B1, the contents of B2 are listed in detail in Appendix B.
6. Cooke, 'Henry Hall', p. [7]. But Cooke also says on p. [4] that his volume contains a 'portion' of Hall's verses.
7. On p. [10] Cooke notes that 'the poem on the Jubilee in 1700', i.e. 'Come beaus virtuosos rich heirs and musicians', which is found in manuscript form only in B1, is also present in his manuscript volume, but he does not transcribe it.
8. In some cases the items in question survive also in other manuscripts (for which see Appendix A), but I restrict references here to the Ottley and Brotherton manuscripts.
9. See Chapter 7.4, below, for other manuscript variations in the opening line of this political satire.
10. Cooke records that he transcribes this poem (to which he adds explanatory notes) 'since it

states a fact in the municipal history of Hereford, not elsewhere recorded, certainly unknown or forgotten in modern days'. Abrahall is possibly to be equated with the John Abraham who served as Mayor of Hereford in 1693.

11. There is further textual variation in that O1a/O2 have an additional couplet between ll. 4 and 5, so that C here aligns with B1 alone.

12. An exception is 'Amphibious John! O John Abr'all', where 'amphibious' bears the meaning of 'having two lives', for which see sense 3 of its entry in *OED*; the only pre-1700 citation is from Sir Thomas Browne, *Religio Medici* (1643). But the phrase 'amphibious John' is not unique to Cooke's transcription: it occurs in the poem's penultimate stanza in O1d/O2, one of those missing from his text.

CHAPTER 4

❖

Poems and Songs with Wider Circulation in Literary Manuscripts

As many as sixty-six of the poems and songs preserved in the Ottley and Brotherton Collection manuscripts — a substantial proportion of Hall's output — are not found elsewhere. Many are on local topics, but several of the 'national' political satires are also among them. Reasons for lack of circulation are likely to include perceived lack of wider interest, perceived unsuitability of content, confidentiality, lack of effort or interest on Hall's part (as discussed in Chapter 2 above), obscurity, and possibly length, which is a significant feature of the local epistles and satires. Thus Hall writes a total of 369 lines to Dr Broughton, 182 lines to Mr Addis, 223 lines lampooning the Mathews family, and 295 lines more generally satirizing the Hereford establishment. The dialogue between Gilbert Ironside and John Birch takes up 92 lines, the political incident at Ludlow, 78, and the satire on the fat woman Jane Mayo, 106. And by far the longest of the political satires, 'Why towering tides submit to constant laws', an outspoken 221-line attack on the Dutch, is not found outside the Ottley manuscripts. Possibly uncirculated because of their obscurity (both are in B1 alone) are a dialogue put into the mouths of a fire-engine and a street-lamp, presented to Hereford by the local MPs Paul Foley and James Morgan, respectively (65 lines), and a lightly satirical account of the writer's imagined career as window-tax collector for Hereford, and his subsequent return to the city as a teacher of handwriting (80 lines).[1]

Some forty-five poems or songs found in the main manuscript collections do, however, occur elsewhere in manuscript or printed form (often in manuscript miscellanies), and there are in addition some thirty-five other items attributed or attributable to Hall, the majority of them songs, that are not represented in the Ottley and Brotherton Collection manuscripts. Attributions to Hall in these other witnesses are inconsistently present. Most of the political satires (of which seventeen account for the great bulk of the sixty-odd manuscript occurrences in question) are not assigned to him, and in the case of songs found with music it is not always certain whether Hall, if mentioned, is being credited with the words or only with the music. The implications of this wide, often anonymous distribution for the confident attribution of poems and songs occurring in the Ottley and Brotherton

Collection manuscripts will be a repeated theme. Conversely, whatever the true situation, there is no doubt that the extant manuscript collections are less than comprehensive in their coverage of Hall's poetic output.

Owing to their special nature, on the one hand, and importance, on the other, the circulation of Hall's songs with music and of his political satires will be treated separately in chapters of their own, with the exception of the special case of the Minnesota manuscript. The other manuscripts to be discussed in this chapter contain what may be characterized as 'miscellaneous' poems by Hall.

4.1. University of Minnesota MS 690235f

The most remarkable instance of manuscript copying of Hall's verse outside the Ottley and Brotherton Collection manuscripts is University of Minnesota MS 690235f, which has by far the largest number of poems by Hall (nineteen) preserved in a miscellany manuscript. All of them occur in one or other of the main manuscript collections. MS 690235f, to be cited here as M, is described by *CELM* as 'a formal folio miscellany of verse and prose, in English and Latin, chiefly on affairs of state, in a single professional hand', datable to the late 1690s. It is indexed, and contains over 220 separate items. Many well-known political satires of the period are represented, and it is likely that the compiler drew on multiple sources.[2]

Only one of the Hall items is attributed to him ('Dunned by the bells I rose from bed') and the nineteen in question are widely distributed within the manuscript. Nevertheless the selection of poems is of great significance, as ten of the nineteen are not found otherwise outside the Ottley and Brotherton Collection manuscripts, and seven are known elsewhere only in B1 (or C). For the purposes of discussion the poems are listed here in some detail:

1. 'An epitaph upon Sir John Fenwick baronet murdered upon Tower Hill by an act of Parliament 97. January 28' ('Here lies the relics of a martyred knight'), p. 96. Also in B1, B2.
2. 'Truth' ('With Job-like patience we've our burthens bore'), pp. 101–02. Also in B1, B2.
3. 'Sent to the House of Commons in 96' ('Ceas hypocrites to trouble heaven'), p. 106. Also in B1, C.
4. 'A satyr upon William' ('Haile happy William thou art strangely great'), p. 106. Also in B2.
5. 'Upon the taxes' ('The parliament thrifty to make up their wages'), p. 107. Also in B1 ('Our government thrifty [...]').
6. 'Upon the [m]onarchy' ('King William concern'd to leave his gull'd loobies'), p. 108. Also in B1 ('Great William concern'd [...]').
7. 'Upon Faux's blowing up the convention' ('When Catesby and Faux with the rest of the gang'), p. 108. Also in O1d, O2, B1.
8. 'The Jacobites quaeries for the thanksgiving 94' ('Are all those lights that gild the street'), pp. 131–32. Also in B1.
9. 'K: William cleared the rebellion laid upon the subjects of England' ('Ne're blame the heroe for the kingdomes fall'), p. 132. Also in B1.
10. 'The Parliament and the Kings management of Eng(land)' ('Six tedious months our senate sitts'), p. 132. Also in B1, B2.

11. 'A health 91' ('To our monarch's return'), pp. 141–42. Also in B1, C.
12. 'Upon the taxes' ('Good people what will ye of all be bereft'), p. 161. Also in B1.
13. '94' ('The author sure must take great pains'), p. 181. Also in B1 (''Twill puzzle much the author's brains').
14. '95' ('Rejoice ye sots the king is come again'), p. 182. Also in B1 ('Rejoice yee fops [...]'), C.
15. 'On Tom: Broades picture Hereford' ('For missing thee how canst thou Burting blame'), p. 208. Also in O1a, O2, B1, C.
16. 'On the Cheshire plott 94' ('No sooner our heroe to Flanders was gott'), p. 209. Also in B1.
17. 'The comparison of love & war' ('Now love & warr the self same art is grown'), p. 210. Also in O1d, O2, B1, B2.
18.   'On the election at Brecknock Sir Rowland Guin being chosen & Mr Jefferies [?] refused' ('Its odd indeed indeed its wounderous odd'), pp. 210–11. Also in B1 (''Tis odd indeed [...]').
19. 'By Hen: H: to E: Chandos's being beat by the E: att gameing' ('Dup'd by the bells I rose from bed'), pp. 211–12. Also in B1 ('Dun'd by the bells [...]'), C.

Although dispersed over more than a hundred pages, the majority of the poems are nonetheless grouped, suggesting that M's compiler may have had access to a collection of Hall's poems on which he drew from time to time. The principal groupings (defined here as having no intervening English poems) are of items 3–4, 5–7, 8–10, 13–14, and 15–19, with 3–4 separated from 5–7 by only a single non-Hall poem. What is more, items 1 and 2 are separated by only four such poems, and 2 and 3 by no more than two.[3]

In terms of subject-matter, the great majority (1–10, 12–14, 16) are political satires on William III and his government, some of them well known from other manuscripts and contemporary printings (see Chapter 7 below). Six of these satires, however (2, 3, 7, 8, 9, 16), are not recorded outside the Ottley and Brotherton Collection manuscripts. In addition, three out of the nineteen Hall poems — the most surprising occurrences — are on topics local to Hereford or the wider region, namely items 15, 18, and 19, here with the strikingly detailed titles quoted above.[4] (Titles more detailed than those in the main manuscript collections are a feature of many of the Hall items in M.) Again, none of these three poems occurs otherwise outside the main collections (or, in two cases, C). It is hard to believe that the compiler, in these several cases, was not copying directly from a collection of Hall's poems.

It is particularly significant that M has been dated to the late 1690s, within Hall's lifetime and before the creation of the Ottley and Brotherton Collection manuscripts. On the basis of no more than titles and opening lines it is clear that M has marked textual differences from B1, and in some cases its readings can be shown to agree with those of various other manuscripts.[5] The conclusion must be that certain of Hall's poems were circulating together at an early stage, and were subject either to the usual textual changes associated with manuscript transmission and/or to his own revisions. Questions of motive and agency in respect of their occurrence in M remain unanswerable.

4.2 Other Literary Manuscripts with Miscellaneous Hall Poems

Nothing compares to M in terms of number of Hall poems, but Bodleian, MS Eng. poet. f.13 is decidedly more personal. This small bound volume is a miscellany of English and Latin verse and university orations compiled in the early eighteenth century by the antiquary William Parry (1687–1756?), student and then Fellow of Jesus College, Oxford, who was born in Hereford.[6] It contains no more than two poems by Hall, both explicitly attributed to him, namely B1's 'Whether those hills that round you spread' (ff. 69r-71v) and 'In vain my fair you strive to cheat the sight' (f. 193r), but it preserves also a unique anonymous tribute to the poet composed after his death. This witty, affectionate little poem, which begins 'When Strephon sorrowing saw the Union past' (f. 74r), is printed and discussed in more detail in Chapter 9.1 below. In addition Parry transcribes, immediately before 'Whether those hills', Latin verses entitled 'Dr Broughtons epitaph made by himself' (f. 68v), and there can be no doubt that this is the same Dr Broughton to whom Hall addresses verse epistles.

The copy of the descriptive and reflective 'Whether those hills' is especially important textually, partly because of the detailed circumstantial information in its title. Whereas B1 has simply 'To Mr. Nicholas Arnold' and O1d/O2 have 'To Mr. Nich. Arnold on the Skerrit', Eng. poet. f.13's title reads: 'Mr. Hall, Organist of Hereford, being induc'd by Captain Arnold of Lantony to take a Prospect of the Country from the Top of the Skirrit; did within a day or two after send him the following lines from Abergavenny' (f. 69r). Parry's copy of the poem is also longer than that in the main manuscript collections, with frequent textual divergences. In particular, the absence in B1 and O1d/O2 of three lines of bawdy suggests that Hall may have revised the poem and that Eng. poet. f.13 preserves a more private earlier version. In contrast, its text of 'In vain my fair you strive to cheat the sight' (which is copied at the end of the manuscript, after the index) is close to that in B1, except that it begins 'Madam in vain you strive to cheat our sight'.

Despite being a generation younger it is conceivable that Parry had met Hall in Hereford and it is clear that he had access to materials relating to him and his circle. The closeness of the association may also be significant from an attributional point of view. One other poem in the manuscript is Daniel Kenrick's 'The great good man whom fortune does displace' (f. 35v), which, as noted earlier, occurs as if Hall's own composition in O1d/O2 (and in B1, to the disgust of the later corrector). Its lack of attribution in Eng. poet. f.13 may well be evidence that Parry, also, had no reason to think it Hall's.[7]

It was suggested in Chapter 2.3 that the younger Adam Ottley may have had a hand in assembling copies of Hall's poems for the Ottley manuscripts, and it is possible that he and Parry knew each other not only from Hereford but at Oxford.[8] As noted earlier, O3b is a letter from Hall, containing copies of several of his poems, addressed to Ottley at Balliol College almost certainly in July 1704. Other manuscripts containing poems or songs by Hall will be seen to have Oxford associations, evidence that his work had some circulation there in both literary and musical circles.[9] Parry would seem to have continued his interest in Hall's verse in that he includes an altered, softer version of the aggressively masculine 'Now love and war the self-same art is grown' (O1d/O2, B1, B2, M) in a volume of letters and other materials that he addressed in later life to his friend Thomas Rawlins; this is now Bodleian, MS Ballard 29, where the poem occurs on f. 145v.[10] But no attribution is given, and it is possible that Parry transcribed it from *A Miscellany of Poems by Several Hands* (Oxford, 1731), where the same version appears, also unattributed, on pp. 60–61.[11] This volume itself, however, is evidence that Hall's verse continued to be known in Oxford. Its compiler, John Husbands, Fellow of Pembroke College, included three poems by Hall, printing them in sequence on pp. 58–62. All unattributed, the other two are 'Phyllis in vain you drop that tear' (pp. 58–59) and 'In vain my fair you strive to cheat the sight' (p. 62), the latter with the same first line as in MS Eng. poet. f.13 ('Madam in vain you strive to cheat our sight').

Another early eighteenth-century private poetical miscellany from Oxford is Yale UL, MS Osborn c.233.[12] Yale's online catalogue suggests that its compiler, and most frequently represented author, may have been one Thomas Holland, who matriculated, also from Jesus College, in 1697. Strikingly, one of the three poems by Hall is again 'In vain my fair you strive to cheat the sight' but with its first line beginning 'Madam in vain you strive', as in MS Eng. poet. f.13, and *A Miscellany of Poems by Several Hands*.[13] The two others are not represented in the main manuscript collections of Hall's verse: one is the drinking song 'Whilst this bumper stands by me' ('An extempore catch on the Vigo expedition'), which is copied immediately after 'Madam in vain you strive' on the same page (p. 99), and the other, the four-line epigram 'To gain dishonour and immense disgrace', an attack on Christopher Wren's design for St Paul's Cathedral (p. 87). Both 'Madam in vain you strive' and 'To gain dishonour' are explicitly attributed to 'H. Hall', which may possibly suggest derivation from a Hereford-related source. 'Whilst this bumper', unattributed in the Yale manuscript, was printed in *The Grove: or, A Collection of Original Poems, Translations, etc.* (1721), but there it is ascribed to 'H. Hall of Hereford' and 'extempore' is missing from its title.[14]

The epigram attacking Wren also appears, without attribution, in Trinity College Dublin, MS 879 (vol. 1, f. 93r), but there it begins with a harder reading, 'To get false fame and infinite dispraise', which is also the form in which it appeared anonymously in *The Diverting Post* in March 1705. As will be shown in Chapter 5.3, it is very likely that Hall himself submitted poems to this journal. MS 879 is a formal three-volume miscellany headed 'The whimsical medley, or a miscellaneous collection of severall pieces in prose and verse', which was compiled by Theophilus Butler (1669–1723), first Baron Newtown of Newtown-Butler *c.* 1720.[15] The items catalogued by *CELM* make it clear that Butler very often copied from printed sources, including *The Diverting Post*, and this is almost certainly the case here. The manuscript also contains three other poems by Hall (none of them attributed), one of them again 'Now love and war' (vol. 3, f. 4r), and this too matches the (shorter) version that was printed in *The Diverting Post* (January 1704/5) — a different softening of the poem from that preserved in MS Ballard 29 and the 1731

Miscellany.[16] The remaining Hall poems are the enigma 'Out of the deep and from the earth', found in B1 but here titled 'Aenigma 48th' and so very likely copied from a printed collection of riddles; and the popular version of 'When Church was mother Anne was then her daughter' (discussed in Chapter 8.1 below), i.e. that beginning 'When Anna was the church's daughter', as printed in *POAS*, IV (1707).[17] It is probable, on balance, that all four of the Hall items in the Dublin manuscript were copied from printed sources.

Three other of the miscellaneous poems in B1 are known to have had a measure of manuscript circulation. One is the bawdy ballad 'All in the land of cider', which makes fun of Sir Edward Harley's attempt to suppress a sexual scandal at his Herefordshire country seat, Brampton Bryan. Harley (1624–1700) would have been a target in Hall's eyes for being a prominent local Puritan, but it was no doubt the explicit subject matter that won the ballad popularity. It occurs, however, in no more than a single manuscript miscellany, Bodleian, MS Eng. poet. e.87, possibly compiled in the 1710s.[18] In contrast it appears in four contemporary printed collections, beginning with *Political Merriment, or Truths Told to Some Tune* (London, 1714), where it has the title: 'The Welsh saint; or a full and true account of burning the defiled bed at Sir Anthony Crabtree's house in Herefordshire. To the tune of When first I laid siege to my Cloris'. There is no attribution. Exactly the same text (and title) then occurs in *A New Collection of Miscellany Poems* (London, 1715). In February 1714 the writer Richard Steele had satirized his political opponent Robert Harley, Earl of Oxford, as 'Sir Anthony Crabtree' in the fourth issue of his periodical *The Lover*, and it appears that someone who knew Hall's poem and its underlying target (Harley's father Sir Edward, who had died in 1700) quickly retitled it.[19] The printed text, it would seem, was then picked up in turn by the diarist Sarah Cowper (1644–1720), who copied this same 'Crabtree' version of the ballad into her 1713–16 diary, shortening it to twenty-four lines perhaps because of its explicit sexual content.[20] The poem next appeared, without title or attribution but with music, in the song book *The Merry Musician* (London, 1716), and then — like 'Whilst this bumper stands by me' — in *The Grove*, as 'A Ballad, by H. Hall of Hereford'.

The text of the poem in MS Eng. poet. e.87, which omits stanza 4, does not appear to have been copied from one of these printed texts but nor does it match the version in B1, which has its own corruption: stanzas 4 and 5 there have the same first line, 'John being so well provided'. (The version printed in *The Grove* also diverges at this point, exchanging the first lines of these two stanzas, and it inserts words throughout, apparently for metrical reasons.) B1's mistake, it may be noted, was not picked up by its later corrector, suggesting that the latter may not have had a copy of the ballad to hand. Surprisingly the poem is left untitled in B1. In Eng. poet. e.87 it is headed 'A ballad in imitation of All in the Land of Essex', a popular poem that Hall may well have known.[21] Overall, this mix of textual variations suggests quite significant manuscript circulation.

Quite different is B1's Jacobite six-line drinking song or catch, 'To our monarch's return'. Treated here as a miscellaneous poem, it tends to keep company with

Hall's political satires, as indeed it does in B1 itself, where it occurs in the middle of the opening sequence of 'national' satires noticed in the previous chapter. The main example — other than its presence in the Minnesota manuscript, for which see above — is its appearance on f. 92r of BL, Add MS 29497 (a folio collection of poems on affairs of state), not many pages away from three of the satires (see Chapter 7.5 below). Another occurrence is in the avowedly Jacobite compilation, Yale UL, MS Osborn b.111 (p. 36), though there it is well separated from Hall's political satire "Twill puzzle much the author's brains'. The isolated copy within the composite volume BL, Add MS 14854 (f. 104r), has the first couplet marked to be repeated and an extra line at the end. Further apparent evidence of textual variation is the transcription that appears in William Cooke's manuscript, where the first two lines of the song are reversed (see Chapter 3.2 above).

Mention may be made here of another political drinking song, 'Our business is drinking a round with a glass', which is attributed to 'Mr Hall' in a booklet now forming the final element of the large scribal collection of satires that is BL, MS Lansdowne 852 (for which see Chapter 7 below). The style and spirit of the poem are very plausibly Hall's, but no other copy is recorded.

Finally there is B1's distinctive 'The progress of the stage by way of epilogue', which begins 'Your primitive players first acted in a cart'. There are two other known manuscripts, namely Folger Shakespeare Library, MS M.b.12 (part 3, ff. 211r–12v), a large professionally written compilation of political satires and lampoons dating from the early 1700s, and Nottingham UL, MS Portland Pw V 44 (pp. 282–86), a related collection from the same period.[22] The poem in question indeed begins with a brief history of the stage, but quite soon passes to the period when women at last began to play female parts and then to a critique of the contemporary London theatre, satirizing Thomas Betterton's company.[23] The Folger and Portland manuscripts, which transmit an unattributed text of sixty-seven lines, both date it 1699, and the latter has a side-note, 'Mrs Batterton', against a line referring to an actress playing Ophelia.[24] B1 lacks these details and has only sixty lines. Where lines are shared, its readings seem preferable to those in Folger and Portland (which are textually very close), but there is no doubt that a rewriting took place, though the direction of revision is unclear. It is very likely that Hall himself was responsible for the changes, and one reason could have been circulation to a wider or different readership.

The manuscript with the largest number of poems by Hall not in the main manuscript collections is Worcestershire Archive and Archaeology Service, Lech-mere Archives 40 (i). This has a clear local provenance, in that it is from the collection of the Lechmere family of Hanley Castle in Worcestershire, twenty-four miles east of Hereford. According to David Newsholme, 'the manuscript appears to have been written over a number of years around the first decade of the eighteenth century by someone closely associated with [Worcester] cathedral who was able to comment skittishly on each of the prebendaries and on many other members of the cathedral community'.[25] The manuscript — which comprises fifty-six damaged pages, repaired and remounted within a modern binding — is indeed all in a single hand, and there are five items attributable to Hall:

- p. 3, a love song 'When I your charms your wondrous charms I see', 'by H. Hall'. The song was printed in *Monthly Mask of Vocal Music* for August 1710 as 'A song set by the late Mr Henry Hall of Herreford'. Its occurrence here is strong evidence that Hall was also responsible for the words.
- p. 4 (i.e. the next item), 'To Silvia mending her nightraill by H. H.', beginning 'A most ungodly work you now begin'; a playful love poem addressed to a lady mending a dressing gown.
- p. 10, 'Quid pro Quo or The Wocester [*sic*] Ballad Burlesk'd by H. Hall of Hereford', beginning 'Since in the last sessions your beau got the better'. The poem made fun of is 'The Worcester Cabal', which immediately precedes it in the manuscript (pp. 8–9).[26]
- p. 10 (i.e. the next item), 'On the King of Spain's presenting the Duke of Marlbrough with his picture', unattributed, beginning 'Accept my lord of this poor glittering thing'. This is the first poem in Hall's autograph letter to Adam Ottley the younger, O3b as described in section 2.3 above.
- pp. 14–15, 'A lampoon on Mrs Ec — y an apothycarys wife in return for one she made on E.W., by H. H.', beginning 'Must Silvia then the brightest nymph in town'.[27]

The second, third, and fifth items are not known elsewhere. The two attributed merely to 'H. H.' are in Hall's style (the latter is a fierce attack on 'Mrs Ec — y') and, given their manuscript context, his authorship seems certain.

The absence of the above poems from the main manuscript collections could be accounted for by their dating from after 1700, certain in the case of 'Since in the last sessions' and 'Accept my lord', which can be assigned to 1701 and 1703, respectively. The same applies to an isolated poem, 'First then we must confess Florella fair', which is preserved in two other of the Portland manuscripts held in Nottingham University Library. In one case, an originally folded sheet addressed 'For Mistress Eliz. Harley, with care' (MS Pw V 249), the poem is entitled 'A lampoon on the Hereford ladies'. In the other (MS Pw V 856, ff. 1v-2r), where it is one of eight poems copied on to two bifolios once part of a larger manuscript, the heading includes an attribution and date, namely 'A lampoon made on the Hereford ladies by Mr Hall, 1706'. The recipient of MS Pw V 249 must have been Elizabeth Harley (m. 1712, d. 1713), daughter of Robert Harley, the future Earl of Oxford, and granddaughter of Sir Edward Harley of Brampton Bryan, the target of Hall's ballad 'All in the land of cider' (see above). The poem is a satire on the pretensions to beauty of thirteen local ladies, each pseudonymous target identified in the margin by her real name.

No more than fifteen separate items have featured in the above survey of manuscript copying of Hall's miscellaneous poems, demonstrating how partial and restricted such copying seems to have been. Perhaps unsurprisingly it is quite often short, witty poems on female subjects that are chosen for copying, presumably for social reasons, but even here one might have expected more manuscripts to have survived.

Notes to Chapter 4

1. 'Here have I lain Lord knows how many years' and ''Twas with regret I left your lovely town'.
2. Relevant poems in M are included in the Index to Harold Love, *English Clandestine Satire, 1660–1702* (Oxford: Oxford University Press, 2004).
3. In addition, items 8–10 are immediately preceded on p. 131 by the non-Hall composition 'Curse on those representatives', which occurs also in O1d, O2, and B1.
4. These poems are all noticed in Chapter 1 above.
5. Thus its item 5 shares its title 'Upon the taxes' and the initial 'The' of its first line with BL, MS Sloane 2717, f. 98, though Sloane then reads 'government', like B1. Its item 13, 'The author sure must take great pains', agrees in its first line with all other witnesses, against B1. The opening words of its item 14, 'Rejoice ye sots', agree with BL, MS Stowe 305, f. 216v. But it may be noted that 'the worshipper', the final words of its item 9, one of the poems found otherwise only in B1, agrees with the latter's scribe against the later corrector, who substitutes 'th'Idolater'.
6. It bears Parry's bookplate dated 1724; cf. the entry in *CELM*. For Parry see Thompson Cooper, rev. Mary Clapinson, 'Parry, William (bap. 1687, d. 1756), Antiquary', in *ODNB*.
7. For further discussion of 'The great good man', see Chapter 9.2 below.
8. Foster, *Alumni Oxonienses*, III, 1096, 1122, records Ottley as matriculating in April 1702 and Parry in February 1706.
9. Hall has no known link with the so-called Christ Church wits of the 1690s (for whom see Griffin, 'The Social World of Authorship, 1660–1714', pp. 48–49, in relation to literary coteries), but Christ Church Library holds his autograph scores, and it may be relevant that his associate Daniel Kenrick was educated at the college.
10. See *CELM*, where the manuscript is dated *c*. 1737–49. The recipient may possibly be the musician Thomas Rawlings, for whom see Graydon Beeks, 'Rawlings [Rawlins], Thomas (c. 1703–1767), Musician and Music Copyist', *ODNB*.
11. The title is also the same, '(Up)on the taking of a mistress'. In citing this 1731 volume I make an exception to the cut-off date of 1721 otherwise used in this study for consideration of printed works.
12. See Yale UL's online catalogue <https://orbis.library.yale.edu/vwebv/> [accessed 11 October 2021].
13. The titles in these three copies vary: 'On a lady that pretended to be a ghost' (Eng. poet.), 'To a lady dress'd like a ghost to fright her lover' (Osborn), 'To Sylvia appearing like a ghost' (*Miscellany*), but they contrast more strongly with B1's 'To a lady that wou'd have put herself for a spright on a gentleman'.
14. For discussion of *The Grove*, see Chapter 9.2 below. Here and elsewhere the place of publication of printed works containing poems or songs by Hall can be assumed to be London unless otherwise stated.
15. As noted in *CELM*.
16. This shorter version was also printed in *A Miscellaneous Collection of Poems, Songs and Epigrams*, 2 vols (Dublin: [for T. M. Gent], 1721), II, 226.
17. With nineteen lines, 'Aenigma 48th' matches the text printed in the *Gentleman's Journal* in 1694 (for which see Chapter 5.1 below), in contrast to the sixteen lines preserved in B1.
18. In *CELM* it is dated *c*. 1742 on the basis of an ownership inscription by John Conyers, of Copt Hall, Essex, but the script and contents argue for earlier in the eighteenth century. *CELM* notes the miscellany's Jacobite sympathies.
19. See Charles A. Knight, *A Political Biography of Richard Steele* (London: Pickering & Chatto, 2009), p. 159.
20. The volume in question is Hertfordshire Archives and Local Studies, DE/P F35, for which reference I am indebted to the entry for Sarah Cowper in the Perdita Project database, <https://web.warwick.ac.uk/english/perdita/html/> [accessed 11 October 2021]. Hall's poem went on to be included in many eighteenth-century manuscript miscellanies, sometimes with the first line ''Twas in the land of cider'. For references, see the *Union First Line Index*.
21. For the poem, see Diana Julia Rose, 'MS Rawlinson Poetical 147: An Annotated Volume of

Seventeenth-Century Cambridge Verse' (unpublished doctoral thesis, University of Leicester, 1992), pp. 475–83.

22. See *CELM*, and the publications referenced in Chapter 7 below, n. 46, where these two manuscripts are discussed. They also both contain 'The great Sir George', a 1704 poem possibly attributable to Hall (see Chapter 8.1).

23. The poem is printed from B1, with detailed commentary, in *The Prologues and Epilogues of the Restoration, 1660–1700: A Complete Edition*, ed. by Pierre Danchin, 4 vols (Nancy: Presses universitaires de Nancy, 1981–88), III, 428–31. As Danchin writes, p. 429, 'there is no certainty that the piece we print here was a real epilogue actually used on stage'. The likelihood seems remote.

24. The first seventeen lines of the Folger text are printed in Maggs's 1923 catalogue *Shakespeare and Shakespeareana* (lot 434), from where the Folger Library purchased the manuscript.

25. David Newsholme, 'The Life and Works of William Davis (c. 1675/6–1745)', 3 vols (unpublished doctoral thesis, University of York, 2013), I, 231.

26. 'The Worcester Cabal' is printed from Yale UL, MS Osborn fb.70 (*olim* Phillipps 8301), in Ellis, VI, pp. 313–17, where it is attributed to the Whig MP and poet William Walsh on the basis of Hall's poem, which names Walsh (Hall's poem is a riposte to Walsh's satire on local Tory politicians). Both poems can be dated to 1701. Ellis, confusing his sigla, mistakenly states (p. 312) that Hall's poem follows 'The Worcester Cabal' in his copy text.

27. 'Mrs Ec — y' is identifiable as the wife of Richard Eckley, an early eighteenth-century apothecary in Worcester; see P. J. and R. V. Wallis, *Eighteenth Century Medics (Subscriptions, Licences, Apprenticeships)*, 2nd edn (Newcastle upon Tyne: Project for Historical Bibliography, 1988), p. 181.

CHAPTER 5

❖

Hall and Print Publication

Absent from the previous chapter is any evidence that Hall himself instigated the manuscript circulation of his verse outside his local area. The one exception might be his letter to the younger Adam Ottley, which appears to be little more than an excuse to send the student three short poems lampooning the Duke of Marlborough, possibly with the hope or expectation that Ottley would share them with his Oxford friends; but out of the three it is only 'Accept my lord this humble glittering thing' that is known from elsewhere (see Chapter 8.1 below).

Hall, in contrast, seems undoubtedly to be the agent responsible (or mainly responsible) for the print publication of what I have called his 'miscellaneous' poems. The instances to be discussed are of three kinds, namely verses printed in the *Gentleman's Journal* in 1694; poems paying tribute to, respectively, Henry Purcell, John Blow, John Dryden, and Henry Playford, published 1698–1702; and verses printed in the *Diverting Post* from 1704 to 1706. In total some twenty-eight poems are in question. Excluded from discussion here, as before, are Hall's songs with music, which began to appear in print in as early as 1685, and his political satires.

5.1. *The Gentleman's Journal*

The importance of the *Gentleman's Journal* (1692–94) as an outlet for authors seeking to get short pieces into print has already been noted.[1] Its enterprising editor, Peter Motteux, described it as 'Consisting of news, history, philosophy, poetry, musick, translations &c.', and created a deliberate mixture of serious and light-hearted contents.[2] Margaret Ezell has argued persuasively that the journal represents the commercialization of coterie manuscript practice, in that the letter format used by Motteux to communicate with his readership 'assists in the creation of a friendly community of readers and more broadly invites their participation in the process of writing the journal'. To this end he made use of 'interactive genres, literary forms which invite the reader's response'.[3]

One such popular genre was the 'enigma', which involved readers, every month, sending in or solving riddles, in both cases in the form of verse. It was this sociable, witty aspect of the journal that seems first to have caught Hall's attention and made him wish to participate, despite Motteux's frequent praise of William and Mary.[4] It may be that he was one of those writers, to use Ezell's words, 'whose only previous literary venue would [have been] a coterie manuscript circle'.[5] Thus the issue for October 1692 records that 'H. Hall' had submitted answers, in verse, to both of the 'ænigmas' published the previous month, the subjects of which were lace on the one hand and a newsletter or gazette on the other. However, these submissions were not printed, and Hall does not appear to have entered the field again until January 1694 when an enigma of his own was successful: 'Out of the deep and from the earth'.

This 19-line riddle occurs also in B1 (where the solution is given as 'A bottle of clarrett'), so Hall's authorship seems assured, but in the *Gentleman's Journal* the lines are given to 'Mr De la Sale' — problematic at first, but almost certainly a witty translation of 'Hall', possibly by the journal's French editor, Motteux, but more likely by Hall himself, given the popularity of pseudonyms amongst the contributors.[6] Five further poems attributed to Mr De la Sale (including two enigmas) then appear in later issues, along with, in May 1694, a couplet sent in as the solution to two enigmas published in April, on 'wit' and 'a bubble'. 'Both were solv'd [...] by Palæmon and Mr De la Sale in verse', writes Motteux, 'thus the latter: "To solve your too [*sic*] riddles will cause no great trouble | Since if life be no more, surely wit's but a bubble"'' (p. 131).

The five poems in question are 'I never did eat yet I'm still at a feast', 'All own the young Sylvia is fatally fair' (both printed in May 1694), 'I love to madness rave t'enjoy' (June 1694), 'We neither are Christians, Turks, Pagans, nor Jews' (August 1694), and 'Too roughly Sir you paint the dear delight' (October 1694). The first and fourth are the riddles, on the subjects of laughter and cards, respectively. The second and third are love songs with music, in the first case as 'A song set by Mr Robert King, the words by Mr De la Sale', in the second as 'The mad lover. The words and tune by Mr De la Sale'. The fifth poem is 'To Mr W. in answer to his verses against injoyment, by Mr De la Sale', which in eighteen lines of couplets wittily recommends sex as the route to happiness.

If 'Mr De la Sale' is accepted as being Henry Hall in the case of 'Out of the deep', then the identification clearly has to apply to all these other items, and there appears to be no evidence for an English poet called 'De la Sale' outside the pages of the *Gentleman's Journal*. Stylistically there is no difficulty in accepting the humorous poems as Hall's, and the riddle on laughter contains a line that could be said to sum him up: 'Yet my greatest delight for the most part's in satire'. The love poems, too, if more conventional in content, have a characteristic exuberance.[7] From the heading to 'I love to madness' the author appears also to be a musician.

It is somewhat surprising, however, that out of five poems in the *Gentleman's Journal* contributed by a 'Mr H.' during 1694, three can be assigned to Hall, showing that he was not uniformly pseudonymous. All appear in either the March or July issue, when nothing by De la Sale was printed. Two of these poems occur also in B1, namely 'Although for every different dress' (March), on how wearing black enhances a young woman's beauty, and 'As Phoebus did with heat pursue' (July), which is headed 'Why the thunder never strikes the laurel'.[8] The latter is also found, with music ascribed to Hall, in Henry Playford's *Deliciae Musicae* [...] *The Second Book* (1695). The third poem (also July) is an enigma beginning 'Like two sage sisters close we dwell', to which the solution is dice. It is not elsewhere associated with Hall, but there is little question that it is his. The style matches that of the other enigmas, and one of the three poetic responses to it printed in the August issue is by Hall's close associate Daniel Kenrick.[9] All four of Hall's riddles, it may be noted — on drinking, cards, dice, and laughter — reflect the kind of social life he evidently enjoyed.

The other two 'Mr H.' poems published in 1694 comprise, mysteriously, John Oldmixon's effusive love poem 'The Grove' (June) (not at all in Hall's style), which subsequently appeared in his *Poems on Several Occasions* (1696); and a short translation of a passage from Horace (March), which can probably be discounted — despite the presence of 'Although for every different dress' in the same issue — because its explicit context is extravagant support for William III's wars (it begins 'The bounteous gods to make you happy joined'). Another poem given to a 'Mr H.' appears in the December 1692 *Gentleman's Journal*, but this is Benjamin Hawkshaw's 'The management' ('Each day I've liv'd I've spent it all in love').

It may be noted finally that the *Gentleman Journal*'s musical supplement for November 1693 had included the love song 'While Galathea you design', in a setting that in Playford's *Thesaurus Musicus* [...] *The Second Book* (1694) is said to be 'by Mr Henry Hall'. In the *Gentleman's Journal*, however, it is described as 'A song set by Mr R. Courtiville', i.e. the London composer Raphael Courteville (*c.* 1673–*c.* 1735). Hall's involvement with the piece is therefore somewhat uncertain, but it is conceivable that Playford's statement represents a correction.[10]

5.2. Poems in Tribute

All four of the poems in question here appeared in volumes closely associated with the London music publisher Henry Playford, with whom Henry Hall apparently formed a close friendship. It is possible, and perhaps likely, that Henry Purcell made the introduction. Hall's enduring affection and admiration for Purcell, following their time together at the Chapel Royal, is evident in a number of poems, and it is plausible that they kept in touch during the intervening years and possibly even met on the occasions when Hall visited the capital. The latter's popular royalist song 'Haste Charon haste' was published in Playford's first important collection, *The Theater of Music* (1685), and Playford there thanks Purcell (and John Blow) for editorial assistance, which may have extended to recommendation of pieces for inclusion. There is little doubt that Playford, Purcell, and Hall shared similar religious and political convictions.[11]

In 1698, when Playford published the first volume of *Orpheus Britannicus*, his famous collection of Purcell's vocal music, it would appear that he invited Hall to write one of the prefatory poems in tribute to the composer. Headed 'To the memory of my dear friend Mr. Henry Purcell' and subscribed 'By H. Hall, organist of Hereford', the poem laments the composer's death, places him in the context of musical development in England, and praises his irreplaceable musical skill. That Hall took considerable trouble with this tribute is demonstrated by the way in which he combined and rewrote elements of two earlier poems in which he had praised Purcell, one preserved in all of O1d, O2, B1, and B2 ('Yes my Palemon 'tis too true'), written after Purcell's death, the other in B1 alone ('Music the chiefest good the gods have given', a first line re-used for the version in *Orpheus Britannicus*). As I have shown in detail elsewhere, the public tribute principally derives from 'Music the chiefest good the gods have given' (in B1 headed 'To Mr Purcell'), in which Hall praises the exceptional abilities of the still-living composer.[12] It must therefore pre-date 1695, the year of his death. The lament 'Yes my Palemon 'tis too true' is drawn on in a more general way in the later stages of the new poem, which then ends with the extravagant autobiographical tribute already quoted in part in Chapter 1 above (I retain the typography of the final couplet, so as to reproduce its effect):

> Hail! and for ever hail harmonious shade!
> I lov'd thee living, and admire thee dead.
> Apollo's harp at once our souls did strike,
> We learnt together, but not learnt alike:
> Though equal care our master might bestow,
> Yet only Purcell e'er shall equal Blow:
> For thou, by Heaven for wondrous things design'd,
> Left'st thy companion lagging far behind.
>
> *Sometimes a* HERO *in an Age appears*;
> *But scarce a* PURCELL *in a Thousand Years*.[13]

This is new material, not found in the manuscript precursors, and it is striking that Hall has here turned to John Dryden as a model, as the six lines beginning 'Apollo's harp' are clearly indebted to Dryden's 1684 'To the Memory of Mr Oldham':

> One common Note on either Lyre did strike,
> And Knaves and Fools we both abhorr'd alike:
> To the same Goal did both our Studies drive,
> The last set out the soonest did arrive,
> Thus *Nisus* fell upon the slippery place,
> While his young Friend perform'd and won the Race. (ll. 5–10)[14]

But these inter-related texts are not the sum of Hall's tributes to the departed Purcell. As will be noted in the following chapter, he adapted the text of the original manuscript version of 'Yes my Palemon 'tis too true' for a musical setting of this lament (now beginning 'Yes my Aminta 'tis too true'), and Purcell's genius is again highly praised in the poem 'From the bright mansions of the blest above', a song for St Cecilia's Day printed in the *Diverting Post* for November 1704 (see section 5.3 below).

Following *Orpheus Britannicus*, other tribute poems appeared in three further Playford-related volumes. The first, published in 1700, was *Amphion Anglicus*, John Blow's collection of his own songs, to which Hall, probably at Blow's request, contributed a 66-line poem ('A publick good, does publick thanks require') not elsewhere recorded. In familiar style, it is headed 'To his esteemed friend, Dr. Blow, upon publishing his book of songs', the volume in this case having been printed for the author, i.e. Blow, with Playford acting as seller.[15] Hall's poem — he is again named as 'Henry Hall, organist of Hereford' — includes satire on the popular ballads and song-writers of the day, a one-line reference to Purcell ('And Britain's Orpheus learn'd his art from you'), praise of Blow's role in reforming English music, and again, a lengthy autobiographical passage as a conclusion. Part of this was given in Chapter 1 above — the lines in which Hall describes himself as cut off from London — but I quote now the final ten lines in which he memorably compares his reaction to hearing a new composition by Blow to that of a knight of old inspired once again to action by news of a 'mighty hero's fame':

> But if by chance some charming piece I view,
> By all carress'd, because put forth by you;
> As when of old, a knight long lost in love,
> Whose Phillis neither brine nor blood cou'd move,
> Throws down his lance, & lays his armor by,
> And falls from errantry to elegy:
> But if some mighty hero's fame he hears,
> That like a torrent, all before him bear's,
> In haste he mounts his trusty steed again,
> And led by glory, scow'rs along the plain;
> So I with equal ardour seize my flute,
> And string again my long neglected lute.[16]

Some lines earlier Hall had written 'Nought of the bard, besides his fame, I hear', which must refer to John Dryden, who died in 1700, the year in which *Amphion Anglicus* was published. His admiration for Dryden as an example to be followed was noted in Chapter 2.1, above, in connection with his poem 'To Mr Charles Hoskins upon my lending him Mr Wallers poems' (B1, B2), but Edmund Waller is praised there as well as Dryden, specifically for having refined the English language into a medium suitable for poetry:

> He first our native language did refine,
> Rugged and rough, like mettle in the mine,
> He purg'd the dross and stampt it into coin. (B1, p. 51)

The triplet in question is a striking example of the frequent intertextuality of Hall's poems, because he re-used the lines — with a simple change of reference from language to music — in the verse tribute to John Blow just discussed:

> You first our modern musick did refine,
> Rugged and rough, like mettal in the mine,
> You purg'd the dross, and stamp'd it into coin.[17]

Here again we see Hall drawing on a presumably earlier manuscript composition when creating a new poem for public consumption.

Dryden in turn was honoured in a volume published by Playford and his fellow-bookseller Abel Roper later in 1700, and Hall was again a contributor. This rather unsatisfactory compilation of tributes, entitled *Luctus Britannici, or The Tears of the British Muses for the Death of John Dryden Esq*, features an unusual preface by the two publishers defending the enterprise from advance criticism. Given the contents of the volume this is perhaps not so surprising, as the contributors appear largely to be undistinguished Oxford and Cambridge men, and (compounding the oddity) the book's typography changes abruptly more than once. The presence of a poem by Hall (named here as 'Henry Hall') is surprising in this context, and it is conceivable that Playford, though attributing the selection of the material to trustworthy 'Learned gentlemen' (sig. A2v), had asked him to support the venture. The poem, headed simply 'To the memory of John Dryden, Esq.', begins 'Greece had a Homer; Rome a Virgil lost', and Hall's effusive, overlong, and yet particularized praise of his fellow-poet and his works stretches to 106 lines, in this case with no apparent textual overlap with other of his compositions. It demonstrates, along the way, the breadth of Hall's reading of English poetry. No other witness is known.

The final item in this sequence of public tributes by Hall is a poem in praise of Playford himself, printed (with others) at the front of the second volume of *Orpheus Britannicus*, published in 1702.[18] The same poem ('Next to the man who so divinely sung') is preserved in O2, the fair copy amongst the Ottley manuscripts, but no source manuscript has survived.[19] The title is the same in both witnesses, 'To Mr Henry Playford on his publishing the second part of Orpheus Britannicus', and the body of the text varies in only minor ways, differing most noticeably in the printed version's omission of the manuscript's inelegant final triplet, which is furnished with an explicatory footnote in O2. Other smoothings suggest that the printed text represents a revision. Not changed, amongst Hall's praise of Playford for having perpetuated Purcell's fame, are his expressions of friendship for the bookseller, as in 'Go on my friend, nor spare no pains nor cost, | Let not the least motett of his be lost'. As in the tribute to John Blow, considerable space is given to adversely comparing the work of young contemporary song-writers, and in this connection both refer, apparently in friendly fashion, to the well-known music engraver Thomas Cross. If there were an embargo on their 'most insipid songs, and sad sonato's', writes Hall in his tribute to Playford, 'Then honest *Cross* might copper cut in vain, | And half our sonnet-sellers starve again'; and in his poem to Blow, 'While at the shops we daily dangling view | False concord, by Tom Cross engraven true'.[20] In both compositions Hall appears to be describing the London musical scene with first-hand knowledge, and it is possible that he himself employed Cross to engrave his song 'Dragoons have a care', *c.* 1700 (see Chapter 6.3).

5.3. *The Diverting Post*

Hall's early eighteenth-century connections with London, and again Henry Playford, are further demonstrated by his frequent contributions to the *Diverting Post*, an unprepossessing 2-page paper that in its main manifestation (nos. 1–36) appeared as a weekly half-sheet folio from October 1704 to June 1705. The imprint of the early issues names only Benjamin Bragg, as printer and seller, but it is Playford who (as 'H. P.') signs the preface to the collected 'First Volume', which is addressed 'To those gentleman and ladies who have been assistants', and who goes on to boast that it was through their 'kind assistance' that he 'began, continued, and completed it'.

As with the *Gentleman's Journal* a decade earlier, the poetic contents of the paper were solicited from its readers. But also like the *Gentleman's Journal*, the title was not long-lasting. A stitched set in the Bodleian, containing the preface and comprising all of nos. 1–36 (up to June 1705), is preceded by a title-page for 'Vol. 1, for the year 1705'.[21] The imprint, however (naming Playford and the bookseller John Nutt), is dated 1706 and is followed by an advertisement for the first part of the *Diverting Post* for 'January', apparently a new monthly series following a hiatus in publication. This issue for January duly appeared, in a more ambitious 10-page format, but Playford's attempt to revive the title evidently failed, as after February 1706 there were no subsequent issues.

Hall's light-hearted political satire beginning 'As man in Westminster to each that comes' is in fact the lead item in this final *Diverting Post*, and bears the expansive heading 'For the entertainment of the gentry of Oxford. A farther explanation of the Oxford Almanack, occasioned by its being laid before the L — ds'. But there is no author statement, the attribution of the poem to Hall dependent on the copy in Thomas Hearne's diary entry for 19 March 1706: 'A silly explanation having been publish'd by some foolish fanatick upon the Oxon Almanack for this year 1706, there is another written by way of banter upon the Whiggs (as 'tis said) by Mr. Hen. Hall of Hereford, call'd A farther explanation of the Oxford Almanack.'[22]

Hall's earlier contributions, totalling fourteen poems or songs, were spread across nine separate issues of the *Diverting Post* from no. 2 (October 1704) to no. 23 (March 1705). He clearly got into the habit of sending verses to be printed. In the circumstances of their friendship it is quite likely that Playford drew Hall's attention to his new venture, and perhaps solicited poems from him. It is of interest that while some of the items are clearly newly written and often occasioned by contemporary events, others are pre-existing compositions. As will be seen, those in the latter group occur also in B1 (and in some cases elsewhere), whereas the newer poems, if not unique to the *Diverting Post*, are found amongst the Ottley manuscripts. I list the fourteen items in question in the order of their publication:

No. 2 (October 1704), p. 2: 'To our arms on earth and seas', a celebration of British success in the wars with France. Its detailed heading, 'A health to the generals. A song for two voices, compos'd and set by Mr H. Hall, Organist of Hereford. Sung by Mr Cook and Mr Davis, at the new Theatre, and at the Temple', makes the printing appear a report of a recent London musical event. If so, it may even be that Hall was present and that Playford solicited the text of the song for the newly established journal. It is preserved in O1e and O2 under the title 'The healths', and another manuscript copy, with music ascribed to 'Mr Henery Hall', exists in Christ Church, Oxford, MS Mus 1219 (F). The text was subsequently printed as 'A new song, set by Mr D. Purcell' on the verso of the single-sheet *A New Ode, Being a Congratulatory Poem on the Glorious Successes of Her Majesty's Arms* [...] *Set to Musick by Mr. Jer. Clark* (London: J. Morphew, 1706).[23]

No. 3 (November 1704), p. 1: 'From the bright mansions of the blest above', another new song (with a 'grand chorus'), again with explicit attribution: 'A Song on St Cecilia's Day, being the 22nd Instant, admirably set by Mr H. Hall of Hereford'.

Given that Henry Purcell is praised equally with St Cecilia it is highly likely that Hall was also responsible for the words. No other copy is known.

No. 3 (November 1704), p. 2: 'Lucinda has the de'l and all', a song putting a sexual value on a girl's beauty, again with an attribution: 'By Mr Henry Hall made and set to musick'. Unrecorded in manuscript, it had already been printed, with music, in the August 1700 issue of Playford's *Mercurius Musicus*. Further information is given in the following chapter.

No. 7 (December 1704), pp. 1–2: 'A good honest farmer by providence blest', an unattributed satire on religious politics, headed 'A fable'. It is preserved under the same title in O1e (in Hall's own hand and beginning 'An honest good farmer') from where it was copied into O2. See further Chapter 8.1 below.

No. 7 (December 1704), p. 2: 'Since the town is our own what it cost us no matter', a song, unattributed, toasting an English victory during the War of the Spanish Succession. Entitled here 'On the taking of Landaw. A song', in O1e and O2 it is headed 'Landau took, Nov. 1704', again making the printing decidedly contemporary.

No. 9 (December 1704), p. 2: 'To Phyllis fools and men of wit resort', an unattributed satire on the lustful attentions paid to a lady of fashion, headed 'On Phillis'. A more sexually explicit version occurs in B1 (headed 'La Coquette'), and Hall may have realised that change was necessary before publication.

No. 12 (January 1704/05), p. 2: 'We heard indeed of glorious actions done', once again a poem celebrating English victory, with a circumstantial title suggesting a recent event: 'On the standards taken at Bleinheim; being carried to Westminster-Hall, and there hung up'. Unattributed, but the poem 'In vain my fair', which follows it directly in the *Diverting Post*, has 'By the same author' appended to its title. The poem is not known elsewhere.

No. 12 (January 1704/05), p. 2: 'In vain my fair you strive to cheat the sight', with the heading 'On a young lady who wou'd have put herself upon him for a spright'. Again with no named author (but see the previous entry), this poem in praise of a lady's beauty begins as in B1, whereas the other known manuscript copies begin 'Madam in vain you strive to cheat our sight', as noted in Chapter 4.2 above. It also bears a similar title to that in B1, again different from those in the other manuscripts. These factors imply a close relationship to what is presumed to be a Hereford copy, perhaps equivalent to Hall's original text.

No. 13 (January 1704/05), p. 2: 'Now love and war the self-same art are grown'. Another poem existing in multiple copies, including all of O1d/O2, B1, B2, and M, this unattributed version differs from the texts just cited in having only seventeen lines and bearing the title 'Love and war: a parallel'.[24] It appears to be a probably authorial shortening and softening, for publication, of their overly masculine version, as noted, again, in Chapter 4.2, there in relation to the copy found in Trinity College, Dublin, MS 879, which was almost certainly copied from the *Diverting Post*.

No. 20 (March 1705), p. 1: 'The jovial crew in piteous plight departed'. Headed 'On a company of strolers that were lately at Hereford. By H.H.', the poem is unusual in recounting, wittily, an apparently contemporary event in Hereford, namely the expulsion from the town of a company of strolling players. It is known only from the *Diverting Post*.

No. 20 (March 1705), p. 1: 'To get false fame and infinite dispraise', an unattributed epigram attacking Christopher Wren's design for St Paul's Cathedral, then in the course of rebuilding. It is headed 'To Sir C — r W — n'. As noted in the previous chapter, a different version, beginning 'To gain dishonour and immense disgrace', survives in Yale UL, MS Osborn c.233. As with 'Now love and war', noted above, the text in Trinity College, Dublin, MS 879 was almost certainly copied from the *Diverting Post*.

No. 21 (March 1705), p. 1: 'Phyllis in vain you drop that tear', but here beginning 'Phillis in vain those tears you shed'. In addition, the unattributed *Diverting Post* text is headed 'To Phillis mourning for the death of her husband' rather than simply 'Song', as in B1 (its only other occurrence), suggesting that a variant manuscript text may have been in circulation.

No. 23 (March 1705), p. 1: 'Once in a reign to increase our causeless fears', headed 'On the two monsterous Fishes, lately taken at Gravesend', and so a poem reacting to another contemporary event. It is again unattributed. As with 'A good honest farmer' (December 1704), Hall links the incident to the current political situation, and the poem is therefore considered in more detail in Chapter 8.1 below. In this case the slightly shorter manuscript version occurs, in Hall's own hand, in O3a.

No. 23 (March 1705), p. 2: 'Hark to the war the trumpet sounds'. In contrast to the previous poem's anonymity, this same issue of the *Diverting Post* contains another celebration of the Duke of Marlborough as war hero, its detailed heading explicitly reflecting Hall's success in getting such songs performed in London: 'On the Duke of Marlborough's approaching campaign, made and set by Mr H. Hall of Hereford, and sung with great applause by the new boy at the Theatre Royal'. No other copy is known.

Assuming that Hall himself submitted the poems on contemporary events to the *Diverting Post*, it is likely that he sent in all fifteen of his contributions, older and newer. Encouragement and input from Playford are, however, distinctly possible in some cases, especially with songs bearing headings that both attribute these compositions to Hall and/or praise their success, including in performance. It may be significant that his first three contributions all fall into this category. If having these songs published had been suggested to him, he may subsequently have sent in other work on his own accord, revising certain established poems but more frequently submitting newly written material. The lack of attribution in the case of most of the items without musical associations is very likely not significant, as the great majority of the poems published in the *Diverting Post* conceal their authors' names. If his verses had no musical context, Hall may not have been concerned about remaining anonymous in an essentially ephemeral print-publication of this kind. As has been said — and leaving aside the 'tribute' poems discussed in section 5.2 above — the evidence seems to show that he remained at heart a manuscript poet, happy to produce verse for the occasion and with no thought of bringing his considerable output together in any lasting form.

Notes to Chapter 5

1. In Chapter 2 above, citing Ezell, *Social Authorship and the Advent of Print*, pp. 87–88.
2. Robert Cunningham, *Peter Anthony Motteux, 1663–1718: A Biographical and Critical Study* (Oxford: Blackwell, 1933), pp. 27–50, and see also David Hopkins, 'Motteux, Peter Anthony [formerly Pierre-Antoine Le Motteux] (1663–1718), Journalist and Translator', in *ODNB*. As stated earlier, when quoting from printed sources of the period, I retain original spelling and (with rare exceptions) punctuation, but apply modern capitalization practice.
3. Margaret J. M. Ezell, 'The *Gentleman's Journal* and the Commercialization of Restoration Coterie Literary Practices', *Modern* Philology, 89 (1992), 323–40 (p. 328).
4. Cunningham, *Peter Anthony Motteux, 1663–1718*, p. 29.
5. Ezell, 'The *Gentleman's Journal* and the Commercialization of Restoration Coterie Literary Practices', p. 332.
6. But in B1 the riddle has only sixteen lines. See the previous chapter for its occurrence also in Trinity College, Dublin, MS 879.
7. 'All own the young Sylvia' and 'I love to madness' were reprinted in the miscellany *Wit and Eloquence* (1697), without author attributions and very likely without Hall's knowledge, but with the former said to be 'A song set by Mr Robert King'. They appear also in *Wit and Mirth*, VI (1720), the only attribution again being to King.
8. The *Gentleman's Journal* text of 'Although for every different dress' omits the first three lines of this poem, presumably in error.
9. 'On dice' (six lines). Kenrick's only other credited contribution to the *Journal*, a poetic 'Dialogue between Dives and Abraham', appears in the same issue. For the relationship between Kenrick and Hall, see Chapter 9.2 below.
10. For fuller information on this song, see the following chapter.
11. For Playford's career, and his relationship with Purcell, see Richard Luckett, 'The Playfords and the Purcells', in *Music and the Book Trade from the Sixteenth to the Twentieth Century*, ed. by Robin Myers, Michael Harris, and Giles Mandlebrote (New Castle, DE, & London: British Library, 2008), pp. 45–67. See also the relevant paragraphs in Robert Thompson, 'Playford, John (1621x23–1686/7), Music Publisher', *ODNB*.
12. Pickering 1994. The text of the poem from *Orpheus Britannicus* is printed in Franklin B. Zimmerman, *Henry Purcell, 1659–1695: His Life and Times*, 2nd edn (Philadelphia: University of Pennsylvania Press, 1983), pp. 309–10.
13. Purcell, *Orpheus Britannicus*, I, vi.
14. *The Poems and Fables of John Dryden*, ed. by James Kinsley (London: Oxford University Press, 1962), p. 324. I am indebted to Paul Hammond for this reference, as also for pointing out that the opening couplet of both poems beginning 'Music the chiefest good the gods have given' shows the influence of John Oldham's own 'An Ode for an Anniversary of Musick on S. Ceclia's Day'; see *The Poems of John Oldham*, ed. by Harold F. Brooks (Oxford: Clarendon Press, 1987), pp. 282–83, and Pickering 1994, p. 23. Hall may have known Oldham's poem from its 1685 setting by John, Blow.
15. See Luckett, 'The Playfords and the Purcells', p. 65, for Playford's having apparently withdrawn from publishing the volume. Hall's tribute to Blow is briefly discussed in Pickering 1994, p. 29.
16. Blow, *Amphion Anglicus*, p. ii.
17. Ibid. For further examples of such intertextuality, see the Conclusion to this study.
18. As with Hall's tribute to Purcell in the first volume of *Orpheus Britannicus*, the text is reprinted in Zimmerman, *Henry Purcell, 1659–1695*, pp. 310–11.

19. In O2 it begins 'Next to the man that so divinely sung'.
20. It may be noted that O2 reads 'sonnet-setters', which seems a less good reading.
21. The title-page may not, however, apply to nos. 25–36, for April-June 1705, each of which is headed 'Vol. II'. For a detailed bibliographical description, see the relevant *Digital Miscellanies Index* entry <https://dmi.bodleian.ox.ac.uk/catalog/miscellany_1147> [accessed 11 October 2021]
22. Bodleian, MS Hearne's Diaries 9, pp. 27–28; printed in *Remarks and Collections of Thomas Hearne*, ed. by C. E. Doble and others, 11 vols (Oxford: Oxford Historical Society, 1885–1921), I, 205.
23. *ESTC* N2304, Foxon N162. The item by Hall, here beginning 'To our arms by land and sea's' and very likely printed without his knowledge, is not noted by Foxon or identified by *ESTC*. The printing in question is item 200 in Robert D. Horn, *Marlborough, a Survey: Panegyrics, Satires, and Biographical Writings, 1688–1788* (New York: Garland, 1975), pp. 231–32, where it is mistakenly given the title 'To Regina be the mutual cry', which is the final line of the preceding song.
24. Cf. 'The New Art of Love' (O1/D, O2), 'Song' (B1), 'Upon the taking of a mistress' (B2, Ballard 29), and 'The comparison of love and war' (M).

CHAPTER 6

❖

Songs with Music

The preceding two chapters have discussed, first, the manuscript copying of Hall's poems by others and then, in contrast, his own involvement in the print-publication of his works. The present chapter concentrates on songs by Hall that are preserved with music, in both manuscript and printed form. As will be seen, some of the manuscript material is in Hall's autograph, notably the formal compositions paying tribute to Henry Purcell and Queen Anne. The non-autograph manuscripts mainly comprise copies of catches (often drinking songs) or love poems, the exception being copies of Hall's popular 'Haste Charon haste'. All of this manuscript activity may be regarded as parallel to the non-Hereford copying of Hall's poems without music in that he himself appears to have had no agency in the matter. His printed songs, on the other hand, which largely appear within contemporary song books, raise once more the question of Hall's links with London booksellers, among whom Henry Playford again features quite prominently.

6.1. Autograph Music

Autograph manuscripts of non-religious vocal music by Hall are preserved exclusively in the library of Christ Church, Oxford.[1] The manuscripts in question contain two compositions, one represented by MS Mus. 1212(A), MS Mus. 1141a, f. 47, and MS Mus. 1142a, ff. 34–37, the other by MS Mus. 1212(B). Mus. 1212(A) is fragmentary, but this deficiency is largely made good by the four leaves in Mus. 1142a and the single leaf in Mus. 1141a, which can be seen to have once been part of it.[2] Both of the compositions are songs, and the presence of corrections in the scribal hand (to both music and words) affords a strong initial presumption that they are autographs.

Mus. 1212(A) and the leaves in Mus. 1141a and 1142a together comprise a lengthy 'Song to the Queen', an ode evidently written to celebrate Anne's accession to the throne in 1702. Mus. 1212(A) consists of two bifolios and one single sheet, stitched together, and a smaller fold-out sheet pasted to the right of f. 4, evidently added when the queen gave birth to another son ('Another royal infant sing'). The two bifolios that form ff. 34–37 of Mus. 1142a belong between f. 2 and f. 3 of Mus. 1212(A), and supply, among other material, the missing opening words of the first section of the ode ('Bless Albion bless thy stars above'). Mus. 1141a, f. 47, supplies no more than an instrumental 'Tune' between other vocal pieces. The song is known nowhere else.

Mus. 1212(B), a separate fascicle of eight bifolios, contains a pastoral lament for the death of Henry Purcell, portrayed as a shepherd, Daphnis. It too is fragmentary, lacking the beginning, including ll. 1–9 of the text; however, a complete copy survives in Bodleian, MS Tenbury 1232, and the song in question ('Yes my Aminta 'tis too true') proves to be an adaptation by Hall of his poetic lament for Purcell ('Yes my Palemon 'tis too true') preserved in the four manuscripts O1d, O2, B1, and B2.[3] It mainly takes the form of a dialogue between a shepherd and a shepherdess, scored for soprano, bass, two recorders, and continuo, but the final seven lines of the text are given to a chorus. The piece was recorded by the Parley of Instruments in 1992 and published in a performance edition by Peter Holman in 2008.[4] The Purcell Society has more recently (2013) published a detailed scholarly edition by Alan Howard, which includes a facsimile of Mus. 1212(B), f. 3v.[5]

These two compositions in Christ Church library are respectively signed 'Henry Hall' (Mus. 1212(A), f. 5v) and 'H. Hall' (Mus. 1212(B), f. 8r). The first subscription, in particular, is clearly the same as the 'Henry Hall' signature at the foot of the letter that is O3b. Even though the words are sometimes written small to fit between the staves of music, the hand that supplied the text of the songs in both manuscripts exhibits plentiful signs of the boldness and exuberance of letter-forms typical of the relevant parts of O1d, O1e, O3a, and O3b. The presence of scores by Hall in Christ Church Library (see below for two further examples) reinforces the impression that his work, both musical and poetical, was well known in Oxford, and it appears that 'Bless Albion bless thy stars above' was performed there.[6]

6.2. 'Haste Charon Haste'

Hall's other most significant pieces of secular vocal music are his royalist song, 'Haste Charon haste', representing his first appearance in print, and (outside the scope of this study) his setting of a Renaissance Latin poem, 'Viderat Adriacis', extolling the supreme beauty of Venice.[7] The latter, to be dated no later than 1695, is likely to be part of the otherwise untraced 'Opera on the Subject of the Doge of Venice's Marriage with the Adriatick-Sea' that Hall is said to have composed.[8]

'Haste Charon haste' is often entitled 'A Dialogue between Oliver Cromwell and Charon', and the words and action of the song glorify Charles I while condemning Cromwell to hell (the three-part chorus begins 'Drag him down'). This appears to have been one of Hall's most popular compositions, presumably partly because of its subject-matter. There are eight known musical manuscripts, usually naming Hall as the composer, many of them datable to the late seventeenth century, and there is a later one with the words alone (BL, Add MS 21544). The song was printed, with music by 'Mr Henry Hall', as early as 1685, in Book 2 of Henry Playford's *The Theater of Music* (reprinted as *The New Treasury of Music*, 1695). As noted earlier, Playford's preface, thanking Henry Purcell and John Blow for their assistance, raises the possibility that they played a part in bringing Hall into Playford's circle.[9]

The words of 'Haste Charon haste' without music were subsequently included in John Nutt's *Deliciae Poeticae* of 1706 (reissued as *Mirth Diverts All Care* in 1708 and 1709), and even feature in vol. 2 of the collection published in 1707 under the title of the *Miscellaneous Works of the Right Honourable the Late Earls of Rochester and*

Roscommon. Both printings contain attributions, respectively to 'Mr Henry Hall' and 'Mr Hall of Hereford'. A particular curiosity, somewhat later, is the occurrence of the words in one of the 1720 printings of *A True and Faithful Narrative of Oliver Cromwell's Compact with the Devil for Seven Years*, a compilation that had first appeared in 1718 as *A Full and Particular Account of Oliver Cromwell's Making a League with the Devil*, and seems to have gone through several expansions. In this 1720 case the text (in corrupted form) is attributed not to Hall but to 'Dr Kendrick', an example, it would seem, of the confusion as to correct attribution of certain works by Hall and Daniel Kenrick, for which see Chapter 9.2 below.[10]

6.3. Printed Song Books

Printed songs by Hall, with music, occur in more than twenty song books dating from 1685 to 1720, and other occurrences from later in the eighteenth century attest to the continuing popularity of certain of his compositions. The subject-matter is sometimes love, but after 1700, when catches were popular and periodical publication begins, Hall turns to providing songs for sociable drinking or patriotic purposes. As will be seen, Henry Playford is often the publisher, especially before 1704, and it may be, as suggested earlier, that Playford solicited material from Hall in some cases. Later on it may more likely have been Hall himself that took the initiative in submitting songs, given that his links with London evidently strengthened after Queen Anne's accession. But with no copyright legislation in place before 1710, the involvement of author or composer would often not have been an issue. It may be assumed that publishers in general would not have scrupled to print songs circulating in manuscript form, especially if demonstrably popular.

I now itemize the relevant song books in chronological order, noting Hall's contributions.[11] As already indicated, the problem of correct attribution affects the words of many of his songs, and a distinction on the grounds of poetic style does not seem possible. Love songs, for example, whose words may be thought too sentimental or conventional for an irreverent satirist like Hall — songs such as 'Enchanted by your voice and face' or 'While Galathea you design' — seem also to have been within his poetic range, judging from the occurrence of 'Charming fair Amoret' in B1 and the attributed 'When I your charms' in Lechmere Archives 40 (i). In what follows, therefore, I treat the words of all songs that are ascribed to Hall, and to no one else, as potentially his — as 'attributable' to him — even though the reality may have been different. Cases where Hall indubitably set to music words by other known writers are listed in an appendix to the present chapter.

The Theater of Music [...] *The Second Book* (1685, Henry Playford; DM 79): 'Haste Charon haste', attributed to 'Mr Henry Hall'; reprinted in *The New Treasury of Music*, 1695.

Comes Amoris [...] *The Second Book* (1688, John Carr; DM 98): 'From a due dose of claret', ascribed to 'Mr Hen. Hall'. Found also, without music or attribution, in the poetical anthology *The Theatre of Compliments* (1689).

Vinculum Societatis [...] *The Third Book* (1691, John Carr; DM 110): 'In vain I strive my flame to hide', first stanza only, no attribution. The ascription to Hall (as 'A new song sett by Mr Henry Hall') appears in the two-stanza version included in John Walsh's bespoke *A Collection of the Choicest Songs and Dialogues Composed by the Most Eminent Masters of the Age* (1703), and which survives also in single-sheet format.[12]

Thesaurus Musicus [...] *The Second Book* (1694, Henry Playford; DM 129): three love songs, namely 'Enchanted by your voice and face', 'In vain my fair Sylvia your presence I shun', and 'While Galathea you design', respectively 'to a ground by Mr Henry Hall', 'set by Mr Henry Hall', and 'by Mr Henry Hall'. The first item occurs also, without music, in the anthology *Oxford and Cambridge Miscellany Poems* [1708], where it is said to be 'A song, set by Mr Dean', but its ascription to Hall is supported in the music manuscript BL, Add MS 31453 ('A song to a ground by Mr Henry Hall').[13] As noted in the previous chapter, the setting of 'While Galathea you design' is attributed in the *Gentleman Journal*'s musical supplement for November 1693 to Raphael Courteville. 'In vain my fair Sylvia' is a unique occurrence.

Deliciae Musicae [...] *The Second Book* (1695, Henry Playford; DM 132): 'As Phoebus did with heat pursue', 'set by Mr Henry Hall, Organist of Hereford'. Its occurrence in the *Gentleman's Journal* was noted in the previous chapter. The words occur in B1.

Mercurius Musicus (for January 1699, Henry Playford; DM 174): 'Charming fair Amoret', 'sett by Mr Henry Hall of Hereford'. Included also in the Library of Congress copy of *A Collection of the Choicest Songs and Dialogues*, where the words and music are both attributed to Hall.[14] Again, the words occur in B1.

Mercurius Musicus (for August 1699, Henry Playford; DM 174): 'While Galathea you design', but here the setting (the same as in *Thesaurus Musicus*, above) is ascribed to 'Mr Courtivill', as it is also in the *Gentleman's Journal* for November 1693 and a BL copy of *A Collection of the Choicest Songs and Dialogues*.[15]

Wit and Mirth, or Pills to Purge Melancholy (1699, Henry Playford; DM 182): 'How happy's the mortal'. It occurs also in subsequent editions of *Wit and Mirth* (including the 1719 *Songs Compleat, Pleasant and Divertive*) and in two different single-sheet printings ('A song made on a mill set for a flute and a voice' and 'A song made on a mill'). The words occur in B1 and in the printed anthology *A New Academy of Complements, or The Lover's Secratary* [sic] (1715).

Mercurius Musicus (for March 1700, Henry Playford; DM 186): 'Sing what shall we sing' (on 'Eliza' being the best choice as the theme of a song), 'sett by Mr Henry Hall organist of Hereford'. A unique occurrence.

Mercurius Musicus (for August 1700, Henry Playford; DM 186): two songs, namely 'Lucinda has the de'l and all' and 'Should a legion of cares', both as 'sett by Mr Henry Hall of Heriford' / '[...] Hereford'. The first of these occurs without music in the *Diverting Post* for November 1704, with attribution to Hall, as noted in the previous chapter; and without attribution in two anthologies printed in 1721, *A Miscellaneous Collection of Poems, Songs and Epigrams* and *The Grove: or, A Collection of Original Poems, Translations, etc.* The second item, a two-part drinking song, is a unique occurrence.

Supplement of New Catches to the Second Book of the Pleasant Musical Companion (1702, Henry Playford; DM 202): 'Tom making a manteau' (a bawdy song about a tailor and a female customer), unattributed, but given to Hall in the 1707 and subsequent editions of *The Second Book of the Pleasant Musical Companion*. Attributed also to 'Mr Henry Hall' in the music manuscript Fitzwilliam Museum, Cambridge, Mu. 120. In contrast, John Walsh's 1709 *The Jovial Companions* (and later of Walsh's catch books) attributes the catch to Henry Purcell, but this ascription is now generally discounted by Purcell scholars. Thus Ian Spink includes it in an appendix to his 2000 edition of Purcell's catches, noting that 'Purcell is probably not the most likely author' of the piece, and adding that 'Perhaps it comes on the scene too late to be Purcell's'.[16]

A Collection of the Choicest Songs and Dialogues Composed by the Most Eminent Masters of the Age (1703, John Walsh (a bespoke collection); Hunter 5), song 105, 'In vain I strive', song 276, 'While Galathea you design', and song 310, 'Charming fair Amoret'. See the references to these songs in preceding entries and the details given in Appendix D.

Monthly Mask of Vocal Music (for March 1704, John Walsh): 'Come take of your liquor', headed 'The King of Spains health: a catch for three voices: the words and notes by Mr Henry Hall Organist of Heriford', as it is also in Walsh's 1709 *The Jovial Companions*. It survives additionally in single-sheet format.

Wit and Mirth, or Pills to Purge Melancholy, IV (1706, William Pearson): 'Come beaus virtuosos' ('A song on the Jubile'), unattributed, as it is also in subsequent editions of *Wit and Mirth* (including the 1719 *Songs Compleat, Pleasant and Divertive*). Pearson had printed the song separately for Henry Playford in 1700 ('A Song on the Jubilee'), but no copies have been traced.[17] It occurs without music in B1, in *Oxford and Cambridge Miscellany Poems* [1708], where it is explicitly a 'Ballad on the Jubilee by Mr Hall of Hereford', and the 1721 *A Miscellaneous Collection of Poems, Songs and Epigrams*, again with attribution ('The Jubilee, a song by Mr H.H.').

Monthly Mask of Vocal Music (for September 1706, John Walsh): 'So glorious a victory not to be sung', headed 'A song upon the late victory over the French in Italy by Prince Eugene of Savoy, set by Mr H. Hall of Heriford'. Found also in single-sheet format.

Monthly Mask of Vocal Music (for October 1706, John Walsh): 'As sharper when his coin grows low', headed 'On the French king's pretended victorys, set by Mr Henry Hall of Heriford', a catch also surviving in single-sheet format. It is preserved in manuscript in the early eighteenth-century York Minster Library, MS M.12.S (largely devoted to catches), where it is also attributed to 'Mr Henry Hall'. Along with two other of Hall's catches (noted below) this manuscript includes the chorus to 'Haste Charon haste'. The words to 'As sharper' occur in B1.

Monthly Mask of Vocal Music (for February 1707, John Walsh): 'Thus while the eight goes merrily round', with the expansive title, 'Eight Bells being Lately Cast at St. Hellens in Worster had these Names given 'em, The 1st Blenheim, 2nd Ramillie, 3rd Barcellona, 4th Menin, 5th Turin, 6th Eugene, 7th Marlbrough, 8th Queen Ann. On which was Made this Catch, by Mr Henry Hall of Hereford. A 3 Voice'. A catch celebrating English victories abroad. As with 'Come take of your liquor', it occurs also in Walsh's 1709 *The Jovial Companions* (with the same title) and in single-sheet format. Two manuscripts with music also survive, one again being York Minster Library, MS M.12.S.[18]

Second Book of the Pleasant Musical Companion (1707, Henry Playford): three catches, namely 'Tom making a manteau', as noted above, along with 'Come all ye high churchmen' ('A catch' by 'Mr Henry Hall'), and 'Dragoons have a care' ('Mr Hall'). All three occur in subsequent editions. 'Dragoons have a care' is also known in an apparently earlier single-sheet format with the heading 'The Muscovite Madrigal — Catch for 3 Voices, or the Czar's Health, Set by Mr. Hall and exactly engrav'd by Tho. Cross' (Bodleian, Harding Mus. G.170 (11), dated *c.* 1700). The words alone appear in the 1715 anthology *A New Academy of Complements*. 'Come all ye high churchmen' (celebrating cross-party support for the Church of England) is copied into York Minster Library, MS M.12.S, as 'A catch by Mr Hall'.

The Jovial Companions, or Merry Club ([1709], John Walsh; Hunter 55 and 55a): three catches, namely 'Tom making a manteau', 'Come take of your liquor', and 'Thus while the eight', all as noted above.

Monthly Mask of Vocal Music (for August 1710, John Walsh): 'When I your charms', described as 'A song set by the late Mr Henry Hall of Herreford'. The occurrence of the words in Lechmere Archives 40 (i) (see Chapter 4.2) is good evidence that Hall also wrote the words.

[*Collection of Catches*] (171c, Luke Pippard?; Hunter 73) : 'Tom making a manteau', unattributed.

Catches for Flutes, or A Collection of the Best Catches (1711, John Walsh): 'Tom making a manteau', unattributed.

Wit and Mirth, or Pills to Purge Melancholy, v (1714, John Young): 'Lucinda has the de'el and all', attributed to 'Mr H. Hall', as it is also in subsequent editions of *Wit and Mirth*.

The Merry Musician, or A Cure for the Spleen (1716, John Walsh; Hunter 99): 'All in the land of cider', as 'A song', unattributed. Its other occurrences, with words alone (including in B1), are discussed in Chapter 4.2 above. The music provided in 1716 is presumably not by Hall

The Pleasant Musical Companion (1720, John Young): four catches, namely 'Come all ye high churchmen', 'Dragoons have a care', 'Tom making a manteau', as above (all here attributed to Hall), along with the new 'Oil and vinegar are two pretty things' (seemingly a drinking song), which is given to 'Mr Henry Hall', as it is also in the musical manuscript Fitzwilliam Museum, Mu. 120. It occurs also, with music but without attribution, in Durham Cathedral Library, Bamburgh Collection, MS M193, datable to as early as 1695–1705.

The twenty-five publications listed above contain a total of twenty-three different songs that have music by Hall and words attributable to him. Up to 1702, and then intermittently up to 1707, the publisher is generally Henry Playford, evidence additional to that presented in the previous chapter that participation in Playford's enterprises was for some years Hall's principal route to publication. From 1704 John Walsh is then the main publisher involved, his *Monthly Mask of Vocal Music* in effect taking over from Playford's periodical, *Mercurius Musicus*.[19] As was said, Hall's say in the matter of where his songs were published may have been limited. After his death in 1707 the only newly published items attributed to him are 'When I your charms', 'All in the land of cider', and 'Oil and vinegar'. The second of these, as noted, is likely to have had music newly written for it.

As mentioned, some half dozen of the above songs also occur in single-sheet format, and it is very likely that others once circulated in similar fashion. Thus *Amphion Anglicus*, John Blow's collection of songs published in 1700, contains an advertisement by Henry Playford (p. [ix]) for 'Two new songs of Mr Henry Hall's of Hereford engraven. Price 6d', which may or may not equate to songs found in the song books. A manuscript song by Hall with music, not found elsewhere, is 'All the follies of love we'll drown in full glasses'; it is attributed to 'Mr Henry Hall' in BL, Add MS 33234, which contains also 'Haste Charon haste'. An ownership inscription in the manuscript is dated 1682, but the contents may have been copied over a number of years. Another music manuscript, BL, Add MS 22100, is also dated to the early 1680s, but the two songs attributed there simply to 'Mr Hall' could conceivably be by the London violinist and composer William Hall (d. 1700). One of the texts is in any case by Abraham Cowley ('These two full hours now have I gazing been') and the other, 'Awake fair goddess of this place', is found also in Yale UL, MS Osborn b.54, a very extensive miscellany dated 1666–81, which seems too early for this song's author to have been Henry Hall.

6.4. Catches and Other Poems to Be Sung

A particular feature of Hall's printed songs is the number of catches: at least seven out of the above twenty-three items, all of them published from 1702 onwards during a period when the market for this genre continued to thrive.[20] The songs in question are 'As sharper when his coin', 'Come all ye high churchmen', 'Come take of your liquor', 'Dragoons have a care', 'Oil and vinegar', 'Thus while the eight', and 'Tom making a manteau'. Ian Spink notes that Henry Purcell was 'by far the most prolific catch composer of his time', with almost sixty attributable to him, followed by John Blow (fourteen), Henry Aldrich (twelve), and Michael Wise (eight).[21] What is intriguing, in Hall's case, is that along with the two printed catches found also, without music, in B1 ('As sharper' and 'Dragoons have a care', the latter also in O1d and O2), that manuscript has another two poems described there as catches: 'Let disputes of the law' ('Catch in the year 1689', known nowhere else) and 'To our monarchs return' ('Catch', which has five other text-only manuscript witnesses). There is in addition the song 'Whilst this bumper stands by me', which in Yale UL, MS Osborn c.233 and *The Grove* (1721) is entitled 'A catch upon the Vigo-Expedition', as noted in Chapter 4. By this measure Hall's number of catches rises to at least ten, and this popular genre can be seen to fit well with his apparently ebullient personality, trenchant views, and love of good company.[22] Olive Baldwin and Thelma Wilson, editors of the facsimile edition of Walsh's *Monthly Mask*, note that 'Come take of your liquor' (March 1704) was the first catch and the first political song to appear in that publication.[23]

It is not only items headed 'Catch' that suggest that other of Hall's manuscript poems for which the words alone survive may also have been sung. Indeed six of these have 'to the tune of' as part of their heading (given here in italics): 'Are all those lights that gild the street', *To the tune of The Children in the Wood* (B1); 'Attend to my verse you whose ears are as long', *To the tune of Packingtons Pound* (B1); 'Good people what will you of all be bereft', *To the tune of the Rummer* (BL, Add MS 69968) and *To a pleasant new tune called A Pot of Good Ale* (Princeton UL, MS RTC01 no. 38); 'See here the confederate train', *To the tune of Old Simon the King* (B1); 'So little being done and so much money spent', *To the tune of Which Nobody Can Deny* (B1); 'Thus o unconstant Jockey', *To the tune of Luxemburgh's March* (B1).

In addition, three poems are described as ballads, namely 'Let old England rejoice' (B1, B2), 'No sooner our hero to Flanders was got' (B1, M), and 'Whilst Clio rehearses' [ii] (B1, B2, O1d, O2), of which the second shares the refrain 'Which nobody can deny' with the poem 'So little being done'. There is also a 'Litany' ('From a peace with new taxes', with the refrain 'Libera nos', B1, O1d, O2) and a 'Health' ('Here's a health whilst the trumpets', B1), whilst two poems contain choruses: 'How happy is this day' and 'The storm grows loud the lightnings flash' (both in the Ottley manuscripts alone). The first of these is a drinking song at the meeting of a 'club', almost certainly in Hereford because the toast is to 'Chandos', i.e. James Brydges, eighth Baron Chandos (mentioned in Chapter 1), who is Hall's gambling opponent in the poem 'Dunned by the bells I rose from bed'. The club in question may conceivably be the Black Lion Club that provides the title of 'Whilst Clio rehearses' [i] ('The Black Lion Club in 1690', a satire of Hereford society found in B1 alone) and which was associated with Hall by the nineteenth-century memoirist William Cooke, drawing on unknown sources:

> Since among his Poems several Songs are inserted, it is presumed, that in his twofold capacity of Poet & Musician, He had no difficulty in giving proof of this combination of talent, by carolling those ditties in the Black Lion Club Room.[24]

Cooke's conjecture is very likely correct. Other poems in B1 and the Ottley manuscripts that are simply entitled 'Song' or 'A song' include the political satire 'Six tedious months' and the love poems 'Charming Sylvia if you knew' (also in B2), 'Come my Sylvia now discover', and 'Phyllis in vain you drop that tear'. Another satire, 'The clergy and the layman' is entitled 'Mock song', as is a drinking song,

'Such command o'er my skull'. Even the widely circulated 'Now love and war the self-same art is grown' (discussed in Chapter 4), a poem discussing love, is headed 'Song' in B1.

The previous chapter drew attention to the words of three songs by Hall printed in the *Diverting Post* in 1704–05, namely 'To our arms on earth and seas', 'From the bright mansions', and 'Hark to the war the trumpet sounds'. The music for all three is said there to have been composed by Hall (and the first and third to have been publicly performed) and indeed music for the first, attributed to 'Mr Henery Hall', survives in Christ Church, Oxford, as MS Mus. 1219 (F), ff. 1v-2r. A fourth item in the *Diverting Post*, 'Since the town is our own', includes 'A Song' in its title, a detail missing from the copies in O1d and O2, though the nature of the poem (another celebratory drinking song) is clear enough. All things considered, it is clear that a significant proportion of Hall's verse output must have been written to be sung, formally or informally.

Appendix: Songs with Music by Hall to the Words of Others

1. 'As on Septimius' panting breast'. Attributed to 'Mr Henry Hall' in Folger Shakespeare Library, Washington, DC, MS W.b.515, pp. 28–29. The words are by Abraham Cowley, and are known elsewhere with the incipit 'Whilst on Septimius' panting breast'. A setting by John Blow of the same text immediately precedes Hall's version.

2. 'Beauty the painfull mothers pray'r'. *Deliciae Musicae* [...] *The Second Book*, 1695, pp. 9–12: 'A song set by Mr Henry Hall, the words by Mr Peter Senhouse' (a fellow Vicar Choral at Hereford).

3. 'Fill the bowl with rosie wine'. Attributed to 'Mr Henry Hall' in Christ Church, Oxford, MS Mus. 350, pp. 12–13. The words are by Abraham Cowley.

4. 'Forbear bold youth'. A setting by Hall of a poem by Katherine Philips, preserved in Folger Shakespeare Library, Washington, DC, MS W.b.515, p. 30. Reproduced in facsimile in Elizabeth H. Hageman and Andrea Sununu, 'New Manuscript Texts of Katherine Philips, the "Matchless Orinda" ', *English Manuscript Studies*, 4 (1993), 174–219 (facsimile, p. 207, discussion of Hall, pp. 206–09).[25]

5. 'I've heard and I've seen and am throughly undone'. 'A New Song', subscribed 'Mr. Henry Hall Organist of Hereford', comprising p. 4 of a four-page printing, in which it follows an unattributed song headed 'A New Dialogue Sung at Mrs. Minn's Booth, this present Bartholomew Fair, 1698' (*RISM*, HH 1906a).[26] The words are attributed to 'Dr Kenrick' in the version printed in *The Grove* (1721), pp. 170–71 (entitled 'On Sylvia singing' and beginning 'I heard and I saw').

6. 'Pallas destructive to the Trojan line'. Fitzwilliam Museum, Cambridge, MS Mu. 120, pp. 120–21: 'A two part song the words per Dr Garth and set to musick by Mr Henry Hall of Hereford'. Printed in the *Diverting Post*, no. 6 (December 1704), p. 1: 'These words of Dr Garth's are set to Musick by Mr H. Hall of Hereford'.

7. 'The bright bewitching Chloe's eyes'. Bodleian, Harding Mus. G.170 (10): 'A Song, the Words by Mr John Andrews, Set by Mr Henry Hall, and exactly engrav'd by Tho. Cross' [n.d.].

8. 'The great good man whom fortune does displace' (words almost certainly by Daniel Kenrick). For the complications surrounding this item's correct attribution, see the discussion in Chapter 9.2 below.

9. 'Too long thou tyrant love', a printed song, with music, item 2314 in the Pilley Collection in Hereford Public Library. 'A song set by Mr H.H., the words by a Gentleman' [n.d.].

10. 'Why fair Armida why so cold'. *Mercurius Musicus* (November 1700), pp. 74–76: 'A Song set by Mr Henry Hall of Hereford. The words by Dr Kendrick'.

11. 'Yee awfull powers of love and wine'. Single-sheet printing, n.d., in the Bibliothèque nationale de France, Paris, Département de la Musique (*RISM*, HH 1909a). 'A Song for 2 Voices set by Mr Henry Hall, the Words by Mr John Andrews'.

Notes to Chapter 6

1. They are described in detail in John Milson, *Christ Church Library Music Catalogue* <library.chch. ox.ac.uk/music/> [accessed 11 October 2021]. For autograph manuscripts of Hall's religious music preserved in Hereford Cathedral Library, especially MSS 30.A.xxx and 30.B.ii, see Barry Cooper, 'Keyboard Sources in Hereford', *RMA Research Chronicle*, 16 (1980), 135–39.
2. Cf. the reconstruction in the catalogue description.
3. See Pickering, 'Henry Hall of Hereford and Henry Purcell' (which wrongly states that the Tenbury manuscript is in the hand of the composer William Croft). The Tenbury manuscript ends: 'This was composd by the Ingenious Mr H. Hall organist att Hereford upon the Death of Mr H. Purcell, who was educated with him in the Chapell Royall in the Reign of K. Charles the Second.' This musical tribute to Purcell, drawing on 'Yes my Palemon 'tis too true' alone, is separate from Hall's blending of that poem and 'Music the chiefest good the gods have given' to create the tribute printed in *Orpheus Britannicus*, for which see Chapter 5.2 above.
4. *Odes on the Death of Henry Purcell*, Hyperion Records, CD A66578; Henry Hall, *A Dialogue on the Death of Henry Purcell*, ed. by Peter Holman (Richmond: Green Man Press, 2008).
5. *Odes on the Death of Henry Purcell*, ed. by Alan Howard, Purcell Society Edition, Companion Series, 5 (London: Stainer & Bell, 2013). See pp. xxvi (manuscript description), xxxiii (facsimile), xxxviii–ix (text of the song), 78–90 (edited text of the music and words), and 108–09 (notes to the edited text).
6. The autograph manuscript is included in a list of 'fowle originalls' of Oxford Act songs and odes printed in Rebecca Herissone, *Musical Creativity in Restoration England* (Cambridge: Cambridge University Press, 2013), p. 73 (her Table 2.2), in this case with the note 'Unclear if composed for Oxford'.
7. BL, MS Music Loan 1C9.12, pp. 65–70, brought to my attention by Dr Bryan White; it was owned in January 1696 by a Thomas Williams. Hall's song occurs amongst a collection of anthems by Purcell and others; see the British Library online manuscripts catalogue <https:// searcharchives.bl.uk> [accessed 18 February 2022].
8. See Thomas Cox, *Magna Britannia Antiqua et Nova: or, a New, Exact, and Comprehensive Survey of the Ancient and Present State of Great-Britain*, 6 vols (London: Caesar Ward and Richard Chandler, 1738), II, 951: 'Mr. Henry Hall, a famous Master of Musick, was Organist of this Cathedral [Hereford]. He understood Compositions well, and wrote several Poems, and an Opera on the Subject of the Doge of Venice's Marriage with the Adriatick-Sea'. Cf. the similar statements in

John Price, *An Historical Account of the City of Hereford* (London: D. Walker, 1796), p. 103 (who credits Hall also with 'several dramatic [...] compositions'), and John Duncumb, *Collections towards the History and Antiquities of the County of Hereford*, 2 vols (Hereford: E. G. Wright and others, 1804–12), I, 586.

9. For this preface, see Luckett, 'The Playfords and the Purcells', p. 55.

10. The printing in question is *ESTC* T135445.

11. I provide the date of publication and the bookseller's name, along with references to Day and Murrie, *English Song-Books, 1651–1702*, in the form DM + song-book number, and to Hunter, *Opera and Song Books Published in England, 1703–1726*, in the form Hunter + song-book number. Page references will be found in the list of publications in Appendix D. The entry for Hall in *The New Grove Dictionary* includes an incomplete list of his songs and catches.

12. For the 1703 collection see Hunter, song-book 5, p. 14, item 105. Details of all the items said here to occur in single-sheet format are given at the end of Appendix D.

13. Another manuscript copy, with music, in Bodleian, MS Mus. d.246, is unattributed.

14. Hunter, song-book 5, p. 18, item 310.

15. Ibid., p. 17, item 276.

16. Henry Purcell, *Catches*, ed. by Ian Spink, in *The Works of Henry Purcell*, 22A (London: Novello, 2000), pp. ix, 66. See also Zimmerman, *Henry Purcell, 1659–1695*, p. 416, item D106.

17. See DM, p. 436.

18. The other is William Andrews Clark Memorial Library, UCLA, MS M1579P98.1720, which has the notes '3 Voc. Mr. Hall', and '8 Bells cast in Worcester, Blenheim, Ramilie, Barcelona, Menin, Turin, Eugene, Marlbro', 2. Ann'.

19. For accounts of song-book publication at this time, see Cyrus Lawrence Day and Eleanore Boswell Murrie, 'English Song Books, 1651–1702, and their Publishers', *The Library*, 4th series, 16 (1936), 355–401, and David Hunter, 'The Publishing of Opera and Song Books in England, 1703–1726', *Notes*, 2nd series, 47 (1991), 647–85.

20. 'A catch is a species of round or canon at the unison in which the voices (usually three or four) come in one after another, a line of verse apart' (Purcell, *Catches*, p. ix; pp. ix–xii discuss the genre, which is associated with all-male drinking clubs).

21. Ibid., p. ix.

22. There is also the case of 'Curse on those representatives', included in O1d, O2, and B1 — in the first case in Hall's own hand and in the other two manuscripts as if Hall's composition — even though it is an adaptation of an earlier poem (see Chapter 7.6, below). It may be that Hall included it in O1d because he had turned it into a 'Catch' (its heading in O1d and O2) and was pleased with the result.

23. *The Monthly Mask of Vocal Music, 1702–1711: A Facsimile Edition*, ed. by Olive Baldwin and Thelma Wilson (Aldershot: Ashgate, 2007), p. 28.

24. Cooke, 'Henry Hall', p. [5], referenced in full (with a longer quotation) in Chapter 1 above.

25. Hageman and Sununu, 'New Manuscript Texts of Katherine Philips, the "Matchless Orinda"', p. 206, report that the song set by Hall that immediately precedes 'Forbear bold youth' (in fact 'As on Septimius' panting breast', as above) is Cowley's 'Oft am I by the women told', but this text, which is unattributed, is the first item in the manuscript (p. 1). I am grateful to Elizabeth DeBold, Curatorial Assistant at the Folger Shakespeare Library, for providing the correct information.

26. Copies are recorded in the Bibliothèque nationale de France, Paris, and in the Humanities Resource Center, University of Texas at Austin.

CHAPTER 7

❖

Political Satires,
1689–1701

7.1. Overview

Hall's political satires deserve separate, extended consideration because they form a major part of his output (and strongly reflect his character) and because they include poems for which his responsibility has been contested in modern times. The satires fall naturally into a larger grouping of thirty decidedly oppositional poems written while first William and Mary together and then William alone occupied the throne, and a smaller, generally more light-hearted group of ten poems written during Queen Anne's reign (the subject of the next chapter). Poems or songs that satirize foreign rulers (Peter the Great, Louis XIV, and the Margrave of Baden-Baden) are excluded from the discussion, as are local political satires.[1] Also excluded is the short Jacobite drinking song 'To our monarch's return', which expresses the wish that only one of the two kings currently abroad will return to England.[2]

From the list below it can be seen that all the oppositional satires are represented in the main manuscript collections, contrary to the distribution of many of Hall's songs and miscellaneous poems, where these collections are nowhere near as comprehensive. The sheer number (twenty-four) of these satires copied into B1, a collection clearly designed to perpetuate Hall's memory, leaves little doubt that they were regarded as an important part of his output. Only four of the satires, however, occur in the Ottley manuscripts. It is B1 and B2 that have the great preponderance of oppositional poems, with Ottley alone (in contrast) preserving the satires of Queen Anne's reign. This accords with the perception that B1 and B2 generally represent Hall's pre-1702 output, whereas the Ottley manuscripts are plausibly to be dated to a time not long before his death. None of the satires was printed until 1703 (in *POAS*, II), and it is clear that they all circulated first in manuscript form, as would be expected from their subject-matter.

I now list and then analyse the thirty oppositional satires, noting their occurrence in the main manuscript collections (and in C); whether they are also in the Minnesota manuscript (M); the number of other manuscript occurrences; and whether they were printed in *POAS*. A list of manuscripts for each poem, along with a brief characterization of subject-matter, is provided in the Checklist in Appendix A. As will be seen, the number of these other manuscripts is considerable, testifying in the case of some poems to great popularity. Hall, it should be said, is never named as author, but anonymity was of course usual with material of this kind. There is in addition no evidence that he played any part in their manuscript circulation (or subsequent printing), but it does not follow that they were copied against his will. As quoted earlier from Harold Love, Hall may consciously have participated in an 'initiatory' act of (manuscript) publication, 'when a private possessor of a text [...] facilitates its first going forth into the world'. Furthermore, and despite quite frequent textual variation, the satires in question clearly possess (to quote Love again) the 'required state of finish' to be seen in public.[3] There is no doubt that Hall was familiar with contemporary verse satire and wished to contribute to the genre.

'Are all those lights that gild the street'	B1, M
'Attend to my verse you whose ears are as long'	B1, B2
'Cease hypocrites to trouble Heaven'	B1, C, M
'Cities of adamant must yield'	B1
'From a peace with new taxes and yet without trade'	B1, O1d, O2
'Good people what will you of all be bereft'	B1, M + 12 + printed (POAS, II)
'Great William concerned to leave his gulled loobies'	B1, M + 9
'Hail happy William thou art strangely great'	B2, M + 16 + printed (POAS, II)
'Here lie the relics of a martyred knight'	B1, B2, M + 11 + printed (POAS, II)
'Here lies our Sovereign Lady Moll'	B1
'In place where men of wealth and wit'	B1
'Let old England rejoice'	B1, B2
'Ne'er blame your hero for the kingdom's fall'	B1, M
'No sooner our hero to Flanders was got'	B1, M
'Our government thrifty to raise up their wages'	B1, M + 1
'Rejoice ye fops your idol's come again'	B1, C, M + 4
'See here the confederate train'	B1
'Since we're undone the matter is not much'	O1d, O2
'Six tedious months our senate sits'	B1, B2, M + 3
'So little being done and so much money spent'	B1
'The clergy and the laymen'	B1 + 1
'Those tokens which avenging heaven sent'	B2
'Thus for his master fell the brave Montrose'	B1
''Twill puzzle much the author's brains'	B1, M + 3 + printed (POAS, III)
'What fast for horrid murder of the day'	B2 + 5 + printed (POAS, II)
'When Catesby and Faux with the rest of the crew'	B1, M, O1d, O2
'When of half a score lasses ten harlots you see'	B1
'Whither ye impious Britons do ye run'	B2 + 4 + printed (POAS, II)
'Why towering tides submit to constant laws'	O1b, O2
'With Job-like patience we've our burdens bore'	B1, B2, M

This varied pattern of circulation divides into thirteen poems found only in the main manuscript collections, six more that are copied also into M alone, and eleven found also in other manuscripts (including eight more in M). This third group ranges from one to eighteen additional manuscripts (with four poems occurring in nine or more) and includes all the instances of printing in the original *POAS*.[4]

It is, one suspects, partly the extent of their manuscript circulation that led William J. Cameron, editor of volume v (*1688–1697*) of the Yale edition of *Poems on Affairs of State* (1971), to question the likelihood of the satires' having been written by a Hereford organist. Cameron, who includes five of the oppositional poems in his edition (and quotes from others), begins with a textual argument. Having consulted B1 and B2, he reports that 'The authority of both MSS is suspect because collation of the poems reveals that the texts are inferior to other MSS in which they occur' (p. 451). B1 is indeed quite often corrupt, and the argument of the present study is that it is more important for gathering up a great many of Hall's poems after their author's death than for its textual fidelity to his words. Cameron goes on to draw attention to an undoubted attributional error in B1 (to be discussed below in Chapter 9) and to a somewhat similar mistake in B2 relating to a poem by Katherine Philips.[5] He concludes: 'One wonders how many poems of different authorship have been included [in B1 and B2] simply because they were associated by subject matter or interest with one of Hall's' (p. 452).

Cameron attempts to undermine Hall further by noting that some of the many songs, catches, and ballads in the two manuscripts 'might represent Hall's attempt to set other men's poems to music', and from this first speculation leaps to another, that 'this common practice of the ballad-makers may lead us to suspect that perhaps Hall also treated some of the 30 poems that belong in our canon of *POAS* in the same way'.[6] In the case of two of the poems he follows this up by referring, somewhat disparagingly, to Hall's status as a musician: on p. 456, 'Perhaps, then, [John Grubham] Howe is a better candidate for the authorship of ['Hail happy William'] than the musical Mr Hall'; and on p. 483, 'In the absence of other evidence, we reluctantly are forced to allow ['Here lie the relics'] to rest in the canon of the organist of Hereford.' Elsewhere Cameron allows that 'Great William concerned' 'may have been written by Henry Hall, organist of Hereford' (p. 517), but largely dismisses his claim to 'Rejoice ye fops' on textual grounds, admitting only 'There is a small possibility that the following epigram was written by Henry Hall' (p. 455). But to be fair to Cameron, there are stylistic reasons for doubting Hall's authorship of 'Hail happy William' (see below), and in the case of 'Good people what will you of all be bereft' (described in several manuscripts as a song) he for once regards Hall as a serious candidate: 'Henry Hall, organist of Hereford, was capable of both the wit and the musical background' (p. 498).[7]

Cameron's appreciation of Hall's wit no doubt derives from his reading of other poems in B1 and B2, where Hall's characteristic quick-firing, conversational style — sarcastic, scurrilous, concise — is often in evidence, as in the outspoken epistles to Dr Broughton and the attacks on the Mathews family. The same irreverent poetic qualities permeate many of the political satires listed above, while allusions to national politics frequently occur in Hall's local poems. To give one example: the local poems and the political satires both contain lengthy passages that use the device of supposedly viewing paintings hung round a room, debunking each subject in turn. Thus the 'national' satire, 'See here the confederate train', which makes fun of the leaders of the countries opposing Louis XIV, naturally lampoons William III, in the form:

> See the heroe of Brittain appears
>   That rallies and runs like a devill,
> And's banish'd within these few years
>   The root and the cause of all evill.
>   And all for to levell Le Grand
>   Who takeing their citties do's sing,
>   Begar me you no understand,
>   Sing hey ding ding a ding ding. (B1, p. 2)

The Hereford poem 'All you who delight and take pleasure in painting', in its turn, slips in a line of personal abuse of William and Mary before the narrator begins his attack on his local opponents (a later hand has filled out the abbreviated names):

> There's a dauber who canvas and nature abuses
> And makes you nine devills of dainty nine muses,
> But I've not a stroak of this stuff to expose,
> Or of M — s fat a — s, or W — s hook nose,
> Mine are all just alike as two bowls to each other
> Or as pretty Miss who'd a whore to her mother. (B1, p. 20)

The metre is different but the two poems share Hall's fluent, abusive mockery. In this case it is the 'national' satire, written as a song ('To the tune of Old Simon the King'), that is the more light-hearted.

'Good people' itself, though again a song, is a more serious piece of work. As will be shown later, it attacks the new coinage and the taxes brought in to pay for the French wars, and can be dated to mid-1696. Amongst its thirteen manuscripts other than B1 are several large anthologies (or miscellanies) of the late seventeenth or early eighteenth century, some of them in professional hands (e.g. BL, MS Lansdowne 852, and M), some apparently written privately (e.g. BL, MS Stowe 305, and Bodleian, MS Rawlinson D.361). Other copies are preserved mounted in guardbooks (e.g. MS Rawlinson D.383, National Library of Scotland, MS 2092) or as separates (e.g. Yale UL, MSS Osborn Poetry Box VII/5 and XIII/80). The poem was also printed in *POAS*, II (1703). This range of distribution is typical of Hall's most popular political satires.

Hall's earliest satires of this kind did not achieve such wide circulation, but with the exception of the four most widely copied poems, which can be dated to 1696–98, there is no correlation between later date and more extensive distribution. In whatever circumstances, individual poems clearly became popular at different times throughout the decade, and Hall himself may or may not have been involved in the process of circulation. In keeping with the overall approach of this study, the following discussion begins with those found only in the main manuscript collections and works outwards to those that were copied more widely. It will be seen, perhaps not surprisingly, that the most egregious expressions of Jacobitism are restricted to the former group (compare the outspoken content of the uncirculated epistles to Dr Broughton). Similarly, it is not possible to demonstrate a correlation between verse form or style and the extent of a poem's distribution, though shorter poems, unsurprisingly, appear to have been copied more often than longer ones. As will be seen, Hall uses a variety of often recurring verse or stanza forms, depending on subject-matter, stance, or genre (for example, song, epigram, lament).[8]

7.2. Satires Found Only in the Main Manuscript Collections

Just as B1 has the highest number of political satires overall, so it has the highest number (seven) of unique occurrences, of which two are songs mocking King William's lack of success in the French wars. These are 'So little being done and so much money spent', on the failure of the naval expedition to attack Brest in June 1694, and 'See here the confederate train', which (as stated above) satirizes the leaders of the various countries allied against Louis XIV; this is dated 1693 in B1.[9] The former has twelve 4-line stanzas (tetrameters followed by the popular refrain 'Which nobody can deny'), the latter, twenty-three 8-line stanzas (trimeters).[10] Similar in style and spirit, and this time found also in B2, is the lengthy 'Attend to my verse you whose ears are as long', a Jacobite song on the king's contrasting fortunes in 1690, first at the Battle of the Boyne and then at the Battle of Beachy Head. A ballad with eleven 10-line stanzas (four-stress and two-stress lines) including a varied refrain, its style resembles that of the widely circulated 'Good people', although with a different rhyme scheme. For example:

> It treats of a warr betwixt father and son,
>   As you'l find when you come to the end of the matter,
> Of the first of these two I shall quickly have done
>   But then my brave boys I've a world of the latter.
>   The ballad is new,
>   Altho' at first view
>   It looks like a lye,
>   Every jott on't is true:
> Tho' truth is not always thought so necessary
> In singing the annalls of W — m and M — y. (B1, p. 5)

A related song found in both B1 and B2 is 'Let old England rejoice' (eight 6-line stanzas, the lines variously of two, three, or four stresses), one of several satires reacting to the official celebrations for William's supposedly triumphant return from the wars. B1's title in this case is 'Ballad on the Thanksgiving Day so solemnly observ'd the 12th of April 1694'. In B1 alone, and contrasting in style, is the sober 12-line poem 'Cities of adamant must yield' (tetrameter couplets and triplets, edited below), in which Hall reflects on the fate of the besieged citizens of Namur who 'find a grave, | Even in their sights who came to save', following William's victory there in 1695.

Three other of B1's unique satires relate to individuals. One, a disparaging mock epitaph on Queen Mary, who died on 28 December 1694 ('Here lies our Sovereign Lady Moll'), has fifteen lines of four-stress triplets, a form that lightens its tone.

Another on the same theme preserved only in B2 ('Those tokens which avenging heaven sent') is decidedly harsher, asserting in eight lines of pentameter couplets that the queen's death from smallpox is divine punishment for her crimes.[11] Also in B1 alone is 'Thus for his master fell the brave Montrose', a fiercely Jacobite poem on the execution of Sir John Fenwick in 1697, attacking also Parliament and William III. In this case there are twelve lines of pentameter couplets, suiting Hall's seriousness and his terseness of expression.[12] Quite different is 'In place where men of wealth and wit', a satire on the decision of the House of Commons, in January 1693, to burn the pastoral letter issued in 1689 by Gilbert Burnet, Bishop of Salisbury, in which he argued that allegiance should be owed to William and Mary on the basis that they were in actual possession of the throne. The poem has ten 4-line stanzas in colloquial light-hearted style, and makes good use of Burnet's name:

> In vain for as I say'd before,
>   They wou'd no more adjourn it,
> But each hott head cry'd out the more
>   Oh Burn it, Burn it, Burn it. (B1, p. 13)

Finally, of political satires unique to B1, is 'When of half a score lasses ten harlots you see', which is headed 'A prophecy found in Ragland Castle in the year 1630'. The subject-matter is the unhappy condition of England in the 1690s, as exemplified by fashion, politics, and religion. The poem, in couplets formed of anapaestic tetrameters, is in a different hand from the rest of the manuscript and has evidently been added later (it is the final item). This might be thought to cast doubt on Hall's authorship, but the handwriting is the same as that responsible for the informal attribution 'Harry Hall's Poems' on the verso of B1's cover, and one couplet is close to lines in another satire, 'Why towering tides submit to constant laws', preserved in O2:

> When every religion, as if 'twere in spight,
> Amongst us shall tolerated be, but the right' (B1, p. 113)

> And yet they seem to serve the Lord in spite
> And authorize all worship but the right. (O2, f. 8v).

This removes any doubt about authorship. The final line of 'When of half a score lasses' might at first seem another obstacle — 'Since the bigotted Father she swopt for the Son' — but Hall's use of 'bigotted' to refer to James II (unless praising this aspect of his character) is presumably ironic. A date of composition in the later 1690s seems likely.

'Why towering tides', which is a long vituperative attack on the Dutch in 221 lines of pentameter couplets, is one of only two poems amongst the 1689–1701 corpus of political satires that are unique to the Ottley manuscripts (O2, with a fragmentary text in O1b). It can be dated to 1701 as it ends with Hall urging Britain not to get involved in the War of the Spanish Succession. The other unique poem is 'Since we're undone the matter is not much', a terse 12-line attack (again in pentameter couplets) on Parliament's treatment of the financier Sir Charles Duncombe in 1698, especially the House of Lords' rejection of a Bill designed to fine him; Hall contrasts this with its approval of the Bill that led to Sir John Fenwick's execution. The poem, which is edited below, survives in O1 and O2, the former text being in Hall's own hand.

A third oppositional satire amongst the Ottley manuscripts (O1d, O2), again edited below, is 'From a peace with new taxes and yet without trade', which is found also in B1. Again the text in O1d is in Hall's hand. The poem is headed 'Litany' and comprises five stanzas of anapaestic tetrameters — the verse form of 'When of half a score lasses', but this time in triplets — followed by the popular refrain 'Libera nos [Domine]'. It laments the state of affairs in England following the 1697 Treaty of Ryswick, but the reference to Peter the Great's visit dates it to early 1698. As the next section will show, there is one other 'national' political satire in the Ottley manuscripts that is to be dated somewhat earlier, but overall it is clear that they preserve a generally later body of material than do B1 and B2.

7.3. Satires Found Also in the Minnesota Manuscript

Next to be considered are six satires, found variously in B1, B2, and Ottley, that were copied also into M but into no other known manuscript, significant support for the supposition that M's compiler had access to a now lost collection of Hall's verse (see Chapter 4.1 above). Four of the six occur only in B1 and M, and two of these are songs similar to 'So little being done' and 'Attend to my verse', discussed above. One of them is 'No sooner our hero to Flanders was got', which satirizes the authorities' failure to mount a successful prosecution against a supposed Jacobite plot in Lancashire and Cheshire. Entitled 'Ballad on the Cheshire Plott 1694', it has nine 4-line stanzas comprising three tetrameters and the refrain 'Which nobody can deny' (as in 'So little being done').[13] The other song is 'Are all those lights that gild the street' (six 4-line stanzas, alternating four- and three-stress lines), which, like 'Let old England rejoice', mocks the celebrations of William's supposed success in the wars, instead drawing attention to English losses and defeats.[14]

Both of the other two items shared by B1 and M are attacks on Hall's political opponents. 'Ne'er blame your hero for the kingdom's fall' concisely but uncompromisingly asserts that those who wanted William to be king should take the blame now things are going badly (referring presumably to the French wars). The title in M is explicit: 'King William cleared, the rebellion laid upon the subjects of England', and the poem proceeds on the basis that kings are godlike and can do nothing wrong, as in the ironic third line, 'God like he reigns and innocent he is' (B1). The poem has twelve lines of rough pentameters, ending tersely, 'The fault's not in the idoll but the worshipper' — a wording shared by the two manuscripts, except that B1's later corrector (though without deleting) substitutes a stronger final term, 'th'idolater'.

Shorter still is the six-line 'Cease hypocrites to trouble Heaven', which is also included in C, William Cooke's nineteenth-century selection of items from a manuscript likely to have been broadly similar to B1. The target now is the hypocrisy of those who pray for forgiveness on the anniversary of Charles I's death while simultaneously seeking the death of the exiled James II:

> Cease hippocrites to trouble heaven,
> How can ye think to be forgiven
> The dismall deed you've done,
> When to the martyrs sacred blood
> This very moment if you could
> You'd sacrifice his son? (B1, p. 15)

B1 and C agree in dating the poem to 30 January 1691, i.e. (almost certainly) 1692 new style.[15] It is not surprising that such oppositional poems should have had restricted circulation.

Common to B1, B2, and M is 'With Job-like patience we've our burdens bore', in which Hall attacks the ruinous cost of the French wars as well as (after seven years of his reign) William III in general. Headed 'Truth' in all three witnesses, this is a serious and impressive poem (edited below) comprising forty-nine lines of pentameter couplets. Hall points to the human as well as the financial cost of the conflict, in lines that are quoted also by Cameron:[16]

> He came to save your throats from Popish knives,
> Yet by his warr, has widdow'd halfe your wives.
> Before Namure there [sic] scatter'd limbs are lay'd,
> At Landen, count the number of your dead,
> Or all the wretched liveing, yet unpaid. (B1, p. 36)

Strongly Jacobite, and explicitly evoking the non-juring bishops Ken and Sancroft, the poem ends with a warning of possible rebellion: 'Least not the taxes but the people rise' (B1, p. 37). It may be noted that the three manuscripts are closely aligned textually.

Finally, of this group, is 'When Catesby and Faux with the rest of the crew', one of a number of poems in which Hall attacks the incompetence and/or corruption of the House of Commons. Preserved in all of B1, O1d, O2, and M, and untitled in the main collections — M in contrast has 'Upon Faukes's blowing up the convention' — it is possibly to be dated to the early or mid-1690s. In twelve lines of anapaestic tetrameters the poem wittily asserts that the nation would happily have given the Gunpowder Plotters the go-ahead if Parliament then had been like it is now, characterized as 'our 500 brib'd blockheads | Pimps, pensioners, collnells, damnd legal pickpocketts' (O1d, p. 32). Of particular textual interest is the revision made to the opening of the poem. Whereas B1 and M begin with the couplet 'When Catesby and Faux, with the rest of the gang | For a horrid design did deservedly hang', O1d (copied without change into O2) reads 'When Catesby, and Faux, with the rest of the crew | Were hangd for a crime of which little they knew', thus exonerating the plotters.[17] The latter version is in Hall's own hand, suggesting that this is the original wording, later modified in the direction of orthodoxy by an unknown reviser. If so, the alteration would again cast doubt on B1's textual authority. Hall, on the other hand, may himself have made the change, deciding that an ironical disguise of his true feelings was better for public circulation. Irony is also apparent in the substitution in B1 of 'loyal' for 'legal' in the line quoted earlier.[18] Little else in the poem is altered, both versions making explicit that the authorities found barrels of powder 'to make the conspiracy clear' (O1d).

7.4. Satires with Wider Manuscript Circulation

The remaining eleven of the total of thirty oppositional satires all exist in at least one non-central witness other than M, evidence of wider circulation. As might be expected, textual variation is now more common. Two of the eleven are likely to date from a time when Hall's first instinct after the events of 1688–89 was to attack the English establishment for replacing King James with King William. The items in question are 'The clergy and the laymen' and the strongly-worded 'Whither ye impious Britons do ye run'. The former poem, which has three 10-line stanzas (in trimeters) and in B1 is headed 'Mock song', is notable for having an almost completely different text in its only other manuscript, Bodleian, MS Rawlinson poet. 207. After censuring the clergy for ignoring their sworn allegiance to James and the navy for allowing the Dutch fleet to land, the version in B1 ends with a stanza attacking Hendrik van Nassau van Ouwerkerk (who from 1689 was William's Master of the Horse) for his part in the plot. In contrast the Rawlinson version (which is in Richard Rawlinson's own hand *c.* 1715 and so almost certainly copied in Oxford),[19] is more outspokenly abusive of William III, criticizes the clergy and the laymen in quite different ways, and ends with the plight of the soldiers now fighting abroad, the dire economic consequences of the war, and a rousing finale even more appropriate to a song:

> But James is still alive Sir
> And his Protector thrives Sir
> Then chear up heart brave boys. (ll. 28–30)[20]

This appears to represent a revision made later in the 1690s, very plausibly by Hall himself.

'Whither ye impious Britons do ye run' had a more definite distribution, preserved as it is not only in B2 but in BL, Add MS 21094, Bodleian, MS Rawlinson poet. 181, and Yale UL, Osborn MSS c.570/2 and fb.207/3, all of which contain other oppositional satires attributable to Hall, as will be seen.[21] It is also included in *POAS*, II (1703), where it is dated 1690. The poem, edited below, represents one of Hall's fiercest attacks on his political opponents, which may account on the one hand for its popularity and on the other (speculatively) for its exclusion from B1, on the assumption that its compiler thought the material too strong. In thirty-two lines of pentameter couplets it attributes on-going English preparations for war in Flanders against Louis XIV, despite the economic ruin it will bring upon the country, to unexpiated guilt for the murder of Charles I. The poem is, however, imitating Horace's Epode VII — in which Rome is said still to feel guilt for Romulus's murder of his brother Remus — and Hall's at times extreme language may in part derive from this model.

Another satire with wider circulation that exists in B2 but not B1 is the 8-line 'What fast for horrid murder of the day', which, in similar vein to 'Cease hypocrites to trouble Heaven' (B1, M, discussed above), attacks the hypocrisy of those who would piously commemorate the anniversary of Charles I's death after expelling his son James II. In B2 the poem (again in pentameter couplets) is headed 'On the 30th of January 1695', i.e. (almost certainly) 1696, but the other five manuscripts (and, again, *POAS*, II) vary the date and occasion in considerable detail, demonstrating its popularity.[22] Space precludes an analysis of the textual variants within the poem, but there are two main versions of the final line, one beginning 'Sins whilst repeated' (cannot be forgiven), the other, 'Sins unrepented'. The latter, represented by *POAS*, II, p. 267, Bodleian, MS Rawlinson poet. 169, BL, Add MS 72479, and Yale UL, MS Osborn c.570/1, is the more straightforward, but 'Sins whilst repeated' (B2, BL, MS Lansdowne 852, and Princeton UL, MS RTC01 no. 38) might be preferred as the harder reading.[23] Support for this, intriguingly, is provided by M's corrupt version of l. 2 of 'Cease hypocrites', namely 'Sins whilst repeated, are ne're to be forgiven', which is clearly an error in context (cf. the text quoted in section 7.3 above). It is striking, too, that the opening line of 'Cease hypocrites' appears in altered form as the penultimate line of 'What fast' ('But cease with prayers and fasts to trouble Heaven', B2), and we may conclude that the latter poem represents Hall consciously recasting his earlier formulation, making it somewhat less outspoken. Perhaps surprisingly, neither 'Cease hypocrites' nor 'What fast for horrid murder' is discussed by Cameron, and he fails even to include the former in his list of relevant political satires, despite knowing B1.

Lighter in mood are three short poems mocking aspects of William III's involvement in the French wars. Epigrammatic in style, it is not surprising that they attracted copying and, in the process, were subject to textual variation. The earliest is the 8-line ''Twill puzzle much the author's brains' (ababcdcd, alternating 4- and 3-stress lines), which relates to British lack of success in the campaigns of 1691 and 1692. B1 stands alone in having this opening line and in addressing the king in the second person:

> 'Twill puzzle much the authors brains
> That is to write your story,
> To know in which of these campagnes
> You have acquired most glory;
> For when you march'd the foe to fight,
> Like heroe, nothing fearing,
> Namur was taken in your sight,
> And Mons, within your hearing. (B1, p. 20)

In contrast the other four manuscripts (M, BL, Add MS 29497, CUL, Add. 5962, and Yale UL, MS Osborn b.111) and *POAS*, III (1704), all read broadly as follows:[24]

> The author sure must take great pains
> Who pretends to write his story
> In which of these two last campaigns
> He has acquired most glory.
> For whilst that he marched out to fight,
> Like hero nothing fearing,
> Namur was taken in his sight
> And Mons within his hearing.[25]

This latter version weakens the satire, reducing the brain-taxing puzzlement needed to discern evidence for any glory at all in William's military exploits to working conscientiously at the task. Hall may or may not be responsible for what appears to be later smoothing.

Dating from 1695, following William's victory at Namur that year, is then the 4-line 'Rejoice ye fops your idol's come again', another satire on the king's homecoming. In this case there are four known manuscripts additional to B1, C, and M, but the poem was not taken up into one of the volumes of *POAS* despite its obvious attractiveness. It has, however, been anthologized in modern times in the *New Oxford Book of Seventeenth Century Verse*, which takes its text from that printed by Cameron, who quotes from BL, MS Stowe 305:[26]

> Rejoice, you sots, your idol's come again,
> To pick your pockets and kidnap your men.
> Give him your moneys, and his Dutch your lands.
> Ring not your bells, ye fools, but wring your hands.

Cameron, as noted earlier, allows the 'small possibility' that this poem was written by Hall, 'although the text that survives in [B1] is not the best one' (p. 455). But B1 (p. 14) reads:

> Rejoice yee fops your idoll's come agen,
> To pick your pocketts, and to slay your men.
> Give him your millions, and his Dutch your lands;
> Don't ring your bells, yee fools, but wring your hands.

This is at least as good, added to which 'fops' and 'millions' are supported by the two Bodleian manuscripts collated by Cameron — which, in addition, read 'destroy', closer to B1's 'slay', rather than MS Stowe's 'kidnap'. One of these manuscripts, the Jacobite MS Rawlinson poet. 181, mentioned earlier, preserves a version expanded by an additional six lines, which are printed by Cameron in his textual notes (p. 592).[27] Elsewhere, Yale UL, MS Osborn c.570 (a four-volume collection of satirical poems to be dated *c.* 1715) begins 'Rejoice ye Whigs' and M, 'Rejoice ye sots the king is come again'. B1's text is also closely supported by C, except that the poem is there said to begin 'Rejoice ye fools'. On balance the Hereford-based compilations of his poetry (as B1 and C seem to be) appear to transmit a relatively good text of the quatrain.

The third epigram (though this is not its form in B1 and B2, where it runs to twenty lines rather than the eight found in M and three other manuscripts) is 'Six tedious months our senate sits'. A light-hearted satire on the cost of the French wars, the reference to the government's 1696 recoinage dates it to that year. Cameron attempts to use the 'song' (as B1 calls it) as an example of B1 and B2's textual unreliability, printing in contrast the text found in BL, Add MS 5540, which, as he points out, is an early manuscript, bound in Bristol in 1696:[28]

> Six winter months our Senate sits
> Five Millions for to raise
> And all the while they wrack their wits
> To find out means and ways.

> Six summer months out hero spends —
>> In what? you'll please to say —
> In finding out of ways and means
>> To squander it away.

He then prints the corresponding part of the poem in B1, in the form:

> Six tedious months our Senate sits
>> Though ready, Sir, to raise,
> And night and day employ their wits
>> In thoughts of means and ways.
>
> Six months abroad our hero spends
>> In what? perhaps you'll say
> Why he too thinks of ways and means
>> To squander it away.

This is followed by two variant readings from B2, namely 1 our] 'the', and 2 Though ready, Sir] 'The ready sum'.

Cameron's conclusion from this evidence, and no more, is that 'The textual unreliability of both MSS can be judged from these variants and casts doubt on the attribution of the poems in the two MSS to Hall'. He seems, however, to regard B1 and B2 (of apparently unrelated provenance) as without independent value as textual witnesses, and thus discounts the occurrence of 'ready' in l. 2 of both; and his case is further undermined by his having misread B1, which in fact reads 'The ready, Sir', a perfectly acceptable colloquialism, as 'ready' as a slang term for money was already current at this time.[29] Hall's poems are notable for their use of colloquial language, and Cameron does not consider the possibility that later scribes may have smoothed such expressions in different ways.

Two other manuscripts of the poem, BL, MSS Lansdowne 852, and Sloane 1731A, share certain readings with Add MS 5540, notably the use of 'millions' in l. 2 ('five' in the case of Lansdowne, 'eight' in the case of Sloane) and the phrase 'Six summer months' in l. 5, though they also have readings that are closer to B1.[30] But Cameron additionally fails to point out that whereas in the three British Library manuscripts the text of 'Six tedious months our senate sits' has only eight lines, in B1 and B2 these represent merely the first two stanzas of a longer poem of more serious attack on William, Parliament, and the cost of the war. Despite its apparently early date, the short version is plausibly an abridgement, deliberately made more epigrammatic, repetitive, and light-hearted, and avoiding all mention of William's campaigns.[31]

Another short satire on Parliament, more of a squib, once again uses anapaestic tetrameters. This is the 12-line 'Our government thrifty to raise up their wages', found in B1, M, and BL, MS Sloane 2717.[32] It can be dated to 1694, when taxes on births, marriages, and burials were brought in. Cameron, in passing, describes the poem as 'flaccid', but it is concisely witty in Hall's usual style, scoring points about each tax in turn (as in 'Nor can they forbear on our pleasures intrenching, | We pay for our Marriage as if it were wenching', B1, p. 101).[33] Variation in the opening line of the three known manuscripts immediately signals a measure of popular circulation (M, 'The parliament thrifty to make up [...]', Sloane, 'The government thrifty to make up [...]').

Four satires, finally, stand out because they survive in far more manuscripts than any other of Hall's poems: 'Great William concerned to leave his gulled loobies' (B1, M, and nine others), 'Here lie the relics of a martyred knight' (B1, B2, M, and eleven others), 'Good people what will you of all be bereft' (B1, M, and twelve others), and 'Hail happy William thou art strangely great' (B2, M, and sixteen others). All four poems are edited by Cameron, who collates variant readings in those manuscripts known to him (detailed analysis of the many variants is not attempted here).[34] All but 'Great William' were printed, anonymously, in *POAS*, II (1703).

'Great William concerned to leave his gulled loobies' is a satire on the nine members of the Council appointed by William III during his absence from England in 1697, a Council that was now dominated by Whigs. The number of lines varies depending on the verse layout, but essentially two couplets at either end (in anapaestic tetrameters) enclose a sequence of short lines each briefly characterizing the supposed virtues of the appointees (except that the ninth is treated in the succeeding long line). Thus, to quote a passage from M (because B1 disguises the names):

> There's Tennison's politicks
> Dorsetts divinity
> Shrewsburys religion
> Sunderlands honesty. (M, p. 108)

Cameron prints the poem from MS Sloane 1731A, which his variants show to be an aberrant choice. The majority of other manuscripts are often ranged against it, and Cameron admits that Sloane may represent a 'sophistication' of the 'nonextant exclusive common ancestor'. It alone begins 'Great William concerned to leave this gulled nation', and has an opening triplet rather than a couplet. Other manuscripts end the first line variously with 'boobies' (the majority), 'loobies' (B1 and M, which may be significant), or 'cullies'. Although the poem is never attributed to Hall, neither is it to anyone else, and the lively final couplet seems typical of his high spirits: 'The K — g was so pleas'd with the rakes he had chosen, | He swore the next year he'd make them a dozen' (B1, p. 103).

In contrast, 'Here lie the relics of a martyred knight' is a compact poem of three triplets (mainly pentameters), which laments the death by execution, on 28 January 1697, of the Jacobite conspirator Sir John Fenwick. Not as angry as Hall's treatment of the same subject in 'Thus for his master fell the brave Montrose' (B1 alone), the tone now is restrained, and the poem's effectiveness derives from its three measured sentences that make Hall's position very clear. I quote it in full from B2:

> Here lyes the reliques of a martyrd knight
> Whose loyalty unspotted as the light
> Sealed with his blood his injured monarchs right.
> His head the state did from his body sever
> Because when living twas his cheife endeavour
> To join the nation & its head togather.
> Boldly he fell girt round with weeping souldiers
> Imploring Heaven for the good of his beholders
> So to cutt of Holl — ds head from En — ds shoulders. (B2, f. 14v)[35]

B1 has a less good text, its seventh line particularly weak ('He dy'd amongst a crowd of weeping soldiers', unique amongst the manuscripts collated by Cameron).

As noted earlier, Cameron describes himself as 'reluctantly [...] forced' to admit 'Here lie the relics' into Hall's canon, and he suggests as a theoretical alternative that Hall's 'general interest in the Jacobite martyr may have prompted him to anthologize the poems' (i.e. this and 'Thus for his master'). He points out that the letter in which the poem is preserved amongst the former Trumbull manuscripts (now BL, Add MS 72479, f. 69) was both written and postmarked on 23 February 1697, showing that the epitaph was in circulation soon after Fenwick's execution, but he does not seek to use this as evidence against Hall's authorship.[36] M, it may be noted, has the most explicit title of any manuscript of the poem: 'An epitaph upon Sir John Fenwick baronet murdered upon Tower Hill by an act of Parliament, 97, January 28'.

'Good people what will you of all be bereft' is different in style again, being a song 'upon the severall payements of taxes', to quote from its title in CUL, MS Add. 7112 (f. 35v). Along with the taxes on births, marriages, and burials dating from 1694 (as in 'Our government thrifty to raise up their wages'), the targets now include the ongoing poll taxes, the new window tax of 1696, and the recoinage introduced that same year. In three stanzas of essentially 8-line tetramers (but variously set out as a mixture of long and short lines), it ends in rousing style very much as a 'satyr on the tymes' (its title in Yale UL, MS Osborn fb.207/3):

> We parted with all our old money, to shew
> That we foolishly hoped for plenty of new.
> But now w'are convinc'd, since it comes to the push,
> That a bird in the hand is worth two in the bush,
>   For now like poor wretches,
>   W'are clapt under hatches,
> At rack, and at manger, like beasts in the Ark.
> Since our lords and our knights make us pay for our lights,
> Why shou'd we, why shou'd we be left in the dark? (B1, p. 96)

The range of its fourteen manuscripts was noticed earlier in the chapter, as was its inclusion in printed collections of writings attributed on their title-pages to the satirists Thomas Brown and Edward Ward.[37] From the plentiful textual variants printed by Cameron it appears that B1 may not always preserve the best readings (Cameron places it in a possibly inferior group), but this is not in itself a reason to doubt Hall's authorship, as it is possible that B1's exemplar was already corrupted as the result of repeated copying. Cameron, as noted above, regards the 'organist of Hereford' as a serious candidate for author. An argument in Hall's favour — along with the song's wit and energy — is the similarity of the writing style and verse form (other than the rhyme scheme) to that of 'Attend to my verse you whose ears are as long', as noted earlier. To quote another stanza from that poem, relating to the Battle of the Boyne:

> When Fate will not have it, how mortals mistake,
>   The bulletts fell thick, yet they kill'd not one soul,

> But by their silk sashes made ducks and fine drakes,
>   Altho' they swam thicker than flocks of those fowl.
>   But when they came o'er
>   Unto the far shoare,
>   Good Lord, how the French
>   And the Irish did scoure!
> Away they ran faster (nor thought fit to tarry)
> Than the news of Will's vict'ry, did to Q — M — ry. (B1, p. 6)

The satire with the widest circulation, finally, is 'Hail happy William thou art strangely great', which is known in a total of eighteen manuscripts, including B2 and M (but not B1).[38] Cameron prints it from *POAS*, II, where its title (as also in BL, Add MS 21094) is 'A Panegyrick, 1696/7'; compare '1696' in BL, MS Stowe 305, and Leeds UL, Brotherton Collection MS Lt q 11, item 14, and '1697' in the transcription in Thomas Hearne's 1706 diary (Bodleian, MS Hearne's Diaries 11, pp. 102–04).[39] Hearne, however, also supplies a different attribution, namely 'Mr Michael Bold's Verse 1697', referring presumably to the scholar who in 1702 published a Latin translation of Book 1 of *Paradise Lost*.[40] Another touted candidate for authorship is 'the honourable J. H. Esq.' to whom the poem is given in the 1704 anthology entitled *Miscellaneous Works Written by His Grace George Late Duke of Buckingham*.[41] As noted earlier, Cameron suggests that the J. H. in question could be the politician and lampooner John Grubham Howe (1657–1722), 'one of William's non-Jacobite opponents' (p. 456).[42]

On stylistic grounds it is not in fact clear that 'Hail happy William' should be attributed to Hall, because over half the satire — in total, twenty-six lines of mainly pentameter couplets — comprises a formal and unusually schematic mock-panegyric, whose repetitions and indeed seriousness seem foreign to Hall's usual manner:

> Hail happy W — m thou art strangely great,
> And whats the cause, thy virtue or thy fate?
> For thee the child the parents heart will sting,
> For thee the favourite will desert his king,
> For thee the patriott will subvert the laws,
> For thee the judge will still decide the cause,
> For thee the prelate will his church betray,
> For thee the souldier fights without his pay. (B2, f. 8v)

Six similar lines follow. The final two couplets, referring to William's subjects, are more typical:

> And that this wonder may more wondrous seem
> Thou never yet didst one kind thing for them.
> Rebells like witches having sign'd the rolls
> Must serve their masters though they damn their souls.

Hall is nothing if not versatile, but 'Hail happy William' appears, to the present writer, the least likely of the oppositional satires to be his work.[43]

7.5. Co-occurrence of the Oppositional Satires

It is of particular interest that as many as sixteen manuscripts (other than the Brotherton Collection and Ottley manuscripts, C, and M) each contain between two and four of the oppositional satires, representing in total no more than nine different poems. The number of occurrences of these poems in the sixteen manuscripts, i.e. with other of the satires present, is as follows:

'Hail happy William thou are strangely great'	11 times
'Good people what will you of all be bereft'	6 times
'Here lie the relics of a martyred knight'	5 times
'Great William concerned to leave his gulled loobies'	5 times
'Rejoice ye fops your idol's come again'	4 times
'What fast for horrid murder of the day'	4 times
'Whither ye impious Britons do ye run'	4 times
'Six tedious months our senate sits'	2 times
''Twill puzzle much the author's brains'	Once

It is striking also how many times the nine poems have been copied adjacent to one another, or are at least no more than a few leaves apart, irrespective of the type of manuscript involved. The following broad (and partly tentative) characterization of thirteen of the relevant manuscripts brings this out:[44]

Professionally written anthologies:

BL, Add. MS 21094: 'Whither ye impious Britons' and 'Hail happy William' adjacent, with 'Great William concerned' close by.

BL, MS Lansdowne 852: 'Good people what will you' and 'Six tedious months' adjacent ('Great William concerned' and 'What fast for horrid murder' occur elsewhere in the manuscript).

Yale UL, MS Osborn fb.207/3: 'Whither ye impious Britons' and 'Good people what will you' adjacent, with 'Hail happy William' one poem apart ('Here lie the relics' occurs elsewhere in the manuscript).

Personal or miscellaneous collections

BL, Add. MS 29497: 'Good people what will you' and 'Hail happy William' adjacent, with ''Twill puzzle much' close by.[45]

BL, MS Stowe 305: 'Good people what will you' and 'Hail happy William' adjacent, with 'Rejoice ye fops' close by.

Bodleian, MS Rawlinson D.361: 'Good people what will you' and 'Hail happy William' adjacent.

Leeds UL, MS BC Lt 79: 'Hail happy William' and 'Here lie the relics' one poem apart.

Leeds UL, MS BC Lt q 40: 'Here lie the relics' and 'Hail happy William' adjacent.

Princeton UL, MS RTC01 no. 38: 'Good people what will you' and 'Hail happy William' one item apart ('Here lie the relics' and 'What fast for horrid murder' occur elsewhere in the manuscript).

'Separates' within composite manuscripts

BL, Add MS 72479: 'Here lie the relics' and 'What fast for horrid murder' adjacent (with three separate copies of 'Hail happy William', all in different hands, positioned straight afterwards).

Bodleian, MS Rawlinson C.586: 'Here lie the relics' and 'Rejoice ye fops' adjacent, and (in the same hand):

Bodleian, MS Rawlinson poet. 169: 'Hail happy William' and 'What fast for horrid murder' adjacent (amounting to four items out of a total of ten poems in these two manuscripts).

Bodleian, MS Rawlinson poet. 181: 'Great William concerned' and 'Rejoice ye fops' close ('Whither ye impious Britons' occurs elsewhere in the manuscript).

Some of this co-occurrence of poems is very likely owing to the phenomenon of scriptorium manuscripts, i.e. anthologies produced commercially on the basis of existing collections, which might be replicated more or less exactly or else modified (possibly to suit a particular customer) by the addition or excision of material.[46] This applies particularly to BL, Add. MS 21094 and MS Lansdowne 852 (listed in the first group above), which were characterized by Cameron as 'made professionally for an interested owner' and, respectively, as 'copy of a scriptorium manuscript with additions' and 'copy of a scriptorium manuscript with corrections'.[47] Manuscripts produced commercially might then go on to influence the contents of privately written miscellanies.

In this light the frequent co-occurrence of a significant proportion of Hall's oppositional satires is not in itself evidence for common authorship, but the extent to which these poems travelled in close proximity is perhaps suggestive. The adjacency noted above is not, however, reflected in the arrangement of poems in B1, which in any case contains only six of the nine poems singled out above. Its twenty-four oppositional satires occur largely in two sizeable groups: those that are restricted in their circulation to B1, B2, and M appear at the beginning of the manuscript, whereas those distributed more widely (including 'Good people what will you', 'Here lie the relics', and 'Great William concerned', separated by other poems) are, by and large, found towards the end. This may suggest that the compiler of B1 was drawing on more than one manuscript source for the oppositional satires. B2, whose seventeen Hall items (nine oppositional satires) include five of the poems discussed above, has 'What fast for horrid murder' and 'Here lie the relics' side by side, with 'Hail happy William', 'Whither ye impious Britons', and 'Six tedious months' all close at hand. M, with fourteen oppositional satires out of its nineteen Hall items, many of which are grouped (see Chapter 4.1 above), has 'Hail happy William' close to 'Great William concerned', and ''Twill puzzle much' and 'Rejoice ye fops' adjacent.

7.6. 'Curse on Those Representatives'

An oppositional satire excluded from all of the preceding discussion is the 12-line 'Curse on those representatives' (two stanzas, aabccb), which occurs in B1, O1d (in Hall's own hand), O2, and M. As noted above (Chapter 2.3), this is a version of a popular 18-line satire 'Curse on such representatives', which usually occurs in manuscript (and in *POAS*, III) as an answer to a poem known as 'The Chequer Inn'.[48] The latter can be securely dated to 1675, as it was occasioned by impeachment proceedings brought that year against Thomas Osborne, Earl of Danby, who was then Lord High Treasurer. The subject-matter of the 'answer' is more general — an attack on Parliament, complaining about taxes and the waste of public money — but another 12-line adaptation of the poem, in BL, MS Harley 7316 (f. 12r), entitles it 'On King Charles the Seconds pension parliament' and changes the usual l. 10 ('So when mine host does money lack') to 'So Rowley when he gold does lack'. There is therefore no possibility that Hall composed the first version of 'Curse on', and his text appears to be an independent abridgement of the 18-line original, the subject-matter equally applicable to the 1690s:

> Curse on those representatives
> That sell us all, our bearns, and wives,
>   Quoth Dick with Indignation;
> All that they doe is, to raise tax,
> And the whole bus'ness of their acts
>   Is to consume the nation.
>
> Thus to our rotten pumps at home
> Wee pour in water when 't wont come
>   And that way get more out;
> So when our lord does money lack
> He money gives among his pack
>   And then it runns full spout. (O1d, p. 29)

In O1d it has the heading 'Catch', and follows immediately on the preceding poem ('Since we're undone the matter is not much') without even a line space. All other poems copied by Hall into O1d begin on a fresh page, with the exception of 'The great good man whom fortune does displace' (again almost certainly of separate authorship), which is discussed in Chapter 9.2 below. Rather than claiming it as his own work, Hall is more likely to have included 'Curse on those representatives' as an appropriate companion-piece to 'Since we're undone', which was occasioned by the proceedings in Parliament against the financier Sir Charles Duncombe. He may have abridged the 18-line original to make it fit on the page, or he may already have turned the poem into a 'catch' for performance purposes, wishing now to preserve this version. Whatever the circumstances, it is clear that 'Curse on those representatives' was subsequently copied as if Hall's work, appearing as it does in all of O2, B1, and M.[49]

Notes to Chapter 7

1. The former comprise 'Dragoons have a care', 'That pleasant prince that strolling northern star' (both about Peter the Great), 'As sharper when his coin grows low', and 'Here's a health whilst the trumpets', although the last of these makes fun also of William III. With the exception of ''Tis odd indeed indeed 'tis wondrous odd', found also in M, all of the latter occur only in the main manuscript collections.

2. Its manuscripts include B1, C, and M, the last headed 'A health 91', dating it presumably to 1691. In B1 it is positioned within a large group of oppositional political satires at the beginning of the manuscript. There are no known printings. See further n. 45 below.

3. See Chapter 2 above for a somewhat longer discussion of manuscript publication of political satires, where I quote more extensively from Love, *Scribal Publication in Seventeenth-Century England*, and provide page references.

4. Many of the manuscripts in question are briefly described in *CELM*, and those relevant to Love's major study, *English Clandestine Satire*, appear in his list of manuscripts on pp. 305–07. None of Hall's poems is discussed by Love, but many of them feature in his first-line index to the contents of these manuscripts (pp. 307–414).

5. See the description of B2 in Chapter 3.1 above.

6. Cameron, p. 452, lists in a footnote, by number (with reference to one of his own indexes), all of these Hall poems not otherwise discussed by him.

7. Cameron notes the poem's inclusion in *The Remains of Mr Thomas Brown, Serious and Comical, in Prose and Verse* (London, 1720), pp. 73–74, but dismisses Brown's claims (pp. 498, 530). It was printed also in a 1712 volume of poems attributed to the London satirist Edward Ward (see Appendix D).

8. For an overview of verse forms and styles occurring in lampoons of the period, including ones apparently to be sung, see Love, *Scribal Publication in Seventeenth-Century England*, pp. 232–35.

9. Cameron, p. 400, notes 'So little being done and so much money spent' in passing (it is his 'S13'), without bothering to mention Hall. It is edited below.

10. Hall's songs of this type generally exhibit an informal mixture of dactyls and anapaests.

11. Cameron notes both poems on p. 439, quoting three lines from the first (which he calls 'mild'), but strangely associates only the second of them with Hall ('One Jacobite (Henry Hall?) callously asserted [...]').

12. 'Montrose' (in B1, 'Montross') is James Graham, Marquis of Montrose (1612–50), who died fighting for the royalist cause in Scotland. Cameron refers to the poem (his 'T39') in two footnotes on pp. 483–84. It is edited below.

13. It is referenced in Cameron, p. 414, as by 'Henry Hall?'. An anonymous poem on the same subject is printed on his pp. 415–20.

14. In both manuscripts the title includes the date 1694, but this is likely to be a mistake for 1693, as suggested in the edition of this song, below.

15. M, in contrast, titles the poem 'Sent to the House of Commons in 96'.

16. Cameron, p. 453; he does not print the poem in full.

17. B1, p. 102; O1d, p. 32.

18. M here reads 'illegal' and has only ten lines overall, omitting a couplet about the annual celebration of 5 November.

19. *A Summary Catalogue of Western Manuscripts in the Bodleian Library at Oxford*, ed. by R. W. Hunt and others, 7 vols (Oxford Clarendon Press, 1895–1953), III, ed. by Falconer Madan (1895), 328–29.

20. Bodleian, MS Rawlinson poet. 207, p. 19.

21. Cameron, p. 537, describes Add. 20194 as 'a carefully transcribed comprehensive anthology made professionally for an interested owner'. *CELM* notes the Rawlinson manuscript's 'Jacobite sympathies'.

22. 'On the 30 of January these were given to the bishop & Dean of Worcester' (BL, MS Lansdowne 852); 'Found on the Church Door at White Hall, January 30th 1696' (Bodleian, MS Rawlinson poet. 169, Yale UL, MS Osborn c.570/1, and *POAS*, II); 'Wednesday March 2 96, This deliverd the 30th of January last to a parson going into the pulpit at Chichester' (Princeton UL, MS RTC01 no. 38); 'Thes 8 verses following were given to the minister who preacht at St Gyleses Church the 30 of Jan. last being the anniversary for the martyrdome of King Charles the First', 'Feb 23 96/7' (BL, Add MS 72479).

23. B2's text is itself corrupt, however, reading 'Since while repeated cannot be forgiving'.

24. I quote from Cameron, p. 388, who prints the epigram in full during a passage of discussion, basing himself on *POAS*, III. He relates the poem to a longer, anonymous verse satire 'The Campaign', printed in *POAS*, II, 203–10 ('When people find their money spent'), suggesting that the author of the epigram 'polished up' its thirteenth and fourteenth stanzas. The lines in question do indeed include 'Namur was taken in our sight', but say that the English forces in general did not participate, not merely the king.

25. M reads 'who writes King Williams story'. The most divergent text is that of CUL, Add. MS 5962 (beginning 'The writer sure must take great pains | When he relates the story' and ending 'And Mons was in his hearing'), possibly the result of an imperfect memory of the poem. Cameron, p. 537, characterizes BL, Add MS 29497 as a private commonplace book, while MS Osborn b.111 comprises avowedly Jacobite 'loyal poems'.

26. *New Oxford Book of Seventeenth Century Verse*, ed. by Fowler, p. 792; Cameron, p. 455. The former prints it with the author heading 'Henry Hall? d. 1713', thus attributing the poem to Henry Hall the younger.

27. The other Bodleian manuscript is Rawlinson C.986, an early eighteenth-century composite miscellany. Cameron regards all the manuscripts he collates as 'corrupt collaterals'. The case against Stowe is strengthened by its copy having the date '96' in the title, as Cameron admits (p. 455).

28. For this discussion, see Cameron, pp. 452–53.

29. The first citation in *OED* (*ready*, D. n.,1) is from Otway's play *The Atheist* (1684).

30. *CELM* characterizes MS Sloane 1731A as 'A folio composite volume of papers, 171 leaves. Assembled by Dr W. Wall. c.1700'.

31. If so, then M may represent an intermediate stage. With minor exceptions its readings agree with those of B1, but it, too, has only the first two stanzas.

32. *CELM* characterizes MS Sloane 2717 as 'A folio composite volume of legal and state papers and poems on affairs of state'.

33. Cameron, p. 499 n. The poem is his 'T18'.

34. Cameron, pp. 516–19, 483–84, 498–500, and 456–57.

35. The final words of the last three lines are heavily abbreviated, as the writer has not left enough space when preparing a frame for the poem. The expansions made here appear to match his or her intentions.

36. Cameron, p. 483. One of the other two poems in the single-sheet letter is 'What fast for horrid murder of the day'.

37. See n. 7 above.

38. Or rather twenty manuscript copies, as BL, Add MS 72479, a collection of separates, contains three copies (ff. 70r-v, 71r, 72r).

39. MS Lt q 11, item 14 is a separate, a single leaf formerly folded and with its title on the dorse, part of a collection of loose sheets almost entirely of English verse in many different hands, dating from the early seventeenth to the early eighteenth century.

40. See John T. Shawcross, 'A Note on Milton's Latin Translator', *Milton Quarterly*, 21 (1987), 65–66, who thinks it most likely that he was the Michael Bold (d. 1742) who, as a non-juror, was ejected in 1692 from his fellowship of Trinity Hall, Cambridge. Hearne's transcription of 'Hail happy William thou art strangely great' was not included in *Remarks and Collections of Thomas Hearne*, ed. by Doble and others.

41. Vol. 1 (London, 1704), p. 492.

42. See A. A. Hanham, 'Howe [How], John Grobham [Jack] (1657–1722), Politician', in *ODNB*.

43. Cameron, though collating only a proportion of the manuscripts, usefully draws attention to the variants surrounding ll. 12–13 of the 27-line *POAS* text — one or other of which is usually omitted by the manuscripts — and to the variant opening words of the poem, although his reading 'Thrive' for Bodleian, MS Rawlinson D.361 should read 'Thrice', as in Leeds UL, Brotherton Collection MS Lt 79, f. 132r, and Yale UL, MS Osborn fb.207/3, p. 12.

44. Other manuscripts having more than one of Hall's oppositional satires, in these cases more widely dispersed, are BL, MS Sloane 1731a ('Six tedious months', 'Great William concerned', and 'Hail happy William'), a private compilation; Holkham Hall, MS 686 ('Great William concerned' and 'Hail happy William'), a scriptorium manuscript; and Yale UL, MS Osborn c.570 ('Rejoice ye fops', 'What fast for horrid murder', and 'Whither ye impious Britons'), probably professionally written.

45. Also not far away is Hall's Jacobite drinking song 'To our monarch's return', which, like ''Twill puzzle much', occurs also (though well separated) in Yale UL, MS Osborn b.111. See further Chapter 4.2 above.

46. See W. J. Cameron, 'A Late Seventeenth-Century Scriptorium', *Renaissance and Modern Studies*, 7 (1963), 23–52; Cameron, pp. 528–38; and Love, *Scribal Publication in Seventeenth-Century England*, pp. 231–83, esp. pp. 271–76. For a detailed study of the manuscript transmission and reception of satirical material of the period, see Love, *English Clandestine Satire*, pp. 249–302.

47. Cameron, pp. 537 and 542. Three members of what Cameron and Love refer to as the 'William' group of scriptorium manuscripts each contain one of Hall's oppositional satires ('Great William concerned'), namely BL, MS Harley 7315, Nottingham UL, MS Portland Pw V 48, and Leeds UL, Brotherton Collection MS Lt q 38. Holkham Hall, MS 686, with two of his satires (n. 44 above), belongs to the same group.

48. See *Poems on Affairs of State: Augustan Satirical Verse, 1660–1714*. I: *1660–1678*, ed. by George deForest Lord (New Haven: Yale University Press, 1963), pp. 252–62, where both 'The Chequer Inn' and 'Curse on such representatives' are printed. Because of an attribution to the Duke of Buckingham the latter is also included in *Plays, Poems and Miscellaneous Writings Associated with George Villiers, Second Duke of Buckingham*, 2 vols, ed. by Robert D. Hume and Harold Love (Oxford: Oxford University Press, 2007), II, 17–18.

49. In M it immediately precedes a sequence of three of Hall's own oppositional satires, namely 'Are all those lights that gild the street', 'Ne'er blame your hero for the kingdom's fall', and 'Six tedious months our senate sits'.

CHAPTER 8

❖

Political Satires,
1702–05

Hall, as has been said, is evidently much happier once Queen Anne succeeds William III. He is no longer in opposition, and his poetic mood lightens. His links with London strengthen, partly, it seems, as a result of getting poems into print, and some of his compositions read as if he himself has witnessed events in the capital. Another major difference is that most of the political poems from this later period, both celebratory and satirical, are found in the Ottley manuscripts, not B1 or B2, which generally reflect Hall's pre-1702 output. The particular manuscripts in question are those designated in Chapter 2.3 as O1e and O3a-b, which contain poems datable to 1703–05 and which are partly in Hall's own hand. As will be seen, some of the items had quite wide manuscript circulation, and four were printed in the original *Poems on Affairs of State*.

8.1. Poems in the Ottley Manuscripts

O1e, a single leaf, has three poems that were taken into the fair copy manuscript O2, namely 'An honest good farmer by providence blest', 'To our arms on earth and seas', and 'Since the town is our own what it cost us no matter' (they are the final three Hall items in O2). As noted in Chapter 5.3, all three were printed in the *Diverting Post*, the second in October and the first and third in December 1704. 'To our arms on earth and seas' and 'Since the town is our own', which are not satires, are headed 'The Healths' and 'Landau Took', respectively. Both celebrate English victories abroad and both raise a glass to (among others) Admiral Sir George Rooke, the English naval commander. Rooke is also the subject of an addition to O1e by another hand, a little poem beginning 'The great Sir George Toulouse did beat', attributionally problematic in that it was not copied into O2. This 8-line verse, in popular ballad style (and using the well-known refrain 'the clean contrary way'), alludes to the indecisive Battle of Malaga of August 1704. It was widely copied, surviving in eleven other manuscripts (with variant opening lines), and it was printed in *POAS*, IV (1707), as the second of two satires 'On the Sea fight between Sir G.R. and Tolouse, 1704'.[1] The poem is possibly not Hall's work, partly because it represents Rooke as having been beaten and running away just as much as the French commander the Comte de Toulouse; Rooke, from Hall's other references to him, was clearly a hero of his (being a known Tory and almost certainly a High Churchman), and the final line of 'Since the town is our own' alludes unfavourably to the House of Lords' refusal to congratulate him on his successful exploits.[2] But the eight lines are essentially light-hearted and they hardly constitute serious criticism of Rooke.[3]

The fourth item in O1e, 'An honest good farmer' (edited below), is distinguished from the others by its satirical subject-matter and in being written in Hall's own hand. Headed 'A fable', and comprising twenty-two lines of couplets, it tells of a prosperous farmer whose flocks were subject to nightly attack by 'a herd of sly Isigrims', i.e. wolves, because his predecessor had filed out their guardians' teeth. He decides in consequence to 'make his fence higher', an action considered by his neighbour (accused of being a 'Low Rascall') to be unnecessary. There is little doubt that Hall is referring to the change of government in April 1704, when the removal of High-Church Tories would have left the Church of England, in his eyes, in danger of despoliation by Low Churchmen. In the slightly changed version of the poem printed in the *Diverting Post* in December 1704, 'a herd of sly Isigrims' becomes instead 'wolves lions and panthers'. The autograph text in O1e contains several corrections, and clearly represents the first version of the poem.

The six political satires preserved in O3a and O3b, none of which was copied into O2, are all in Henry Hall's own hand. O3b, as described in Chapter 2.3 above, is a letter from Hall, dated simply 'July 26', replying to one he had received from Adam Ottley the younger, then resident at Balliol College, Oxford, who matriculated in 1702 at the age of seventeen. The bulk of the letter — which exemplifies Hall's easy informality of style and address, and the way in which verse-making was apparently second nature to him — comprises three poems mocking John Churchill, Duke of Marlborough, principally for achieving success in battle without endangering himself. All three consist of six lines of couplets. The first two, 'Accept my lord this humble glittering thing' and 'Your awkward Austrian phiz with joy I take', are a linked pair in which Archduke Charles of Austria, the Allies' candidate for the Spanish throne, addresses Marlborough (presenting him with his portrait and a sword), following which Marlborough replies. The imagined occasion is presumably the ceremonial welcome laid on for the Archduke when he visited England in November 1703.

The third poem, 'Strike you new medals to your hero's fame', is headed 'To my Lord G — n, who struck the medal to the D — e of M — last year'. The allusion is presumably to Marlborough's political ally Sidney, Earl Godolphin, and 'last year' is likely also to be 1703. 'Accept my lord' is found also in BL, Add MS 40060 (f. 50v, dated at end 'Feb. 1703/4), where it is preceded on f. 50r by a much-copied anonymous poem, again satirizing Marlborough, beginning 'The glory of our English arms retreiv'd', dated at the end 'Mar 1703/4'. The heading to this poem is 'On the new medal with the Queen on one side and the Generall on horseback on the other with this motto Sine clade victor'. The medal in question, with its motto meaning 'A conqueror without slaughter', was struck in 1703 to commemorate allied victories at Bonn, Huy, and Limbourg, and there can be little doubt that

'Strike you new medals' — which ends 'Yet not one drop of M — gs [blood] was lost' — is referring to the same special medal.[4] All three poems in O3b being therefore concerned with events in 1703, including late in 1703, Hall's letter to Ottley can confidently be dated 26 July 1704.

The poems in O3b are immediately preceded, as already quoted in Chapter 2.3, by the words 'You know Sir, 'tis the juce of the grape, and not of the apple inspires the poet, and to justify the assertion, read these epigrams' — strong evidence that Hall is claiming all the verses that follow as his own. But there is a marked contrast, in terms of circulation, between the latter two poems, 'Your awkward Austrian phiz' and 'Strike you new medals', which are unknown elsewhere, and 'Accept my lord this humble glittering thing', which was widely copied: eleven other manuscripts are known (including BL, Add MS 40060, as above), and it appeared in print in *POAS*, IV.[5] As usual, none of these sources attributes the poem to Hall (or indeed to anyone else). Given its different circulation, it could conceivably be an existing composition now being passed off as Hall's own, included in the letter for the sake of the witty 'Answer', but there is a sense throughout that Hall is showing off to a much younger man, the son of a close friend, and 'Accept my lord' and 'Your awkward Austrian phiz' are extremely similar in style. It may be noted also that the former occurs in the Worcestershire manuscript Lechmere Archives 40 (i) alongside other of Hall's poems (see Chapter 4.2 above), although it is not there attributed to him. Assuming it is his, it is possible it achieved circulation through being sent independently to another correspondent, perhaps before the answer was written.

O3a, a single folio leaf, has three satires in Hall's own hand written on one side only. 'Once in a reign to increase our causeless fears' and 'Two noble earls long since the court forsook', in that order, fill the vertical writing space, but Hall subsequently squeezed 'When church was mother Anne was then her daughter' sideways into the left-hand margin.

'Once in a reign', which is edited below, was first entitled 'On the whale lately taken at Greenwich', but Hall then altered 'whale' to 'two monstrous fish'. This matches the poem's heading when printed in the *Diverting Post* in March 1705, except that the place of taking is different: 'On the two monstrous fishes, lately taken at Gravesend'. It may be that Hall received the news in stages, leading to a series of corrections.[6] The poem itself, nineteen lines of largely pentameter couplets, is a successful, confident display of wit (and loyalty to Queen Anne) that relates the whales' appearance to the current national situation.[7] Hall's initial conceit is that Britain has no need of prodigies warning of disasters to come when it is already suffering heavy taxation and war, 'which ne're but with the world will end', added to which 'Low Church triumphant does already ride'. Thus 'The monsters might as well have staid at home'. Hall's subsequent wish is that 'God preserve our mild and matchless queen | And guard his Church from Whigs and mod'rate men'. Conscious of the quarrelsome state of the country, he concludes:

> For if kind Heav'n wou'd once our jarrs unite
> Whole shoals of whales we'd gaze on with delight,
> Nor cou'd Leviathan himself affright.

'Two noble earls', found nowhere else, is a more perfunctory piece. Headed 'On the late alterations at court', the first of its five couplets ('Two noble earls long since the court forsook | Seymour long since laid down, and lately Rook') dates its composition again to 1705. The references are to the Earls of Rochester and Nottingham, who left high office respectively in 1703 and 1704, Sir Edward Seymour, who relinquished his post also in 1704, and (once again) Sir George Rooke, who was omitted from the 1705 Privy Council. Hall laments their departure — all four of them leading Tories — regretting that 'Men with hard names the hero now succeed, | And Goths, and Vandalls, govern in their stead'. He ends the poem by contrasting their 'hearts intirely [*sic*] Dutch' with 'hearts entirely English', a phrase that picks up Queen Anne's declaration in her first speech from the throne, 'I know my own heart to be entirely English'. It was evidently natural for Hall to continue viewing his political opponents in terms of the 1690s.[8]

The third poem in O3a achieved wide circulation and deserves quoting in full:

> When Church was mother Ann was then her daughter,
> Then Ann did only what her mother taught her,
> But now since Anna's mother of the Church
> She fairly leaves her daughter in the lurch.

As was said, it is written in Hall's own hand, and further evidence for his authorship is provided by an annotation 'H. Hall in a letter 1703', which is in the hand of the person responsible for the attributions to Hall in O2 (see Chapter 2.3 above).

Stating Hall's claim to the poem (and seemingly its date of composition) was possibly important to the annotator given that it achieved popularity in a textually different version that at first sight appears superior. The usual first line as it appears elsewhere is 'When Anna was the Church's daughter', and it is this version that was printed by F. H. Ellis in the Yale *Poems on Affairs of State* on the basis of lines quoted by Daniel Defoe in a footnote to his 1706 poem, *Jure Divino*:

> When *Anna* was the Church's Daughter,
> She acted as her Mother taught her;
> But now she's Mother of the Church,
> She's left her Daughter in the Lurch.[9]

The poem subsequently re-appeared in print (in the same tetrameter form) in *POAS*, IV.[10]

The occasion of the poem is the contemporary perception, by High Churchmen, that Queen Anne had failed in her promise to defend the Church of England after the hopes placed in her at the beginning of her reign. The situation came to a head in Parliament in December 1705, resulting in the passing of a government-sponsored resolution that the Church was in no danger under Queen Anne. 'When Anna was the Church's Daughter' was clearly popular at the time, with the text preserved in BL, MS Lansdowne 852, headed 'Upon the vote that pass'd that the Church was not in danger', and Defoe, in his 1706 printing, referring to it as 'the common Song of the [High Church] Party'.[11]

The early date of 1703 attached to the epigram in O3a is therefore striking, as it was in February of that year that Anne first dismissed a High Churchman —

the Earl of Rochester — from her government. It is perfectly possible that Hall, certainly of High Church persuasion, was at once disillusioned and reacted with the form of words that he subsequently copied into O3a two years later, when the furore about Queen Anne and the Church was at its peak.[12] It seems probable that Hall's presumed original version, which has longer lines and more cumbersome syntax than the received text, was later rewritten in an easier, shorter-lined form for popular consumption, quite possibly by somebody else, given that this is not the form that Hall transcribes in 1705. Of the known manuscript copies, six transmit the popular version.[13] The text as found in O3a is, however, copied twice (by the same hand) in the contemporary composite miscellany Bodleian, MS Smith 23, while a more doggerel version preserved in BL, Add MS 21094, would seem, on the basis of line length and word order, to derive from Hall's text rather than that printed by Defoe.[14]

8.2. 'To Give the Last Amendments to the Bill'

A quite different poem related to religious politics is the long and much-copied 'To give the last amendments to the bill', often known by the title *The Mitred Club*. Only one of its fourteen known manuscripts (and none of its printings) assigns it to Henry Hall,[15] but the copy in question, in the composite manuscript BL, Add MS 25490 (where it occupies ff. 13r–14r, a separately mounted bifolio), has a double attribution: at the end, the subscription 'H. Hall Organist of Hereford', and on f. 14v, 'Mr Henry Hall's poem on the Bill of Conformity'. It does not occur in the Ottley and Brotherton Collection manuscripts.

The Mitred Club, written in pentameter couplets, is set during the debate concerning the Bill to put an end to the practice of occasional conformity with the Church of England, which was introduced into Parliament in November 1702. It was aimed at those Nonconformists who were allowed to hold public office so long as they took the sacrament according to Anglican rites once a year, as required by the Test Act. The Tory-dominated Commons were heavily in favour of the Bill, but the Lords, with much support from the episcopal bench, introduced numerous wrecking amendments, and it eventually failed.[16] Frank Ellis, who edited *The Mitred Club* for the Yale *Poems on Affairs of State*, dates it 'January (?) 1703', while the debate was at its height (he accepts Hall's authorship, although also with a question mark). The 148-line poem takes the form of an imagined private conference of twelve of the bishops, all but one of them appointed by William III. The bulk of it comprises four speeches, the first and last by the outspoken Whig (and opponent of the Bill) Gilbert Burnet, the second and third by the ghosts of Archbishop Laud (in favour) and William III (against). Between the second and third speeches the bishops' opinion moves in favour of support for the Bill, but by the end, persuaded by Burnet that allowing it would not be in their financial interest, they decide to throw it out.

That, at least, is the content of the poem as printed by Ellis, whose copy text is *The M — 'd C — b: or the L — th Consultation. Et tu, Brute?* [...] *From a correct copy* (London, 1704; *ESTC* T39072, Foxon E480/481). This edition aside, all other copies, both manuscript and printed, end the poem at the point when William III's ghost vanishes (with the words, 'In Shapeless Air the Royal Bubble broke, | And that thin Form their wond'ring Eyes forsook', ll. 93–94, Ellis, VI, 514–15), even though this leaves the poem — and the dramatic situation — without a resolution.

As to the priority of the two versions, the phrase 'From a correct copy' on the title-page of the printed text just cited implies that an imperfect version of the poem circulated earlier, and indeed another 1704 printing, comprising no more than ll. 1–94, was issued under the title *Et tu Brute? or, the M — 'd C — l* (no imprint; ESTC T129593, Foxon E479, which also notes 'Title in half-title form'). The British Library copy has the word *C — l* filled in as 'Cabal', a possibly more original wording found also in the heading to the poem in BL, MS Lansdowne 852 (where the poem is dated 1703), and Leeds UL, Brotherton Collection, MS Lt q 55. On this basis it is possible that ll. 1–94 represent an unfinished state of the poem that was 'released' with or without the author's blessing and yet was clearly regarded as worth copying (and printing), despite its apparent imperfection. Five of the manuscript texts are also headed 'Et tu Brute', suggesting a possibly close connection with Foxon E479.[17] The version of the poem, again of no more than ninety-four lines, that was quickly included in *POAS*, III (1704), is entitled 'A Consultation of the Bishops', a title shared by three manuscripts.[18] It is curious that no manuscript copies of the completed poem appear to survive.

ESTC lists twenty-one printed copies of the 'correct copy' (as opposed to nine of Foxon E479), and suggests that the London imprint possibly disguises Edinburgh publication. If correct, this may be thought to lessen the likelihood of Hall's having been responsible for more than the opening 94 lines. But *ESTC* has here amalgamated two Foxon items, E480 and E481, the latter number used by Foxon to distinguish an edition in which the rules in the phrase 'M — 'd C — b' 'are each composed of three short sections' rather than being printed continuously, as in E480. On this basis he suggests that E481 is 'probably an Edinburgh reprint from the location of copies' (four of the nine that he lists are held in Edinburgh libraries). The case for the first edition of the 'correct copy' having been printed elsewhere than in London therefore disappears.[19]

Its probable London publication is, however, unlikely to have any bearing on the question of authorship. As mentioned above, the copy of the (shorter) version of the poem in BL, Add MS 25490, names Henry Hall as author, and this seems very plausible, given that its content conforms closely to his known religious and political proclivities, especially his loathing of Gilbert Burnet. In addition, the metaphorical reference in ll. 44–45 to the need to fence in the flock from prowling wolves (and the unusual use of the verb 'cot' to describe the protection) recalls the poem 'An honest good farmer', discussed above.[20] However, there remains the question of the longer, 'finished' version of the poem, and on stylistic grounds it may well be that Hall's responsibility ended with l. 94. Lines 95–148 lack his usual lightness of wit, and the four-line parenthetical comparison of Burnet to a 'Debauchee' in ll. 102–05, in formal Augustan mode, is an unexpected stylistic feature.[21] All things considered, it is likely that another writer obtained a copy of the unfinished poem, in print or manuscript, and brought it to a conclusion. Foxon, it may be noted, records that the copy of E480 in the William Andrews Clark Memorial Library at the University of California, Los Angeles, has an early manuscript note, 'Suppos'd by Prior'.

A final point of interest is that 'To give the last amendments to the bill' is at times found copied in the near company of certain of Hall's oppositional satires from the previous decade. Thus in BL, MS Lansdowne 852, it appears immediately before the adjacent poems 'Good people what will you of all be bereft' and 'Six tedious months our senate sits', while in Leeds UL, Brotherton Collection MS Lt q 40, it is copied straight after the adjacent pair 'Here lie the relics of a martyred knight' and 'Hail happy William thou art strangely great'.[22] It also shares a manuscript, Yale UL, MS Osborn c.111, with two of the other satires considered in the present chapter, namely 'The great Sir George Toulouse did beat' and 'Accept my lord this humble glittering thing', but in this case the three poems are widely spaced.

8.3. Other Poems

Finally, from this period, there are three further poems celebrating the success of British arms abroad and one light-hearted satire. The earliest of the celebrations is a 4-line epigram 'While fame with pleasure shall the story tell', found only in B1 where it is headed 'To the Queen on the success of her arms in Spain'. The occasion is seemingly the English victory at Vigo Bay in 1702. (A song wholly devoted to praising Queen Anne is the ode with music beginning 'Bless Albion bless thy stars above', discussed in Chapter 6.1 above.) Dating from three years later are 'We heard indeed of glorious actions done' and 'Hark to the war the trumpet sounds', known only from their publication in the *Diverting Post* in January and March 1705, respectively (see Chapter 5.3 above).

The satire is the 32-line poem 'As man in Westminster to each that comes', printed in the final, February 1706 issue of the *Diverting Post*. From that source, almost certainly, it was taken into Thomas Hearne's diary for 19 March 1706, again as noted earlier in Chapter 5.3; it is Hearne who provides the attribution ('as 'tis said') to Henry Hall. The poem is given over to a light, Whig-baiting interpretation of the subject-matter of the engraving published in the 1706 *Oxford Almanack*, in answer to, in Hearne's words, 'A silly explanation having been publish'd by some foolish fanatick'.[23] The final three lines show the subject of the Church in danger to be a continuing preoccupation of Hall's (I quote from the *Diverting Post*):

> But where to find the figure out, I trow,
> That does the Church in so much danger show
> Their L — d — ps, only and the L — d does know.

Notes to Chapter 8

1. It is edited in Ellis, VII, 18, with discussion, 15–17, and textual variants, 628–29. Ellis's copy text is wrongly said to be the 1707 printing, but (from the variants) it is evidently either Folger Shakespeare Library, MS M.b.12, p. 304, or Nottingham UL, MS Portland Pw V 44, p. 432. Both these copies state that the poem is 'In imitation of Sternhold and Hopkins', i.e. the popular

sixteenth-century versification of the Psalms, widely sung in Church of England services. The assertion is thus a possible pointer to Hall's authorship.

2. For a detailed account of his career, including of the Whig party's hostility to recognising his achievements, see *The House of Commons, 1690–1715*, ed. by Eveline Cruickshanks, Stuart Handley, and D. W. Hayton, 5 vols (Cambridge: Cambridge University Press, 2002), V, 298–304.

3. It may be noted that Daniel Defoe quotes a version of the lines in his *Tour through the Whole Island of Great Britain* during his account of Canterbury, where he mentions Rooke. But Defoe has confused French naval commanders: he refers instead to 'The great Tourville', who had indeed encountered Rooke at sea, but in 1693, when the French were decisive victors.

4. See the British Museum's catalogue description of a specimen in its collections, available at <https://www.britishmuseum.org/collection/object/C_G3-EM-245> [accessed 24 Nov 2021].

5. Its other manuscripts include two belonging to or derived from Cameron and Love's 'Restoration' group of scriptorium-related manuscripts, namely BL, MS Harley 6914, and Nottingham UL, MS Portland Pw V 43; see Love, *Scribal Publication in Seventeenth-Century England*, p. 274.

6. John Stow, *A Survey of the Cities of London and Westminster* (London: for A. Churchill and others, 1720), confirms 1705 as the year in question, but names a different location: 'In the Year 1705 were two Whales of different Sorts brought and cut up at Blackwal' (Book IV, Chapter 2, p. 44).

7. The text in the *Diverting Post* has an additional couplet after l. 6, for which see the edition below.

8. One oddity in the poem is a reference to a plan for Gilbert Burnet, Bishop of Salisbury, to replace Peter Mews as Bishop of Winchester: 'Sarum's to fill the loyall prelates place', with Hall himself glossing (in the margin) 'loyall prelate' as 'Winchester'. But William Shippen's long poem *Faction Display'd*, written 1702–04, has Burnet speak the line 'For since my hope of Winton [i.e. Winchester] is expir'd', the modern editor explaining in a note that 'the possibility of Burnet's translation to the rich bishopric of Winchester was lost when Peter Mews (1619–1706) failed to predecease William III' (Ellis, VI, 654).

9. Ellis, VII, 147; Daniel Defoe, *Jure Divino: A Satyr in Twelve Books* (London, 1706), p. 262 (Book XI). Defoe, whose text has 'she' rather than 'Anna', had earlier quoted a version of the first two lines in his *Review* of 21 July 1705.

10. On p. 17, perhaps significantly as 'Suppos'd to be writ by a Dignify'd Clergyman'. Strikingly, it is there printed on the same page as 'Accept my Lord this humble glittering thing', although another poem separates them.

11. See the useful summary of the situation in Ellis, VII, 146–47.

12. Cf. Ellis, VII, 146, 'So it was a very disillusioned high churchman who wrote the present epigram'. As has been shown, 1705 is the date of composition of the other two poems in O3a.

13. Four begin 'When Anna [...]' (BL, MS Lansdowne 852, Bodleian, MS Eng. poet. c.9, Trinity College Dublin, MS 879/1, and Harvard UL, MS Eng 606), while two begin 'When she [...]', as in Defoe (Bodleian, MS Rawlinson poet. 81, and Yale UL, MS Osborn b.90, the latter dated 1705). The short-lined version was quoted by Agnes Strickland, *Lives of the Queens of England from the Norman Conquest*, with the comment 'The following witty *jeu d'esprit* was handed through the literary coffee-houses in London, and dropped in manuscript in the thoroughfares by night' (1904 edition, VI, 253–54), but no supporting reference is given.

14. It reads as follows (f. 153r): 'When mother church had Ann for her daughter | Anna was good, observd those rules shee taught her | Now a great Q — n and mother of the church | By Sid — and Sarrah for it, she leaves it in the lurch.' As a marginal note to the last line makes clear, the references are to Sidney, Lord Godolphin, and Sarah, Duchess of Marlborough.

15. I exclude from the count a partial copy made by the collector Joseph Haslewood probably in the early nineteenth century, now Huntington Library, MS HM 183 ff. 31r-32v.

16. See the detailed summary in Ellis, VI, 505–08.

17. BL, Add MS 27407, Nottingham UL, MS Portland Pw V 41 (the second copy, pp. 137–38), Princeton UL, MS RTC01 no. 38, and Yale UL, Osborn MSS c.111 and b.204.

18. BL, Add MS 27408, Yale UL, MS Osborn c.189, and Bodleian, MS Rawlinson poet. 173.

19. Eight of the twenty-one copies listed in *ESTC*'s merged entry are held in either Edinburgh or Glasgow libraries. *ESTC*, it may be noted, describes E481 as a 'reprint' of E479, and Foxon also fails to record that the 'correct copy' has a longer text than what was first printed.

20. 'To Cote the Flock, to Fence from out the Fold | The Proling Wolf [...]' (Ellis, VI, 512); compare 'To cott 'em himself was each ev'ning his care' ('An honest good farmer', l. 3, and see the edition of this poem, below).

21. 'Thus 'midst his Pain a Debauchee Diseas'd | Grew Penitent, and Piety profess'd; | But once Reliev'd, again the Gods he brav'd, | Disown'd his Short-liv'd Grace, and swore he Rav'd: | Thus Burnet [...]' (Ellis, VI, 515).

22. For these manuscripts see Chapter 7.5, above. It is present also in BL, MS Stowe 305, and Princeton UL, MS RTC01 no. 38, but in these cases widely separated from Hall's oppositional satires.

23. For a discussion of the engravings in early eighteenth-century editions of the *Oxford Almanack*, including that for 1706, see Neil Guthrie, *The Material Culture of the Jacobites* (Cambridge: Cambridge University Press, 2013), pp. 76–78.

CHAPTER 9

❖

Hall's Contemporary Poetic Reputation

The existence of the Ottley and Brotherton Collection manuscripts leaves no doubt that Henry Hall's poetry was highly valued by certain people in the Hereford area, but how well known was his work elsewhere, and what did his contemporaries think? As has been made clear, the great majority of manuscripts preserving copies of Henry Hall's verse make no mention of him, but occasionally his name is there, with sometimes an identity added ('Organist of Hereford' or simply 'of Hereford'). Thomas Hearne, for example, appears to have some knowledge of him when recording the poem discussed at the end of the previous chapter, 'written [...] (as 'tis said) by Mr. Hen. Hall of Hereford', but he makes no judgement. Explicit references are much more common in the case of printings, especially those involving music, but the question of Hall's reputation as a verse writer has still largely to be inferred.[1]

The exceptions to these generalizations are Bodleian, MS Eng poet. f.13, where there can be no doubt that Hall is more than just a name to the compiler of this personal collection, and, in the case of printings, *The Grove, or a Collection of Original Poems, Translations, etc* (1721).[2] This latter anthology is particularly important because 'Mr Hall of Hereford' is named on the title-page (next after Walsh, Donne, and Dryden) as one of the poets represented, and he is characterized in the Preface (pp. 3–4) as 'well-known to the present age'. It is important too in having been 'Collected and published by Mr. Theobald', i.e. the London-based poet and man of letters Lewis Theobald (1688–1744), as is revealed on the new title-page of a 1732 reissue of the anthology, now entitled simply *A Miscellany of Original Poems, Translations, etc*. The collection is discussed further in section 9.2 below, partly in relation to Hall's fellow poet Daniel Kenrick.

9.1. Contrasting Opinions of Hall's Verse

MS Eng. poet. f.13, compiled by the Oxford antiquary William Parry (see Chapter 4.2 above), contains one of two highly conflicting contemporary opinions of Hall's poetic achievement. As well as the evidence for detailed knowledge of Hall and his circle presented earlier, it preserves an accomplished short poem, almost an epigram, 'On the death of Mr Henry Hall, Organist of Hereford', which praises his achievements in both wit and music, and demonstrates the affection in which his friends clearly held him. Hall died in the year of the Act of Union, 1707, and the anonymous author alludes wittily to what must have been his subject's reaction:

> When Strephon sorrowing saw the Union past,
> And organs like 'eer long to breath their last;
> Must I outlive my livelyhood, he cry'd?
> No, first I'll quit my place; and so he dy'd.
> Living admir'd by all for wit and love,
> Matchless in ev'ry choir, but that above. (f. 74r)

In contrast, a much longer appraisal of Hall's poetry from quite another point of view (and central also to the question of authorial attribution) occurs in the anonymous poem *A Tryal of Skill; or, A New Session of the Poets*, 'printed for the booksellers of London and Westminster' in 1704.[3] In the way of the genre, the 600-line poem presents, and satirizes, twenty-four candidates for the 'poetical crown', and one of them is Henry Hall, who is introduced between Richard Steele and Nahum Tate. Hall, however, is rapidly discounted, partly (implicitly) on the grounds of plagiarism from Daniel Kenrick:

> Harry Hall was attentive to what was declar'd,
>   And deliver'd as Matter of Fact,
> And Requested he might have a Poet's Regard,
>   Since he like a Poet could Act.
>
> For thanks to Dan Kendrick who wrote what he sent
>   To his Friends as his own up to Town,
> For a Poet among certain Judges he went,
>   And deserv'd the Poetical Crown. (ll. 237–44)

The admission in ll. 241–42, apparently put into Hall's own mouth, is that it was Kenrick who wrote what Hall sent to his friends in London as if it were his own. Despite the satirical distortions of poems in the mode of *A Tryal of Skill*, there is possibly something in this charge, as is discussed further below. But Hall's inclusion in this session of poets shows, at the least, that he had a recognized place among the writers of the time, and the lines about him that then follow reinforce strongly, if in part obscurely, his undoubted reputation as a (scandalous) personality:

> What! to Game it away? said Apollo, 'Tis plain
>   My Lord Shandois will never admit,
> Though he flung at his Clothes, that he set him a Main
>   So small as the Trophies of Wit.
>
> What if just now we put by a Man of the Sword,
>   Must we needs chuse a Man of the Gown?
> You a Candidate fit for a Place? You a Turd;
>   We must have a more Worthy or None.
>
> Not but if any Muse, that was Fleshly Inclin'd,
>   Would have what makes a Virgin be Spoil'd,
> She need not go very much farther to find
>   A Parson would get her with Child.

> But as for this Office to which you lay claim,
> Sweet Sir, you are hugely mistaken,
> It belongs to a Person of Learning and Fame,
> And not to a Scandalous Deacon. (ll. 245–60)

Hall is exposed first as a notorious gambler (ll. 245–48),[4] and it is very likely that his sessions with 'Lord Shandois' — James Brydges, 8th Baron Chandos (1642–1714)[5] — were well known as a result of his poem 'To your Lordship after being ruin'd at Play' ('Dunned by the bells I rose from bed'), in which Hall gives a lively account of the results of a night out with Chandos in Hereford and acknowledges his financial debt to him.[6] The *Tryal of Skill* then continues (ll. 249–56) with references to Hall's status as a priest and his apparent reputation for sexual promiscuity, a passage that may again show knowledge of 'Dunned by the bells I rose from bed', as Hall there makes much of his success as a lover and the frequent unfortunate result some nine months later.[7] As a result of these various charges the final estimation of Hall as 'a Scandalous Deacon' (l. 260) does not seem inappropriate. Hall himself may not have been too displeased with this character sketch, it being so similar to some he paints of himself. As has been suggested, it may be that he began to spend more time in London — and to build a London reputation as a wit and rake — in the more sympathetic political climate that followed the accession of Queen Anne in 1702.

9.2. Questions of Attribution: Hall and Daniel Kenrick

Did Hall really pass off some of Kenrick's poems as his own, as *A Tryal of Skill* alleges? There is no doubt that they knew each other well. Daniel Kenrick (sometimes 'Kendrick') was born in Gloucestershire in 1649 or 1650, the son of a clergyman.[8] After education at Christ Church, Oxford (BA 1670, MA 1674), he held clerical appointments in the Diocese of Worcester, and preached a controversial Assize sermon in the cathedral in 1688, when Vicar of Kempsey.[9] Though generally Tory in stance, and loyal to the king, the sermon was condemned by the bishop for advocating tolerance towards Catholics and Nonconformists,[10] and in consequence Kenrick, now also accused of drunkenness and incest (in fact marrying his late wife's sister), was in 1689 deprived of his living.[11] He was able, however, to embark on a new career in medicine, practising as a physician in Worcester (*The Grove* states that he 'took his Degrees in both Divinity and Physick', p. iv), and he had his bewigged portrait splendidly engraved by Robert White (1645–1703) with the legend 'Daniel Kenricus Medicus'.[12] He did not, however, remain free of controversy, for in October 1693 he was accused of drinking James II's health in a Worcester tavern.[13]

It has not previously been noticed that 'Daniel Kendrick Master of Arts' was admitted as a Commoner to the College of Vicars Choral at Hereford Cathedral on 4 February 1681, old style, i.e. 1682. Two subsequent entries in the College Act Book, in April and July of the same year, refer to aspects of his accommodation, but he then disappears from the records.[14] He was therefore a close colleague of Hall's at Hereford, if a temporary one, and their acquaintance no doubt dates from this time.

In this connection it is striking that Lewis Theobald's Preface to *The Grove*, which is the principle repository of Kenrick's poetry, describes him in terms that would seem equally applicable to Hall:

> Dr Kenrick [...] being a Person of Vivacity and Wit, entertain'd his Leisure Hours in Poetical Compositions. His Talents seem equal in Panegyrick, Satire, and Lyric: There is a Fire and Sprightliness of Thinking which runs thro' all his Copies, and to this, perhaps, he ow'd that haste in his Writing, which made him sometimes Negligent of Harmony both in Rimes and Numbers. (p. iv)

It would not be surprising if such similarities led to friendship and possibly collaboration. Kenrick did not, however, include Hall as one of the candidates in his own *A New Session of the Poets, Occasion'd by the Death of Mr Dryden* (1700) (by far his longest poem) and Hall, in turn, refers to Kenrick only in passing, during the poem 'Dunned by the bells I rose from bed': there, as part of a catalogue of things supposedly to be bequeathed to others, we find 'To Kendrick, rhimeing well and drinking' (B1, p. 35).[15] It may be noted that Kenrick, unlike Hall, does not feature as a candidate for the poetical crown in the 1704 *Tryal of Skill*.

Two possible collaborations between Hall and Kenrick (though their contributions could have been independent) are the songs 'Why fair Armida why so cold' and 'I've heard and I've seen', both noted in the Appendix to Chapter 6 above. The first was printed in *Mercurius Musicus* (November 1700) as 'A song set by Mr Henry Hall of Hereford. The words by Dr Kendrick'. The second, with music attributed to Hall, occurs within a printed bifolio of c. 1698; there is no mention of Kenrick, but the words are given to him in the text published in *The Grove*. Another potential case is Hall's popular royalist song 'Haste Charon haste' (1685 or earlier), discussed in Chapter 6.2 above. The words as well as the music are usually attributed to Hall, but in a 1720 printing without music the author is named as 'Dr Kendrick'. This at first appears without foundation, but given the two men's early association the attribution may be plausible. It is possible that the two men worked together on the song, but that following successful performance it came to be associated primarily with Hall. While not evidence of collaboration, it is noteworthy also that the riddle 'Like two sage sisters close we dwell', printed in the *Gentleman's Journal* of July 1694 as by 'Mr H.' and attributable to Hall, is answered in verse in the August issue by 'Mr Kenrick', to which Kenrick also contributes a poem of his own (see Chapter 5.1 above).[16]

A more complicated and intriguing instance is the 10-line poem (in couplets) beginning 'The great good man whom fortune does displace', which was engraved and printed as 'A New Song' by Thomas Cross *c.* 1700, without attribution (Wing K306); this printing was then included in a bespoke album of printed songs entitled *A Choice Collection of Songs by Several Masters*, which has a manuscript title page dated 1704 in which the music is ascribed to Hall (BL, K.7.i.2). Kenrick's claim to the words is supported by attribution in *The Grove* (pp. 260–61) and in B1, as will be explored below. Bodleian, MS Rawlinson poet. 203, however, where 'The great good man' occurs within 'A Collection of Loyal Poems and Songs written in the year MDCCXV', attributes the words to 'Henry Hall Senior, Organist at the Cathedrall of Hereford' (f. 4v), as does Thomas Hearne ('by H. Hall of Hereford') in a diary entry for 21 April 1715.[17] Both these sources state the subject of the poem to be King James II, whereas the copy in MS Eng. poet. f.13 is headed 'On Bishop Kenn' (f. 35v), i.e. the prominent non-juring bishop Thomas Ken (1637–1711). This is the manuscript demonstrating particular knowledge of Hall, and in this case there is no attribution to him, which may be significant.[18]

The style of the poem, too, appears to be more formal, and more focused on praise of a man of principle, than would be expected of Hall:

> The great, good man whom fortune does displace,
> May into scarseness fall, but not disgrace.
> His sacred person none will dare profane,
> He may be poor, but never can be mean.
> He holds his value with the wise, and good,
> And prostrate, seems as great, as when he stood.
> So ruind temples doe an awe dispence,
> They loose their height, but keep their reverence.
> The pious crowd the fallen pile deplore,
> And what they fail to raise, they still adore. (B1, p. 90)

That such a straight-faced style was not Hall's way of writing was so apparent to the later annotator of B1 (as noted in Chapter 3.2 above) that he expressed amazement at the scribe's mistake in transcribing the poem as if it were a continuation of 'To Phyllis fools and men of wit resort', which occupies the upper part of the same page: 'The ignorance of the transcriber has clapp'd these two pieces of poetry by Hall and Kendrick, though of so different a nature, into one. Which I have sever'd with a line.' The clapping together is especially odd considering that the first poem ends 'Snuff up the sav'ry scent and piss against the door', and the page overall is headed 'La Coquette'. Nevertheless the scribe ends the page by attributing his merged poem explicitly to 'D. Kendrick'; that is to say, rather than attributing 'The great good man' to Hall, he is in effect attributing 'To Phyllis fools and men of wit resort' to Daniel Kenrick. Somehow the two poems must have become linked in his exemplar.

As was shown earlier, B1's annotator frequently demonstrates greater knowledge of the correct wording of Hall's poems than does the transcriber, and there can be little doubt that he is right in asserting that 'The great good man' was not composed by Hall, being 'of so different a nature'. It is therefore all the more unexpected that Hall himself copied the poem into O1 (on p. 32, without any heading or accompanying note) from where it was taken into O2 as if it were his work. Seeing that it clearly enjoyed some popularity, on account of its subject-matter, is this proof that Hall was not averse to claiming someone else's work as his own — evidence of the plagiarism from Kenrick held against him in *A Tryal of Skill*? A mitigating circumstance may lie in the fact that Hall undoubtedly set 'The great good man' to music. Cameron, as noted in Chapter 7.1, attempted to explain away some of the songs, catches, and ballads in B1 as possibly representing 'Hall's attempt to set other men's poems to music', and he may well be right in implying that Hall's activities as a musician increased the chances of confusion on the part of those trying to transmit his canon.[19] In this case (if they were indeed collaborators) he and Kenrick may have worked on 'The great good man' together, with Hall, responsible for the music, possibly also having some input into the wording. Given, in addition, the poem's crypto-Jacobite position, it was very likely a piece with which he was pleased to be associated.[20]

To return to *The Grove*, the title-page of this miscellany names nine poets as represented in the volume, and refers also to contributions by other 'eminent hands', but according to its Preface it is Kenrick's 'posthumous pieces, together with those of Mr Hall and Mr Walsh' that 'make up a considerable part of this collection'.[21] It is also Kenrick who is judged most in need of an introduction, 'the two latter' (Henry Hall and William Walsh) being 'well known to the present age'. Unlike Walsh, however, who is said to have 'distinguish'd himself in Poetry', Hall is characterized not as a poet or any other kind of writer, but as 'having been an organist of Hereford and in much esteem for his musical compositions', and indeed in contrast to the twenty or so poems ascribed to Kenrick (who is clearly central to the miscellany) no more than three are attributed to '(Mr) H. Hall of Hereford'. These are a light-hearted epistle to a creditor, Robin Clayton, beginning 'If rhyme for rhino could atone' (pp. 53–55); the bawdy ballad 'All in the land of cider' (pp. 98–101); and the drinking song celebrating English victory at Vigo Bay, 'Whilst this bumper stands by me' (p. 126).[22] One other item elsewhere associated with Hall, 'Lucinda has the de'll and all', appears on pp. 95–96, but is here ascribed to 'A Gentleman of Oxford', which may cast some doubt on Theobald's detailed knowledge of Hall's writings.[23] Indeed so small, unrepresentative, and unbalanced is the selection of his poetry, it would seem that Theobald had little to go on, and that Hall's place in the miscellany derives rather from his known association or friendship with Kenrick.

The Grove is nevertheless important from a textual point of view because the epistle to a creditor, which is found otherwise only in B1, receives a heading that includes what is clearly a harder reading: compare 'To Mr R — C — , who every year sent him a dun, a little before St Paul's Day' (*The Grove*) with 'A copy of verses to Mr Clayton after done at St Pauls Fair Bristoll' (B1, p. 112). There can be little doubt that B1's 'done' is a corruption of 'dun', i.e. demand for payment, and B1's text of the poem is also four lines shorter than *The Grove*'s, apparently by omission.[24] Even if Theobald was unable to lay hands on very much of Hall's verse, he at least appears to have had access to a good copy of this specimen.

Notes to Chapter 9

1. Cf., in contrast, commendations of his musical achievements, as in Bodleian, MS Tenbury 1232, the principal manuscript of 'Yes my Aminta 'tis too true' (Chapter 6.1, above), which is annotated 'This was composd by the ingenious Mr. H. Hall'; and the *Diverting Post*, 3 (Nov. 1704), where a song for which he probably wrote the words ('From the bright mansions of the blest above') is described as 'Admirably Set by Mr. H. Hall of Hereford' (Chapter 5.3, above).

2. Given the number of poems by and attributions to Hall in Lechmere Archives 40 (i) (Chapter 4.2, above), it is probable that he was known also to the compiler of this personal anthology, at least by reputation.

3. It was published as a folio booklet, *ESTC* N64318, Foxon T475, the text beginning 'Apollo perplext with poetical duns'. The poem is edited in Ellis, VI, 679–711, from where I quote (the

lines about Hall occur on pp. 693–94). The only recorded copy is held in Yale UL, and there are no known manuscript versions.

4. Ellis, VI, in a note, explains ll. 246–48 as follows: 'even though Hall might be willing to wager his very clothing to win the laurel crown, Lord Chandos, as banker, would never set a stake so low' (p. 694), but the point may rather be that Chandos, when gambling with Hall, would never wish to set a stake of such small value as the crown itself. As Ellis points out, in the game of hazard it is not the 'main' (a number from five to nine called by the thrower) that is 'set' (as in l. 247), but the stake. Ellis attributes the use of 'main' in this line to 'the exigencies of rhyme', probably correctly.

5. The Chandos in question cannot be the eighth lord's better-known son, James Brydges, first Duke of Chandos (1673–1744), later satirized by Pope, as he did not become Lord Chandos until his father's death in 1714.

6. The poem is discussed in Chapter 3.2 above, in relation to the inclusion of an extract from it in the Cooke manuscript and to scribal corrections to its text in B1. It occurs also in the Minnesota manuscript (Chapter 4.1), testifying to wider circulation.

7. Lines 21–26, partly quoted by Ellis, VI, 694.

8. For details of his life, see Nicholas Jagger, 'Kenrick, Daniel (b. 1649/50), Poet and Physician', in *ODNB*.

9. *CCED* records him as minister at Worcester St Clement in 1675, a detail not in *ODNB*.

10. Daniel Kenrick, *A Sermon Preached in the Cathedral-Church of Worcester, at the Lent Assize, April 7th, 1688* (London: David Mallet, 1688). See the *ODNB* entry, and especially the discussion of Kenrick in Scott Sowerby, *Making Toleration: The Repealers and the Glorious Revolution* (Cambridge, MA: Harvard University Press, 2013), pp. 133–35.

11. Paul Kléber Monod, *Jacobitism and the English People, 1688–1788* (Cambridge: Cambridge University Press, 1989), p. 239.

12. Copies of the portrait in the National Portrait Gallery and elsewhere are readily available online, without a date other than 'Late 17th century'. Kenrick receives an entry as 'Physician, poet', Worcester, with a date from 1688, in Wallis and Wallis, *Eighteenth Century Medics*, p. 340. The original *DNB* records that the portrait in question was engraved when Kenrick was only thirty-two (*ODNB* does not mention it), but this appears to be a misunderstanding of the brief account of Kenrick (as a physician) in James Granger, *A Biographical History of England*, 5th edn, 6 vols (London: Baynes, 1824), V, 137.

13. Monod, *Jacobitism and the English People, 1688–1788*, p. 239.

14. HCA, 7003/1/3, pp. 96, 99, 101; an earlier entry, dated 9 September 1681 (p. 94), shows him witnessing an indenture and so already associated with the Vicars at that time.

15. Daniel Kenrick, *A New Session of the Poets, Occasion'd by the Death of Mr Dryden* (London: for A. Baldwin, 1700); 'by a Person of Honour'; ESTC R179198. See also Ellis, VI, 679–80, and, for a full description, Hugh MacDonald, *John Dryden: A Bibliography of Early Editions and of Drydeniana* (Oxford: Clarendon Press, 1939), item 307, pp. 298–99. The poem was reprinted in *The Grove*, pp. 129–44.

16. A decade later issue 21 of the *Diverting Post* (March 1705), which prints a version of Hall's 'Phyllis in vain you drop that tear', also contains a poem 'On a suit of old arras hangings filled with scripture stories' attributed to a 'Dr K.', who may possibly be Daniel Kenrick.

17. Bodleian, MS Hearne's Diaries 53, pp. 133–34; printed in *Remarks and Collections of Thomas Hearne*, ed. by Doble and others, V, 50.

18. For other manuscripts and printings of the poem, see the *Union First Line Index*.

19. Cameron, p. 452.

20. It may count in Hall's favour that in O1d 'The great good man' does not begin a fresh page, a feature otherwise shared only with 'Curse on those representatives', which was shown earlier to be not Hall's own composition even though also copied by him into O1d (see Chapter 7.6, above).

21. The poets listed on the title-page of *The Grove* are 'W. Walsh, Esq., Dr J. Donne, Mr Dryden, Mr Hall of Hereford, The Lady E — M — , Mr Butler, Author of *Hudibras*, Mr Stepney, Sir John Suckling, Dr Kenrick'.

22. The latter two items are both discussed in Chapter 4.2, above.
23. See especially 'By Mr Henry Hall made and set to musick', the attribution in the *Diverting Post* of November 1704.
24. The poem is edited below, with the version in *The Grove* used as copy text.

CONCLUSION

❖

Verse in Flux

Difficulties with attribution fit with what can be perceived as Hall's frequently casual attitude to the business of verse-making, of which another element is his habit of using the same lines in more than one composition. A small example is the occurrence of a very similar couplet within two short informal epistles addressed to cathedral colleagues: 'From dinner then excuse my missing, | Tho' not at tennis, or a-fishing' in that to Dr Ottley; and 'From prayers forgive my often missing, | Either at tennis or a-fishing' in that to Dr Richard Bulkley.[1] But this tendency can also act as a stimulus to fresh composition, as most obviously in his sequence of poems paying tribute to Henry Purcell. In this case 'Music the chiefest good the gods have given', written before the composer's death, is combined both with new material and with elements of the lament for Purcell beginning 'Yes my Palemon 'tis too true', the outcome being the public tribute printed in *Orpheus Britannicus*. A longer, re-worked version of 'Yes my Palemon 'tis too true', now beginning 'Yes my Aminta 'tis too true', then formed the text of Hall's subsequent musical tribute.[2] Creative in the same way are instances of poems with markedly revised versions, notably the address to Nicholas Arnold beginning 'Whether those hills around you spread' and the epistle to his friend and fellow-Jacobite Edmund Addis requesting a load of wood.

The latter is a particularly good example of Hall's re-use of material, in that his subject-matter is partly the act of presenting poetry to a potential benefactor in the hope of obtaining a favour (cf. 'If rhyme for rhino could atone', in which he wishes that verse could count as a form of payment). His first appeal to Addis, written one cold April, begins 'Though rhyme of late's no more my talent', quickly followed by 'even my doggrell days are done' (l. 4), assertions that Hall immediately proceeds to demonstrate in a pair of decidedly awkward couplets, possibly deliberate:

> Yet once for all in meeter thus do
> For your burnt offerings blunderbuss you,
> Best measures to be understood in,
> Since verse is, like the subject, wooden. (B1, p. 98)

The poem then runs through ways in which people contrive to keep warm in cold weather (excluding for himself, since his marriage, the possibility of passionate love-making), before returning to the desired gift of firewood.[3] It ends obscurely with an admitted afterthought ('As at that stroak I thought to end', l. 60) in the shape of fourteen further lines relating to an unidentified local personage known to both

Hall and Addis. The weakness of this passage may possibly have contributed to Hall's decision to rewrite the poem.

Going by the revised version ('This Sir's to you the second time'), likely to have been written the following autumn, it seems clear that Hall did not receive Addis's wood the first time round and so decided to try again.[4] The opening lines, however, refer to a 'first petition' as having been for 'fruit' (l. 3), which must allude to an earlier epistle to Addis, the light-hearted and much shorter 'Although to petition has been out of fashion' (B1, edited below), in which Hall and an associate, Nat Priest, request a consignment of cider. That seems also to have been unsuccessful, but Hall now appears to have received at least a promise of wood ('That nere came to me to this day; | Pray Heav'n the promisd timber may', ll. 5–6). It has to be said, however, that the fresh appeal is not markedly more successful as a poem, because the new material principally comprises twenty-nine lines in which Hall, in effect, wishes Addis well, especially in relation to a long-standing court case in which the latter is embroiled. Furthermore, the eighteen lines directly taken over from 'Though rhyme of late's no more my talent' (the latter's ll. 42–59) are now redistributed less satisfactorily in the form of smaller blocks of couplets, not always well positioned. For example, the lines 'Then quickly send the loaden team, | At once my reall want and theam' (ll. 25–26), placed originally after a digression, now simply continue with the subject in hand. Hall, at the end, returns to his real or pretended loss of poetic talent ('But now my muse [...] verse as dull as D'Urfey sings', ll. 73, 76), but he at least finishes where he should have done on the first occasion, by appealing to Addis with the adage 'Quick giving doubles still the blessing' (l. 78; originally l. 59), this time adding its Latin source: *Bis dat (tu scis) qui cito dat*' (l. 80).

This reworking, as with the other examples mentioned above, is very much a case of deliberate revision. At other times, when lines found in one poem appear scarcely changed in a quite different one, Hall seems rather to be saving himself poetic effort. Thus not only do lines in his tribute to John Blow ('A public good does public thanks require') recall words and phrases in his poems praising Purcell, three lines from the same poem directly repeat a triplet from 'Not Waller read and yet so well to write', merely altering the reference from 'native language' to 'modern musick', as already noted in Chapter 5.2 above.[5] Another poem with repetition of wording found elsewhere is 'Of all the bards that e're were bent on fame', a light-hearted tribute 'To Mr John Grub on his inimitable ballad'; Grubb (the usual spelling) was the author of the deliberately doggerel *The British Heroes*.[6] Most strikingly, ll. 6–9 of 'Of all the bards' match ll. 16–19 of, once again, the tribute to John Blow. In the former poem the passage appears as:

> Let humble sonateers for Sylvia's sake
> Some merry madrigal to musick make,
> Then print the names of those that set and wrote 'em
> With lords o'top, and blockheads at the bottom. (O2, f. 1r)

The only difference in the poem to Blow is that the opening line there reads 'Let 'em sing on — and for fair Sylvia's sake'.[7] A smaller reminiscence occurs in l. 4, 'And to divert would'st be extreamly odd', which echoes 'What e're hits thee must be extremely odd', a line in a poem making fun of a Hereford colleague, Tom Broad ('For missing thee how canst thou Burren blame').[8]

According to *ESTC*, Grubb's *The British Heroes* was not published until 1707, which would suggest that 'Of all the bards' was one of Hall's final poems, written in the year of his death — perhaps explaining and excusing its apparent verbal borrowings.[9] But according to Percy's *Reliques of English Poetry*, in which it was reprinted, Grubb's poem had first been published in Oxford in 1688.[10] Seeing that Hall addresses Grubb as if still alive, it appears that he must have had access to this first edition or perhaps to a manuscript copy (Percy states that 'This diverting poem was long handed about in manuscript'),[11] and given that Grubb died in 1697 it would seem that 'Of all the bards' predates the tribute to John Blow — showing that Hall in that poem therefore drew on two of his earlier compositions.[12]

'Of all the bards' also brings us back to Daniel Kenrick, in that it contains a couplet that occurs in one of *his* poems, further complicating his poetic relationship with Hall. Who in this case is the borrower? Given that Hall is capable of unblushing self-borrowing, might he not also have lifted, if not whole poems, then at least individual lines from Kenrick? Alternatively, the co-occurrence might be an example of the latter's apparent propensity for borrowing, as recorded by James Granger in his *Biographical History of England*, where he writes that Kenrick, 'like many others, seems to have fathered some lines which he never wrote, and probably borrowed wit as freely as he did receipts', citing a couplet apparently taken from a poem printed in 1653.[13]

The lines in question occur in Kenrick's *A New Session of the Poets* (noted in the previous chapter) during a passage in which Sir Richard Blackmore is being satirized as a pretender to Dryden's poetical crown: 'In which thy Rhymes a constant Cadence keep, | At once they make us smile, and make us sleep'.[14] The almost exactly equivalent couplet in Hall's 'Of all the bards' (ll. 16–17) reads: 'His murm'ring rhymes a constant Cadence keep | At once they make us smile, and make us sleep' (O2, f. 1ᵛ). Hall is here contrasting certain other poets unfavourably with John Grubb, and the lines in question conclude a six-line passage on the sleep-inducing effects of a writer characterized as 'haughty Esculapius' (perhaps again Blackmore). The immediately preceding couplet demonstrates the continuity of thought in the passage — 'That still will mingle opium with his ink | At pages six, we dose, at seven, we wink (ll. 14–15) — whereas the couplet as it appears in Kenrick's poem stands isolated from what precedes it, suggesting that he was the borrower.

A charge of plagiarism cannot therefore easily be laid against Hall in this instance. Whether either of the two writers would have been troubled by the borrowing is another matter. Given their known associations, verses in a more or less finished state may quite often have passed backwards and forwards between them. Even though Hall's tribute to John Grubb now survives only in the fair copy preserved in O2, it must have had other manuscript circulation, and it is conceivable that Hall, pleased with the poem, sent Kenrick a copy without any concern about the use he might make of it.

Hall's seemingly unbothered attitude to the reuse of earlier material, by himself or others, is of a piece with one of the principal conclusions of this study of the circulation of his poems and songs, namely that he was not greatly concerned about his poetic reputation. As has been said, despite his great facility with words, his biting wit, and the evident approbation of his friends, he was apparently content to remain a social poet, with no interest, it would seem, in gaining a reputation on the basis of an identifiable body of work. He was, after all, a professional musician. This is not to say he played no part in circulating his verses. In the early 1690s he sent material to the *Gentleman's Journal* (but initially because of his pleasure in 'enigmas') and in the early 1700s to the *Diverting Post* (but very likely, at least in part, to please Henry Playford). He was evidently happy to see a series of 'tribute' poems appear in print, though here again he may have been responding to requests. He participated in local Hereford efforts to make fair copies of at least some of his compositions, and he may have been instrumental in getting some or all of his political satires into manuscript circulation, no doubt aware that these (perhaps along with his conversational epistles to friends) represented some of his best work.

But these, it seems, were sporadic initiatives, not part of any campaign. Hall's status as a social poet means that, as a writer, he was almost certainly happiest when turning out verses for these friends, and producing new versions of them as occasion demanded. His body of work can be said to represent verse in flux, shifting in shape, making an edition of his 'collected poems' (if appropriate) far from easy. While the content of his most hard-hitting political satires is undoubtedly sincere, it could be argued that he was essentially an unserious writer, with no great interest in producing finished or final texts of his poems. And his friends, after his death, appear to have regarded manuscript — that is, the making of further manuscript copies of what they could get hold of — as the natural medium by which to remember him.

Notes to the Conclusion

1. The poems in question are 'Ye gods what gulfs are set between' and 'Though now in station to adjust us'.
2. See above, Chapters 5. 2 and 6.1.
3. Together with Hall's assertion that his verse-making days are at an end, the reference, in ll. 34–37, must be to Hall's second marriage (to Anne Gower), which dates the poem to later than October 1696.
4. 'Nor the so wish'd-for gift delay | Till I've no need on't, that's next May' (O1d, ll. 17–18). The revision is preserved only in O1d and O2. Compare, in the earlier version, 'This month call April if you will; | To me 'twill be December still' (B1, ll. 16–17).
5. See Pickering 1994, p. 29. Hall's tribute to Henry Playford, 'Next to the man who so divinely sung' (Chapter 5.2 above), also repeats ideas found in the poems about Purcell (ibid, p 28).
6. The unique witness to 'Of all the bards' is MS O2, f. 1r-v, where it is directly followed by a transcript of Grubb's ballad (ff. 2r-6r).
7. The poem to Blow also reads 'point' rather than 'print' in l. 3, but this may be a misprint.
8. Quoted here from the copy in O2, f. 6r.
9. Foxon G303, *ESTC* T95838; two other undated editions.
10. By a known Oxford bookseller, Henry Clements. See *Reliques of Ancient English Poetry*, ed. by Thomas Percy, 3rd edn, 3 vols (London: J. Dodsley, 1775), III, 313. *ESTC* does not list the edition, copies of which appear not to have survived.

11. Ibid, p. 312. A comparison of the text of Grubb's poem in O2 with that printed in 1707 reveals differences in wording.

12. For Grubb's date of death, see Foster, *Alumni Oxonienses*, II, 616.

13. Granger, *A Biographical History of England*, V, 137 n.

14. Kenrick, *A New Session of the Poets*, p. 6.

SELECTED EDITION OF
POEMS AND SONGS

❖

Principles of selection

For the following selected edition I have chosen all eight of Henry Hall's verse epistles to Dr Broughton; four epistles addressed to other friends; ten political satires; and three love poems.

Most of the epistles, particularly those to Broughton (which are a remarkable record of an enduring and intimate friendship), show Hall speaking freely to men he knows well, in colloquial, conversational language. Many exhibit a fluid and markedly informal interplay of narrative and argument, enlivened by a wide range of contemporary, historical, and literary reference, and the great majority, despite sometimes being driven by other motives, were undoubtedly written for the private pleasure of their recipients. None can have been intended for print publication. Chapter 2.1 above discusses aspects of their verse style, with particular reference to the epistle to Dr Broughton beginning 'These grateful lines are doubly Sir your due'. As noted there, and as would be expected with verse epistles, all twelve poems are in couplets, but Hall uses three different forms: four-stress, mainly iambic lines for lighter material, slower pentameters for more serious subject-matter, and in one case a mixture of four-stress dactyls and anapaests ('Although to petition has been out of fashion'). Only one of the twelve has ever appeared in print ('If rhyme for rhino could atone', in 1721).

The ten political satires, presented here in chronological order of their presumed date of composition, are a representative selection of some forty in this genre. They have been chosen to illustrate Hall's reaction to events as the 1690s and 1700s proceed, once again his range of verse forms, and (which is linked) the satires' varying degree of levity or seriousness. Indeed, one of the chosen items ('Cities of adamant must yield') is not properly a satire at all, being serious reflections on the fate of Namur and its citizens after the stronghold was taken in 1695. Its success partly derives from its brevity and the simplicity of its four-stress couplets. Pentameters, in contrast, are used for Hall's habitual attacks on the political establishment or, in the case of 'Whither ye impious Britons do ye run' (an imitation of Horace), on his fellow-countrymen in general. Quite different are three stanzaic poems, all of them songs and two having popular refrains — appropriate verse forms for comparatively light-hearted satire mocking first the failure of military and naval campaigns and then the condition of England following the restoration of peace. The sequence of poems as presented here ends with two datable to the reign of Queen Anne.

One, a political-religious fable, mixes four-stress anapaests and dactyls (as do the two refrain poems), while the other, in pentameter couplets, finishes with Hall in relatively buoyant mood, despite renewed unhappiness at the state of the country. Three of the ten poems were printed during Hall's lifetime: 'Whither ye impious Britons do ye run' (1703, but written 1690), 'An honest good farmer by providence blest' (1704), and 'Once in a reign to increase our causeless fears' (1705).

Omitted from the selection of satires are those that were included in the Yale edition of *Poems on Affairs of State* (in two cases with variant first lines), that is to say 'Good people what will you of all be bereft', 'Great William concerned to leave his gulled loobies', 'Hail happy William thou art strangely great', 'Here lie the relics of a martyred knight', 'Rejoice ye fops your idol's come again', 'To give the last amendments to the bill', ''Twill puzzle much the author's brains', and 'When Church was mother Anne was then her daughter'. Bibliographical details are provided in Appendix A, below. Four of these poems have, however, been quoted in full in the course of the above study, for purposes of discussion: 'Here lie the relics', 'Rejoice ye fops', ''Twill puzzle much', and 'When Church was mother'. The same applies to two other of the political satires, 'Cease hypocrites to trouble Heaven' and 'Six tedious months our senate sits'.

The three love poems describe three different situations, seen, as would be expected, from the man's point of view. The action of the third, the *jeu d'esprit* ''Twas in the temple first I saw', is placed autobiographically by Hall within Hereford Cathedral, with much extravagant circumstantial detail.

Copy text and editorial policy

The copy text for the chosen items is in almost all cases one or other of the Brotherton or Ottley manuscripts, these being deliberate compilations of Hall's poems. B1 alone contains all of the epistles to Dr Broughton (in three cases uniquely), and therefore, for consistency, provides the text for all eight items in this group. It also serves as copy text for two of the other epistles (one uniquely), five of the political satires (three uniquely), and all three of the love poems. B2, however, supplies the text of 'Whither ye impious Britons do ye run', a satire that survives in four other manuscripts (and a printed text) but not in B1. The Ottley manuscripts in turn serve as copy text for five poems, four of them in Hall's autograph, which in the one case where they overlap has been chosen ahead of the corresponding text in B1. Finally, the 1721 printed text of 'If rhyme for rhino could atone' (from *The Grove*) has been preferred to the clearly less good version in B1.

Where B1's later annotator has made corrections to the text, these have been silently accepted, with notes provided in the commentary as appropriate. Emendation overall has been kept to a minimum, affecting no more than six poems. In three of these the corrections are of small scribal mistakes affecting sense or grammar, along with the conjectural expansion of an unusual abbreviation ('So little being done and so much money spent', l. 27). More substantively, in two poems I have incorporated readings supported by both B1's later annotator (in marginal notes) and the nineteenth-century Cooke manuscript; see 'Dunned by the bells I rose from bed', l. 19, and ''Twas in the temple first I saw', ll. 13 and 18. In a sixth case ('Whither ye impious Britons') I have emended on four occasions where a variant reading is strongly supported by other witnesses. Emendation throughout has been carried out silently in the edited texts, but is signalled and explained in the commentaries.

Presentation of the edited texts

The spelling of the copy text has been preserved, but punctuation and word division are editorial. Paragraphing, where it occurs, is also editorial. In the case of stanzaic poems the indentation of lines approximates to that of the source text. Each poem is followed by a detailed commentary (to bring out the meaning and explain allusions), sometimes preceded by discussion of the content, structure, context, and/ or textual state of the poem, as necessary. Variant readings from other witnesses are recorded when substantive, in almost all cases within the line-by-line commentary. The exception is 'Whither ye impious Britons', where the variants are grouped at the end because of the number of other witnesses involved.

Epistles to Dr Broughton

And art thou faith a true recluse become   (34)

Title in copy text: 'To Dr Broughton confineing himself to avoid takeing the Oaths'.
Summary: Hall takes issue with Broughton's scruples about swearing the Oath of
Allegiance to William III and Mary II.
Date: Very likely 1689.
Copy text: B1, pp. 85–86.

[*p. 85*]   And art thou, faith, a true recluse become?
    I thought long since you'd had enough of Rome;
    Besides you know, my friend, the devil's at home.
    Is it for fear of swearing that you mew?
    'Sbud, what's a triviall oath to me or you?   5
    View well the clergy, nicely count 'em all,
    How few you'l find that have not bow'd to Baal.
    Of thousands who the sacred ephod wear,
    Shew me a hundred who refus'd to swear.
    Some fools stood off, whose friends their fortune mourn'd,   10
    Butt 'twas but till the Sessions was adjourned,
[*p. 86*]   And tho' they unlawfull did the Act allow,
    In conscience then, and more by honour now,
    Yet as when martyr sees the crackling flame,
    Altho' resolved to perish in't he came,   15
    Denies his god and turns Mahometan,
    So fear of looseing makes all doctrines clear,
    And heaven at distance is and pencoin near.
    Wee see the clergy with all oaths dispence:
    Why not a man of pleasure, then, and sence?   20
    To see you suffer wou'd a scandall give
    For that which all conclude you don't beleive.
    We've heard of one that did for humor's sake;
    I hope you won't the second martyr make.
    Shame to thy mighty master and to me: 25
    What says your fam'd *Religio Medici*?
    'Where three physitians, there two atheists be'.
    But if you'l needs be holyer than the rest,
    And Broughton only stand the penall test,
    These lasting lines, my friend, when thou art dead,   30
    With pious praise shall o're thy tomb be read:
    'Broughton the gay, who laughd and lov'd, lies here.
    Learning and loy'lty both his talents were,
    Yet had been damn'd, but that he would not swear'.

Commentary

Title: Dr Broughton, a physician and Hall's close friend, is addressed in eight epistles. He is very likely Dr Edward Broughton of Kington, fifteen miles north-west of Hereford, as noted in Chapter 1 above. The 'oaths' refers principally to the Oath of Allegiance to the new sovereigns, required of every person carrying out a public function, and so of physicians like Broughton as well as the clergy. A main reason for refusing to swear was continued allegiance to James II, on the basis of his enduring divine right as king.

1–2. Hall begins by comparing Broughton's act of seeming concealment with the decision of a Roman Catholic contemplative to shut himself away from the world.

3.   *the devil's at home*: proverbial. See Morris Palmer Tilley, *A Dictionary of the Proverbs in England in the Sixteenth and Seventeenth Centuries* (Ann Arbor: University of Michigan Press, 1950), D 243.

4.   *mew*, 'conceal (yourself)'. *OED* (*mew*, v.², 3) does not record this intransitive use.

5.   *'Sbud*: an abbreviated version of an oath invoking Christ's blood, i.e. 'by his blood'; cf. *OED 'Sbud*, n., recorded from 1676.

6–9. Hall is right that the great majority of the clergy took the oath of allegiance, but a substantial minority (the nonjurors) refused to do so. For some account of oppositional clerical attitudes, see the chapter 'Religion and Loyalty: Jacobitism and Religious Life', in Monod, *Jacobitism and the English People*, pp. 126–58. Monod notes (p. 146) that 'West Midlands clergy were particularly abusive to the new rulers in 1692–93', leading to prosecutions for sedition in Herefordshire, Shropshire, and Worcestershire. According to Howard Tomlinson, 'Restoration to Reform, 1660–1832', in *Hereford Cathedral: A History*, ed. by Aylmer and Tiller, pp. 109–55 (pp. 120–21), eleven ordained clergy in the Hereford diocese lost their livings for refusing to swear new oaths to William and Mary, including three from the cathedral, all of them members of the chapter. Hall, not a man of principle and apparently not publicly oppositional, asserts in ll. 47–50 of 'As in a pump we water put' that he and Broughton both swore the oaths verbally but managed to avoid signing.

6.   *nicely*, i.e. carefully, precisely.

7.   *Baal*, a heathen god ('the chief male deity of the Phoenician and Canaanitish nations', *OED*), here applied to the illegitimate new regime.

8.   *ephod*, a characteristic priestly garment (*OED*, *ephod*, n., 2).

10. *stood off*, i.e. held themselves aloof, refused to cooperate.

11. *Sessions*: the Quarter Sessions, at which Justices of the Peace administered the oaths.

12. *Act*, i.e. *An Act for the Abrogating of the Oathes of Supremacy and Allegiance and Appointing other Oathes*, promulgated in late 1688, which required the oath to be taken before 1 August 1689.

14. The manuscript has a long dash after *when*, possibly indicating a problem with the copy-text, though the line is metrically complete as it stands. But the scribe

then ends the line, unexpectedly, with 'the flame crackling', a mistake that the later annotator puts right by deleting 'crackling' and inserting it instead before 'flame'.

17. *looseing*, apparently 'perdition', 'destruction', as in *OED*, *losing*, n., a., not recorded there after 1612.

18. *pencoin*, an old spelling of 'pension' (cf. *OED*, *pension*, n.). Hall is saying that at such a juncture the prospect of a pension if one stays in office outweighs that of 'heaven' or adherence to conscience.

19. *with* [...] *dispence*, i.e. disregard.

20. Hall now turns back to Broughton's particular case.

21–22. That is, it would be scandalous if you had to suffer for something that everyone knows you don't believe in.

23. *did for humor's sake*, i.e. suffered punishment on account of a whim or particular state of mind (*OED*, *humour*, n., 6). Hall is seemingly referring to a specific case (cf. l. 24).

25. *mighty master*: on the basis of the following line, Sir Thomas Browne (1605–82), physician and author of *Religio Medici*, represented here as a hero of Broughton.

27. A version of the medieval Latin proverb 'Ubi tres medici, duo athei', quoted near the beginning of the *Annotations upon Religio Medici* (by Thomas Keck), published with the work itself from 1656 onwards. Unlike in 'These grateful lines are doubly Sir your due', where he urges belief in God on Broughton, Hall is maintaining that a doctor should not take matters of belief so seriously.

34. i.e. 'Were it not that he wouldn't swear [the oath], he would have been damned'.

Calling at Fountain's late last night   (86)

Title in copy text: 'To Dr Broughton'.
Summary: Hall hears an account of a young ex-prisoner named Will Fountain who is in need of a coat, and asks Broughton to send him one of his. He then advises Broughton not to worry about a summons but to spend time on love-making, encouraging him with tales of women who were very desirous of sexual intercourse.
Date: Probably 1689 or 1690.
Copy text: B1, pp. 66–68.

[*p. 66*]   Calling at Fountain's late last night
(Cynthia and I at once being bright)
And blundering thro' the ill-pav'd entry,
Lo, Hannah with a lamp stood centry,
But so ill-dress'd that when I ken'd her   5
I took her for the Witch of Endor.
A mantle her vast balk hung o're,
Her cheeks were swoln, her eyes were sore,
A very unelligible — .
Being satt, we fell to various chatt,   10

From that to this, from this to that;
All stories traced, or false or true:
Who pimp'd last night and who loves who.
At length with tears (which eyes much sore-
rer made appear than were before)   15
And many a sigh she thus began
After a hearty glass t'harangue:
'In vain alas! and ill-bestow'd
Ar'th favours you to Fountaine shew'd.
In vain you bail'd him from the bastille   20
And brought him home to's proper castle.
In vain yourself and friends you've troubled
To gett him shent of stony dublett,
Since want of promis'd coate or taylor
Makes him t'himselfe a harder jayler.   25
The doctor has of coats enough,
Bin cloy'd with silk as well as buff;
He's choice of all surtouts to wear,
From silver down to humble hair.
[p. 67]   Not that poor Will pretends to putt on   30
The coat till he pulls off each button,
And then if he'l vouchsafe to stoop
To's fleshly one I'le find a loop;
And when poor Fountaine enters in
His coat, he may my wider skin.'   35
Thus Hannah pleaded for her youth,
And, faith, to tell the naked truth,
He wants, he wants a coate in sooth,
And only stays for th'Irish garment
In England to look out preferment.   40
He vows for work he'l search the nation,
And have his spouse t'her old vocation.
Then send the thing he does so dote on,
And lett him sett thy rusty coat on;
So you each night may taste the blessing   45
And cloy yourselfe whilst supper's dressing,
Unravell all the law has done
By putting Cook on Littleton,
Ne're vallue Brett, or care a t — d
For that starch'd Spaniard Abram Seward,   50
Since whilst you are in Cælia's graces
What signifies a *scire facias*?
But vigourously push on your passion;
You'l find even flaws i'th'Declaration.
I did, my dear, and still do wish ye   55

Never at barr, but bed joyn issue.
Improve the time that fate has lent,
Use the convinceing argument,
The only charming thing we find
Prevailes with easie womankind.   60
'Twas this that made the Ephesian matron
So hack and hew her lord and patron,
And cutt from's belly, sans remorse,

[p. 68]

What had so often been in hers.
'Twas this occasion'd so much grief   65
To'th lass that long'd for liveing beif,
And when her pregnant womb was full
Part by her husband, part by bull,
At length shee teem'd, and brought forth halfe
A man, and all the rest was calfe.   70
The want of this delicious progg
Makes 'em take up with dil. or dogg.
So once a Presbyterian curr
To th'Elder's maid was paramour,
For which her shoulders had the lash,   75
And for which too they hanged Swash.
For this, when Spark is found more able,
Wives pawn the matrimoniall bable,
Forgett the witty poesy,
'In Christ and thee my comfort be'.   80
For this — but hold, I've writt enough
For'th coate, altho' it were of buff.
What is't that makes you then so prize
A very humble one of frize?
Then quickly send the long'd-for rayment;   85
Thanks to the rich is always payment.

Commentary

1.   *Fountain's*: the description in ll. 3–4 at first suggests it may be some kind of club, but it is clearly a private dwelling.
2.   *Cynthia*: like *Cælia* (l. 51), a conventional poetic name for an attractive young woman. *bright*, 'animated' (*OED*, *bright*, adj., 16b), probably here 'in high spirits'.
5.   *ken'd*, 'caught sight of', 'scanned' (*OED*, *ken*, v.¹, 6).
6.   *the Witch of Endor*: the Old Testament necromancer, who makes the dead Samuel appear to Saul (1 Samuel 28), but here merely evoking a generally ugly appearance.
12. i.e. 'we recounted stories in detail, whether false or true' (cf. *OED*, *trace*, v.¹, 6a).
20. *bastile*, i.e. prison (*OED*, *bastille*, n., 4b, this sense first recorded in Samuel Butler's *Hudibras*).

23. *shent of*: apparently 'freed from'. Obscure, but perhaps a miswritten form of 'shet', a possible dialectal form of 'shut', for which see *OED*, *shut*, v., 11a, 'set a person free from'. *stony dublett*, i.e. prison; see *OED*, *doublet*, n., 1d, *stone doublet*, slang, first recorded in 1698 (quot., 'We say metaphorically, when any is in Prison, He has a Stone Doublet on'). The normal meaning of doublet, 'garment', is then picked up in the next line.

25. Presumably the lack of a coat makes Fountain keep himself indoors.

27. *Bin*, '(which) are' (probably deliberately dialectal). *cloy'd*: probably from *OED*, *cloy*, v.¹, 6, 'weigh down'. *buff*, i.e. buff-leather (*OED*, *buff*, n.², 2).

28. *surtouts*, i.e. overcoats (*OED*, *surtout*, n., a).

29. *silver*, i.e. 'one ornamented with silver thread' (*OED*, *silver*, n., 4).

30. *pretends*, 'intends' (*OED*, *pretend*, v., 10).

32–35. Concentrated sexual innuendo, 34–35 referring to sexual intercourse.

33. *fleshly one*, presumably penis. *loop*: playing on two senses of the word, *OED*, n.¹, 1, relating to ornament or fastening on a garment, and n.², relating to an opening or hole.

35. *wider*: cf. *OED*, *wide*, adj., 13a, for connotations of lack of moral or sexual restraint.

39. *th'Irish garment*: See note to l. 84 below.

42. *her old vocation*: presumably prostitution.

44. *rusty*, 'shabby', 'worn' (*OED*, *rusty*, adj.¹, 8b, recorded from 1709).

45. *the blessing*, i.e. resulting from having done good.

46. *cloy*, 'satiate' (*OED*, *cloy*, v.¹, 8). *dressing*, 'being prepared' (cf. *OED*, *dress*, v., 4b).

48. *Cook on Littleton*: 'Coke upon Littleton' was the common name for *The Institutions of the Laws of England*, the famous commentary by Sir Edward Coke (1552–1634) on the *Tenures* of the fifteenth-century judge Sir Thomas Littleton, which had become a standard text book of English law. The reference is probably connected to the summons mentioned in l. 52.

49. *Brett*: possibly a local magistrate, if connected with the summons.

50. *Spaniard*: obscure, but clearly derogatory. *Abram Seward*: Abraham Seward (d. 1698) was Chapter Clerk at Hereford Cathedral from September 1672 (see Tomlinson, 'Restoration to Reform', p. 116), and served as Mayor of the city in 1676. He may have continued as a magistrate.

52. *scire facias*: a judicial writ requiring the person named to come to court. It is likely that Broughton is being summonsed in connection with the Oath of Allegiance, and is concerned at the prospect; cf. the preceding poem, 'And art thou, faith, a true recluse become?'.

53–56. Hall's advice is that Broughton should follow his example and concentrate on love-making rather than worrying about the court case, noting that there were flaws even in the 1687 Declaration of Indulgence.

56. *joyn issue*, 'come to agreement', 'reach unity', first with reference to a legal matter, then in a general sense (*OED*, *issue*, n., P2, (a) and (d)). Hall, however, is again recommending sexual intercourse.

57. It would seem that Broughton has been granted time before being brought to court.

58–60. Hall now moves into a lengthy, obscene, and very masculine account of what he represents as women's overriding desire for sexual intercourse, extending to l. 80. The *convinceing argument* and the *charming thing* must both refer to at least the offer of sex, but the references to 'this' in ll. 61, 65, 71, and 77 suggest the terms may refer directly to the penis.

60. *Prevailes*, i.e. that prevails. *easie*, 'compliant', 'soon yielding' (*OED, easy*, adj., 12a).

61–64. The story of the *Ephesian matron* (or the Widow of Ephesus), from Petronius's *Satyricon*, sections 111–12, ends with the widow helping her lover fix the body of her dead husband to a cross, as if crucified. Hall's lines represent an obscene addition to the already sensational elaboration of the story by John Ogilby (in his *Aesopic's: A Second Collection of Fables Paraphras'd in Verse*, published in 1668), in which the widow first mutilates parts of the corpse to make it more resemble the crucified body which it is to replace.

65–70. A reference to the Greek myth in which Pasiphaë, wife of Minos, lusts after a bull, with the result that she gives birth to the Minotaur, part bull and part man.

69. *teem'd*, 'gave birth' (*OED, teem*, v.[1], 2).

71. *progg*: the word carries the double meaning of food (*OED, prog*, n.[2]), picking up from 'beef' in l. 65, and more obviously that of a piercing instrument (*OED, prog*, n.[1], 1).

72. *dil.*, i.e. dildo.

73–76. Possibly a local scandal.

74. *Elder's*, referring to an Elder in the Presbyterian church.

76. *Swash*: the name of the dog involved. Cf. also l. 77, *Spark*.

78. *pawn the matrimoniall bable*, i.e. set aside their matrimonial vows (*bable*, 'bauble', in this case a wedding ring).

79–80. The reference is to a motto inscribed within a wedding ring. Cf. the quotation from 1575 under *OED, poesy*, n., 3, 'A Wedding Ring with this Poesie ('In thee my Choice, I do rejoyce')'.

84. *frize*, a type of coarse woollen cloth (*OED, frieze*, n.[1], 1, where it is associated especially with Irish manufacture).

From college hall where thirsty vicar   *30*

Title in copy text: 'To Dr Broughton' (B1).
Summary: Hall, having just finished lunch, arranges a meeting at an inn with Dr Broughton and Captain Jones, alluding to their shared Jacobite and Catholic beliefs.
Date: Probably 1689 or 1690.
Copy text: B1, p. 79. Also in O1/D, pp. 17–18, and O2, f. 20r-v ('To Dr Broughton and Captain Jones', in both).

[*p. 79*]   From colledge hall, where thirsty vicar
            To cool his draught letts down much liquor,
            I, namesake to't, doe send you greeting
            With greasy fists, just come from eating,
            And if the rimes prove something dull,   5
            It is because my belly's full.
            At one precisely at th'King's Head
            Who was by's subjects murdered
            (And not content when they had don
            Have lately sent away his son)   10
            I'le meet both you and Captain Jones,
            I'le meet you, tho' I build a sconce.
            What there wee drink can't make us sick,
            The wine and drawer's Catholick,
            Tho' all the rest, to make no jest on't,   15
            Of ale and cyder's true Protestant.
            A wonder 'tis, these many years,
            The celler, just like doggs and bears,
            Fell not together by the ears,
            And butts themselves to fighting goe   20
            As wee when full of 'em doe so.
            'Tis strange to see the Monsieur lye
            As still as night, yet Rhenish by,
            Or that the Spaniard shou'd abide
            Forbidden clarett by his side,   25
            Or cyder, which wee hearty call,
            Shou'dn't rather abdicate 'em all.
            The time is short or more I'de send,
            But what (and that 'tis makes me end)
            I gett in rime I loose in friend.   30

Commentary

Title: the 'Captain Jones' included in the poem's title in O1d and O2 is very likely Dr Broughton's brother-in-law, as noted in Chapter 1 above.

1.   *colledge hall*: the dining hall at the College of Vicars Choral.

2.   *draught*, i.e. *OED*, *drought*, n., 4, 'thirst'. This spelling, not recorded there, may be the result of mistaken association with *OED*, *draught*, n., 14, 'quantity of drink'. O1d also has 'draught', but O2 reads 'drought'.

3.   *namesake to't*, i.e. to the hall.

7–10. Hall is referring, of course, to the execution of Charles I in 1649 and the exiling of James II in 1688.

7.   *King's Head*: the name of the inn suggests that the meeting was to take place in Kington, where Broughton lived, as there was formerly a King's Head in the town.

12.   *build a sconce*, 'run into serious debt' (at a tavern). *OED*, *sconce*, n.³, 1c.

13–16. As elsewhere, Hall positions himself clearly on the Catholic side of the religious divide, though for the sake of his conceit (or perhaps also ironically) he makes out that cider, at least in this tavern, is Protestant.

14.   *drawer*, i.e. the tapster (*OED*, *drawer*, n.¹, 2).

17–27. Hall fancifully affects surprise that the various drinks stored in the tavern cellar have not fought amongst themselves, given their different religious and national allegiances.

19.   For the phrase 'to fall by the ears', i.e. fight, see *OED*, *ear*, n.¹, P1, c. (d).

25.   *Forbidden clarett*: possibly a reference to French wine no longer being officially imported while Britain was at war with France.

26.   *hearty*: an evidently local term for cider, not recorded in *OED* or in Joseph Wright's *English Dialect Dictionary*. Hall uses it also in 'Once in a week a letter's due', l. 32, and in the title and l. 19 of 'Although to petition has been out of fashion'. Cf. his adjectival use of the word in 'After a hearty glass t'harangue' in 'Calling at Fountain's late last night', l. 17, possibly with the more general sense of 'intoxicating', and also the recorded Scottish usage meaning 'tipsy' (*OED*, *hearty*, adj., 3b).

27.   *abdicate*, 'depose' (*OED*, *abdicate*, v., 2).

29–30. i.e. 'except for the fact that [...] what I would gain in terms of verse I would lose in terms of a friend'.

Coming from place where you have seen   (33)

Title in copy text: 'To Dr Broughton'.

Summary: Hall, returning to college after a night out, meets a post boy apparently celebrating an English victory against France, but discovers on further enquiry that this is a distortion of the truth.

Date: Probably 1693–94.

Copy text: B1, p. 26.

[*p. 26*]   Comeing from place where you have seen
             More postures than in Arretin
             — Where mortalls prate to slydeing wood
             As if the engine understood

Their sence as well as flesh and blood;   5
Where fools for reasons wagers lay
And oaths and money throw away
(That's Hannah's harvest, Peasey's prop,
A better income than his shop,
The Collonell's folly, Robin's ruine,   10
Nat's walk, to take a turne or two in);
Where Club, more biass'd than his bowl
In what relates to Will and Moll
Each night of Hawley takes his toule —
And steering early to the colledge,   15
Credit at once to gett, and knowledge,
I mett the postboy blowing horn,
With horse's head like unicorn
(For really, Doc, without a joak-a,
He'd full three foot of pure fioca;   20
When Turk wou'd money get, or force,
They still expose the tail o' th'horse
But we trick up the head of ours).
I could not fancy, for my soul,
But Nam. was tane, or Pignerol,   25
Or that St Malloes wee'd gott in,
Maugre the nightly *gaurd de cheines.*
T'enquire the truth I straight took a turn
T'th'house yclep'd the wheel call'd Cathern,
Where soon I found we'd mist the matter   30
And, 'stead of vict'ry, caught a Tartar.
Thus Hogens make the mobb obey 'em,
And for a basteing sing Te Deum.

Commentary

Hall begins with an extended, complex subordinate clause — full of circumstantial detail of the disreputable 'place' he has visited — eventually arriving at a main verb in l. 17. The satirical subject-matter of the latter part of the epistle receives more extended treatment in 'Are all those lights that gild the street' (edited below) and 'Let old England rejoice'.

1. *place*: from the description that follows, clearly a gambling and drinking establishment in Hereford, with shows of a sexual nature. *you* implies that Dr Broughton has also been a visitor.

2. *postures* [...] *Arretin*: a reference to the sets of obscene engravings associated with the name of Pietro Aretino (1492–1556); they are referred to in, for example, Jonson's *The Alchemist* (II.2) and Wycherley's *The Country Wife* (I.1). See David Foxon, *Libertine Literature in England, 1660–1745* (New York: University Books,

1965), pp. 19–25, and Patrick J. Kearney, *A History of Erotic Literature* (London: Macmillan, 1982), pp. 24–29.

3–4.   *slydeing wood* [...] *engine*: ll. 3–5 together suggest some kind of semi-dramatic performance in which the participants address a moving wooden construction, perhaps a wooden figure; cf. *engine* in the sense of the mechanism used to present gods, etc., in the theatre (*OED, engine*, n., 7).

8.   *Hannah* [...] *Peasey*: evidently people (in one case a local shopkeeper) working in the club and gaining from the money thrown away by the *fools* (l. 6) who visit.

11.   *walk*, perhaps in the sense of 'place of resort' (*OED, walk*, n.[1], 11a).

12–14.   *Club*: seemingly another personal name, on account of the repeated *his* (the occurrence in l. 14 inserted by B1's later corrector) and the mention of his having an opinion about the reigning monarchs (*Will and Moll*). Given the reference to a biased *bowl* (presumably some kind of ball used in a gambling game) he is likely to be employed to cheat regular losers like *Hawley* out of their money (*toule*, i.e. toll, 'payment').

15.   *colledge*, i.e. the College of Vicars Choral.

16.   *credit*, presumably money (or promise of money) on which Hall can draw. *knowledge*, i.e. news.

17–23.   From Hall's description, the head of the post boy's horse has been decorated with a tassel on a pole, as a sign of public celebration (cf. ll. 24–27).

19.   *joak-a*, i.e. joke, here in the form of a nonce word to enable a rhyme.

20.   *fioca*: see *OED, fiocco*, n., 'tassel' (two quotations, from 1694 and 1714).

21–22, a reference to the horsetail banners commonly displayed by Turkish armies.

23.   *trick up*, 'adorn' (*OED, trick*, v., 5b).

25.   *Nam.*, i.e. Namur in Belgium, captured by the French in 1692 and eventually re-taken by William III's forces in 1695. *Pignerol*, i.e. Pinerolo in northern Italy, at this time in French hands.

26.   *St Malloes*, i.e. St Malo, another target for the English forces during the war with France.

27.   *Maugre*, 'despite'. *gaurd de cheines*: St Malo was traditionally defended by guard dogs.

29.   *yclep'd*, 'called', a deliberate archaism. *the wheel call'd Cathern*, i.e. the former Catherine Wheel inn in Hereford. See Herefordshire Archive Service, BG11/17/5/86, 'Information against a tavern called the Catherine Wheel as being the resort of Jacobites, 1694' (available online).

31.   *caught a Tartar*: see *OED, tartar*, n.[2], 4, 'to catch a Tartar', said of a situation where one's opponent proves to be much more formidable than expected.

32–33.   For extended satire of the government's practice of organizing public celebrations when victory has not in fact been achieved, see 'Are all those lights that gild the street', edited below.

32.   *Hogens*, a derogatory term for people from the Netherlands (*OED, hogen-mogen*, n., 3), more usually in the self-rhyming form, as in 'Whither ye impious Britons do ye run', also edited below. It is here applied contemptuously to William III and his ministers in general. *mobb*: inserted by B1's later corrector.

33.   *basteing*, 'thrashing' (*OED, basting*, n.[3]).

As in a pump we water put (50)

Title in copy text: 'To Dr Broughton desireing him to send me some verses of mine which I had forgott'.
Summary: Hall asks Broughton to send him a copy of a poem of his (Hall's) that he has forgotten, going on to wish that there were not now so many bad writers, especially poets and clergymen.
Date: Probably 1694.
Copy text: B1, pp. 70–71. Also in O1d, pp. 15–16, and O2, f. 19r-v ('To Dr Broughton for a Coppy of Verses I had wholly forgot', in both).

[*p. 70*] As in a pump wee water put
 Only that more we may gett out,
 So I, my friend, by way of letter
 In rime petition you for meeter,
 And that you'l let m'amanuensis   5
 Transcribe what's quite forsook my sences.
 To me the stanzas and their theams
 Are all like Neb'cadnezar's dreams,
 Yet you, who joak at prophecy,
 Shall Belteshazer be to me   10
 If in your hand a book you take,
 The book that makes Old Mathews quake,
 The book that me'll imortall make,
 Not for the loyalty or witt
 But, Sir, because by you 'tis writ,   15
 Altho' I fear the world will say
 Friendship your judgement did o'resway.
 I ask not, Sir, for all you've wrott;
 Some better much were quite forgott.
 Bad women kill their bratts, we know;   20
 Wou'd all bad poetts too doe so.
 The spurious offspring of the pen
 As soon as born shou'd dye agen,
 For 'tis but just a law was made:
 Those ne're shou'd write whom none will read.   25
 Then less lampoons had plagu'd the times,
[*p. 71*] Nor had we seen Tom Shadwell's rimes.
 Saffold content in prose had slew,
 Not murder'd us and poesy too.
 'T had muszel'd all the muses' foes,   30
 Nay, halfe the church and all the beaus.
 Guilt paper less wou'd be in use,
 And Phillis freed from *billett doux*

(Who minds the witt within the lines,
Tho scented glitt'ring paper shines).   35
Tho' priests (and, faith, they're in the right)
In one in ten take huge delight,
Scarce in a thousand one shou'd write.
Less sermons then wou'd come abroad
With nought but th'text, the word of God,   40
Nor damn to hell that doctrine now
That came from heaven seven years agoe.
But now our blest association
Has writers made of halfe the nation.
Clean and unclean, like beasts i'th Ark,   45
Some sett their hand and some their mark,
Tho' this wee wisely both forbore,
And wou'd not sign, altho' we swore,
For words will soon blow off again,
Whilst letters oft too long remain.   50

Commentary

For the circumstances that led Hall to send this epistle to Broughton, and what it reveals about his writing practices, see the discussion in Chapter 2.2 above. Having deplored the existence of so many bad writers, Hall ends the poem by bringing the argument round to the Oath of Allegiance, which 'has writers made of halfe the nation' — but which he and Broughton apparently did not sign.

1–2. Similar to lines from the poem 'Curse on those representatives', discussed and quoted (in Hall's version) in Chapter 7.6 above. In that case it is money that is compared to the water needed for mechanical pump priming; here it is poetry.

2. *we may get*: O2, 'may come'.

5. *m'amanuensis*, i.e. my amanuensis. 'Emanuensis', O1d, O2.

8. *Neb'cadnezars dreams*: the dreams forgotten by the Old Testament king, Nebuchadnezzar, but nevertheless interpreted for him by the prophet Daniel (Daniel 2:5).

10. *Belteshazer*: the name by which Daniel was known in the king's court (Daniel 1:7). Hall is confident that Broughton, like Daniel, will be able to restore what has been forgotten.

12. *Mathews*: in B1 written as 'Ma — ws', filled in by the later annotator. O1d, O2 have the full form. Hall is clearly referring here to a collection of his local satires, in which the Mathews, father and son, members of the Hereford Protestant establishment, occur more than once as targets of satire and derision. As well as the discussion in Chapter 2.2, see Chapter 1 and Chapter 3.2 (b). The reference here suggests that the elder Mathews is aware that the book exists, and is scared (or so Hall likes to think) that its contents would, if known, expose him to ridicule.

13.   Perhaps an indication of real poetic ambition on Hall's part, although the lines that follow (14–17) are characterized by self-deprecation and irony.

15.   The reference shows that Broughton was deliberately maintaining a volume of fair copies of Hall's poems, perhaps at the latter's request.

19.   i.e. 'some (poems) were much better quite forgotten'.

22.   *spurious*: not just 'unauthentic', and so 'worthless', but also bearing its original meaning of 'illegitimate', 'bastard' (*OED*, *spurious*, adj., 1), anticipated in l. 20.

27.   *Tom Shadwell's rimes*: Thomas Shadwell (1642?–92), famously satirized by Dryden in *Mac Flecknoe*, ended his life as Poet Laureate.

28.   *Saffold*: a reference to the astrologer and quack physician Thomas Saffold (d. 1691), who had premises in Blackfriars, London, and allegedly died under his own treatment; he advertised his nostrums by means of doggerel verses (see T. A. B. Corley, 'Saffold, Thomas (bap. 1620?, d. 1691), Astrologer and Nostrum Seller', in *ODNB*).

30.   *'T had* , i.e. 'It [the proposed law] would have'.

32.   *Guilt paper*, i.e. writing paper with gilt edges (*OED*, *gilt*, adj., C3, *gilt-paper*).

33.   *Phillis*, a conventional name for an attractive young woman. O2 reads 'Phillips'.

34–35. Apparently, 'Who pays attention to any wit in the verses as long as [...]' (cf. *OED*, *though*, 4). In l. 35 B1's initial 'The' has been altered by the later annotator to 'Tho', almost certainly the original reading, despite O1/D and O2 both reading 'The'.

37.   *In one in ten*, i.e. in their entitlement to tithes.

40.   A critical allusion to preaching wholly based on biblical texts, as favoured by Puritans.

41–42. Very likely a reference to James II's 1687 Declaration of Indulgence, which granted freedom of religious observance to Catholics as well as the majority of Nonconformists. Hall's private Catholicism, despite his employment in an Anglican cathedral, is often apparent in his poems. In the 1690s the Declaration of Indulgence was attacked by many in the established church.

43–50. Hall turns finally to the imposition of the Oath of Allegiance on clergy and other public figures; see 'And art thou, faith, a true recluse become', above.

43.   *association*: an ironic reference to the Oath of Allegiance as a physical object to be signed. Cf. *OED*, *association*, n., 3, 'a document setting forth the common purpose of a number of persons, and signed by them as a pledge that they will carry it into execution'.

47–48. It appears from this that both Hall and Broughton managed to get away with swearing the oaths verbally, avoiding signing the document.

49–50. Hall is alluding to the Latin epigram 'Litera scripta manet, verbum ut inane perit', i.e. the written letter remains while the empty (i.e. spoken) word perishes.

From place where long to lie does tire one (20)

Title in copy text: 'To Dr Broughton' (B1).
Summary: Hall, suffering from an illness, appeals to Dr Broughton for an emergency supply of the iron pills that the doctor has prescribed.
Date: Presumably 1690s.
Copy text: B1, p. 83. Also in O1d, p. 21, and O2, ff. 21v-22r ('To Dr Broughton desiring some of his steel pills', in both).

[*p. 83*] From place where long to lie does tyre one,
Where pillow does my head inviron,
I rose in haste to eat cold iron,
A pretty breakfast for a sinner
To gett a stoomack to his dinner!   5
For spiritts lost, you, to restore 'em,
Extracts prescribe of mettallorum,
And that my pulse may beat the quicker
You make an ostridge of a vicar,
And as with paste we cram a pullett,   10
So you do paunch with iron bullett:
My gutts a magazeine become,
Fill'd full with carcasses and bomb.
Butt pitty now my sad condition
For want this morn of ammunition.   15
Since Morse's man has not been here,
That queer chalybiate engineer,
Just four of yours will serve this time
At once to charge his gun and prime
Who's muchly yours in prose and rime.   20

Commentary

Hall's illness here may be the same as that from which he has recovered in 'These grateful lines are doubly Sir your due', edited below. If so, 'From place where long to lie' was probably also written no later than 1695. The two poems are adjacent, the present poem placed first, in all three manuscripts.

1.   *From*: O1d, O2 read 'In', but l. 3's 'I rose' suggests that *From* is correct.
2.   *inviron*, 'surround' (*OED*, environ, v., 1a).
3.   *cold iron*, i.e. the iron (or steel) pills that Dr Broughton has prescribed for Hall's illness.
5.   *stoomack*, 'appetite' (*OED*, stomach, n., 5).
7.   *mettallorum*: a pseudo-scientific word probably made up by Hall for the occasion, borrowed for rhyming purposes from the Latin genitive plural 'metallorum'.

9. *an ostridge*: ostriches were commonly supposed to eat iron and other hard substances.
10. *we*: O2 reads 'you'.
11. *So you do paunch with*, i.e. 'in the same way you cram a paunch with'.
12. *magazeine*, in the military sense, a storehouse for arms or ammunition (*OED*, *magazine*, n., 2).
13. *carcasses*: see *OED*, *carcass*, n., 7, a particular type of explosive shell. Hall uses the word again (in a literal sense) in 'So little being done and so much money spent', below (l. 14).
15. Hall's supply of steel pills has evidently run out.
16–18. *Morse's man*: Morse is presumably the apothecary (described in l. 17) who has been providing the pills prescribed by Broughton; in the circumstances Hall makes a direct appeal to the latter for temporary supplies.
17. *chalybiate*: see *OED*, *chalybeate*, adj., 'impregnated or flavoured with iron', usually referring to liquid preparations. Cf. the occurrence of 'calybiat' in 'Once in a week a letter's due', below (l. 5).
19. Hall ends with a further application of the idea of iron pills as ammunition, necessary to restore him to health and vigour. There may also be a sexual reference.

These grateful lines are doubly Sir your due *(70)*

Title in copy text: 'To Dr Broughton after a fitt of sickness'.
Summary: Hall, writing to thank Broughton for curing him of an illness, extravagantly praises his medical skill and the generosity with which it is practised, describing it as a godlike gift that should persuade doubters (like Broughton himself) of the existence of God.
Date: No later than 1695 (see note to ll. 32–33).
Copy text: B1, pp. 72–74. Also in O1d, pp. 1–3, and O2, ff. 13r-14r (same title, in both, as in B1).

[*p. 72*]   These gratefull lines are doubly, Sir, your due,
Both as my friend and my physitian, too.
The trembling hand you see does steady grow,
To render thanks to him that made it so.
Phantomes and sprites, those melancholly theams   5
We wakeing think but clearly see in dreams,
Hobgoblings, ghosts, and all the sooty train
Disorder'd spiritts stamp upon the brain
You've utterly dispell'd, and I'm agen
As free from fayries as a Magdalen.   10
The wondrous cures the sages have of old
Of mighty Galen and his master told
Are like our modern saints which cross the seas,

Whilst with the miles the miracles increase:
Beyond Japan Xavier was all divine,   15
With Jacob's Ladder heaven to earth cou'd joyn,
But legend silent is this side the line;
So cou'd we once those antient mists remove,
Physitians' tales wou'd like their poetts prove.
But your diviner art each day is shown   20
I'th spight of all, that all your power might own,
And farther then your loyalty is gone.
Had Heaven thought fitt you shou'd those days have seen,
The fam'd Bethesda sure had useless been.
No more wou'd men expecting there have stood   25
The constant kind disturber of the flood;
An angell in your hand had been as good.

[p. 73]   Your skill and wondrous power your friends confess,
And ev'n your enemies must own success.
You need no apochryphall recorded proof;   30
You've upright liveing witnesses enough.
If e're a patient on the bier you bore,
Dunstan had slain him certainly before;
You came indeed, and saw, and own'd death's mighty power.
(Dunstan, whose useless care is cruelty,   35
Who ne'er kills one but let's whole hundreds dye.)
Whilst spring and autumn lasts you'l greater grow
In spite of ignorance, thy mortall foe.
A Whig, when well, crys out he'l ne're employ
A man that wou'd the government destroy.   40
No sooner had he say'd it but the sott
A surfett at the last election gott;
Urg'd on by pungent pains and pittying friends,
In far more haste then once he shun'd thee, sends,
Where with thy noble remedies divine   45
Thou gav'st him life that wou'd have taken thine.
Says Bigott, full of Dutch divinity,
'I'de rather then thy heathenish prescripts try
Be sent by quack to him thou dost deny',
Not knowing those who oft our insides see   50
Can never atheist and physitian be.
The deity does sure nowhere appear
So evident, so wonderfull as there.
Without a paradox it may be say'd
We own th'Almighty less alive, than dead.   55
The fool in's heart no God wou'd own, we know,
Mark well, sage friend, 'tis only fools say soe;
Those who the paths of providence have trod

[p. 74]   Have ever yet and still must own a God.
            Our banisht prince who did his subjects cure   60
            Of lesser evills then he does endure,
            Full of compassion and repleat with zeal,
            'I only touch', said he, ''tis Heaven does heal.'
            The mighty tenet then dispute no more,
            Since godlike kings still own a greater power.   65
            Higher then any should thy incense rise,
            Fatter and fairer be thy sacrifice,
            Since Heaven almost a miracle has shown
            In giveing mighty thee a power alone
            To cure all maledyes, to kings but one.   70

Commentary

The present poem is a good example of the fluency and speed of thought of Hall's verse-making (and the wide range of his references), as discussed in Chapter 2.1 above. From thanking and praising Broughton, and contrasting his demonstrable medical skill with unauthenticated claims of miraculous cures in stories, Hall passes to his friend's willingness to treat anyone who needs his help, including his political and religious opponents, forced in the end to call on his services. The poem concludes with Hall asserting that doctors, familiar with the wonders of the human body, cannot but acknowledge the existence of God, and that Broughton, in particular, should give thanks for having such a godlike gift.

7.   *the sooty train*, i.e. all the other terrifying black figures.
10.   *a Magdalen*: presumably in the sense of a reformed prostitute (cf. *OED*, *Magdalen*, 2), but also with reference to the biblical Mary Magdalene 'out of whom went seven devils' (Luke 8:2). *fayries*, in this case malevolent spirits.
11–19. Before returning, in l. 20, to praise Broughton's great and demonstrable skill as a healer, Hall, sceptically, contrasts stories of supposed miraculous cures by others, in both ancient times (ll. 11–12) and modern (ll. 13–17).
12.   *Galen and his master*: Galen, the famous physician of antiquity. *His master* is very likely a reference to his predecessor Hippocrates.
13–14. i.e. stories of miraculous cures by modern 'saints' become more numerous the further away they are supposed to have happened.
15–17. As an example, Hall picks out the Spanish saint Francis Xavier (1506–52), the Christian evangelizer of India and parts of the Far East, to whom many healing miracles were attributed. The triplet is apparently saying that Xavier was regarded 'beyond Japan' as so godlike he could have erected a Jacob's Ladder between heaven and earth, but nearer home no such story is told. *the line*, i.e. the equator (*OED*, *line*, n. 2, 10b), here used loosely with a meaning closer to hemisphere.
18–19. i.e. stories about ancient physicians, if we could know their true nature, would prove to be like the works of poets, made up.

21. Obscure, but probably 'in spite of everyone who might admit the fact of your great abilities' (*OED*, *own*, v., 5a), i.e. but chooses not to do so, very likely with reference to Broughton's difficult position in the Hereford area because of his oppositional views.

22. Seemingly, 'and (your skill is manifested) more widely than your loyalty has been exhibited'; that is to say, Broughton, as a doctor, treats those — the members of the local establishment — whose political views he does not share.

23. *those days*: i.e. New Testament times, as is made clear in the following lines.

24–27. A reference to the pool at Bethesda described in John 5:2–4, where it is said that those wishing to be healed wait for an angel to come and 'trouble the water' (cf. l. 26). In l. 27 Hall's pun on the word *angel* as gold coin is likely to allude to the fee for treatment that Broughton would theoretically receive for doing just as good a job.

30. *apochryphall*, i.e. of doubtful authenticity (*OED*, *apocryphal*, adj., A).

31. *You've*: in B1 altered by the later corrector from 'Your', which is the reading also in O1d and O2.

32–33. Hall makes out that even if one of Broughton's patients dies, another doctor, 'Dunstan', will in effect have killed him through his previously administered treatment. Cf. the extravagant satire of ll. 35–36. O1d, O2 both supply a marginal gloss 'Old Dr Harford', the 'Dr' in O1d (inserted above the other words) being almost certainly in Hall's own hand. The doctor in question is Bridstock Harford (1607–95), who had been a staunch Parliamentarian in mid-century and so was very likely a political opponent of Hall and Broughton. His grandson, another Bridstock (1654–1713), also practised medicine in Hereford, hence, no doubt, the 'Old Harford' of the marginal note (who would appear to be still alive). See Henry Connor, 'Mistress Joyce Jeffreys and her Physician, Dr Bridstock Harford (1607–1695)', *Journal of Medical Biography*, 24 (2014), 545–50.

36. In both B1 and O1d *ne'er* (O1d *ner'e*) has been corrected from *never*, in the latter case almost certainly by Hall himself.

39–40. A reference to Broughton's opposition to William and Mary and consequently the governing Whig establishment. For the supposed strength of feeling against Broughton, cf. 'Thou gav'st him life that wou'd have taken thine', l. 46.

42. *surfett*, i.e. illness attributed to excessive eating or drinking (*OED*, *surfeit*, n., 4).

43. *pungent*, 'piercing' (*OED*, *pungent*, adj., 1).

44. *sends*, i.e. summons Dr Broughton.

47. *Bigott*, personified bigotry, similar to the ignorant, vindictive Whig of the previous example. *Dutch divinity*, probably a general reference to the kind of rigid Protestantism that Hall associates with the Dutch William III and his adherents in Hereford.

48. *then*, i.e. than, as also in l. 66. *prescripts*, 'prescriptions'.

49. 'be sent to God [i.e. killed] by an ignorant doctor'. Bigott's belief that Broughton is an atheist is then refuted by Hall (speaking of doctors in general) in the lines that follow.

50–55. Hall argues that a dissected dead body reveals the wonder of God's creation more than does a live one.

55. *own*, 'acknowledge [the existence of God]', as elsewhere in the poem.

56. Psalms 44:1 and 53:1: 'The fool hath said in his heart, There is no God.'

57. Hall now turns to arguing the existence of God to Broughton (in contrast to 'And art thou, faith, a true recluse become', above, where Hall urges his friend not to take religion too seriously). *say*: O1d, O2, 'says', B1 (here emended).

58. Possibly, in context, those whose health has been preserved (implicitly by divine assistance) in their journey through life.

60. *Our banisht prince*: James II, in exile since 1688.

61–64. The references here are to the belief that kings were able to cure their subjects of scrofula, known as the king's evil. The practice of the monarch 'touching' people with the disease continued until the death of Queen Anne in 1714.

64. *tenet*, i.e. belief in the existence of God. B1's later annotator has corrected the word from 'tenent', which is a reading shared also by O1d and O2.

65. i.e. 'since kings, who are like gods, acknowledge that there is a power greater than theirs'.

66–70. Hall, imagining Broughton as an ancient Israelite, argues that his sacrificial offering to God should be more splendid than any other, on account of the exceptional gift he has been given.

Once in a week a letter's due   *(46)*

Title in copy text: 'To Dr Broughton'.
Summary: Hall reflects that age will eventually bring about impotence, making love-making impossible. In consequence he recommends living for the moment and enjoying the pleasures of inebriation.
Date: Presumably 1690s.
Copy text: B1, pp. 84–85. Also in O1d, pp. 22–23, and O2, f. 22r-v (untitled in both).

[*p. 84*]   Once in a week a letter's due,
             As once a night to spouse from you.
             But ah, my friend, I sigh to speak,
             The time will come when once a week
             The tough calybiat teeth of time   5
             Will spoile thy loveing and my rime.
             Age will bind o're and rudely seize
             The very maker of our peace.
             Then it no more at Silvia's eyes
             Than graileing at my fly will rise.   10
             You may perhaps for Parl'ment man
             — You may, but that will never, stand.
             There is we read for flesh and bone,

For that, no resurrection.
Then kind soft words and many a kiss   15
We give in leiu of greater bliss.
No more will Syl your rudeness blame;
Strephon will then be wondrows tame.
Our pitty Scandrett has, and praise,
For fasting out his forty days,   20
But when our oyle of love is spent
We keep an everlasting Lent.
Then you'l recite to listening son
The glor'ous deeds that thou hast done;
On your past life with joy look back,   25
As men from land behold a wrack.
Since nothing we can do or say
Can keep the stalking fiend away,
Let's, dearest doctor, live today.
[*p. 85*]   Oft fill the moveing glass to th'brim;   30
As oft, my friend, wee'l empty him.
Round lett imortall hearty flow,
Till all things else with it do soe.
Then Silvia seems to me a goddess,
Tho' pent within vast Giles's boddice,   35
And if my Sylvia wou'd but drink,
She'd even Giles a Feilding think;
Brib'd by the god, she'd ne'r espie
His wooden legg or christall eye,
But frankly own, I mean when mellow,   40
He was *sur-tout* a pretty fellow.
This is to you the second time
Without return I've wrot in rime.
As I am yours, so you're my debtor:
I owe you vissitts, you me meeter,   45
And so, dear Doc, here ends my letter.

Commentary

5.   *calybiat*: cf. the use of the same word in l. 17 of 'From place where long to lie does tire one', above, there more normally spelt 'chalybiate', as in O1d, O2 here. In that poem it has the usual medicinal connotations, but here it seems simply to mean 'made of iron'.

8.   From what follows — a prediction that age will lead to impotence — *The very maker of our peace* must refer to the penis, with no doubt a play on 'piss', urine.

9–18. These lines, with their frequent references to the male erection, are omitted from O1d, O2, and the same passage is marked with a cross at beginning and end in B1, plausibly for excision when copying.

10. *graileing*, i.e. the fish, as also in 'Dunned by the bells I rose from bed', l. 38.

11. *for Parl'ment man*, i.e. in the presence of a Member of Parliament.

18. *Strephon*: a conventional pastoral name for a male lover.

19. *Scandrett*, characterized here as scrupulously careful to fast throughout Lent, is evidently the same person as is lightly satirized in 'Dunned by the bells I rose from bed', below, l. 38. A Philip Scandrett was Mayor of Hereford in 1708.

28. *stalking fiend*, i.e. age.

32. *hearty*, cider. See the note to 'From college hall where thirsty vicar', above, l. 26.

33. i.e. as it appears to one's senses, as the result of inebriation.

34. *me*: O2, 'be'.

35. *vast Giles's boddice*: presumably a local allusion.

37. *Feilding*: probably a reference to Robert Fielding (1651?–1712), the scandalous (Jacobite) womanizer and bigamist, known as Beau or 'Handsome' Fielding.

38. *the god*, presumably Bacchus, the god of drinking.

39. *christall eye*, i.e. glass eye.

40. *mellow*, '(mildly) drunk' (*OED*, *mellow*, adj., 6).

41. *sur-tout*, i.e. for the most part.

43–45. As noted in Chapter 2.2 above, it appears that the verse-making was meant to be reciprocal, with Broughton also contributing.

Epistles to Other Friends

Dunned by the bells I rose from bed $\left(52\right)$

Title in copy text: 'To your Lordship after being ruin'd at play'.

Summary: Hall describes his life of unsuccessful gambling and loose living, and wittily acknowledges his debt to Lord Chandos following his latest loss.

Date: *c.* 1692–94.

Copy text: B1, pp. 34–35. Also in Univ. Minnesota 690235 (M), pp. 211–12 ('By Hen: H: to E: Chandos being beat by the E: att gameing').

[*p. 34*]	Dun'd by the bells I roase from bed,	
	With empty fobb and aching head,	
	With dirty hands and nasty linnen,	
	Th'effects of sitting up and sinning.	
	I cou'd not but reflect upon	5
	What mighty crimes of late I'd done,	
	Eternally to loose l'argent;	
	To throw out is a common evill,	
	But still ams-ace is sure the devill.	
	Was eight the maine, I threw eleven,	10
	And still ungodly twelve nick'd seven.	
	I'le Fortune fickle call no more,	
	To me she prov'd a constant whore;	
	I did her backward favours share	
	From tenn at night to morning prayer.	15
	She's been of late, to my dear knowledge,	
	A very Jew unto the college,	
	Witness your Milk Lane recreation,	
	Where lansquenet, so much in fashion,	
	Gave Alderson some perturbation.	20
	In love than play, my greater skill is,	
	And Fortune's more a gilt than Phillis.	
	The bargain here is quickly driven,	
	And Miss turns sooner up than seven.	
	Besides 'tis much the sweeter sinn:	25
	Here you throw out, there always in,	
	Tho' some nine months, or thereabouts,	
	What you threw in too oft comes out,	
[*p. 35*]	Altho' wee're ruin'd either way,	
	To gett by love or loose by play.	30
	I'le fairely therefore both give o're,	
	And shutt in time the stable door,	

Leave fighting to our great comanders,
Scurrillity to Samuell Saunders,
To Luxembourg, the art of beating,   35
To our great Prince, that of retreating,
To surly Guil. the guift o' raileing,
To Scandrett, that of takeing graileing,
To Kendrick, rhimeing well and drinking,
To your Lordship, talking just and thinking,   40
To whom this awkard doggrell letter
Is offer'd by your humble debtor.
To prove I'm poor, in verse I choose
T'accost your Honour in, not prose.
Plenty of rime, both you and I know,   45
Supposes scarecity of rhino,
While all these words in order meet
By way of bond to own the debt,
Tho' this you'l say's the only time
That ever bond was wrott in rhime,   50
In which I own I'm at your mercy,
By force of *Noverint universi.*

Commentary

The epistle is addressed to James Brydges, eighth Baron Chandos (1642–1714), for whose gambling sessions with Hall see the discussion (in Chapter 9.1 above) of the 1704 poem *A Tryal of Skill*; Hall is one of the featured poets, very likely with reference to the present poem. 'Dunned by the bells' can be dated to between 1692, the year of the Duke of Luxembourg's military victories (l. 35) and January 1695, the date of Luxembourg's death. The copy in M, which has few textual differences, is mistaken in referring to Chandos as E., i.e. Earl. For the altered 11-line extract in the lost Cooke manuscript (C), discussed at ll. 12–20 below, see also Chapter 3.2 above.

1. *Dun'd by*, 'bombarded with noise by'; *OED, din*, v.,2, here in the variant form *dun* (*OED, dun*, v.²), no doubt to pun on the latter's primary meaning, 'make insistent demands on for money' (*OED, dun*, v.³, 1). M, less satisfactorily, reads 'Dup'd by'.
2. *fobb*, a small pocket for valuables (*OED, fob*, n.², 1).
7. *l'argent*, i.e. money, well attested in English at this time (*OED*).
8. *throw out*, i.e. make a losing throw in hazard, the game of dice being played (*OED, throw out*, 7, within *throw*, v.¹).
9. *still*, 'always'. *ams-ace*, i.e. two aces (*OED, ames-ace*, n.), the lowest throw possible.
10. *Was eight the maine*. In a game of hazard the 'main' is the number (from five to nine inclusive) called by the person casting the dice before the throw is made.

11. *ungodly*, perhaps with the meaning of cursed or damned. M reads 'unhappy'. *nick'd*, at hazard, made a winning throw of a specified number (*OED*, *nick*, v.², 6b). The rules by which Hall and Chandos are playing are unclear, but it is certain that Hall loses.

12–20. C contains a version of these lines, transcribed by William Cooke as part of his memoir of Hall's colleague Barnabas Alderson (a Vicar Choral since 1686); see Chapter 3.2 (a) above. The extract begins with four lines apparently representing an expansion of ll. 12–13: 'Miss Fortune's not a fickle dame, | To me, she's evermore the same; | Smiling on gamblers of the town, | On me she casts a constant frown.' They very likely represent a bowdlerization of the original, possibly by Hall himself.

14. *backward*, possibly 'disinclined to help' (*OED*, *backward*, adj., B.6), but very likely with a sexual connotation, in view of the collocation with *favours* and with what follows. In C the line reads 'Her backward favours I must share'.

16. *dear*, 'costly'. C begins 'Of late she has been'.

17. *Jew*: presumably in the sense of someone who drives a very hard bargain, to the point of financial ruin. *colledge*, i.e. the College of Vicars Choral.

18. *Milk Lane*: Cooke introduces his extract from the poem as follows: 'One of Mr. Hall's M.S. poems describes the effects of the card parties then so numerously attended at the coffee house in Milk Lane (now St John Steet), where much money & time were recklessly squandered' (HCA 7003/4/3).

19. *Lansquenet*: B1's scribe has the evidently corrupt reading 'Banc. Filett', for which the later corrector supplies the marginal gloss 'Lansquenet', which is also the term found in C (ll. 18–20 are omitted by M, possibly for reasons of obscurity to a non-local readership). See *OED*, *lansquenet*, n, 2, a game of cards of German origin.

20. *Alderson*: in B1 written as A — n, filled in by the annotator. C reads 'Gave Alderson such perturbation'.

22. *gilt*, i.e. jilt.

24. *turns* [...] *up*, i.e. consents to sex; cf. *OED*, *turn up*, 28 (within *turn*, v.), with reference to prostitution. *seven* refers back to the game of hazard.

26. *Here* again refers to hazard, where *throw out* means lose. In the case of love one throws 'in', the term for winning at hazard.

27–28. Cf. again *A Tryal of Skill* (as discussed in Chapter 9.1), in which Hall's apparent reputation for sexual promiscuity may reflect knowledge of the present poem.

30. *gett*, i.e. beget.

34. *Samuell Saunders*: an asterisk against this line in B1's inner margin relates to local information provided by the later annotator on the manuscript's inside front cover: 'This Saunders was a Presbyterian ironmonger, whose sister was Michael Brampton's mother.'

35. The Duke of Luxembourg, one of Louis XIV's most successful military commanders, played a major role in the French seizure of Namur and victory at the battle of Steenkerque, both in 1692 during the Nine Years' War. As in the next line, Hall is taking some pleasure in William III's military setbacks.

37. *Guil.*: very likely a reference to Gilbert Ironside (1632–1701), Bishop of Hereford since 1691 and a strong supporter of William III. Hall satirizes him in the argumentative dialogue, 'How durst thou thus disturb that surly shade'. *raileing*, i.e. speaking abusively.

38. *Scandrett*: probably the Philip Scandrett who was Mayor of Hereford in 1708, as also in 'Once in a week a letter's due', above, l. 19. *graileing*, i.e. the fish.

39. *Kendrick*: Daniel Kenrick of Worcester, clergyman, physician, and poet, for whose life and probable friendship with Hall see Chapter 9.2 above. Given that all these 'bequests' by Hall clearly refer to accomplishments already possessed by their subjects, it follows that Kenrick already 'rhymes well', in Hall's eyes. *drinking*: corrected from 'thinking' by the later annotator (M reads 'drinking').

41. *awkard*: an acceptable contemporary spelling for 'awkward'.

43. *choose*: M, 'chose', for the sake of the rhyme, but the present tense is needed.

46. *rhino*, 'money' (*OED*, *rhino*, n.¹).

49. *own*, 'acknowledge', as frequently in 'These gratefull lines', edited above.

52. *Noverint universi*, i.e. 'Let all men know', the opening words of a legal writ, such as Chandos would issue against Hall if he wished to pursue the debt.

Although to petition has been out of fashion (27)

Title in copy text: 'The humble piticion of Nat Priest and Henry Hall to Edmund Addys Gent for a load of hearty, vizt. red muss'.

Summary: Hall requests a gift of cider from a friend, Edmund Addis, partly to enable him and his fellow 'petitioner', Nat Priest, to drink the health of the exiled James II and his son.

Date: Probably the mid-1690s.

Copy text: B1, pp. 94–95.

> [*p. 94*] Altho' to petition has bin out of fashion
> Since we play'd an old trick by a new abdication,
> Yet change being so takeing, as now the world goes, Sir,
> You may prize that in rhime you wou'd laugh at in prose, Sir.
> Thus hearing your trees in a laden condition,   5
> For a load of your liquor wee humbly petition,
> For since Madam Fortune has bin our provider,
> And stock'd us with vessells, as you, Sir, with cyder,
> Wee solemly swear, if you please but to fill 'em,
> That not the least drop shall be drank to K — g W — m;   10
> Tho' not very rich wee are loyall *ambobus*,
> And all the whole load we'll devote to Jacobus.
> The devill a man in the roome shall be sober
> On the first day of June or 14th of October,
> [*p. 95*] To whose sacred healths such a loyall train follows   15
> As wou'd reach yee from Alderman Holmes to All Hallows.

The juice that wee ask for is not that of redstrake,
Least it makes, Sir, your heart just as much as our heads ake.
Wee only on hearty pretend to be merry;
You'l not give us pippin nor will we take perry.   20
Then freely assigne us that smileing sweet liquor
That even to an abbot wou'd raise a poor vicar.
But lay your comands and the business is done, Sir,
So your priest will have two and your clerk but just one, Sir.
And tho' we in English do it every day, Sir,   25
Yet since you think Latin's the antienter way, Sir:
Your peticoners in duty henceforward will pray, Sir.

Commentary

Title: *Nat Priest* must be 'the Priest [Christian name unknown] recommended by Henry Hall of Hereford to be Organist at Bangor Cathedral and noted in the Chapter minutes on 14 June 1705 [...]. He might well be the Nathaniel Priest who served as Organist at Bristol Cathedral from Michaelmas 1710 to Michaelmas 1734' (Ashbee and others, *Biographical Dictionary of English Court Musicians*, II, 921). He was perhaps Hall's Assistant Organist, but he appears not to have been a Vicar Choral or in holy orders. His Jacobitism is demonstrated by a 1692 document in the care of the Herefordshire Archive Service (BG11/17/5/80, available online) in which a Walter Wall deposes 'that he heard Nathaniel Priest, at the "Swan and Falcon", drink to King James and his Queen, wishing her a safe return; and that some others that were drinking with Priest, said that he also drank to the Pope and spoke against King William's army and government'. (This 1690s date shows that Priest cannot be the Child of the Chapel [Royal], 1702–06, with whom Ashbee and others tentatively link the organist.) A 'Nat', possibly again Nat Priest, features in 'Coming from place where you have seen', l. 11, as another habitué of the disreputable club there visited by Hall. *Edmund Addys*, or Addis, clearly a friend of Hall and Priest, is also petitioned in 'Though rhyme of late's no more my talent' (later revised into 'This Sir's to you the second time'), as discussed in the Conclusion to this study, above. See also the commentary to 'If rhyme for rhino could atone', below. The present poem is unlikely to much predate 'Though rhyme of late's no more my talent', in which Hall alludes to what must be his second marriage in October 1696. *hearty* (also in l. 19): for this term for cider, see the note to 'From college hall where thirsty vicar', above, l. 26. *muss*: a recorded dialect spelling of *OED*, must, n.¹, 3, *must apple*, referring to varieties of apple (including 'red must') used for making cider. The reference here is to the *liquor* (l. 6) derived from the apples, so that *vizt. red muss* very likely means 'that is to say, made from red must apples'.

2.   A reference to the removal of James II as King of England.
3.   *takeing*, 'appealing' (*OED*, taking, adj, 2).
10.   Addis, like Hall and Priest, is clearly also a Jacobite.
11.   *ambobus*: dative plural of Latin *ambo*, i.e. 'to both', used for the sake of the rhyme, here referring to both James II and his son James Stuart (expressed

together as *Jacobus* in l. 12), and anticipating ll. 14–15, where the health of both is drunk.

13. *The devil a man in the roome*, i.e. 'Not a man in the room'. See *OED*, *devil*, P1, e. (b), 'expressing strong negation' when placed before a noun.

14. Hall must intend the birthdays of, respectively, James Stuart and James II, correct in the case of the latter but the former was born on 10 June.

16. *All Hallows*, i.e. All Saints Church, Hereford.

17. *redstrake*, i.e. the redstreak, a famous Herefordshire cider-apple. Cf. the couplet that Hall includes in a letter to Adam Ottley of Pitchford (O3b): 'Since witt no more will in our country live | Than will our redstreaks when they're out on't thrive.' Hall, however, makes it clear in ll. 17–21 that his and Priest's preference is for hearty.

19. *pretend*, 'intend', as in 'Calling at Fountain's late last night', l. 30.

20. *pippin*: another cider-apple, in this case the resulting drink; *perry*: liquor derived from pears.

23. *lay your comands*, presumably 'give your orders', i.e. to your workmen to fill the *vessells* that Hall and Priest will bring (ll. 8–9).

24. The request for *two* and *one* jokingly reflects the different status of a priest and a clerk, but Hall is no doubt also punning on the lower-status Nat Priest's surname.

25. *do it*: corrected from *do't* by B1's later hand, no doubt for the sake of the metre.

25–27. Hall is here referring to, and in l. 27 using, the traditional form of words at the end of a petition, although despite l. 26 they are given in English.

Ye gods what gulfs are set between *(22)*

Title in copy text: 'To the Reverend Dr Oatly'.
Summary: Hall excuses himself from a dinner invitation on account of the previous night's over-indulgence.
Date: Possibly *c*. 1698.
Copy text: O1c (a single leaf). Also in O2, f. 12v ('To the Revd Dr Ottley. A letter').

[*p. 53*]   Ye Gods, what gulfs are set between
The things we doe and what we ween!
Last night, repairing to my house
With poesie to divert, and spouse,
I was (by partial Fate) pickt up   5
By a rich, queere Carmarthen tupp,
And did so long with Brittain stay
That I can eat no ling today,
Nor head of boar, for all its stuffing,
Nor sturgeon, or its brother puffing,   10
Nor is my vitiating pallat
Mov'd at my own imortal sallad.

> My stomach's just as queere and odd
> As either Richard or Tom Broad.
> From dinner then excuse my missing,   15
> Tho' not at tennis, or a-fishing.
> Let me obtain your wonted pardon
> And all the blame lay on Carmarthen.
> Forgive this morning's little flights
> Which Muse invents and Harry writes,   20
> And the so maukish, sleepy sinner
> Invite another day to dinner.

Commentary

Title: taken from the verso of O1c, which is in the form of a letter; it is therefore properly the address for delivery. In O2 it becomes a title, given as 'To the Revd Dr Ottley. A letter'. Dr Adam Ottley (1653–1723; Davies, in *ODNB*) held appointments in the diocese and cathedral of Hereford from 1682 until his appointment as Bishop of St David's in 1713. In particular, he was Archdeacon of Salop from January 1687.

2.   *ween*: *OED*, *ween*, v., 2, 'anticipate', here used in an absolute sense.

4.   Probably both 'to divert myself with poetry' and 'to divert my spouse'. Hall's first wife, Catherine, died in 1690. He is here referring almost certainly to his second wife, Anne, whom he married in October 1696.

5.   *partial*, 'biased', 'having a liking for'. Cf. *OED*, *partial*, adj., 4.

6.   *queere*, 'odd', 'eccentric', with the possible additional sense of 'of dubious character' (*OED*, *queer*, adj.[1], 1a). O2 reads *queen*. *tupp*: *OED*, *tup*, n., 'ram', applied to a person. *OED*'s quotations (1b) suggest the sense of 'cuckold', but this may not apply here.

7.   *Brittain*: presumably the name of Hall's acquaintance, from Carmarthenshire.

10.   *puffing*, presumably 'puffin', which bird was then classified as a fish; see C. Anne Wilson, *Food and Drink in Britain from the Stone Age to Recent Times* (London: Constable, 1973), p. 37.

11.   *vitiating*, presumably 'impaired' or 'defective'; cf. *OED*, *vitiate*, v., 1 and 4, but this adjectival form is not recorded.

14.   *Richard or Tom Broad*: Thomas Broad was a fellow Vicar Choral and a long-standing colleague of Hall, his name appearing frequently in the Vicars Choral act book for the period (HCA 7003/1/3). Hall makes fun of his odd, changeable nature in the short poem 'For missing thee how canst thou Burren blame', one copy of which (O1a) is in Dr Ottley's own hand, and he mentions him also in ''Twas in the temple first I saw', edited below. Richard Broad (assuming Broad is implied) has not been traced.

15–16. Cf. ll. 29–30 in Hall's poem 'Though now in station to adjust us', in which he congratulates another cathedral colleague, Dr Richard Bulkley, on becoming a canon: 'From prayers forgive my often missing, | Either at tennis or a-fishing.' Bulkley's appointment took place in 1698, and the poem to Ottley may have been written at much the same time.

19. *little flights*, i.e. flights of fancy, with reference to the present poetic apology.
21. *maukish*, 'queasy', 'without appetite' (*OED*, *mawkish*, adj., 1).

If rhyme for rhino could atone   (32)

Title in copy text: 'To Mr R — C — who every year sent him a dun, a little before St Paul's Day'.
Summary: Light-hearted epistle to a creditor, Robin Clayton, wishing that verse could be a substitute for money.
Date: Probably 1701–02.
Copy text: *The Grove: A Collection of Original Poems, Translations, etc.* (London: for W. Mears, 1721), pp. 53–55. Also in B1, p. 112 ('A copy of verses to Mr Clayton after done at St Pauls Fair Bristoll').

[*p. 53*]	If rhime for rhino could attone	
	Or wit stave off an ardent dun,	
	If words, in sweetest numbers chose,	
	Would but wipe off our ticking prose,	
	How bless'd a life would poets lead,	5
	And ah! how punctual you'd be paid.	
	But since the greatest stroke of wit	
	Will not compound the meanest debt,	
	Nor fifty feet in Congreve's muse	
	Tick with old Tranter for two shoes,	10
[*p. 54*]	Nor all the rhimes great Dryden wrote	
	Prevail to trust him for a coat,	
	Know, Robin, I design you money	
	To face the fair now falling on you.	
	But of the saints both great and small	15
	There's none torments me like Saint Paul,	
	Who yearly persecutes the poor	
	As he did Christians heretofore,	
	For still about that holy tide,	
	When folk to fair of Bristol ride,	20
	More dunning bills to me are brought	
	Than e'er the saint epistles wrote.	
	But here the difference is, we see,	
	He wrote to heathens, they to me,	
	Nor can I blame their cleanly calling	25
	So often from their faith for falling	
[*p. 55*]	Since many a one, thro' sly deceivers	
	Have been undone by being believers.	
	But, Robin, this is not your case,	
	Whom heav'n some coin has giv'n and grace,	30

> Who, gruff when sober, bright when mellow,
> Art in the main a pretty fellow.

Commentary

For a discussion of the copy text, the anthology *The Grove*, see Chapter 9.2 above. On its p. 53 an attribution 'By Mr H. Hall of Hereford' follows straight after the title. Page 54 then has a footnote 'Bristol-Fair', defining 'the fair' mentioned in l. 14. On p. 55 ll. 29–32 are spaced off from the preceding lines. The less good text in B1 is the final item in the main scribal hand. As noted in Chapter 9.2, the unsatisfactory 'after done' in B1's titling of the poem is clearly a corruption of *The Grove*'s precise 'a dun', i.e. demand for payment (*OED*, dun, n.², 2). B1 also omits ll. 7–8 and 19–20, conceivably to fit the poem on to a single page. B1, on the other hand, identifies the recipient of Hall's epistle. Robin Clayton is apparently a person of some wealth, who has either lent Hall money or supplied goods for which payment is owing. Although associated here with Bristol, he is likely to be the merchant Robert Clayton, who was Mayor of Hereford in 1707. It is of interest that Herefordshire Archive Service holds an undated assignment (Q/RD/14/12) conveying property in Canon Pyon, a village north-west of the city, in which Robert Clayton is appointed to act by Edmund Addis (for whom see 'Although to petition', above), possibly suggesting a social circle of which Hall is a member.

1.   *rhino*, 'money, as in 'Dunned by the bells', l. 46, above. *attone*, 'make amends for (the lack of)' (cf. *OED*, atone, v., 4b).
4.   *ticking*, 'dealing in credit', 'running into debt' (*OED*, ticking, adj.²; a single quotation from 1673). B1 reads 'our ticks in prose'.
7–8. Omitted in B1, but necessary to the sense.
10.   *Tranter*: possibly a local pawnbroker.
11.   *wrote*: the use of the past tense suggests Hall is writing after Dryden's death in 1700.
12.   *Prevail to trust*: B1, 'Make thee believe'.
14.   *now falling on you*: B1, 'that's falling on ye', 'ye' very likely the original rhyme.
15.   In this case *But of* is clearly preferable to B1's 'Of all'.
17–20. St Paul's Fair in Bristol was held annually on 25 January, marking his feast day in the Book of Common Prayer. Lines 19–20 are omitted in B1, but they give explanatory context to ll. 21–22.
23.   'This difference only in't I see', B1.
25–26. Obscure, but apparently 'Nor can I blame their conversion to Christianity for their so often falling short of their (new) faith', with implied reference to the reason for St Paul writing so many epistles. B1 reads 'thy' in place of 'their' in l. 25.
31–32. B1's final couplet is syntactically separate: 'Thou'rt gruff when sober, bright when mellow, | And in the main an honest fellow.'

Political satires

Whither ye impious Britons do ye run   *(32)*

Title in copy text: 'An imitation of the 7 epod. of Horace. Quo quo scelesti ruitis'.
Summary: Jacobite attack on the English for continuing to support William III's wars despite the ruin it has caused the nation, blaming it on unexpiated guilt for the murder of Charles I.
Date: 1690.
Copy text: B2, ff. 11r–12r. Also in BL Add 21094, ff. 57v–58r; Bod Rawlinson poet. 181, f. 1r; Yale UL, Osborn c.570/2, p. 131; Osborn fb.207/3, p. 9; and *POAS*, II (1703), pp. 322–23. All have versions of B2's title (Add. 21094 and *POAS* read 'allusion to' in place of 'imitation of', and the latter adds the date '1690'), except for Osborn c.570/2 ('A poem') and Rawlinson, which is untitled.

[*f. 11r*]	Whither yee impious Brittains do ye run	
	As if already not enough undone?	
	Your sea has oft run purple to the shoar	
	And Flanders is manured with English gore,	
	Yet still yee arm and are prepared to fight	5
[*f. 11v*]	Against your king, his country, and his right.	
	If you must arm, unite the British powers,	
	Destroy your rivall Holland's lofty towers	
	And be her ruin as she has been yours,	
	Holland decreed to be this nation's curse,	10
	Bad as a foe but as a friend much worse.	
	These Hogans Mogans with a grinning pride	
	Your present ills and future hopes deride,	
	And well they may for they can only boast	
	Because your credit, wealth, and trafick's lost;	15
	Theirs is the gain and they may trihumph most,	
	Pleased with a natural malitious joy	
	To see yourselves none but yourselves destroy.	
	'Tis obvious! But infatuated you	
	Still court your ruin and contrive it too.	20
	Tell me, is madness this, or hope of gain,	
	Or doe the sons the fathers' crimes sustain?	
	Why are yee pale and speechless, why appears	
	This trembling, and why flow those guilty tears?	
	Sure there's a cause, a monstrous cause indeed	25
	You fain would hide, too horrid to be hid.	
	Yes, Brittains, yes, ye groan beneath the weight	
	Of Charles the Martyr's undeserved fate.	

[*f. 12r*]   You feel it still and still ye must deplore
    His pallace walls cemented with his gore.   30
    Too well yee know his unrepented fall
    Entayls this curse and will confound yee all.

Commentary

'Whither ye impious Britons' loosely imitates Horace's seventh epode, which begins 'Quo quo scelesti ruitis' ('Whither, whither do you villains rush?'). Whereas Horace inveighs against the madness of possible civil war in Rome, which would satisfy the desires of its enemies, the Parthians, Hall urges his countrymen not to fight in Flanders against (implicitly) the French — an action that he characterizes as civil war in that it would involve fighting against their rightful king, James II (now resident in France), and both Britain's and his economic interests. Instead, says Hall, if Britain has to take up arms it should be against their real enemies, the Dutch. who will only gloat at witnessing England's self-inflicted ruin.

In the latter part of the poem Hall follows Horace more closely in exposing the cause of the crisis, except that whereas Horace identifies the urge to civil war in Rome as a consequence of Romulus's long-ago murder of his brother Remus, Hall blames the rush to war on his contemporaries' unexpiated guilt for their fathers' crime in executing Charles I.

The 1690 date given above is taken from the title of the poem as printed in *POAS*, II. This version, which omits ll. 29–30, sets out the text as five separate sections, consisting respectively of 6, 7, 7, 6, and 4 lines.

Given the number of other witnesses, substantive variant readings are collected below. O2 serves as copy-text on the basis of being a deliberate collection of Hall's poems, but (as elsewhere) its readings can be unreliable, and I have emended its text on five occasions, in ll. 1, 7, 11, 13, and 24.

12. *Hogans Mogans*: a derogatory term for the Dutch, which Hall uses elsewhere (e.g. in the satire 'Let old England rejoice', l. 17), and compare 'Coming from place where you have seen' (edited above), l. 32. See *OED*, *hogen-mogen*, n., 3.
15. *trafick*, 'trade', 'commerce'.
18. i.e. to see you destroy no one but yourselves.
23–24. Cf. Horace's Latin: 'Tacent, et albus ora pallor inficit | mentesque perculsae stupent' ('They are silent, a white pallor infuses their faces | And their terrified minds are stunned').
28. Charles I was executed on 30 January 1649.

Substantive variant readings in the other witnesses

1 do] Add 21094, c.570, *POAS*, will B2, fb.207, Rawl. 181.
5 are prepared] still prepare *POAS*.
7 must] Add 21094, Rawl. 181, c.570, fb.207, *POAS*, will B2.
10 decreed] deserv'd *POAS*; this] our c.570, the fb.207.

11 a (x2)]   Add 21094, c.570, fb.207, *POAS*, your B2, our Rawl. 181; much] still
        c.570.
12 These Hogans Mogans]   See the Batavians Add 21094, c.570, fb.207, *POAS*.
13 Your]   Add 21094, c.570, fb.207, *POAS*, Our B2, Rawl. 181; present [...] hopes]
        future hopes and present ills fb.207.
15 creditt [...] and trafick's]   wealth your trade & credit's c.507.
17 naturall]   selfish dull *POAS*.
18 yourselves (x2)]   themselves fb.207.
19–20 *omitted* c.507.
19 infatuated]   most infatuate fb.207.
24 flow]   Add 21094, Rawl. 181, c.570, fb.207, *POAS*, *omitted* B2.
25 Sure]   Since *POAS*.
29–30]   *omitted POAS*.
30 His]   The c.570.
31 Too]   Soe fb.207.

Are all those lights that gild the street   *(24)*

Title in copy text: 'The Jacobites quaeres for the Thanksgiving Day in 1694. To the
tune of the Children in the Wood'.
Summary: A song mocking national celebrations of William III's supposed success
in the French wars.
Date: Very likely 1693.
Copy text: B1, p. 10. Also in M, pp. 131–32 ('The Jacobites quaeries for the Thankes-
giving 94')

[*p. 10*]   Are all those lights that guild the street,
            Are all those shouts of joy,
            For takeing of your Turkey fleet
            Or loss of Charleroy?

            Poor Hidleburgh perhaps may be   5
            The near resembling theme on't,
            Or long ago the fate of Huy
            Or lately that of Pidemont.

            Or rather when in paine for Leige
            To show his understanding,   10
            Goeing, brave Prince, to raise the Seige
            Was forced to run from Landen.

            Or if some millions more to gett
            In coming o're most certaine,
            Scap'd very near being overset   15
            And nearer much Dubarting.

> If then for all of these or one
> You now so hector or'e us
> Pray what the devill wou'd you've done
> Had he return'd victorious?   20
>
> If citties three and battailes twain,
> One fleet, you did so boast on't,
> If loss of these you reckon gaine,
> Mobb cn and make your most on't.

Commentary

Title: *quaeres*, 'questions' 'queries'. See *OED*, *quaere*, B, n., where the quotations do not include the plural form. The public thanksgiving of 1694 was one of a series of such events held annually (by royal proclamation) in the late autumn, to enable the public to celebrate the king's supposed success in arms during that year's campaign against France and to give thanks for his safe return from the continent. Hall's song, however, looks back to events in 1693, making it very likely that 1694 in the title is a mistake, especially as there is no mention of the failed attack on Brest in June 1694. (That fiasco is mocked in the next edited poem, 'So little being done and so much money spent', and here too B1's scribe gets the date in the title wrong, ascribing the event to 1592.) Cameron prints ll. 1–4 of 'Are all those lights' on his p. 401, commenting that 'Even Jacobites like Henry Hall could not [...] make much capital out of the latest campaign', which would indeed be the case if the poem dated from autumn 1694.

Another thanksgiving satire, 'Let old England rejoice', headed 'Ballad on the Thanksgiving Day so solemnly observ'd the 12th of April 1694', similarly mocks the king's supposed successes and again looks back to earlier events. In this case the matter is complicated by the dating to April, when there appears to have been no public thanksgiving.

3.   *your Turkey fleet*: the reference is to a convoy of English and Dutch merchant ships, with a naval escort, that set out for Smyrna (Ismir) in Turkey in late May 1693. It was intercepted by the French fleet, the resulting engagement leading to the loss of a large number of the merchantmen.

4.   *Charleroy*: a town in Belgium besieged and captured by the French in summer 1693.

5.   *Hidleburgh*, i.e. Heidelberg in Germany, virtually destroyed by the French in successive attacks in 1689 and 1693. 'Heydelbourgh', M.

6.   *near*: M, 'poor', seemingly repeated from l. 5.

7.   *Huy*: Huy, in Belgium, was repeatedly attacked during the Nine Years' War, but 'long agoe' suggests Hall may be referring to when it was besieged and taken by the French in 1675 during the Franco-Dutch War. *fate*: M, 'state'.

8.   *Pidemont*: probably a reference to the victorious French campaigns in Piedmont-Savoy in the summer of 1690.

9–12. William III was able to prevent the seizure of Liège in July 1693 by sending sizeable reinforcements, but his remaining forces were heavily outnumbered at the subsequent Battle of Landen, decisively won by the French.

13–14. William returned to England at the end of each campaigning season partly to raise more funds for the conduct of the war. *if*: omitted, M.

15. *scap'd*, emended with reference to M from B1's miswritten 'stap'd'. By *oversett* Hall may be referring to the considerable opposition to England's participation in the war as expressed in Parliament in Autumn 1693, if the poem is to be dated then.

16. *Dubarting*: apparently a playful allusion to the Flemish naval commander and privateer Jean Bart, or Dubart (1650–1702), who had great success as a French naval commander in the 1690s, frequently harassing shipping in the Channel. M has the same reading, which probably includes a pun on 'departing'.

18. *You*, i.e. those celebrating the Thanksgiving Day. *hector*, 'brag, bluster, domineer' (*OED, hector*, v.).

24. *Mobb on*, 'carry on crowding or thronging'. See *OED, mob*, v.², 2b, where the intransitive use of 'mob' is not recorded before 1711.

So little being done and so much money spent   *(48)*

Title in copy text: 'On the business of Brest in 1692. To the tune of Which nobody can deny'.

Summary: A song mocking the failure of the naval expedition to attack Brest in 1694.

Date: 1694.

Copy text: B1, pp. 8–9.

[*p. 8*]   So little being done and so much money spent
Was the cause wee resolv'd on this second descent
While Brest was the place, Sir, it seems that we meant,
        Which nobody can deny.

Now Brest you must know was a plaguy strong town,   5
But where there's more danger more honour is won,
So we wisely intended to make it our owne,
        Which nobody can deny.

But as we did always surprizing abhorr,
And least we should fright 'em approaching their shoar,   10
We gave them good notice on't two months before,
        Which nobody can deny.

From court straight went Vauban to view all the passes,
New engins invented and swinging carcasses,
Made double redoubts and of us agen asses,   15
        Which nobody can deny.

While we were embarking our horse and our foot,
Ball, powder, and mortars, and well-boats to boot,
And swoar if not this, surely nothing wou'd do't,
    Which nobody can deny.   20

[p. 9]   When a gale blew for Brest as if Neptune did guide it,
But first we all knew that they'd well fortify'd it,
For 'twoud have been base to've tane't unprovided,
    Which nobody can deny.

As soon as wee came within shott of the shoare,   25
Good Lord how their bulletts our vessells did bore,
And cutt all our rigging, for we came, Sir, therefore,
    Which nobody can deny.

When Talmarsh debarqued a thousand brave men,
But 'stead of poor one, had he landed with ten   30
The devill a man had return'd back agen,
    Which nobody can deny.

While our fleet at the castle at distance did fire,
For as it is say'd, we had been something nigher
But their sixty-six pounders soon made us retire,   35
    Which nobody can deny.

A Dutchman whose captain and crew were quite drunk,
Approaching too near was by one of 'em sunk,
Every man in his way, Sir, for down went Van Dunk,
    Which nobody can deny.   40

The admiralls seeing how thick their dead lay
Call'd a councell in which 'twas thought fitt to convey
Their living as fast as they cou'd to Torbay,
    Which nobody can deny.

So ended our famous adventure at Brest,   45
For what could we doe when with odds so opprest?
Thus what's meant in earnest of't proves but a jest,
    Which nobody can deny.

Commentary

Title: '1692' is clearly an error. The expedition to land troops at Camaret Bay, just south of Brest, was the biggest allied failure of the 1694 campaign against France, partly because the French knew what was planned and had time to make preparations. With much use of irony Hall's song covers these and other main features of the engagement, including the fate of the troops who made it to shore (though he fails to mention the fatal wounding of General Talmarsh), the sinking of one of the Dutch ships, and the English retreat.

2. *descent*: 'A sudden hostile invasion or attack, esp. from the sea, or from high ground' (*OED*, *descent*, n., 9a).

4. *Which nobody can deny*: a refrain used in many popular songs of the period, including also by Hall in 'No sooner our hero to Flanders was got', a song satirizing the authorities' failure to mount a successful prosecution against Jacobites in Lancashire and Cheshire.

5. *plaguy*, 'annoyingly' (*OED*, *plaguey*, 2).

7. *we*: not in the manuscript, but inserted here for grammatical reasons.

13. *Vauban*: the French military engineer Sebastien Leprestre de Vauban (1633–1707), famous particularly for the effectiveness of his fortifications. *passes*, strategically important points for defence or attack (*OED*, *pass*, n.^{1}, 4b).

14. *swinging*, probably, in context, *OED*, *swinge*, v.^{2}, to singe or scorch. *carcasses*, shells, with holes, filled with inflammable material (*OED*, *carcass*, n., 7).

15. *redoubts*, protruding strengthened fortifications (*OED*, *redoubt*, n.)

18. *well-boats*, flat-bottomed boats for landing troops and stores (*OED*, *well-boat*, n., 2, first recorded in 1690). *to*, written as 'too' by the scribe, here emended.

23. *unprovided*, 'not in a state of readiness' (*OED*, *unprovided*, adj.^{1}).

25. *shot*, i.e. the range of a cannon or other kind of shot (*OED*, *shot*, n.^{1}, 8).

27. *Sir*: conjectural. In abbreviating the word, B1's scribe has used a form different from either of the other two abbreviations of 'Sir' in the poem, so another word may be intended ('south', 'straight'?). The clause is in any case difficult, but Hall may mean 'because we came for this reason', with heavy irony.

29. *Talmarsh*: Thomas Talmarsh, the general in command of the troops who were to be put ashore near Brest. *debarqued*, 'disembarked', here used transitively (*OED*, *debark*, v.^{1}, a).

30. i.e. even if he'd landed not with (a poor) one thousand but with ten thousand.

31. *The devill a man had*, i.e. 'not a single man would have'. For the usage see 'Although to petition has been out of fashion', above, note to l. 13.

39. *Van Dunk*: a collective name for Dutchmen found also, in a similar context, in the immediately preceding song in B1, 'Attend to my verse you whose ears are as long' ('And when they were sunk, | Both sober and drunk, | Were food for the herring | As well as Vandunk', B1, p. 8).

Cities of adamant must yield   *(12)*

Title in copy text: 'On K — W — ms takeing of Namur, 1695'.
Summary: Reflections on the fate of Namur after its fall to William III's army after a siege.
Date: 1695.
Copy text: B1, p. 14

[*p. 14*]   Citties of adamant must yield
             When foes reign monarchs of the field,
             For odds in war like play will winn

> And valour sure had useless been
> 'Gainst mines without and bombs within.   5
> Unhappy builder of that town
> Whose walls are once a year beat down!
> And what must needs inhance their grief,
> Still from those walls to view releife.
> What worse can happen to the brave   10
> Than to be left and find a grave
> Even in their sights who came to save.

Commentary

3.   i.e. if the odds are stacked in one side's favour, that side will win, like in gambling.
7.   An exaggeration, but this was the second time in three years that Namur had been besieged and captured, the victors in 1692 having been the French.
9, 12. The allied forces eventually retook the citadel in early September 1695 after a full-scale bombardment, with French forces in entrenched positions further away.

With Job-like patience we've our burdens bore *(49)*

Title in copy text: 'Truth'.
Summary: Jacobite attack on William III and his conduct of affairs, especially the costs of the war with France.
Date: 1696?
Copy text: B1, pp. 36–37. Also in B2, ff. 12v-13v ('Truth'), M, pp. 101–02 ('Truth', but an earlier title, now largely unreadable, has been scribbled through).

[*p. 36*]   With Job-like patience wee've our burthens bore,
> And that they might be less we wish'd them more.
> Our pole and stripping taxes flow'd so fast
> We thought each tedious year had been the last.
> Never was senate yet so prone to give,   5
> Never was prince so ready to receive
> That in his seven years' reign has cost us more
> Than all the kings that ever reign'd before.
> Yet with this mighty dole what has he done
> But every year in Flanders lost a town?   10
> For what is all this bussle, all this stirr,
> But who shall last say Mass within Namur?
> He came to save your throats from Popish knives,
> Yet by his warr has widdow'd halfe your wives.
> Before Namure, there scatter'd lymbs are lay'd,   15
> At Landen, count the number of your dead,

Or all the wretched living, yet unpaid.
Tell me a virtue fills his Belgick breast
With which his father's was not more posest,
But ah! those faults that have the sire undone   20
Become most shining virtues in the sonn.
     One pious prince for granting toleration
Receiv'd a strange unheard-of abdication,
For which this has the eugies of the nation.
[*p. 37*] One prince in haste was hurrying on to Rome,   25
But t'other wisely brought Geneva home.
Calvin accouter'd now in lawn appears
And many a meager saint the sacred ephod wears.
Of such a faith's defender, such a head,
Our living Kenn shall speak and Sandcroft dead.   30
Nor does Albania less her loss deplore,
E're since he loos'd the Caladonian boare.
Up by the roots his tusks the vine do's tear,
And everything's more common than their prayer.
     Our shipps of warr to distant climates roame,   35
And naked leave their native shoars at home.
Did all the vessells we have lost this warr
Rang'd on the Channell in a line appear,
From shoar to shoar their bowsprits wou'd advance
And one might safely go on foot to France.   40
     Our Belgick friends their kindness to evince
Sent us some years agoe a mungrell prince
And every day his clipt vile image since,
In which if e're the soldeiry are paid,
That and their swords are of one mettle made.   45
Six millions more are to be rose 'tis say'd;
Yee sotts, you may as soon even raise the dead.
Beware of giveing still such large supplys
Least not the taxes but the people rise.

Commentary

'With Job-like patience' is a wide-ranging Jacobite attack on William III and his conduct of affairs, beginning with the multitude of taxes, the king's excessive expenditure on the war with France, and his lack of military success (ll. 1–21). Contrasting William with the exiled James II, Hall then laments the changes forced on the church in both England and Scotland (ll. 22–34). Next he deplores British naval failures, especially the loss of so many ships (ll. 35–40). Finally Hall turns to the debased nature of the coinage, and warns that any attempt to raise further millions of pounds may provoke a popular uprising (ll. 41–49). Paragraphing is editorial.

2. Cf. the proverb 'The greater grief (sorrow) drives out the less', G446 in Tilley, *A Dictionary of the Proverbs in England in the Sixteenth and Seventeenth Centuries*. *might*: B2, 'may'.

3. *pole*: M, 'sole'. William III's first poll tax, in 1689, was followed by several others between 1690 and 1698. By *stripping taxes* (i.e. taxes stripping people of money) Hall is likely to mean the taxes on births, deaths, and marriages, imposed in 1694, which he attacks explicitly in 'Our government thrifty to raise up their wages'.

7. *seven years reign*: William III was crowned king in April 1689, making it likely that Hall was writing in 1696. M reads 'nine' in place of seven, suggesting that that copy (or its immediate source) may have been made in 1698,

9. *this*: B2, 'our', M, 'his'. *mighty dole*: ironic, in that Hall regards the king's huge expenditure as benefiting no one.

12. *Mass*: the term presumably reflects Hall's crypto-Catholicism, as it would seem inappropriate after a Protestant capture of the town.

13. Hall now addresses his fellow-countrymen, deliberately sensationalizing the motive for William of Orange's invasion.

15. *Before*: M, 'Att'. B1's *there* is grammatically correct, given that the troops themselves have not yet been mentioned, but it is conceivable that Hall wrote 'their', as in M. Even though the capture of Namur in 1695 was a considerable success for the king, thousands of troops were lost in the assault.

16. *your*: B2, 'the'. The battle of Landen (or Neerwinden) in 1693 was an English defeat, with very heavy losses.

17. i.e. the surviving soldiers, not yet paid for their services.

19. *was*: B2, 'were'. The reference is to William II, Prince of Orange (1626–50), who married Mary Stuart, eldest daughter of Charles I.

20–21. In context Hall is probably referring to William II's extravagance and belligerence, which included an attempt to capture Amsterdam in 1650. Line 21 is thus heavily ironic. *most*: M, 'more'.

22. The reference is to James II's 1687 Declaration of Indulgence, granting toleration to various Christian denominations including Roman Catholics.

23. *abdication*: James II did not abdicate, but fled to France in December 1688.

24. *this*, i.e. the other prince, William III. *eugies*, see *OED*, *euge*, n., 'approval, commendation' (rarely attested; from the Latin *euge*).

25. A reference to James II's conversion to Catholicism.

26. By the end of 1691 sixteen of the twenty-six bishoprics were filled by supporters of the new regime, whose religious inclinations Hall (with an ironic 'wisely') here associates with Calvinism and its spiritual home, Geneva. Cameron, p. 311, prints ll. 25–28 as demonstrating effectively 'the resentment felt at the nature of the new regime's ecclesiastical preferments' (he quotes from B1 but does not name Hall).

27. *lawn*, the fine linen used for the sleeves of a bishop's robes, the usage pre-dating *OED*'s first citation (a1732, *lawn*, n.^{1}, 2).

28. *meager*, 'thin', 'lean', but here with the underlying sense of deficient, unworthy. *saint*, i.e. one of the Puritan elect, here applied derogatively. *sacred*: omitted

by M, possibly to restrict the line to the usual five stresses. *ephod*, properly a Jewish priestly vestment, but applied here to bishop's robes.

29. *faith's defender*, i.e. William III.

30. *Kenn*: Thomas Ken, 1637–1711, a prominent non-juror, Bishop of Bath and Wells until deprived of his see in 1691. By *shall speak* Hall possibly may have in mind Ken's letter to Archbishop Thomas Tenison criticizing the adulatory nature of the sermon he had preached in 1695 at Queen Mary's funeral, perhaps hoping that Ken would in time write against William III. *Sandcroft*: William Sancroft (1617–93), also a non-juror, Archbishop of Canterbury until deprived of his post in 1690. Later that same year he published *A Vindication of the Arch-Bishop and Several Other Bishops*.

31–34. Obscure, but the adjacency of *Albania* and the *Caladonian Boare* makes it likely that the former refers to Scotland (for the etymology, see the discussion at *OED*, *Albanian*, adj.¹ and n.³) and the latter to one of Hall's frequent targets, Gilbert Burnet (1643–1715), Scottish by birth, who was Bishop of Salisbury from May 1689. If so, the characterization of Burnet as the *Caladonian boare* (the term clearly derived from the Calydonian boar of Greek mythology) tearing up the 'vine' (probably the metaphor for the Church in John 15) possibly refers to the abolition of episcopacy in Scotland in July 1689, which would then be Albania's *loss*. But although Burnet had been advising William III on ecclesiastical affairs, it is not clear that he played a part in bringing about the abolition, though Hall may have believed he had.

32. *he*: M, 'she'.

34. *their*: M, 'our'. The line apparently alludes to the continuing controversy in Scotland regarding the Book of Common Prayer.

40. *might*: B2, 'may' (as also B1 before alteration by the later corrector), M, 'might'.

42. *mungrell*, i.e. mongrel, probably in the sense of someone born to parents of different nationalities (*OED*, *mongrel*, n. and adj., A.2).

43. Presumably, 'has since then been in circulation', because at this time the debased English coinage, rather than being imported, was being exported for melting down as bullion.

45. Hall's charge is apparently that the currency is debased so much that its metallic content is comparable to that used for making swords.

46. *rose*: B2, M, 'raised'.

47. *raise*: B2, M, 'rise' (as also B1 before the corrector's alteration). Cf. *OED*, *rise*, v., 2b, 'restore to life'.

Thus for his master fell the brave Montrose (12)

Title in copy text: 'Another'.
Summary: Fiercely Jacobite poem denouncing Parliament for enabling the execution of Sir John Fenwick.
Date: 1697.
Copy text: B1, p. 102.

[*p. 102*]   Thus for his master fell the brave Montross,
Nor do we, Fenwick, less lament thy loss,
The first that perish'd sure for want of proof;
'Tis fatal not t'have evidence enough.
The Co — ns quickly put it to the vote   5
And by a bold resolve they cut thy throat,
And least the Upper House shou'd do thee right,
Levi at last threw in his murthering mite.
The king, consenting to his enemies fall,
With Nero wish'd the neck contain'd them all,   10
Nor cou'd he think the crown sate firm enough
Upon his own, till thy bold head was off.

Commentary

Sir John Fenwick, an active Jacobite, was involved in the planned rising against William III that was to coincide with an invasion from France in early 1696. He was captured in June, but his trial was delayed in the hope that he would reveal information about members of the government that he had suggested were also involved in the plot. When one of the two witnesses needed to convict him of high treason absconded, the government had recourse to a Bill of Attainder as the only other legal method of securing his execution. After long and acrimonious debates, and with small majorities, the Bill passed the Commons and the Lords in November and December 1696 respectively, following which Fenwick was beheaded on 28 January 1697. 'Thus for his master fell the brave Montrose' is a companion piece to Hall's widely circulated 'Here lie the relics of a martyred knight', which, in nine lines (three triplets), concentrates on his execution and is more explicit about Fenwick's Jacobitism. It is printed in Cameron, pp. 483–84. In B1 it immediately precedes 'Thus for his master', hence the latter's title, 'Another'.

1.   *Montross*: James Graham, Marquis of Montrose (1612–50), who was executed after fighting for the royalist cause in Scotland during the Civil War.
3–4.   Not of course the case, but Hall's ironic point is that Fenwick was denied a trial because the authorities had insufficient evidence against him.
8.   *Levi*: derogatory term for a priest. Thomas Tenison, Archbishop of Canterbury, and Gilbert Burnet, Bishop of Salisbury, led the debate against Fenwick in the Lords, so it is likely that Hall is again targeting Burnet. See Ruth Paley, 'Justice and Sir John Fenwick', *King's Law Journal*, 19 (2015), 507–24 (p. 523).

10.   i.e. the king wished that cutting Fenwick's neck would simultaneously bring about the death of all his enemies. The remark 'I wish all of you Romans had only one neck' was originally said of the emperor Caligula by the biographer Suetonius, but was applied to Nero in James Harrington's *The Commonwealth of Oceana* (1656) and several other English works of the seventeenth century. See William B. Gwyn, 'Cruel Nero: The Concept of the Tyrant and the Image of Nero in Western Political Thought', *History of Political Thought*, 12 (1991), 421–55 (p. 439).

From a peace with new taxes and yet without trade   *(20)*

Title in copy text: 'Litany'.
Summary: Song lamenting the state of affairs in England, satirizing William III and Parliament.
Date: 1698.
Copy text: O1d, p. 33 (autograph). Also in O2, f.27v, and B1, p. 105 (both with the same title).

[*p. 33*]   From a peace with new taxes and yet without trade,
            For the good of Old England by a forreigner made,
            From building his house till his debts be first paid,
                Libera nos Domine.

            From an Act lately made that there ne're was the peer on't,   5
            To free us from danger when there was no fear on't,
            That hangs up poor mortalls before they can hear on't,
                Libera nos Domine.

            From a Senate that whilst they're with one hand a-giving,
            In the space of a creed are with t'other receiving,   10
            Whilst by the fine trade half the House get their living,
                Libera nos Domine.

            From times that are harder by much than the weather,
            From a Czar that's a-stroling the Lord knows yet whither
            And has with himself too his climate brought hither,   15
                Libera nos Domine.

            From generous clarett brought o're from the Rhine,
            From making a peace with a wicked design,
            Since wee're freinds with the French but at warrs with their wine,
                Libera nos Domine.   20

Commentary

Hall runs through a number of familiar grievances (new taxes, the king's extravagance, parliamentary corruption), with the addition of more light-hearted targets

(Peter the Great's visit to England and imported French wine). Satirical 'litanies' with verses beginning 'From' and ending 'Libera nos domine' [Deliver us, Lord] were a popular genre of the time.

1. *peace with new taxes*: the war with France was ended by the Treaty of Ryswick, finally signed in October 1697. The 'new taxes' are presumably the poll taxes levied in 1698 to pay off the debts and arrears built up by the armed forces.

2. *forreigner*, i.e. William III.

4. O1d and O2 render the well-known refrain simply as 'Libera', after the first verse, and then as 'Libera nos' at the end, but the full version found in B1 has been adopted here. Hall, in O1d, also fails to leave space between the third and fourth verses (see the frontispiece, above), a mistake corrected by O2's scribe.

5. *peer*: B1, 'pair'. The Act in question is presumably *An Act for Granting to His Majesty the Su[m]m [...]. for Disbanding Forces Paying Seamen and Other Uses Therein Menc[i]oned* (9 Will 3, c. 10), which came into force in April 1698 and set out in detail the levies to be paid.

6. The reference is probably to the king's speech to Parliament on 3 December 1697, arguing for the retention of a sizeable standing army for reasons of national security.

7. *hangs up*: presumably 'is burdensome to', as in *OED*, *hang*, v., 15, but *OED* does not record the phrase 'hang up' with this meaning.

11. *Whilst*: B1, 'For'. *the fine trade*: very likely a reference to the then flourishing export/import trade in silver bullion, to the detriment of the British economy; see David Ogg, *England in the Reign of James II and William III* (London: Oxford University Press, 1955), pp. 422–25. Cf. *OED*, *fine*, n.², 1.

14. *a-stroling*: B1, 'a-rambling'. Peter the Great, Tsar of Russia, visited England as part of his 1697–98 Grand Embassy to Europe. He was in the country from 11 January to 21 April. Hall satirizes his drinking habits in the song 'Dragoons have a care' and his supposed sexual prowess in 'That pleasant prince that strolling northern star'.

15. 1698 is well known for having had an exceptionally cold winter and spring, with snow continuing into May, hence Hall's comparison with Russia.

17–19 refer to the re-importation of French wines following the end of the war, clearly not to Hall's liking.

17. *generous*, 'rich', 'full-bodied' (*OED*, *generous*, adj. 5). *brought o're from the Rhine* seems out of place, and may be for the sake of the rhyme.

19. *Since*: B1, 'Whilst'.

Since we're undone the matter is not much *(12)*

Title in copy text: 'On the Lords throwing out Duncombs Bill'.
Summary: Primarily an attack on the House of Lords for having allowed the Bill against Sir John Fenwick but rejecting that against the financier Charles Duncombe.
Date: 1698.
Copy text: O1d, p. 29 (autograph). Also in O2, f.25v.

[*p. 29*]   Since we're undone the matter is not much
          Whether by Bent — g, Duncomb, or the Dutch.
          Whilst others from the Crown expect their pelf
          That prudent Member wisely paid himself.
          For spite you punish, not the nation's good,   5
          Since all of you'd bin Duncombs if you cou'd.
          But still in vain you teize the wealthy knave
          And damn a man the Lords resolve to save:
          When but to fine they can reject the Bill
          But quickly cotten when it is to kill.   10
          By int'rest now but then by passion led,
          This keeps his cash and Fenwick lost his head.

Commentary

Charles Duncombe (1648–1711) was a rich financier and Tory MP who early in 1698 admitted in Parliament to having profited from improper manipulation of £10,000 worth of Treasury bills. The Whig-dominated Commons proceeded against him with a Bill of Pains and Penalties, but this was rejected by the Lords. For full details of the episode and his career in general, see G. E. Aylmer, 'Duncombe, Sir Charles (bap. 1648, d. 1711), Financier', in *ODNB*. Hall, indifferent to Duncombe's own behaviour, castigates the Commons but mainly attacks the Lords: his point is that when only a financial penalty was at stake they chose not to act, in contrast to their approval of the Bill of Attainder against Sir John Fenwick that resulted in his execution (see 'Thus for his master fell the brave Montrose', above).

Text: unlike in 'From a peace with new taxes', which is also an autograph, Hall here makes changes while writing out the poem: in l. 4 he originally wrote 'Our' instead of *That*, and in l. 9, 'for a' and 'you' instead of *but to* and *they*. O2, as usual a careful copy of its source text, silently accepts these changes of mind.

2.   *Bent — g*: William Bentinck, Earl of Portland (1649–1709), Dutch by birth and a close friend of the king.
3.   *pelf*, 'money', no doubt in *OED*'s depreciative sense 3, '(esp. viewed as a corrupting influence)'.
7.   *teize*, i.e. tease, here probably in the stronger sense of 'irritate', 'vex' (*OED*, *tease*, v.[1], 2a).
10.   *cotten*, 'work harmoniously' (i.e. with the Commons); *OED*, *cotton*, v.[1], 5.

11. *int'rest*, probably the financial self-interest of the Lords, in contrast to the *passion*, i.e. strongly opposed feelings, that had led them to send Fenwick to his death.

An honest good farmer by providence blest *(22)*

Title in copy text: 'A fable'.
Summary: The tale of a farmer (representing a High Churchman) whose flocks were repeatedly attacked at night by wolves because his predecessor had filed out their guardians' teeth. In response he decides to build a higher fence, a decision considered by his neighbour (condemned by the farmer as 'a Low Rascall') to be unnecessary.
Date: 1704.
Copy text: O1e recto (autograph). Also in O2, f. 30r, and the *Diverting Post*, no. 7 (2–9 December 1704), pp. 1–2, both with B1's title but the latter beginning 'A good honest farmer by providence blest'.

[*O1e*^r] An honest good farmer by providence blest
Of a house, of some kine, and of sheep was possest.
To cott em himself was each ev'ning his care,
No flock was so thriving, no fleeces so fair.
Yet round him a herd of sly Isigrims prol'd,   5
Who oft in the night to his loss leapt the fold,
For tho their brave gaurdians seemd surly and stout
His sly predessessor had fil'd their teeth out;
Who wisely consid'ring if thus they went on
In process of time the whole flock wou'd be gone   10
Resolv'd with himself that as soon as he cou'd
He'd make his fence higher, let it cost what it wou'd.
Sais a neighbour that saw him his project pursue,
'What i'th name o' the Lord are you going to doe?
The fold I have known many a year by the Mass   15
And 'tis now just as high, Sir, as ever it was.
'Twill last you your life without any repair,
And what it shal want may be done by your heir,
Besides now for building is no proper season.'
Sais the farmer, 'How like a Low Rascall you reason   20
For if I my own self don't take care of the matter
I'm sure those will never that are to come after.'

Commentary

Text: as in 'Since we're undone', Hall's autograph text displays a number of corrections, notably *seemd* interlined above *look'd* (l. 7), *predessessor* immediately replacing a miswritten *predessour* (l 8), *year* immediately replacing a possibly miswritten *fair*

(l. 15), and *now* interlined above *still* (l. 16). The public version of the poem printed in the *Diverting Post* contains further differences, partly, it would seem, to aid understanding, and so some, at least, may be Hall's doing. These changes are as follows: 1 *honest good*, 'good honest'. 5 *a herd of sly Isigrims*, 'wolves lions and panthers too'. 6 *Who oft in the night to his loss*, 'and oft to his loss in the night'. 7 *their brave gaurdians*, 'its bold guardians'. 8 *fil'd*, 'knockt'. 9 *Who wisely*, 'The good man'. 10 *the*, 'his'. 16 *'tis now*, 'now 'tis'. 18 *what*, 'when'. 19 *now*, 'this'. 20 *Sais*, 'Quoth'.

3. *cott*, 'put in a sheepfold'. *OED*, *cot*, *v.*¹, 2, does not record this usage before 1804.

5. *Isigrims*, i.e. wolves. *OED*, *Isegrim*, n. (the name of the wolf in the medieval Reynard the Fox stories), does not record any instances later than 'a1640' and Hall, when revising his poem for publication (as it would seem), may have realised the word might not be understood and so made the change to 'wolves lions and panthers'. Dryden had used the form 'Isgrim' to refer to Presbyterians in his *The Hind and the Panther* (1687), and Hall may have copied the term from there (Part 1, l. 449).

9. *Who*, to make sense, must refer back to the farmer. The possible confusion may have led Hall to replace it with 'The good man' when the poem came to be published.

13–22. The opposing stances of the farmer and his neighbour, representing High Church and Low Church, reflect contemporary religious politics, and very likely date the poem to the period after the removal of High-Church Tories from the government in April 1704. To High Churchmen like Hall it appeared that Queen Anne was failing in her promise to defend the Church of England. Cf. the discussion in Chapter 8.1 of Hall's poem 'When Church was mother Ann was then her daughter'.

15. In context it is inappropriate for the neighbour to swear *by the Mass*, which is open to criticism as a lazy rhyme for l. 16's *was*.

18. *shal*: O2, 'doth'.

20. The capitals letters given to 'Low Rascall' have been retained, given that they are written boldly with a broad nib.

Once in a reign to increase our causeless fears *(19)*

Title in copy text: 'On the two monstrous fish lately taken at Greenwich'.
Summary: On how two whales landed at Greenwich cannot portend national afflictions, as England is already suffering from war, taxation, and Low Church dominance.
Date: 1705.
Copy text: O3 recto (autograph). Also in the *Diverting Post*, no. 23 (24–31 March 1705), p. 1, where the text differs by the inclusion of an extra couplet after l. 6, printed here within square brackets. For the published version's different title, see below.

[O3']   Once in a reign t'encrease our causeless fears
         A monster of the scaly kind appears,
         But prodigies on us away are thrown:
         What need a nation fear long since undone?
         Can they yet greater taxes e're portend,   5
         Or war which ne're but with the world will end?
         [Or to the Church do they betoken ill?
         E'er they appear'd the L — ds had damn'd the Bill.]
         Can the unhappy breach be made more wide?
         Low Church triumphant does already ride.   10
         If then for nought they needs must hither come
         The monsters might as well have staid at home.
         Now God preserve our mild and matchless queen,
         And guard his Church from Whigs and mod'rate men.
         God bless the loyall Commons when they sitt,   15
         God bless their L — ships too if he thinks fit,
         For if kind Heav'n wou'd once our jarrs unite
         Whole shoals of whales we'd gaze on with delight,
         Nor cou'd Leviathan himself affright.

Commentary

Title: in O3 Hall first wrote 'On the whale lately taken at Greenwich', but subsequently changed it to read as above. In the *Diverting Post* the title is given as 'On the two monsterous Fishes, lately taken at Gravesend'. As noted in Chapter 8.1 above, it may be that Hall received the news of the incident piecemeal, with resulting corrections. Stowe's *Survey of the Cities of London and Westminster* (1720) confirms 1705 as the date of the incident but places it at Blackwall, unless his 'brought and cut up at Blackwal' (Book IV, Chapter 2, p. 44) refers to a change of location from where the whales were first 'taken'.

Text: given that ll. 7–8, supplied from the *Diverting Post*, provide context and coherence to ll. 9–10, otherwise relatively obscure, it may be that Hall accidentally omitted them when copying the poem into O3. But the nature of O3's text, which contains several autograph changes in addition to the altered title, suggests that it may represent an early state of the poem, still being worked out. Significant changes are *ne're* written straight after an erased *never* in l. 6; an original *her* altered to *his* (as in the *Diverting Post*) in l. 14; and *our* (as in the *Diverting Post*) substituted for an original *their* in l. 17. If this is the case, Hall may have added ll. 7–8, for the sake of clarity, before submitting the poem for publication.

2.   *scaly*: Hall appears here to betray ignorance of the nature of whales' bodies.
6.   *war*: since 1702 Britain had again been at war with France (the War of the Spanish Succession).
7–10. Hall, as a High Churchman, elsewhere reveals his concern at the rise of Low Church tolerance and moderation in his epigram 'When Church was mother

Anne was then her daughter' and especially in the lengthy satire 'To give the last amendments to the bill', both to be dated to 1703 (see the discussions in Chapter 8). In question then was the (High Church) Bill designed to end the practice of occasional conformity with the Church of England, which failed to find support in the Lords; and Hall, writing now in 1705, is apparently referring back to the same occasion and declaring Low Church already 'triumphant' on that basis. As with the preceding questions, the answer to that posed in l. 7 is no: the Church as Hall would wish it has already been harmed.

13–16. Despite the earlier swipe at Low Church, the essentially buoyant, light-hearted nature of the poem is reflected in these lines asking God's blessing on the queen, the Commons, and the Lords, though no doubt still ironically in the latter two cases.

Love poems

Charming Sylvia if you knew (22)

Title in copy text: 'Song'.
Summary: Love song to a beautiful girl, urging present enjoyment.
Date: 1690s?
Copy text: B1, p. 29. Also in B2, f. 12r-v ('A song').

[*p. 29*]   Charming Sylvia, if you knew
              All the pains I feel for you,
              'Twou'd so much your tender move
              You'd pitty him you cou'd not love.
                    Pitty is a gift you know,   5
                    Wee on th'unhappy still bestow,
                    Then pitty him you've render'd soe.

              Think not those sweetest eyes were given
              Only to gaze, my fair, on Heaven,
              Or yet those luscious lips so red,   10
              To ask this day our daily bread.
                    Nature sure shou'd teach you this,
                    Eyes are to ogle, lips to kiss,
                    And both, to heighten future bliss.

              Never heed those common rules   15
              Given by age, obey'd by fools,
              But in the paths of pleasure move
              And take advise of youth and love.
                    Tho' bright your beauty, just your mein,
                    Yet always you'l not be fifteen.   20
                    And age, your sexes worst disease,
                    Will leave more mind, than power, to please.

Commentary

3.   *tender*, '(potential) tender feeling' (*OED*, *tender*, n.³, 2).
5.   *gift*: B2, 'greife'.
14. *heighten*: B2, 'lighten'.
16. *age*, i.e. older people.
19. *just*, 'aesthetically pleasing' (*OED*, *just*, adj., 1a). *mein*, i.e. mien, 'appearance'.
22. i.e. will result in physical pleasure becoming more of a theoretical than an actual possibility. *Will*: B2, 'Still'.

Phyllis in vain you drop that tear *(20)*

Title in copy text: 'Song'.
Summary: Love song, hoping that the grief of bereavement felt by a lady will soon give way to new desire for love.
Date: Mid-1690s?
Copy text: B1, p. 28. Also in the *Diverting Post*, no. 21 (March, 1705), p. 1 ('To Phillis mourning for the death of her husband').

[*p. 28*]   Phillis, in vain you drop that tear,
        In vain in broaken sighs you grieve.
    The dead, the one no more can hear
        Than t'other, Phillis, wee beleive.

    Yet since the wicked world has made   5
        Fashion in grief as well as dress,
    Enough of conscience you have paid,
        Enough I fancy too, you guess.

    Grief in those eyes but raise desire
        Whilst pitty does to passion turn.   10
    Spight of the floods, we feel the fire
        As bombs amidst the water burn.

    Of old, the fam'd Ephesian lass,
        Who sighing satt and mourn'd like you,
    Admitted of a warm embrace   15
        Where night and endless horror grew.

    Her lord once dead was soon forgott
        For with his life her love too fled.
    She wisely chose the luckier lott
        And for the quick forsook the dead.   20

Commentary

The altered text in the *Diverting Post* may possibly represent Hall's own revision, but B1 has been preferred here, partly for consistency of copy-text and partly because of the inferior nature of the printed text's first stanza, which removes both B1's subtlety and the abab rhyme scheme.

1.   *DP*, 'Phillis in vain those tears you shed'.
3–4. i.e. the fall of a tear and sighs are equally inaudible to the dead.
3.   *can hear*: *DP*, 'will move'.
4.   *wee beleive*: *DP*, 'us deceive'.
5.   *Yet*: *DP*, 'But'.
8.   *I fancy too, you guess*, i.e. I fancy that you too have guessed as much.
9.   *raise*: *DP*, 'whets'.
11.   *floods*, i.e. the lady's tears.
12.   The simile recalls the 'carcasses', i.e. shells with holes filled with inflammable

material, said to have been deployed by the French against the British in 'So little being done and so much money spent', l. 14 (edited above).

13–20. Hall again invokes the story of the Widow of Ephesus, here in standard fashion. Contrast the obscene use to which he puts the tale in 'Calling at Fountain's late last night', ll. 61–64 (addressed to Dr Broughton and edited above).

14. *DP*, 'That greatly greiv'd and wept like you'.

15–16. In Petronius's story the widow, watching beside her husband's corpse, eventually succumbs to the amorous advances of the soldier who has sought refuge in the underground tomb.

16. *DP*, 'The lovely corps she mourn'd in view'.

19. *luckier lott*, 'more favourable destiny' (or possibly 'prize').

<h2 style="text-align:center">'Twas in the temple first I saw (28)</h2>

Title in copy text: 'To Mrs Robins'.
Summary: Love poem to a beauty seen in church in Hereford (presumably the cathedral), who regularly distracts Hall whenever she appears.
Date: 1690s?
Copy text: B1, p. 91. Lines 1–4, 13–20 are also preserved in C, the Cooke manuscript ('Lines to Lesbia, Miss .... of Hereford').

[*p. 91*]   'Twas in the temple first I saw
        What I shall ne're enough admire,
    The nymph that keeps the beaus in awe
        And doubly gilds the gazing quire.

    Exalted like a deity   5
        She shone above the humble crowd,
    And while she to the altar, I
        To Lesbia just as lowly bowd.

    Careless as cupids laid to rest
        Yet still with due reservrie clad,   10
    She's all the vertues of the best
        Joyn'd with the beauties of the bad.

    Is Lesbia not at church today?
        The organ's dull, the musick's flat,
    The prayers goe down too like chopt hay,   15
        Nor can I tast Magnificat.

    Who preaches next is not my care
        Or if they yerk or loll at ease;
    Provided I but see my fair
        Wilcox or duller Price will please.   20

With her in desarts cou'd I dwell,
   With salvages my fortune take;
For her at home I could rebell
   And with the world my Prince forsake.

Her to behold is all my bliss,   25
   Such mighty power to Lesbia's giv'n.
Kings make their court, and where she is
   For ever will to me be Heav'n.

Commentary

4.   Presumably, sheds a (figuratively) golden light over the cathedral choir, i.e. the chancel, doubling its beauty, but *gazing* expands the reference to include the watching members of the choir.

8.   *Lesbia*: as with Sylvia and Cynthia elsewhere, a conventional name for an attractive young woman.

10.   *reservrie*, 'reserve', in the sense of propriety. Not in *OED* and quite possibly created by Hall for metrical reasons.

13.   *church*: C. B1 reads 'quire', but seeing that Lesbia is a member of the congregation and would therefore sit in the nave, C's reading has been preferred.

15.   *like chopt hay*: a proverbial phrase for something that goes down smoothly, in this case presumably 'without having any effect'. Cf. John Ray, *A Collection of English Proverbs*, 2nd edn (London: John Hayes, 1678), p. 235: 'It goes down like chop't hay', though there without definition.

16.   *tast*, 'appreciate', 'take pleasure in' (*OED*, *taste*, v., 8).

18.   *yerk* (C), 'jerk', probably with reference to jerky physical movement (i.e. in the pulpit, contrasting with *loll at ease*), for which see *OED*, *yark*, v.^{2}, 6b (= *jerk*, v.^{1}, 3). B1 has the more usual 'jerk', but the later annotator has a marginal note 'In orig. it seems to be <u>yerk</u>', a reading attested by C, and *yerk* has therefore been preferred here.

20.   Here again there is both a marginal comment by B1's later annotator ('Tom Broad & Page stood originally in this poem but were afterwards eraz'd', implicitly by Hall) and a corresponding reading in C ('Provided I see Lesbia there | Tom Broade may in the pulpit please') — intriguing evidence of Hall's propensity to revise his poems after their first circulation, and so not a reason for emendation. For Tom Broad, a fellow Vicar Choral, see 'Ye gods what gulfs are set between', above, l. 14. John Page, who became a prebendary of Hereford Cathedral in 1692, is attacked by Hall in 'The sly designing patriot in convention' as the recipient of undeserved promotion. As for *Wilcox or duller Price*, the latter is probably the John Price of Hereford who was ordained deacon in 1695 and priest in 1697 (*CCED*). Wilcox has not been traced.

22.   *salvages*, 'savages' (an acceptable contemporary spelling).

24.   *my Prince*, i.e. the exiled James II.

APPENDIX A

❖

Checklist of Poems and Songs Attributable to Henry Hall

The checklist is arranged alphabetically by first line, using modernized spelling based on the first-cited source. The concluding line is given immediately afterwards, within parentheses. Then follow the number of lines, the verse form (where 'couplets' does not exclude the presence of triplets), a brief indication of content, the likely date of composition, and page references to mention or discussion of the item within the body of the book. In this case '(text)' indicates places where the full text of an item is quoted, while '(edited text)' signals that an item is included in the ⊕ selected edition of Hall's poems and songs.

Page references are then given for occurrences of items within the Brotherton Collection and Ottley manuscripts (cited by the abbreviations used throughout this study), to enable their quick location in the contents lists provided in Appendix B, where their titles in these manuscripts are also given. Page references for occurrences in other manuscripts and in printed books are held over until Appendices C and D, to reduce the amount of detail in the present list. As throughout, occurrences of Hall poems in printed books are not cited beyond 1721.

Shelfmarks of items in the British Library and the Bodleian Library are preceded by BL and Bod, respectively. The National Library of Scotland and Trinity College Dublin Library are cited as NLS and TCD. To save space, the following collections are not preceded by the names of their holding libraries: Brotherton [Leeds UL], Portland [Nottingham UL], Osborn [Yale UL]. The presence of Brotherton in such cases denotes a Brotherton Collection manuscript other than B1 and B2. British and Irish repositories are listed before American ones. University of Minnesota MS 690235f, often cited as M earlier in this study, appears here as Minnesota. Occurrences of items in the nineteenth-century Cooke manuscript (not included in the manuscript count) are noted at the end of the citation list, as 'plus C'. *POAS*, as usual, denotes the original *Poems on Affairs of State*.

A mighty voice rolled down the flood
(And Guil. out of his garden)
16 ll., 4 stanzas, abab. Satire on Gilbert Burnet, Bishop of Salisbury, accusing him
    of lack of reverence before God. 1690s?
1 ms: B1 p. 15.

A most ungodly work you now begin
(My thin-spun thread of life I'm sure but's short)
16 ll., couplets. Playful love poem addressed to a lady mending a dressing gown.
    1700s? See p. 47.
1 ms: Worcestershire Archive and Archaeology Service, Lechmere Archives 40 (i).

A public good does public thanks require
(And string again my long neglected lute)
66 ll., couplets. In praise of the musical skill of the composer John Blow. 1700. See
    pp. 5, 53, 111.
Printed in Blow, *Amphion Anglicus* (1700).

Accept my Lord this humble glittering thing
(When the Archduke's a King then you Archduke shall be)
6 ll., couplets. Satire on the ambitions and lack of real military prowess of Archduke
    Charles of Austria and the Duke of Marlborough. 1703. See pp. 27, 47, 50,
    94–95, 99 n. 10.
12 mss: O3b, BL Add 40060, Add 72479, Harley 6914, Bod Smith 23, pr. bk.
    Firth b.21, Brotherton Lt 81, Portland Pw V 43, Worcestershire Archive and
    Archaeology Service Lechmere Archives 40 (i), Harvard UL Eng 834, Osborn
    b.201 (twice), Osborn c.111.
Printed in *POAS*, IV (1707).

All in the land of cider
(Himself a bed to lie on)
40 ll., 10 stanzas, abcb (or 50 ll. abccb, depending on layout). Bawdy ballad satirizing
    Sir Edward Harley's attempt to suppress a sexual scandal at Brampton Bryan.
    1690s? See pp. 45, 47, 67, 107.
3 mss: B1 pp. 96–97, Bod Eng. poet. e.87, Hertfordshire Archives and Local Studies
    D/EP F35 (= Sarah Cowper's diary; an abridged text).
Printed without music in *Political Merriment, or Truths Told to Some Tune* (1714), in *A
    New Collection of Miscellany Poems* (1715), and in *The Grove* (1721); with music
    in *The Merry Musician; or, A Cure for the Spleen* (1716).

All own the young Sylvia is fatally fair
(By a Je ne say Je ne say quoy)
16 ll., 2 stanzas, ababcdcd. Love song on Sylvia's irresistible charms. 1694? See p. 51.
Printed in the *Gentleman's Journal*, May 1694, in *Wit and Eloquence* (1697), and in
    Wit and Mirth, VI (1720).

All the follies of love we'll drown in full glasses
(For business and love we no longer have leisure)
10 ll., 1 stanza, aabbccc, with chorus, aaa, each including refrain. Drinking song,
    banishing all thought of love in favour of drink. 1680s-90s. See p. 67.
1 ms: BL Add 33234 (with music).

All you who delight and take pleasure in painting
(Since so basely he left both his God and his lord)
95 ll., couplets. Satirical description of paintings of various establishment figures in
    Hereford, including the mayor, a physician, an apothecary, and a squire. 1690s?
    See p. 15 nn. 48 & 50, and p. 75.
1 ms: B1 pp. 20–23.

Although for every different dress
(The crepe's thrown always off at night)
24 ll., couplets. Love poem, on how wearing black enhances a young woman's
    beauty. 1694? See pp. 51–52, 59 n. 8.
1 ms: B1 p. 30.
Printed in the *Gentleman's Journal,* March 1694 (omitting ll. 1–3).

Although to petition has been out of fashion
(Your petitioners in duty henceforward will pray Sir)
27 ll., couplets. Light-hearted request to Edmund Addis, a fellow-Jacobite, for a
    quantity of cider with which to drink James II's health. Mid-1690s? See pp. 15
    n. 46, 111, 115, 126, 143–45 (edited text).
1 ms: B1 pp. 94–95.

An honest good farmer by providence blest
(I'm sure those will never that are to come after)
22 ll., couplets. Political fable, in which a High Church farmer is determined to
    secure his sheepfold against Low Church wolves. 1704. See pp. 26, 57, 93–94,
    98, 101 n. 20, 116, 164–65 (edited text).
2 mss: O1e, O2 f. 30r.
Printed in the *Diverting Post,* no. 7, December 1704, beginning 'A good honest farmer'.

And art thou faith a true recluse become
(Yet had been damned but that he would not swear)
34 ll., couplets. Conversational epistle to Dr Broughton, taking issue with the
    latter's scruples about swearing the Oath of Allegiance to William III and
    Mary II. Very likely 1689. See pp. 29, 118–20 (edited text).
1 ms: B1 pp. 85–86.

Are all those lights that gild the street
(Mob on and make your most on't)
24 ll., 6 stanzas, abab. Jacobite satirical song on William III's lack of success in the
    war against France, at a time of public celebration at his return home. Very
    likely 1693. See pp. 41, 73, 78, 92 n. 49, 127–28, 151–53 (edited text).
2 mss: B1 p. 10, Minnesota.
Modern printing: Cameron, p. 401 (ll. 1–4 only, from B1).

As in a pump we water put
(Whilst letters oft too long remain)
50 ll., couplets. Conversational epistle asking his friend Dr Broughton to send a
    copy of a poem of Hall's, of which he himself no longer has a copy. Probably
    1694. See pp. 15 n. 50, 23, 28, 119, 129–31 (edited text).
3 mss: B1 pp. 70–71, O1d pp. 15–16, O2 f. 19r-v.

As man in Westminster to each that comes
(Their Lordships only and the Lord does know)
32 ll., couplets. Light-hearted anti-Whig satire, naming prominent party members.
    1706. See pp. 56, 99.
1 ms: Bod Hearne's Diaries 9.
Printed in the *Diverting Post*, n.s. no. 1, February 1706.
Modern printing: *Remarks and Collections of Thomas Hearne*, ed. by Doble and others,
    I, 205.

As Phoebus did with heat pursue
(Who hast resisted mine)
10 ll., 2 stanzas, abaab. An explanation, with reference to the legend of Apollo and
    Daphnis, of why the laurel tree is never struck by thunder and lightning. 1695?
    See pp. 51, 64.
1 ms: B1 p. 48.
Printed in the *Gentleman's Journal*, July 1694, and, with music, in *Deliciae Musicae*
    [...] *The Second Book* (1695).

As sharper when his coin grows low
(Be sure you sing Te Deum)
12 ll., 3 stanzas, abab. Song satirizing Louis XIV, defeated in war, behaving as
    though he had won. 1697? See pp. 65, 67, 89 n. 1.
2 mss: B1 p. 106, York Minster Library M.12 S (with music).
Printed in the *Monthly Mask of Vocal Music*, October 1706, and as an undated single-
    sheet song (BL, G.316.m.(18)), both with music.

Attend to my verse you whose ears are as long
(A Dutchman that's drowned for William or Mary)
110 ll., 11 stanzas, ababccdcee (varied refrain). Detailed satirical song about the
    Battle of the Boyne, in particular the actions of William III's forces. 1690? See
    pp. 73, 78, 85, 155.
2 mss: B1 pp. 5–8, B2 ff. 1r-2v, 6r.

Bless Albion bless thy stars above
(Come to offer and obey)
45 ll., irregular ode. In praise of Queen Anne on her accession to the throne,
    celebrating allied success in Europe and her giving birth to another son. 1702.
    See pp. 11, 61–62, 99.
1 ms: Christ Church Oxford Mus. 1212(A) / 1141a / 1142a (with music).

Bright justice is a thing divine
(Or than unjust undone)

8 ll., 1 stanza, ababcdcd. In defence of justice, in answer to an extract from a song from Katherine Philips's play, *Pompey* (here headed 'If justice be a thing divine'), reworking her lines. 1690s? See pp. 33–34.

2 mss: B1 p. 50, B2 f. 15v.

Modern printing: Hageman and Sununu, 'New Manuscript Texts of Katherine Philips', p. 209, from B2.

Calling at Fountain's late last night
(Thanks to the rich is always payment)

86 ll., Couplets. Conversational appeal to Dr Broughton, partly bawdy, for a coat to be sent to a poor man named Fountain. Probably 1689 or 1690. See pp. 21, 30 n. 23, 120–24 (edited text), 126, 145, 170.

1 ms: B1 pp. 66–68.

Cease Amintor to pursue me
(Till you are in the matrimonial gin)

16 ll., 2 stanzas, ababccb. Song in answer to 'Come my Sylvia now discover' (q.v.), requiring marriage first. 1690s?

1 ms: B1 p. 33.

Cease hypocrites to trouble Heaven
(You'd sacrifice his son)

6 ll., 1 stanza, aabccb. Attack on those who would commemorate the anniversary of Charles I's death for wanting also to kill James II. 1692. See pp. 35, 41, 73, 78–79 (text), 80–81.

2 mss: B1 p. 15, Minnesota, plus C, p. [7].

Charming fair Amoret that dear undoer
(Lost in the mighty joy yet still desiring)

12 ll., 2 stanzas, aabbcc. Love song, expressing constant devotion to a disdainful beloved. 1699? See pp. 63–65.

1 ms: B1 p. 109.

Printed in *Mercurius Musicus*, January 1699, and in the bespoke *A Collection of the Choicest Songs and Dialogues* (1703), both with music.

Charming Sylvia if you knew
(Will leave more mind than power to please)

22 ll., 3 stanzas, aabbccc (twice), aabbccdd. Love song, urging present enjoyment. 1690s? See pp. 68, 168 (edited text).

2 mss: B1 p. 29, B2 f. 12r-v.

Cities of adamant must yield
(Even in their sights who came to save)

12 ll., couplets. Reflections on the fate of Namur after its fall to William III's army after a siege. 1695. See pp. 73, 76, 155–56 (edited text).

1 ms: B1 p. 14.

Come all ye high churchmen come all and rejoice

(And if you han't faith to believe it you're asses)

6 ll., couplets. Song celebrating cross-party support for the Church of England. 1705? See pp. 66–67.

1 ms: York Minster Library M.12 S (with music).

Printed in *The Second Book of the Pleasant Musical Companion*, 5th edn (1707), and *The Pleasant Musical Companion*, 6th edn (1720), both with music.

Come beaus virtuosos rich heirs and musicians

(That your heirs will do just so an hundred years hence-a)

42 ll., 7 stanzas, ababcc. Light-hearted satire on the Catholic Church's Jubilee in the year 1700, and the fashionable society flocking to Rome to see it. 1700. See pp. 16 n. 65, 38 n. 7, 65.

1 ms: B1 pp. 110–11.

Printed in *Wit and Mirth* IV (1706), and *Songs Compleat, Pleasant and Divertive*, V (1719), both with music; and in *Oxford and Cambridge Miscellany Poems* ([1708]), and *A Miscellaneous Collection of Poems* (1721), without music. Advertised in the *Post Boy*, 5 November 1700, as separately published, but this printing not traced.

Come my Sylvia now discover

(And leave the world and mortal cares behind)

16 ll., 2 stanzas, ababcccb. Love song, urging present enjoyment, followed by an answer ('Cease Amintor to pursue me', q.v.). 1690s? See p. 68.

1 ms: B1 p. 32.

Come take of your liquor fill fill it about

(With resounding huzzahs we'll add to the wind)

12 ll., couplets. Drinking song, toasting 'the new king' of Spain. 1704? See pp. 65–66, 68.

Printed in the *Monthly Mask of Vocal Music*, March 1704, in *The Jovial Companions* ([1709]), and as an undated single-sheet song (Chetham's Library Manchester no. 1900, Hereford Public Library Pilley Collection 2314), all with music.

Coming from place where you have seen

(And for a basting sing Te Deum)

33 ll., couplets. Satire addressed to Dr Broughton on the practice of organizing public celebrations despite William III's lack of success in the war against France. Probably 1693–94. See pp. 30 n. 23, 126–28 (edited text).

1 ms: B1 p. 26.

Deep in the earth and hid from human eyes

(And soothe his slumbers into endless sleep)

18 ll., couplets. Description of the god of sleep's imagined dwelling. 1690s?

1 ms: B1 p. 109.

Dragoons have a care

(And the cordial I wot on within Sir)

18 ll., 3 stanzas, aabccb. Satirical song toasting Peter the Great, Tsar of Russia, satirizing especially his drinking habits. 1698. See pp. 30 n. 34, 55, 66–67, 89 n. 1, 162.

3 mss: B1 p. 107, O1d p. 31, O2 f. 27r.

Printed in *The Second Book of the Pleasant Musical Companion*, 5th edn (1707), in *The Pleasant Musical Companion*, 6th edn (1720), and as a single-sheet song (Bod Harding Mus. G.170 (11)), all with music. Printed also, without music, in *A New Academy of Complements* (1715).

Dunned by the bells I rose from bed

(By force of Noverint universi)

52 ll., couplets. Epistle to a noble creditor, Lord Chandos, describing the writer's gambling and loose living, and acknowledging his debt to Chandos. 1690s? See pp. 2, 9, 36–37, 41, 68, 104–05, 117, 139, 140–43 (edited text), 148.

2 mss: B1 pp. 34–35, Minnesota, plus C, Memoir of Barnabas Alderson (an 11-line extract).

Enchanted by your voice and face

(Whene'er they please can raise the dead)

8 ll., 2 stanzas, abab. Love song. 1690s. See pp. 63–64.

1 ms: BL Add 31453, with music.

Printed in *Thesaurus Musicus* [...] *The Second Book* (London, 1694), with music, and in *Oxford and Cambridge Miscellany Poems* ([1708]), without music.

First then we must confess Florella fair

(Left off by all and e'en below lampoon)

42 ll., couplets and triplets. Satire on the pretensions to beauty of thirteen ladies, each target identified in a marginal note. 1706. See p. 47.

2 mss: Portland Pw V 249 and Pw V 856.

For missing thee how canst thou Burren blame

(For to be like thee would not be like Tom Broad)

8 ll., couplets. On the changeable nature of Tom Broad, Vicar Choral of Hereford, making it unfair of him to blame an artist, Burren, for not having captured his likeness. 1690s? See pp. 9, 25–26, 36, 42, 112, 146.

4 mss: B1 p. 31, O1a, O2 f. 6r, Minnesota, plus C, Memoir of Thomas Broad, beginning 'For missing thee, the painter wilt thou blame'.

From a due dose of claret no mortal shall shrink

(And sure there's no harm to be warm and grow wise)

9 ll., aabbc (verse), ddd (chorus). Drinking song. 1688? See p. 63.

Printed in *Comes Amoris* [...] *The Second Book* (1688), with music, and in *The Theatre of Compliments* (1689), without music.

From a peace with new taxes and yet without trade
(Libera nos [domine])
20 ll., 5 stanzas, aaab (including refrain). Song lamenting the state of affairs in
England, satirizing William III and Parliament. 1698. See pp. iv, 68, 73, 78,
161–62 (edited text), 163.
3 mss: B1 p. 105, O1d p. 33, O2 f. 27v.

From college hall where thirsty vicar
(I get in rhyme I lose in friend)
30 ll., couplets. Conversational autobiographical epistle addressed to Dr Broughton
and Captain Jones, arranging a meeting at an inn. Probably 1689 or 1690. See
pp. 9, 20–21, 125–26 (edited text), 139.
3 mss: B1 p. 105, O1d p. 33, O2 f. 27v.

From place where long to lie does tire one
(Who's muchly yours in prose and rhyme)
20 ll., couplets. Witty epistle to his physician friend Dr Broughton, appealing for an
emergency supply of the steel pills that Broughton has prescribed. 1690s. See
pp. 21, 30 n. 15, 132–33 (edited text), 138.
3 mss: B1 p. 83, O1d p. 21, O2 ff. 21v–22r (both beginning 'In place').

From the bright mansions of the blest above
(Just as he sang below now sings above)
30 ll., couplets (irregular). Song in praise of music, St Cecilia, and the genius of
Henry Purcell, followed by a 'Grand Chorus' repeating the final eight lines.
1704. See pp. 53, 56, 107 n. 1.
Printed in the *Diverting Post* no. 3, November 1704.

Good people what will you of all be bereft
(Why should we why should we be left in the dark)
30 ll. (varies with layout), 3 stanzas, aabbccdeed. Song attacking the new coinage
and the multitude of taxes brought in as a result of the wars with France. 1696.
See pp. 42, 68, 73–75, 84–85, 87–88, 99.
14 mss: B1 pp. 95–96, BL Add 29497, Add 69968, Lansdowne 852, Stowe 305, Bod
Rawlinson D.361, Rawlinson D.383, CUL Addit 7112, NLS 2092, Minnesota,
Princeton UL RTC01 no. 38, Osborn fb.207/3, Poetry Box VII/5, Poetry Box
XIII/80.
Printed in *POAS*, II (1703), in Edward Ward, *Miscellaneous Writings in Verse and
Prose*, 2nd edn, III (1712) and in *The Remains of Mr Thomas Brown, Serious and
Comical, in Prose and Verse* (1720).
Modern printing: Cameron, pp. 498–500, from the 1720 printing.

Great William concerned to leave his gulled loobies
(He swore the next year he'd make them a dozen)
16 ll. (varies with lay-out), irregular couplets. Satire on the nine members of the
Council appointed by William III during his absence in 1697. See pp. 41,
73–74, 84, 87–88, 91 n. 44, 92 n. 47.

11 mss: B1 p. 103, BL Add 21094, Harley 7315, Lansdowne 852, Sloane 1731A, Bod Eng. poet. e.50, Rawlinson poet. 181, Holkham Hall 686, Brotherton Lt q 38, Portland Pw V 48, Minnesota.

Modern printing: Cameron, pp. 517–19, from Sloane 1731A.

Greece had a Homer; Rome a Virgil lost

(Must to their father ocean backward go)

106 ll., couplets. Effusive elegy in praise of the poetry of John Dryden, following his death. 1700. See p. 55.

Printed in *Luctus Britannici* (1700).

Hail happy William thou art strangely great

(Must serve their masters though they damn their souls)

26 ll. (varies), couplets. Satirical panegyric on William III, accusing him of bringing oppression and poverty to England and her people. 1696 or 1697. See pp. 41, 73–74, 84, 86–88, 91 n. 44, 99.

18 mss: B2 f. 8v, BL Add 21094, Add 29497, Add 72479 (three copies), Sloane 1731A, Stowe 305, Bod Hearne's Diaries 11, Rawlinson D.361, Rawlinson poet. 81, Rawlinson poet. 169, Holkham Hall 686, Brotherton Lt 79, Lt q 11, Lt q 40, Huntington Library EL 8911, Minnesota, Princeton UL RTCo1 no. 38, Osborn fb.207/3.

Printed in *POAS*, II (1703), and *Miscellaneous Works Written by His Grace George Late Duke of Buckingham,* I (1704).

Modern printing: Cameron, pp. 456–57, from the 1703 printing. Lines 1–8 also in Monod, *Jacobitism and the English People,* p. 56, from Cameron.

Hark to the war the trumpet sounds

(And with impatience seeks the Seine)

8 ll., couplets. Song celebrating the Duke of Marlborough's preparations for a new military campaign, following the previous year's victory at Blenheim. 1705. See pp. 16 n. 62, 58, 69, 99.

Printed in the *Diverting Post*, no. 23, March 1705.

Haste Charon haste 'tis Nol commands thy speed

(Proud tyrants on earth shall be slaves here below)

55 ll., irregular. Royalist song, condemning Cromwell to hell and glorifying Charles I. 1685. See pp. 8, 18, 52, 61–63, 65, 67, 105.

9 mss, all except the first with music: BL Add 21544, Add 33234, Christ Church Oxford Mus. 49, Mus. 389, Fitzwilliam Museum Mu. 120, York Minster Library M.12 S (chorus only), Folger V.b.197, UCLA William Andrews Clark Memorial Library fo235M4, Univ Chicago 446.

Printed with music in *The Theater of Music* [...] *The Second Book* (1685); without music in *Deliciae Poeticae* (1706), in *Miscellaneous Works of the Right Honourable the Late Earls of Rochester and Roscommon,* II (1707), and in *A True and Faithful Narrative of Oliver Cromwell's Compact with the Devil for Seven Years* (1720).

Here have I lain Lord knows how many years
(He'll kindle greater flames than you care e'er put out)
65 ll., couplets. Humorous dialogue put into the mouths of a fire-engine and
a street-lamp, presented to the town respectively by Paul Foley and James
Morgan, Members of Parliament for Hereford, 1689–99 and 1695–98. 1695–
98? See pp. 15 n. 45, 40.
1 ms: B1 pp. 23–25.

Here lie the relics of a martyred knight
(So to cut Holland's head from England's shoulders)
9 ll., triplets. Outspoken Jacobite lament for the death by execution of Sir John
Fenwick, 28 January 1697. See pp. 41, 73–74, 84–85 (text), 87–88, 99, 160.
14 mss: B1 p. 101, B2 f. 14v, BL Add 28253, Add 47608, Add 70454, Add 72479, Bod
Rawlinson C.986, Brotherton Lt 79, Lt q 40, Portland Pw V 171, Minnesota,
Princeton UL RTC01 no. 38, Osborn c.171, fb.207/1.
Printed in *POAS*, II (1703).
Modern printing: Cameron, pp. 483–84, from the 1703 printing.

Here lies our sovereign Lady Moll
(Well may the nation put on mourning)
15 ll., triplets. Disparaging Jacobite mock epitaph on Mary II. 1694–95. See pp. 73,
76.
1 ms: B1 p. 103.

Here's a health whilst the trumpets and hautboys all cease
(Not only old claret but back us our king)
6 ll., couplets. A mock Jacobite health or drinking song to the Margrave of Baden-
Baden for advocating peace during the French wars. 1690s. See pp. 68, 89 n. 1.
1 ms: B1 p. 100.

How durst thou thus disturb that surly shade
(There's nothing got by arguing with a ghost)
92 ll., couplets. Argument, in dialogue form, between the ghost of Colonel
John Birch and Gilbert Ironside, Bishop of Hereford, who had defaced his
monument. 1690s. See pp. 15 n. 52, 143.
1 ms: B1 pp. 60–62.

How happy is this day
(Yet all the whole world but one Chandos can show)
34 ll., 2 stanzas, ababcdcdee, with repeated chorus, aabbccc. Drinking song at a
meeting of a club, on the occasion of a feast in honour of Lord Chandos shortly
before Britain's entry into the War of the Spanish Succession. 1701? See pp. 15
n. 35, 31 n. 38, 68.
1 ms: O2 f. 7v.

How happy's the mortal that lives by his mill
(And all the while the health does so the mill goes round)
25 ll., 5 stanzas, aabbb (refrain). Bawdy Jacobite drinking song about a miller loyal
    to James II. 1690s. See p. 64.
1 ms: B1 p. 41.
Printed (three stanzas only, in all cases) in *Wit and Mirth* (1699), *Songs Compleat,*
    Pleasant and Divertive, III (1719), and as an undated single-sheet song (two
    different engravings) in Bod Harding Mus. G.234 (8) and BL Music H.1601
    (214), all with music; and without music in *A New Academy of Complements*
    (1715).

I love to madness rave t'enjoy
(For that dear hour I'd give tomorrow)
16 ll., 2 stanzas, ababcdcd. Love song, declaring readiness to give up everything for
    one hour with Celia. 1694? See 51, 59 n. 7.
Printed in the *Gentleman's Journal*, June 1694, *Wit and Eloquence* (1697), and *Wit and*
    Mirth, VI (1720).

I never did eat yet I'm still at a feast
(Too much of the enig be bestowed on the poet)
12 ll., couplets. An enigma, or riddle, on the subject of laughter. 1694? See p. 51.
Printed in the *Gentleman's Journal*, May 1694.

If Reverend Sir
(She did the trick for pleasure thou for gain)
7 ll., 1 line, then couplets. Satirical comment on the acceptance by a Mr Lewis of an
    ecclesiastical appointment in Hereford Cathedral. 1692? See p. 15 n. 51.
1 ms: B1 p. 78.

If rhyme for rhino could atone
(And in the main an honest fellow)
32 ll., couplets. Light-hearted epistle to a creditor, Robin Clayton, wishing that
    verse could be a substitute for money. Probably 1701–02. See pp. 10, 107, 110,
    116, 144, 147–48 (edited text).
1 ms: B1 p. 112 (lacking four lines).
Printed in *The Grove* (1721), from where it was reprinted in Hawkins, *A General*
    History of the Science and Practice of Music, V, 21–22.

In place where men of wealth and wit
(Than one pastoral letter)
40 ll., 10 stanzas, abab. Satire on the decision of the House of Commons, in January
    1693, to burn the pastoral letter issued in 1689 by Gilbert Burnet, Bishop of
    Salisbury, in which he argued in favour of owing allegiance to William III and
    Mary II. 1693. See pp. 73, 77.
1 ms: B1 pp. 12–13.

In vain I strive my flame to hide
(Forbids us all that's dear)
16 ll., 2 stanzas, ababcdcc. Love song, in the form of a dialogue between a man and
   a woman. 1691? See pp. 64–65.
Printed, with music, in *Vinculum Societatis* (1691) (first stanza only), in copies of the
   bespoke *A Collection of the Choicest Songs and Dialogues* (1703), and as an undated
   single-sheet song (BL G.304 (78) and Bod Harding Mus. E. 118 (84)).

In vain my fair Sylvia your presence I shun
(The infection once taken to fly from the town)
6 ll., couplets. Love song, on the impossibility of escape once love has taken hold.
   1694? See p. 64.
Printed, with music, in *Thesaurus Musicus* (1694).

In vain my fair you strive to cheat the sight
(And easier lay than represent the devil)
15 ll., couplets. In praise of a lady's beauty, which makes it impossible for her to
   disguise herself as an evil spirit. 1690s? See pp. 43–44, 57.
3 mss: B1 p. 31, Bod Eng. poet. f.13, Osborn c.233, in the latter two cases beginning
   'Madam in vain you strive'.
Printed in the *Diverting Post*, no. 12, January 1704 (i.e. 1705).

Let disputes of the law and religion alone
(He that takes off his liquor will take off the test)
6 ll., couplets. Song praising drinking as better than arguing about religion or
   politics. 1689. See pp. 8, 68.
1 ms: B1 p. 25.

Let old England rejoice
(But never no never upon his returning)
48 ll., 8 stanzas, aabccb. Satirical Jacobite song, at a time of public celebration for
   William III's return home, on his lack of success in the war against France.
   1694. See pp. 73, 76, 78, 127, 150, 152.
2 mss: B1 pp.16–17, B2 ff. 10r–11r.

Like two sage sisters close we dwell
(Yet we were never partial yet)
20 ll., couplets. An enigma, or riddle, on the subject of dice. 1694? See pp. 51–52,
   105.
Printed in the *Gentleman's Journal*, July 1694.

Lucinda has the de'l and all
(Damn all the gold in Lombard Street)
10 ll., couplets. Song questioning the value of a girl's beauty if she refuses to give in
   to her lover. 1700? See pp. 57, 64, 66, 107.
Printed with music in *Mercurius Musicus*, August 1700, and in *Wit and Mirth*, v
   (1714); and without music in the *Diverting Post*, no. 3, November 1704, *The
   Grove* (1721), and *A Miscellaneous Collection of Poems* (1721).

Moggey for shame what mean ye
(For my Moggey)
34 ll., 2 pindaric stanzas, aabcddbceefgfgfga, aabcccbdddefefefg. Song in which a
    Scotsman, Jockey, spurns his lover's plea not to fight in William III's wars. An
    answer to 'Thus o unconstant Jockey' (q.v.). 1690s?
1 ms: B1 p. 19.

Music the chiefest good the gods have given [i]
(That all thy truths will like his fables seem)
33 ll., couplets. In praise of Henry Purcell (while still alive) as an incomparable
    modern composer, placing him in the context of the development of musical
    art in England. No later than 1695. See pp. 53, 59 n. 14, 70 n. 3, 110.
1 ms: B1 p. 80.

Music the chiefest good the gods have given [ii]
(But scarce a Purcell in a thousand years)
58 ll., couplets. In praise of Henry Purcell (following his death in 1695) as an
    incomparable modern composer. An expanded version of the preceding item,
    using also material from the lament 'Yes my Palemon 'tis too true' (q.v.). 1698?
    See pp. 12 n. 8, 36, 52–53, 59 n. 14, 110.
Printed in *Orpheus Britannicus* (1698), p. vi.
Reprinted from *Orpheus Britannicus*, 3rd edn (1721), in Zimmerman, *Henry Purcell,
    1659–1695*, 2nd edn, pp. 309–10.

Must Sylvia then the brightest nymph in town
(But of all loves fair Sylvia let alone)
45 ll., couplets. Fierce attack on a woman who had lampooned a female friend of
    Hall. 1700s? See p. 47.
1 ms: Worcestershire Archive and Archaeology Service Lechmere Archives 40 (i).

Ne'er blame your hero for the kingdom's fall
(The fault's not in the idol but th'idolater)
12 ll., couplets. Criticism of those who wanted William III to be king, asserting
    that they should take the blame now that things are going badly. 1690s? See
    pp. 41, 73, 78, 92 n. 49.
2 mss: B1 p. 104, Minnesota.

Next to the man that so divinely sung
(With him that made it barely but to rise)
33 ll., couplets. In praise of Henry Purcell and his posthumous publisher, Henry
    Playford. 1702. See pp. 36, 55, 60 n. 19, 113 n. 5.
1 ms: O2 ff. 6v–7r.
Printed (without the final three lines) in *Orpheus Britannicus: The Second Part* (1702),
    p. ii.
Reprinted from *Orpheus Britannicus*, 3rd edn (1721), in Zimmerman, *Henry Purcell,
    1659–1695*, 2nd edn, pp. 310–11.

No sooner our hero to Flanders was got
(Which nobody can deny)
36 ll., 9 stanzas, aaab (refrain). Satirical song on the authorities' failure to mount a
  successful prosecution against Jacobites in Lancashire and Cheshire. 1694. See
  pp. 42, 68, 73, 78, 155.
2 mss: B1 pp. 11–12, Minnesota.

Not Waller read and yet so well to write
(He equalled living and surpasses dead)
26 ll., couplets. Address to a friend, Charles Hoskins, praising Edmund Waller and
  John Dryden as the greatest modern English poets. 1690s? See pp. 10, 19, 111.
2 mss: B1 p. 51, B2 ff. 13v-14r.

Now love and war the self-same art is grown
(Revel in blood and triumph o'er the slain)
24 ll. (varies), couplets. Wooing and love-making compared to laying siege to and
  attacking a town. 1690s? See pp. 28, 42, 44, 57, 69.
7 mss: B1 p. 49, B2 f. 8r, O1d p. 26, O2 f. 24r, Bod Ballard 29, TCD 879/3,
  Minnesota.
Printed in the *Diverting Post*, no. 13, January 1704 (i.e. 1705), and in *A Miscellaneous
  Collection of Poems* (1721).

Of all the bards that e'er were bent on fame
(He slew the serpent you record the story)
34 ll., couplets. Humorous praise of John Grubb's ballad *The British Heroes*. 1690s?
  See pp. 19, 111–12, 113 n. 6.
1 ms: O2 f. 1r-v.

O John O John O John Abrahall
(That is he died a mayor)
32 ll., 8 stanzas, abab. Light-hearted admonitory satire addressed to the Rev. John
  Abrahall, on the occasion of his election to the corporation of Hereford in
  1686. See pp. 8, 28, 35–36, 39 n. 10.
3 mss: B1 pp. 45–46, O1d pp. 24–25, O2 f. 23r-v, plus C, pp. [10–11], this having a
  variant text beginning 'Amphibious John! O John Abr'all'.

Oil and vinegar are two pretty things I swear
(And so fight dog fight bear)
5 ll., abbaa. A catch on the irreconcilability of opposites. 1700s? See pp. 66–67.
2 mss: Durham Cathedral Library Bamburgh MS M193/1, Fitzwilliam Museum
  Mu. 120, both with music.
Printed with music in *The Pleasant Musical Companion*, 6th edn (1720).

On the borders of Salop still stands a find town
(And always beware how he drove to a meeting)
78 ll., couplets. Description of the intolerance shown by the people of Ludlow in
    breaking up a Presbyterian meeting organised by a local squire, Mr Littleton,
    in 1692. See p. 15 n. 56.
1 ms: B1 pp. 87–89.

Once in a reign to increase our causeless fears
(Nor could Leviathan himself affright)
19 ll., couplets. On how two whales landed at Greenwich cannot portend national
    afflictions, as England is already suffering from war, taxation, and Low
    Church dominance. 1705. See pp. 26, 58, 95, 116, 165–67 (edited text).
1 ms: O3a.
Printed in the *Diverting Post*, no. 23, March 1705.

Once in a week a letter's due
(And so, dear Doc, here ends my letter)
46 ll., couplets. Conversational epistle to Dr Broughton, looking ahead to the
    weakness of old age and consequently urging present enjoyment. 1690s? See
    pp. 24, 126, 133, 137–39 (edited text).
3 mss: B1 pp. 84–85, O1d pp. 22–23, O2 f. 22r–v (abridged in O1d and O2).

Our business is drinking a round with a glass
(Let who will rule the land so we're lords of the main)
6 ll., couplets. Scorning all talk of politics — specifically the question of the Spanish
    succession — in favour of drinking. 1700? See p. 46.
1 ms: BL Lansdowne 852.

Our government thrifty to raise up their wages
(It follows us after death like to damnation)
12 ll., couplets. Light-hearted complaint about the multitude of taxes imposed by
    the House of Commons. 1694. See pp. 41, 73, 83, 85, 158.
3 mss: B1 p. 101, BL Sloane 2717, Minnesota.

Out of the deep and from the earth
(But ah your funeral proves mine)
16 ll., couplets. An enigma, or riddle, on the subject of a bottle of claret (the solution
    is given in the manuscripts). 1694? See pp. 45, 51.
2 mss: B1 p. 69, TCD 879/3.
Printed in the *Gentleman's Journal*, January-February 1694.

Phyllis in vain you drop that tear
(And for the quick forsook the dead)
20 ll., 5 stanzas, abab. Love song, hoping that the grief of bereavement expressed
    by a lady will soon give way to new desire for love. 1690s? See pp. 44, 58, 68,
    169–70 (edited text).
1 ms: B1 p. 28.
Printed in the *Diverting Post*, no. 21, March 1705, beginning 'Phillis in vain those
    tears you shed'.

Poor Pug had loosed or broke his chain
(Mad pranks to play and fools to fright)

113 ll., couplets. Satirical dispute, partly in dialogue form, between a monkey
belonging to the College of Vicars Choral in Hereford, and the Protestant
apothecary Mathews, one of whose family shot and mortally wounded it.
1690s? See p. 15 nn. 43 & 49.

2 mss: B1 pp. 75–78, B2 ff. 3r–5v.

Rejoice ye fops your idol's come again
(Don't ring your bells ye fools but wring your hands)

4 ll., couplets. Satirical comment on the enthusiastic reception given to William III
on his return home after the victory at Namur in 1695. See pp. 1, 3 n. 4, 35,
42, 48 n. 5, 73–74, 82 (text), 87–88, 91 n. 44.

6 mss: B1 p. 14, BL Stowe 305, Bod Rawlinson C.986, Rawlinson poet. 181,
Minnesota, Osborn c.570/1, plus C, p. [7], beginning 'Rejoice ye fools'. Stowe
and Minnesota begin 'Rejoice ye sots', while Osborn begins 'Rejoice ye
Whigs'.

Modern printings: Cameron, p. 455, from Stowe 305, and *The New Oxford Book of
Seventeenth Century Verse*, ed. by Fowler, p. 792, from Cameron.

See here the confederate train
(Sing hey ding ding a ding ding)

184 ll., 23 stanzas, ababcdcd (refrain). Satirical song on the leaders of the nations at
war with France, including satire of William III. 1693. See pp. 68, 73, 75–76.

1 ms: B1 pp. 1–4.

Should a legion of cares once beleaguer my fort
(Fill the trenches with wine they sink and they drown)

6 ll., aabbcc. Drinking song, celebrating wine's power to banish cares. 1700? See
p. 64.

Printed with music in *Mercurius Musicus* [...] *for August* (London, 1700).

Sylvia and Leah were of widows a pair
(For Leah's a Rachel when tacked to her jointure)

39 ll., couplets. Light-hearted satire on a clergyman named Page, torn between
marrying for love or money; he chooses the former but when rejected opts for
the latter. 1690. See pp. 15 n. 51, 35, 38.

1 ms: B1 p. 27, plus C, p. [8], beginning 'Belinda and Leah'.

Since coat of arms your race ne'er wore
(As Shobdon does Bernithon)

32 ll., 8 stanzas, abab. Scurrilous satire on the heraldic pretensions of the apothecary,
Mathews of Hereford. 1690s? See pp. 15 n. 49, 37.

1 ms: B1 pp. 82–83.

Since in the last sessions your beau got the better
(And Walsh is now taken in Packington's Pound)

26 ll., couplets. Burlesque satire on the Worcestershire Whig MP and poet William

Walsh, in answer to Walsh's satire on local Tory politicians ('The Worcester Cabal'). 1701. See p. 47.

1 ms: Worcestershire Archive and Archaeology Service Lechmere Archives 40 (i).

Since the town is our own what it cost us no matter
(Though the Lords won't allow it nor the Paris Gazette)

7 ll., couplets. Drinking song, toasting the English victory over the French at Landau during the War of the Spanish Succession. 1704. See pp. 26, 57, 69, 93–94.

2 mss: O1e, O2 f. 30v.

Printed in the *Diverting Post*, no. 7, December 1704.

Since we're undone the matter is not much
(This keeps his cash and Fenwick lost his head)

12 ll., couplets. Satirical attack on the House of Lords' rejection, in 1698, of a Bill designed to punish the financier Sir Charles Duncombe, contrasted with its speedy approval of that which led to Sir John Fenwick's execution. 1698. See pp. 29, 73, 77–78, 89, 163–64 (edited text).

2 mss: O1d p. 29, O2 f. 25v.

Sing what shall we sing
(And we will sing no other name)

c. 28 ll. plus chorus: irregular 1st stanza, then 2nd stanza abababab, 3rd and 4th stanzas abab, each followed by chorus abb. In praise of Eliza's power to inspire love, choosing her above all others as the theme for a song. 1700? See p. 64.

Printed with music in *Mercurius Musicus* [...] *for March and April* (1700), with opening line set in the form 'Sing sing sing sing what shall we sing'.

Six tedious months our senate sits
(Would better seem above it)

20 ll., 5 stanzas, abab. Satirical song on the heavy financial cost of William III's wars against France. 1696. See pp. 41, 68, 73, 83, 87–88, 91 n. 44, 99.

6 mss: B1 p. 81, B2 f. 15r, BL Add 5540, Lansdowne 852, Sloane 1731A, Minnesota (in the last four cases having only 8 ll. and beginning, except in Minnesota, 'Six winter months').

Modern printing: Cameron, p. 452 (in part), from Add 5540.

So glorious a victory not to be sung
(We wish every glass were as deep as the Po)

14 ll., aabb, aabbcb, aabb. Song celebrating a victory over the French in Italy by Prince Eugene of Savoy. 1706. See p. 65.

Printed in the *Monthly Mask of Vocal Music*, September 1706, and as an undated single-sheet song (BL G.316.0.(5), Hereford Public Library Pilley Collection 2314), all with music.

So little being done and so much money spent
(Which nobody can deny)

48 ll., 12 stanzas, aaab (refrain). Satirical song on the failure of the naval expedition
to attack Brest in 1694. See pp. 68, 73, 76, 78, 90 n. 9, 116, 133, 152, 153–55
(edited text), 170.

1 ms: B1 pp. 8–9.

Strike you new medals to your hero's fame
(Yet not one drop of Marlborough's was lost)

6 ll., couplets. Satire on the Duke of Marlborough's achieving victory in battle
without endangering himself. 1703. See pp. 27, 94–95.

1 ms: O3b.

Such command o'er my skull
(Said a hair of the very same dog would do best)

9 ll., triplets. Drinking song, expressing determination not to weaken the strength
of the liquor. 1690s? See p. 69.

1 ms: B1 p. 46.

That pleasant prince that strolling northern star
(I'll raise thee Russ a regiment of women)

24 ll., couplets. Bawdy satirical account of the sexual prowess of Peter the Great,
Tsar of Russia, during his visit to England in 1698. See pp. 89 n. 1, 162.

1 ms: B1 pp. 105–06.

The clergy and the laymen
(Which cheered this hero's heart)

30 ll., 3 stanzas, aabbcddbbc. Jacobite song satirizing the English establishment for
replacing James II with William III. 1689? See pp. 8, 68, 73, 80.

2 mss: B1 p. 47, Bod Rawlinson poet. 207 (variant text).

The great Sir George Toulouse did beat
(The clean contrary way Sir)

8 ll., 1 stanza, ababacac. Light-hearted satire on the confrontation between the
British admiral Sir George Rooke and the French commander the Comte de
Toulouse during the indecisive Battle of Malaga in August 1704. See pp. 26,
49 n. 22, 93–94, 99.

12 mss (often with variant opening line): O1e, Bod Montagu e.13, Carlisle Archive
Centre D LONS/L, Essex Record Office D/DW Z4, Herts Archives DE/P,
Longleat House MS PO/vol. XI, NLS 3807, Portland Pw V 44, Chicago UL
PR1195.M73, Folger M.b.12, Harvard UL Eng 606, Osborn c.111.

Printed in *POAS*, IV (1707), beginning 'As brave Sir Rooke Thoulouse did beat'.

The jovial crew in piteous plight departed
(And cried 'Tis safer fighting on the stage)

17 ll., couplets. On the ignominious departure from Hereford of a company of
travelling players. 1705? See p. 58.

Printed in the *Diverting Post*, no. 20, March 1705.

The sly designing patriot in convention
(But fools are marked for all mankind to know)
21 ll., couplets. Satirical complaint that fools are promoted while men of worth are
neglected, targeting especially the Hereford Cathedral clergyman John Page.
1690s? See pp. 15 n. 51, 28, 171.
2 mss: O1d p. 30, O2 f. 26r.

The storm grows loud the lightnings flash
(And she saves him at sea to enchant her at land)
46 ll., irregular. Song describing a storm at sea in which a shipwreck is averted only
by Venus's intervention. Lines 43–46 are marked for 'Chorus'. 1690s? See pp.
28–29, 68.
2 mss: O1d pp. 27–28, O2 ff. 24v-25r.

The vacant chair the House no sooner view
(Their speaker Sir for ever must be you)
16 ll., couplets. In praise of Paul Foley, MP for Hereford 1689–99, on his election as
Speaker of the House of Commons in 1695. See pp. 15 n. 45, 34.
1 ms: B2 f. 14r.

These grateful lines are doubly Sir your due
(To cure all maladies to kings but one)
70 ll., couplets. Conversational epistle to Dr Broughton, extravagantly praising his
skill as a physician, describing it as a godlike gift that should persuade doubters
of the existence of God. 1690s, not later than 1695. See pp. 21–23, 120, 132,
133–37 (edited text).
3 mss: B1 pp. 72–74, O1d pp. 1–3, O2 ff. 13r-14r.

This Sir's to you the second time
(Bis dat (tu scis) qui cito dat)
80 ll., couplets. Conversational epistle to a friend (Edmund Addis), urging him to
keep his promise to send him a gift of wood. A revised version of 'Though
rhyme of late's no more my talent' (q.v.). Later 1690s. See pp. 15 n. 46, 111, 144.
2 mss: O1d pp. 36–38, O2 ff. 28v-30r.

Those tokens which avenging Heaven sent
(Heaven sent you hence to give it you below)
8 ll., couplets. Outspoken attack on Mary II, asserting that her death from smallpox
is divine punishment for her crimes. 1695. See pp. 34, 73, 77.
1 ms: B2 f. 14v.

Though now in station to adjust us
(And die though late at least a dean)
33 ll., couplets. Conversational address to Dr Richard Bulkley, congratulating him
on becoming a canon of Hereford Cathedral in 1698. See pp. 15 n. 47, 28, 146.
2 mss: O1d pp. 34–35, O2 f. 28r-v.

Though rhyme of late's no more my talent

(His like was ne'er bred at Hogsnorton)

75 ll., couplets. Conversational epistle to a friend (Edmund Addis), urging him to keep his promise to send him a gift of wood. An earlier version of 'This Sir's to you the second time' (q.v.). 1690s, after October 1696. See pp. 15 n. 46, 110–11, 144.

1 ms: B1 pp. 98–100.

Thus for his master fell the brave Montrose

(Upon his own till thy bold head was off)

12 ll., couplets. Fiercely Jacobite poem denouncing Parliament for enabling the execution of Sir John Fenwick. 1697. See pp. 73, 77, 84, 90 n. 12, 160–61 (edited text), 163.

1 ms: B1 p. 102.

Thus o unconstant Jockey

(Sweet Jockey)

34 ll., 2 pindaric stanzas, aabcaabceefbfbfba, aabbccbbdddefefef. Song in which a Scottish girl pleads with her lover not to fight in William III's wars. Followed by his answer, 'Moggey for shame what mean ye' (q.v.). See p. 68.

1 ms: B1 p. 18.

Thus while the eight goes merrily round

(Then drink and wish the bells your glass)

9 ll., triplets, plus refrains. Drinking song or catch, celebrating English victories abroad. 1707? See p. 66.

2 mss: York Minster Library M.12 S, UCLA William Andrews Clark Memorial Library M1579P98.1720, both with music.

Printed, with music, in the *Monthly Mask of Vocal Music*, February 1707, *The Jovial Companions* ([1709]), and as an undated single-sheet song (Hereford Public Library Pilley Collection 2314).

'Tis odd indeed indeed 'tis wondrous odd

(So here's a Roland for your Oliver)

18 ll., couplets. Reflections on the successful return to Parliament of a candidate advocating higher taxation (Sir Rowland Gwynne, MP for Brecknock, 1689–90 and 1698). 1698? See pp. 15 n. 56, 42, 89 n. 1.

2 mss: B1 p. 89, Minnesota.

To get false fame and infinite dispraise

('Tis nobler to destroy than thus to build)

4 ll., couplets. Epigram attacking Christopher Wren's design for St Paul's Cathedral. 1700s? See pp. 44, 58.

2 mss: TCD 879/1 f. 93r, Osborn c.233 p. 87, in the latter beginning 'To gain dishonour and immense disgrace'.

Printed in the *Diverting Post*, no. 20, March 1705, beginning as in TCD.

To give the last amendments to the bill

(And the thin form their wondering eyes forsook)

94 ll., couplets. A satire on the bishops who voted against passing the Bill to prevent occasional conformity with the Church of England. 1703. See pp. 97–99, 167.

14 mss: BL Add 25490, Add 27407, Add 27408, Lansdowne 852, Stowe 305, Bod Rawlinson poet. 173, Brotherton Lt q 40, Lt q 55, Portland Pw V 41 (two copies), Univ Limerick Moyaliffe Papers P6/2035, Princeton UL RTC01 no. 38, Osborn b.204, c.111, c.189.

Printed as *Et tu Brute? or, the M — 'd C — l* (London, 1704?) and in *POAS*, III (1704), pp. 392–95. Expanded version (148 ll.) printed as *The M — 'd C — b: or the L — th consultation. Et tu Brute?* (London, 1704) and ('London', 1704).

Modern printing: Ellis, VI, 510–16, from *The M — 'd C — b.*

To our arms on earth and seas

(Next year we'll drink it in champagne)

12 ll., 3 stanzas, abab. Drinking song, toasting the successful British generals during the War of the Spanish Succession. 1704. See pp. 16 n. 62, 56, 60 n. 23, 69, 93.

3 mss: O1e, O2 f.30v, and, with music, Christ Church Oxford Mus. 1219 (F).

Printed, without music, in the *Diverting Post*, no. 2, October–November 1704, p. 2, and as 'A new song, set by Mr D. Purcell' on the verso of the single-sheet *A New Ode, Being a Congratulatory Poem on the Glorious Successes of Her Majesty's Arms* (1706, Foxon N162).

To our monarch's return we our glasses advance

(Send one into England and both are at home)

6 ll., couplets. Jacobite song, hoping for the return of James II. 1691. See pp. 8 (text), 35, 42, 45–46, 68, 91 n. 45.

5 mss: B1 p. 11, BL Add 14854, Add 29497, Minnesota, Osborn b.111, plus C, p. [7], beginning 'While one is in Flanders the other in France' (the usual second line).

To Phyllis fools and men of wit resort

(Snuff up the savoury scent and piss against the door)

18 ll., couplets. Satire on the lustful attentions paid to a lady of fashion by men of all kinds. 1690s? See pp. 57, 106.

1 ms: B1 p. 90.

Printed in the *Diverting Post*, no. 9, December 1704.

Tom making a manteau for a lass of pleasure

(Yet all too short to reach her swinging hances)

6 ll., couplets. Bawdy song or catch about a tailor's attempts to measure a female customer. 1702? See pp. 65–67.

1 ms: Fitzwilliam Museum Mu. 120 p. 321, with music.

Printed with music in *Supplement of New Catches* (1702), *Second Book of the Pleasant Musical Companion* (1707), *The Jovial Companions* (1709), [*Collection of catches*] (1710), *Catches for Flutes* (1711), and *The Pleasant Musical Companion* (1720).

Too roughly Sir you paint the dear delight

('Tis the discovery only proves the devil)

18 ll., couplets. Wittily recommending sex as the route to happiness. 1694? See p. 51.

Printed in the *Gentleman's Journal*, October 1694.

'Twas in the temple first I saw

(For ever will to me be heaven)

28 ll., 7 stanzas, abab. Love poem to a beauty seen in church in Hereford. 1690s?
    See pp. 36–37, 116–17, 146, 170–71 (edited text).

1 ms: B1 p. 91, plus C, Memoir of Thomas Broad (a partial variant text).

'Twas with regret I left your lovely town

(Repair by shadows what I lost by light)

80 ll., couplets. Lightly satirical account of the writer's imagined career as window-
    tax collector for Hereford, and his subsequent return to the city as a teacher of
    handwriting. 1690s? See pp. 40, 48 n. 1.

1 ms: B1 pp. 92–94.

'Twill puzzle much the author's brains

(And Mons within your hearing)

8 ll., 1 stanza, ababcdcd. Satire on William III's lack of success in the war against
    France in 1691 and 1692. 1692? See pp. 42, 46, 73, 81–82 (text), 87–88, 91 n. 45.

5 mss: B1 p. 20, BL Add 29497, CUL Addit 5962, Minnesota, Osborn b.111, the last
    four manuscripts all beginning 'The author sure must take great pains'.

Printed (with the same variant opening line) in *POAS*, III (1704).

Modern printing: Cameron, p. 388, from the 1704 printing.

Two noble earls long since the court forsook

(But not to hearts entirely Dutch by Jove)

10 ll., couplets. Complaint about the departure from court of various leading Tory
    statesmen. 1705. See pp. 26, 95–96.

1 ms: O3a.

We heard indeed of glorious actions done

(Proclaimed the action and confirmed the event)

15 ll., couplets. On the celebrations in London for the English victory at Blenheim.
    1704. See pp. 11, 57, 99.

Printed in the *Diverting Post*, no. 12, January 1704 (i.e. 1705).

We neither are Christians Turks Pagans nor Jews

(Though but for us you often would miss of the light)

14 ll., couplets. An enigma, or riddle, on the subject of a pack of playing cards.
    1694? See p. 51.

Printed in the *Gentleman's Journal*, August 1694.

What fast for horrid murder of the day
(Sin[s] while repeated cannot be forgiv[en])
8 ll., couplets. Attack on the hypocrisy of those who would piously commemorate
    the anniversary of the death of Charles I after having expelled his rightful heir
    James II. 1696? See pp. 73, 80–81, 87–88, 91 nn. 36 & 44.
6 mss: B2 f. 14r, BL Add 72479, Lansdowne 852, Bod Rawlinson poet. 169,
    Princeton UL RTC01 no. 38, Osborn c.570/1.
Printed in *POAS*, II (1703).

When Catesby and Faux with the rest of the crew
(And far from preventing set fire to the train)
12 ll., couplets. Attack on the House of Commons, asserting that the nation would
    not have rejoiced at the failure of the Gunpowder Plot if Parliament then had
    been like it is now. 1690s? See pp. 41, 73, 79–80.
4 mss: O1d p. 32, O2 f. 26v, B1 p. 102, Minnesota, in the latter two cases reading
    '[...] with the rest of the gang'.

When Church was mother Anne was then her daughter
(She fairly leaves her daughter in the lurch)
4 ll., couplets. Epigram critical of Queen Anne's treatment of the Church of
    England. 1703? See pp. 26–27, 95–97 (text), 165–66.
9 mss: O3, BL Add 21094, Lansdowne 852, Bod Eng poet. c.9, Rawlinson poet.
    81, Smith 23 (two copies), TCD 879/1, Harvard UL Eng. 606, Osborn b.90,
    in most cases beginning with versions of 'When Anna was the Church's
    daughter'
Printed in Daniel Defoe, *The Review*, 21 July 1705 (first two lines only), and in
    his *Jure Divino: A Satyr* (1706), XI; also in *POAS*, IV (1707), in all these cases
    beginning with versions of the variant first line.
Modern printing: Ellis, VII, 147, from the 1706 printing.

When I at Rome the Jubilee shall see
(And jubilees create where'er you come)
6 ll., couplets. Hyperbolic praise of an unnamed nobleman on the occasion of the
    Catholic Church's Jubilee in 1700. Prefaced by 'My lord'. 1700? See p. 16
    n. 65.
1 ms: B1 p. 110.

When I your charms your wondrous charms I see
(But who enjoys you is all o'er a god)
6 ll., couplets. Love song. 1700s? See pp. 47, 63, 66–67.
1 ms: Worcestershire Archive and Archaeology Service Lechmere Archives 40 (i).
Printed in the *Monthly Mask of Vocal Musick*, August 1710, and as an undated single-
    sheet song (Bod Harding Mus. G.435 (9)), both with music.

When it pleased the late prince to the world to make known
(You confess him the Queen's and I think that's enough)
20 ll., couplets. On the rejoicing that accompanied the birth in 1688 of James Stuart,

son of James II and Mary of Modena, dismissing claims that the birth was an imposture. 1688.

1 ms: B1 p. 108.

When of half a score lasses ten harlots you see
(Since the bigotted father she swopped for the son)

19 ll., couplets. Supposed prophecy of the unhappy conditions in England during the 1690s. Later 1690s? See pp. 33, 73, 77–78.

1 ms: B1 p. 113.

Whether those hills that round you spread
(But of a mouse be brought to bed)

129 ll., couplets. Description of climbing the Skerrit (Skirrid Fawr) in Monmouthshire, with resulting reflections, partly on religion. 1690s? See pp. 10, 43, 110.

4 mss: B1 pp. 54–57, O1 pp. 4–9, O2 ff.14v-16v, Bod Eng. poet. f.13, the last of these having a longer variant text.

While fame with pleasure shall the story tell
(They drove the Moors and you the Gauls from Spain)

4 ll., couplets. Epigram praising Queen Anne, seemingly on the occasion of the English victory at Vigo Bay in 1702. See p. 99.

1 ms: B1 p. 107.

While Galathea you design to gain
(Which for your lover you prepare)

8 ll., ababccdd. Song, warning of the dangers of falling in love. 1694? See pp. 52, 63–65.

2 mss: BL Add 31453, Bod Mus. d.246, both with music.

Printed, with music, in the *Gentleman's Journal*, November 1693, in *Thesaurus Musicus* [...] *The Second Book* (1694), in *Mercurius Musicus*, August 1699, and in the bespoke *A Collection of the Choicest Songs and Dialogues* (London, 1703).

Whilst Clio rehearses [i]
(Or Mahomet worship or Jesus)

120 ll., 20 stanzas, aabccb. Light-hearted satirical ballad, partly in relation to current political and religious affairs, on prominent named figures in Hereford society who meet at the Black Lion Club. 1690. See pp. 15 nn. 36, 43, 48 & 50, pp. 32, 68.

1 ms: B1, pp. 38–40.

Whilst Clio rehearses [ii]
(Ne'er invade Iles his empire, the water)

78 ll., 13 stanzas, aabccb. Satirical ballad in which a Jacobite miller, Iles, puts to flight several young men of Hereford society who had come fishing in his part of the River Wye. 1690s? See pp. 28, 31 n. 37, 68.

4 mss: B1 pp. 63–65, B2 ff. 6r-7v, O1d pp. 10–14, O2 ff. 17r-18v.

Whilst this bumper stands by me brimfull of cidero
(We'll be as becomes us exceedingly drunk boys)
6 ll., couplets. Drinking song celebrating the English naval victory over the Spanish
   at Vigo Bay in 1702. See pp. 44–45, 68, 107.
1 ms: Osborn c.233.
Printed in *The Grove* (1721), from where it was reprinted in Hawkins, *A General
   History of the Science and Practice of Music*, v, 22.

Whilst thus I sing the largest creature
(Oh say you so then Jane farewell)
106 ll., couplets. Good-natured satire on the physical features of the fat woman Jane
   Mayo of Newant, but alluding also to William III's war with France. 1690s?
   See pp. 10, 15 n. 57.
1 ms: B1 pp. 42–44.

Whither ye impious Britons do ye run
(Entails this curse and will confound ye all)
32 ll., couplets. Jacobite attack on the English for continuing to support William
   III's wars despite the ruin it has caused the nation, blaming it on unexpiated
   guilt for the murder of Charles I. 1690. See pp. 73, 80, 87–88, 91 n. 44, 115,
   117, 128, 149–51 (edited text).
5 mss: B2 ff. 11r-12r, BL Add 21094, Bod Rawlinson poet. 181, Osborn c.570/2,
   fb.207/3.
Printed in *POAS*, II (1703).

Why towering tides submit to constant laws
(Created not to conquer but to keep)
221 ll., couplets. Long vituperative attack on the Dutch, finally urging England not
   to get involved, on their account, in the War of the Spanish Succession. 1701?
   See pp. 25, 29, 40, 73, 77.
2 mss: O1b (a fragment of 87 lines), O2 ff.8r-12r.

With Job-like patience we've our burdens bore
(Lest not the taxes but the people rise)
49 ll., couplets. Jacobite attack on William III and his conduct of affairs, especially
   the costs of the war with France. 1696? See pp. 41, 73, 79, 156–59 (edited text).
3 mss: B1 pp. 36–37, B2 ff. 12v-13v, Minnesota.
Modern printing: Cameron, p. 453 (ll. 13–17 only, from B1).

Ye gods what gulfs are set between
(Invite another day to dinner)
22 ll., couplets. Conversational epistle to Dr Adam Ottley, Archdeacon in the
   diocese of Hereford, excusing himself from a dinner invitation on account of
   the previous night's over-indulgence. c. 1698. See pp. 15 n. 47, 25, 110, 113 n. 1,
   145–47 (edited text).
2 mss: O1c, O2 f. 12v.

Yes my Aminta 'tis too true

(Break your pipes and sing no more)

64 ll., couplets. Pastoral lament on the death of Henry Purcell, principally in the form of a dialogue between a shepherdess and a shepherd, celebrating Purcell's musical skill and describing his funeral. An expanded version of the following item. 1695? See pp. 1, 53, 62, 107 n. 1, 110.

2 mss: Bod Tenbury 1232, Christ Church Oxford Mus. 1212B (fragmentary), both with music.

Modern sound recording by the Parley of Instruments on Hyperion CDA66578 (1992), as one of a number of *Odes on the Death of Henry Purcell*.

Yes my Palemon 'tis too true

(But scarce a Daphnis in a thousand years)

46 ll., couplets. Pastoral lament on the death of Henry Purcell, in the form of a dialogue between a shepherdess and a shepherd, celebrating Purcell's musical skill. Cf. the previous item. 1695? See pp. 53, 62, 70 n. 3, 110.

4 mss: B1 pp. 52–53, B2 f. 9r-v, O1d pp. 19–20, O2 ff. 20v-21v.

Your awkward Austrian phiz with joy I take

(And when you're king Sir I'll betray you too)

6 ll., couplets. Answer to the immediately preceding 'Accept my Lord this humble glittering thing' (q.v.), satirizing the Duke of Marlborough's acquisitiveness and success in battle without endangering himself. 1703. See pp. 27, 94–95.

1 ms: O3b.

Your primitive players first acted in a cart

(Than those against the state you should conceal)

67 ll., couplets. On the development of the English stage, ending with satire of present theatrical practice. 1699. See pp. 11, 16 n. 59, 37, 46.

3 mss: B1 pp. 59–59, Portland Pw V 44, Folger M.b.12 (part 3).

Modern printing: *The Prologues and Epilogues of the Restoration, 1660–1700*, ed. by Danchin, III, 428–31, based on B1.

4860 lines
in toto

APPENDIX B

❖

The Contents of the Main Manuscript Collections

The Brotherton Collection manuscripts are listed first, then the Ottley manuscripts. Unlike in Appendix A, all entries are given in manuscript spelling. Titles of poems are now given prominence, with opening lines following in parentheses.

B1   Leeds University Library, Brotherton Collection MS Lt q 5

1.   'On the pictures of the confederates hung round a room in 1693. To the tune of Old Simon the King' ('See here the confederate train'). 184 lines, pp. 1–4.

2.   'The Battle of the Boyne. To the tune of Packingtons Pound' ('Attend to my verse you whose ears are as long'). 110 lines, pp. 5–8.

3.   'On the business of Brest in 1692. To the tune of Which Nobody Can Deny' ('So little being done and so much money spent'). 48 lines, pp. 8–9.

4.   'The Jacobites quaeres for the Thanksgiving Day in 1694. To the tune of The Children in the Wood' ('Are all those lights that guild the street'). 24 lines, p. 10.

5.   'Catch' ('To our monarchs returne we our glasses advance'). 6 lines, p. 11.

6.   'Ballad on the Cheshire Plott 1694' ('No sooner our heroe to Flanders was got'). 36 lines, pp. 11–12.

7.   'On the burning of Dr Burnetts book entitled a Pastoral Letter' ('In place where men of wealth and witt'). 40 lines, pp. 12–13.

8.   'On K — W — ms takeing of Namur, 1695' ('Citties of adamant must yield'). 12 lines, p. 14.

9.   'On K — g W — ms returne out of Flanders' ('Rejoice yee fops your idoll's come agen'). 4 lines, p. 14.

10. 'An account of an odd accident that happen'd to the Right Reverend' ('A mighty voice roll'd down the flood'). 16 lines, p. 15.

11. 'On the observing the 30th of January 1691' ('Cease hippocrites to trouble heaven'). 6 lines, p. 15.

12. 'Ballad on the Thanksgiving Day so solemnly observ'd the 12th of April 1694' ('Let old England rejoice'). 48 lines, pp. 16–17.

13. 'A Pindarick ballad to the tune of Luxemburgh's March' ('Thus oh unconstant Jockey'). 34 lines, p. 18.

14. 'Jockey's answer' ('Moggey for shame what mean yee'). 34 lines, p. 19.

15. 'Upon K — g W — ms two first campagnes' ("Twill puzzle much the authors brains'). 8 lines, p. 20.

16. 'The auction' ('All you who delight and take pleasure in painting'). 95 lines, pp. 20–23.

17. 'A dialogue between the engine and the lamp given by Mr Morgan and Mr Foley' ('Here have I layn Lord knows how many years'). 65 lines, pp. 23–25.

18. 'Catch in the year 1689' ('Let disputes of the law and religion alone'). 6 lines, p. 25.

19. 'To Dr Broughton' ('Comeing from place where you have seen'). 33 lines, p. 26.

20. 'On Mr Page's marriage' ('Silvia and Leah were of widows a paire'). 39 lines, p. 27.

21. 'Song' ('Phillis in vain you drop that tear'). 20 lines, p. 28.

22. 'Song' ('Charming Sylvia if you knew'). 22 lines, p. 29.

23. 'To Sylvia advising her always to wear black' ('Altho' for ev'ry different dress'). 24 lines, p. 30.

24. 'To a lady that wou'd have put herself for a spright on a gentleman' ('In vain my fair you strive to cheat the sight'). 15 lines, p. 31.

25. 'On Tom Broads picture' ('For missing thee how canst thou Burren blame'). 8 lines, p. 31.

26. 'Song' ('Come my Sylvia now discover'). 16 lines, p. 32.

27. 'Answer' ('Cease Amintor to pursue me'). 16 lines, p. 33.

28. 'To your Lordship after being ruin'd at play' ('Dun'd by the bells I roase from bed'). 52 lines, pp. 34–35.

29. 'Truth' ('With Job like patience wee've our burthens bore'). 49 lines, pp. 36–37.

30. 'The Black Lion Club in 1690' ('Whilst Clio rehearses' [i]). 120 lines, pp. 38–40.

31. 'The loyall miller' ('How happy's the mortall that lives by his mill'). 25 lines, p. 41.

32. 'On Jane Mayo the fatt woman of Newant' ('Whilst thus I sing the largest creature'). 106 lines, pp. 42–44.

33. 'On John Abrahall being elected into the corporation, he being a priest of the Church of England' ('O John O John O John Abrahall'). 32 lines, pp. 45–46.

34. 'Mock song' ('Such command o're my skull'). 9 lines, p. 46.

35. 'Mock song' ('The clergy and the laymen'). 30 lines, p. 47.

36. 'Why the thunder never strikes the lawrell' ('As Phebus did with heat pursue'). 10 lines, p. 48.

37. 'Song' ('Now love and warr the selfesame art is grown'). 24 lines, p. 49.

38. 'If justice be a thing divine'. By Katherine Philips. 8 lines, p. 50.

39. 'Answer' ('Bright justice is a thing divine'). 8 lines, p. 50.

40. 'To Mr Charles Hoskins upon my lending him Mr Wallers Poems' ('Not Waller read and yett so well to write'). 26 lines, p. 51.

41. 'A dialogue between Palemon and Alexis lamenting the death of the incomparable Mr Henry Purcell' ('Yes my Palemon 'tis too true'). 46 lines, pp. 52–53.

42. 'To Mr Nicholas Arnold' ('Whether those hills that round you spread'). 129 lines, pp. 54–57.

43. 'The progress of the stage by way of epilogue' ('Your prim'tive play'rs first acted in a cart'). 60 lines, pp. 58–59.

44. 'Dialogue between the Bishop and Coll' Birch's ghost' ('How durst thou thus disturb that surly shade'). 92 lines, pp. 60–62.

45. 'Ballad on the miller's beating Mob Hill and young Mathews at Hereford Wear' ('Whilst Clio rehearses' [ii]). 78 lines, pp. 63–65.

46. 'To Dr Broughton' ('Calling at Fountain's late last night'). 86 lines, pp. 66–68.

47. 'Aenigma' ('Out of the deep and from the earth'). 16 lines, p. 69.

48. 'To Dr Broughton desireing him to send me some verses of mine which I had forgott' ('As in a pump wee water put'). 50 lines, pp. 70–71.

49. 'To Dr Broughton after a fitt of sickness' ('These gratefull lines are doubly Sir your due'). 70 lines, pp. 72–74.

50. 'Dialogue between Old Mathews and the Colledge monkey' ('Poor Pugg had loos'd or broak his chain'). 113 lines, pp. 75–78.

51. 'On Mr Lewis's accepting of Mr Bensons prebendary' ('If Reverend Sir'). 7 lines, p. 78.

52. 'To Dr Broughton' ('From colledge hall where thirsty vicar'). 30 lines, p. 79.

53. 'To Mr Purcell' ('Musick the cheifest good the gods have given'). 33 lines, p. 80.

54. 'A song' ('Six tedious months our senate sitts'). 20 lines, p. 81.

55. 'Mathews's coate of arms' ('Since coat of arms your race ne'r wore'). 32 lines, pp. 82–83.

56. 'To Dr Broughton' ('From place where long to lye does tyre one'). 20 lines, p. 83.

57. 'To Dr Broughton' ('Once in a week a letter's due'). 46 lines, pp. 84–85.

58. 'To Dr Broughton confineing himself to avoid takeing the oaths' ('And art thou faith a true recluse become'). 34 lines, pp. 85–86.

59. 'On Mr Littletons meeting at Ludlow in the year 92' ('On the borders of Salop still stands a fine town'). 78 lines, pp. 87–89.

60. 'On the election at Brecknock, Sir Rowland Gwyn being chosen, and Mr Jeffrys put by' (''Tis odd indeed indeed 'tis wondrous odd'). 18 lines, p. 89.

61. 'La coquette' ('To Phillis fools and men of witt resort'). 18 lines, p. 90.

62. 'The great good man whom fortune does displace'. 10 lines, p. 90. Transcribed as a continuation of the previous item, followed by the attribution 'D. Kendrick', in the scribal hand. Almost certainly by Daniel Kenrick, not Henry Hall.

63. 'To Mrs Robins' (''Twas in the temple first I saw'). 28 lines, p. 91.

64. ''Twas with regrett I left your lovely town'. 80 lines, pp. 92–94.

65. 'The humble Piticion of Nat Priest and Henry Hall to Edmund Addys Gent for a load of hearty (viz.) red muss' ('Altho' to petition has bin out of fashion'). 27 lines, pp. 94–95.

66. 'Good people what will you of all be bereft'. 30 lines, pp. 95–96.

67. 'All in the land of cyder'. 40 lines, pp. 96–97.

68. 'A poem by Mr Hall sent to a person that promised him a load of wood' ('Tho' rythme of late's no more my talent'). 75 lines, pp. 98–100.

69. 'A health to the Prince of Baden' ('Here's a health whilst the trumpets and hautboys all cease'). 6 lines, p. 100.

70. 'On the thrift of the H — e of C — ns' ('Our government thrifty to raise up their wages'). 12 lines, p. 101.

71. 'An epitaph upon Sir John Fenwick' ('Here lyes the relicks of a martyr'd knight'). 9 lines, p. 101.

72. 'Another' ('Thus for his master fell the brave Montross'). 12 lines, p. 102.

73. 'When Catesby and Faux with the rest of the gang'. 12 lines, p. 102.

74. 'An epitaph' ('Here lyes our Sove — gne L — dy M — ll'). 15 lines, p. 103.

75. 'Upon the nine commissioners' ('Great W — m concern'd to leave his gull'd loobys'). 16 lines, p. 103.

76. 'A poem' ('Ne're blame your hero for the kingdom's fall'). 12 lines, p. 104.

77. 'Upon the representatives' ('Curse on those representatives'). 12 lines, p. 104. For its authorship, see Chapter 7.6 above.

78. 'A litany' ('From a peace with new taxes and yet without trade'). 20 lines, p. 105.

79. 'A poem on the courage of the Czar' ('That pleasant prince that strouling northern star'). 24 lines, pp. 105–06.

80. 'Upon the French kings singing Te Deum for being beat' ('As sharper when his coyne grows low'). 12 lines, p. 106.

81. 'A health to the Czar' ('Dragoons have a care'). 18 lines, p. 107.

82. 'To the Queen on the success of her arms in Spain' ('While fame with pleasure shall the story tell'). 4 lines, p. 107.

83. 'A poem on the birth of the Chevalier' ('When it pleas'd the late prince to the world to make known'). 20 lines, p. 108.

84. 'Fair Amorett, a song' ('Charming fair Amorett that dear undoer'). 12 lines, p. 109.

85. 'The palace of the God of Sleep' ('Deep in the earth and hid from human eyes'). 18 lines, p. 109.

86. 'My lord | When I at Rome the Jubile shall see'. 6 lines, p. 110.

87. 'A song on the Jubilee, 1700' ('Come beaus virtuoso's rich heirs and musicians'). 42 lines, pp. 110–11.

88. 'A copy of verses to Mr Clayton after done at St Pauls Fair Bristoll' ('If rythme for rhyno cou'd attone'). 28 lines, p. 112.

89. 'A prophecy found in Ragland Castle in the year 1630' ('When of half a score lasses ten harlotts you see'). 19 lines, p. 113. In a separate hand.

B2   Leeds University Library, Brotherton Collection MS Lt 6

1. 'Upon the Battle of the Boyne' ('Attend to my verse you whose ears are so long'). 110 lines, ff. 1r-2v, 6r.

2. 'A dialogue between the Coll. monkey and Mr Mathews whose son shot him'

('Poor Pugg had loosed or broke his chain'). 113 lines, ff. 3r-5v (in two parts, the second with separate heading, 'Dialogue', f. 4r).

3.   'A song' ('Whilst Clio rehearses' [ii]). 78 lines, ff. 6r-7v.

4.   'Upon the taking of a mistress' ('Now love and war the selfsame art is grown'). 24 lines, f. 8r.

5.   'Upon King William' ('Hail happy W — m thou art strangely great'). 26 lines, f. 8v.

6.   'A dialogue between Palamon and Alexis upon the death of the unimitable Purcell' ('Yes my Palemon 'tis too true'). 46 lines, f. 9r-v.

7.   'A song upon Kink [sic] W — ms Thanksgiving Day' ('Let old England rejoyce'). 48 lines, ff. 10r-11r.

8.   'An imitation of the 7 epod. of Horace. Quo quo scelesti ruitis' ('Whither yee impious Brittains will ye run'). 32 lines, ff. 11r-12r.

9.   'A song' ('Charming Sylvia if you know'). 22 lines, f. 12r-v.

10. 'Truth' ('With Job like patience ne've [sic] our burthens bore'). 49 lines, ff. 12v-13v.

11. 'To my freind Mr Charles Hoskins upon borrowing Mr Wallers poems' ('Not Waller reads and yet so well to wright'). 26 lines, ff. 13v-14r.

12. 'On Mr Foleys being chose Speaker' ('The vacant chair the house no sooner veiu'). 16 lines, f. 14r.

13. 'On the 30th of January 1695' ('What fast for horrid murther of the day'). 8 lines, f. 14r.

14. 'Upon Sir John Fewick [sic] a martyrd knight' ('Here lyes the reliques of a martyrd knight'). 9 lines, f. 14v.

15. 'On the Queens having the small pox' ('Those tokens wich avenging Heaven sent'). 8 lines, f. 14v.

16. 'Six tedious months our senate sitts'. 20 lines, f. 15r.

17. 'Justice' ('If justice be a thing divine'). By Katherine Philips. 8 lines, f. 15v.

18. 'Bright justice is a thing divine'. 8 lines, f. 15v (as if a continuation of Katherine Philips's poem).

O1–3   The Ottley manuscripts of Hall's verse, held within National Library of Wales, Pitchford Hall (Ottley) English Literary MSS (uncatalogued)

O1a

1.   'For missing thee how canst thou Burren blame'. 8 lines on a scrap of paper.

O1b

1.   Lines 135–221 of the poem 'The paradox' ('Why towering tides submit to constant laws'), here beginning 'Now of the Boors again my muse shall treat'. On three sides of a bifolio.

O1c

1.   'Ye gods what gulfs are set between'. 22 lines, within a letter to Dr Ottley.

O1d (items 12–19 are in Hall's autograph)

1. 'To Dr Broughton after a fitt of sickness' ('These gratefull lines are doubly Sir your due'). 70 lines, pp. 1–3. Hand 1.
2. 'To Mr Nich. Arnold on the Skerrit' ('Whether those hills that round you spread'). 129 lines, pp. 4–9. Hand 1.
3. 'Whilst Clio rehearses' [ii]. 78 lines, pp. 10–14. Hand 1.
4. 'To Dr Broughton for a coppy of verses I had wholly forgot' ('As in a pump wee water put'). 50 lines, pp. 15–16. Hand 1.
5. 'To Dr Broughton and Captain Jones' ('From colledge hall where thirsty vicar'). 30 lines, pp. 17–18. Hand 1.
6. 'On the death of Mr Henry Purcell' ('Yes my Palemon 'tis too true'). 46 lines, pp. 19–20. In dialogue form with abbreviated speech prefixes. Hand 1.
7. 'To Dr Broughton desiring some of his steel pills' ('In place where long to lye does tyre one'). 20 lines, p. 21. Hand 1.
8. 'Once in a week a letter's due'. 46 lines, pp. 22–23. Hand 1.
9. 'On John Abrahall being elected into the Corporation of Hereford, he being a preist of the Church of England' ('O John O John O John Abrahall'). 32 lines, pp. 24–25. Hand 1.
10. 'The new art of love' ('Now love and warr the self same art is grown'). 24 lines, p. 26. Hand 1.
11. 'The storme' ('The storme grows loud the lightnings flash'). 46 lines, pp. 27–28. Hand 1.
12. 'On the Lords throwing out Duncombs Bill' ('Since wee're undone the matter is not much'). 12 lines, p. 29. Hand 2.
13. 'Catch' ('Curse on those representatives'). 12 lines, p. 29. Hand 2. For its authorship, see Chapter 7.6 above.
14. 'Merit not rewarded and fools preferd' ('The sly designing patriot in convention'). 21 lines, p. 30. Hand 2.
15. 'The Czarr's health or the Muscovite madrigall. A Catch' ('Dragoons have a care'). 18 lines, p. 31. Hand 2.
16. 'When Catesby and Faux with the rest of the crew'. 12 lines, p. 32. Hand 2.
17. 'The great good man whom fortune does displace'. 10 lines, p. 32. Hand 2. Almost certainly by Daniel Kenrick, not Henry Hall.
18. 'Litany' ('From a peace with new taxes and yet without trade'). 20 lines, p. 33. Hand 2.
19. 'To Dr Buckley upon his commencing cannon — hoping that you'l nere forget' ('Tho' now in station to adjust us'). 33 lines, pp. 34–35. Hand 2.
20. 'To Mr Addis for a load of wood' ('This Sirs to you the second time'). 80 lines, pp. 36–38. Hand 1.

O1e

1. 'A Fable' ('An honest good farmer by providence blest'). 22 lines. On one side of a single sheet of paper, in Hall's autograph.
2. 'The healths' ('To our arms on Earth and seas'). 12 lines. On the other side of the same sheet of paper and in a different hand (as also for items 3–4).

3. 'Landau took Nov. 1704' ('Since the town is our own what it cost us no matter'). 7 lines.
4. 'The great Sir George Tholouse did beat'. 8 lines.

O2

1. 'To Mr John Grub on his inimitable ballad' ('Of all the bards that e're were bent on fame'). 34 lines, f. 1r-v.
2. 'Mr John Grubbs ballad' ('The story of King Arthur old is very memorable'). Ff. 2r-6r. By John Grubb of Christ Church, Oxford.
3. 'Henry Hall's plea for Burren, to Mr T. Broad' ('For missing thee, how canst thou Burren blame'). 8 lines, f. 6r.
4. 'To Mr Henry Playford, on his publishing the second part of Orpheus Brittanicus' ('Next to the man that so divinely sung'). 33 lines, ff. 6v-7r.
5. 'How happy is this day'. 34 lines (including repeated chorus), f. 7v.
6. 'The paradox' ('Why towring tides submit to constant laws'). 221 lines, ff. 8r-12r.
7. 'To the Revd Dr Ottley, a letter' ('Ye gods what gulfs are set between'). 22 lines, f. 12v.
8. 'To Dr Broughton after a fit of sickness' ('These gratefull lines are doubly Sir your due'). 70 lines, ff. 13r-14r.
9. 'To Mr Nich. Arnold on the Skerrit' ('Whether those hills about you spread'). 129 lines, ff. 14v-16v.
10. 'Whilst Clio rehearses' [ii]. 78 lines, ff. 17r-18v.
11. 'To Dr Broughton for a copy of verses I had wholely forgot' ('As in a pump we water put'). 50 lines, f. 19r-v.
12. 'To Dr Broughton and Captain Jones' ('From college hall where thirsty vicar'). 30 lines, f. 20r-v.
13. 'On the death of Mr Henry Purcell' ('Yes my Palemon 'tis too true'). 46 lines, ff. 20v-21v.
14. 'To Dr Broughton desiring some of his steel pills' ('In place where long to lye does tyre one'). 20 lines, ff. 21v-22r.
15. 'Once in a week a letter's due'. 46 lines, f. 22r-v.
16. 'On John Abrahall being elected into the Corporation of Hereford, he being a priest of the Church of England' ('O John O John O John Abrahall'). 32 lines, f. 23r-v.
17. 'The new art of love' ('Now love and war the selfe same art is grown'). 24 lines, f. 24r.
18. 'The storme' ('The storme grows loud the lightnings flash'). 46 lines, ff. 24v-25r.
19. 'On the Lords throwing out Duncombs Bill' ('Since we're undone the matter is not much'). 12 lines, f. 25v.
20. 'Catch' ('Curse on those representatives'). 12 lines, ff. 25v-26r. For its authorship, see Chapter 7.6 above.
21. 'Merit not rewarded and fools preferd' ('The sly designing patriot in convention'). 21 lines, f. 26r.

22.   'When Catesby and Faux with the rest of the crew'. 12 lines, f. 26v.
23.   'The great good man whom fortune does displace'. 10 lines, f. 26v. Almost certainly by Daniel Kenrick, not Henry Hall.
24.   'The Czarr's health or the Moscovite madrigall. A Catch' ('Dragoons have a care'). 18 lines, f. 27r.
25.   'Litany' ('From a peace with new taxes and yet without trade'). 20 lines, f. 27v.
26.   'To Dr Buckley upon his commencing canon — hoping that youl n'ere forget' ('Tho' now in station to adjust us'). 33 lines, f. 28r-v.
27.   'To Mr Addis for a load of wood' ('This Sir's to you the second time'). 80 lines, ff. 28v-30r.
28.   'A fable' ('An honest good farmer by providence blest'). 22 lines, f. 30r.
29.   'The healths' ('To our arms on Earth and seas'). 12 lines, f. 30v.
30.   'Landau took Nov. 1704' ('Since the town is our own what it cost us no matter'). 7 lines, f. 30v.
31.   'Charlettus Percivalio suo' ('Hora dum nondum sonuit secunda'). F. 31r-v. In Latin. Not by Hall. This and the next item, both by Anthony Alsop, were printed together, anonymously, as a single-sheet broadside (London, 1706; *ESTC* T30516, Foxon A177).
32.   'Percivallus Charletto suo' ('Qualis ambabus capiendus ulnis'). Ff. 31v-32v. In Latin.
33.   'The serv — r a poem' ('When Phoebus shone with warmest rays'). Ff. 32v-36r. Not by Hall. Printed London, 1709, as *The Servitour: a Poem*, by 'a servitour of the University of Oxford' (*ESTC* T47969, Foxon S222).
34.   'On the fall of a pis-pot' ('Of wastful havock and destructive fate'). Ff. 36v-38r. Not by Hall. Printed London, [1713], as *A Poem on the Memorable Fall of Chloe's P — s Pot, Attempted in Blank Verse* (*ESTC* T1001, Foxon P627). 'Variously attributed to Jonathan Swift and to John Philips' (*ESTC*).

O3a (in Hall's autograph)

1.   'On the two monstrous fish lately taken at Greenwich' ('Once in a reign t'encrease our causeless fears'). On one side of a single sheet of paper. 17 lines.
2.   'On the late alterations at court' ('Two noble earls long since the court forsook'). On the same page (as also for item 3). 10 lines.
3.   'When church was mother, Ann was then her daughter'. 4 lines.

O3b (in Hall's autograph)

1.   A couplet (not treated in this study as a separate poem) 'Since witt no more will in our country live | Than will our redstreaks when they're out on't thrive', preceded by: 'Sir, If the Muses don't dwell in Oxford, I'm sure you must not expect 'em in Herefordshire', and followed by: 'You know Sir, 'tis the juce of the grape, and not of the apple inspires the poet, and to justify the assertion, read these epigrams.' On the right-hand side of the inside of a folded letter (as also for items 2–3).
2.   'On the Arch Duke's presenting his picture and sword set with diamonds to

the Duke of Marlborough' ('Accept my Lord this humble glitt'ring thing').
6 lines. The words 'Duke' (twice) and 'Marlborough', initially written in
abbreviated form, have been filled out by a later hand.

3.   'His Graces answer' ('Your awkward Austrian phiz with joy I take'). 6 lines.

4.   'To my Lord G — n, who struck the medall for the D — e of M — last
year' ('Strike you new medalls to your heros fame'). 6 lines. In this case
the abbreviated words have not been filled in. Following the poem: 'I was
unluckily making the Welch tour when your letter came to Hereford, so
receivd it not till last Saturday', and then Hall's subscription ('I am Sir your
most obedient and humble servant Henry Hall'), with date, 'July 26th;'. On
the left-hand side of the inside of a folded letter.

APPENDIX C

❖

Other Manuscript Witnesses of Poems and Songs Attributable to Henry Hall

Both here and in Appendix D I employ shortened versions of the first lines of poems and songs. I exclude the nineteenth-century Cooke manuscript, for which see Chapter 3.2 above.

Literary manuscripts (British and Irish repositories)

British Library, London

Add 5540, f. 26v, 'Six tedious months'. See pp. 82–83.

Add 14854, f. 104r, 'To our monarch's return'. See p. 46.

Add 21094, ff. 57v–58r, 'Whither ye impious Britons'; f. 58r-v, 'Hail happy William'; f. 65r, 'Great William concerned'; f. 153r, 'When Church was mother'. See pp. 80, 86–88, 97, 149–51.

Add 21544, f. 125r, 'Haste Charon haste'. See p. 62.

Add 25490, ff. 13r–14r, 'To give the last amendments'. See p. 97.

Add 27407, f. 41r-v, 'To give the last amendments'. See p. 100 n. 17.

Add 27408, f. 138r-v, 'To give the last amendments'. See p. 100 n. 18.

Add 28253, f. 83r, 'Here lie the relics'.

Add 29497, f. 92r, 'To our monarch's return'; f. 100r, ''Twill puzzle much' (beginning 'The author sure must take great pains'); ff. 105v–06r, 'Good people what will you'; f. 106r-v, 'Hail happy William'. See pp. 46, 81, 87, 91 n. 25.

Add 40060, f. 50v, 'Accept my Lord'. See pp. 94–95.

Add 47608, f. 190r, 'Here lie the relics'.

Add 69968 f. 35r, 'Good people what will you'. See p. 68.

Add 70454, f. 50r, 'Here lie the relics'.

Add 72479, f. 69r, 'Here lie the relics'; f. 69v, 'What fast for horrid murder'; ff. 70r-v, 71r, 72r (i.e. three copies), 'Hail happy William'; f.85r, 'Accept my Lord'. See pp. 81, 85, 88, 90 n. 22, 91 n. 38.

Harley 6914, f. 106v, 'Accept my Lord'. See p. 100 n. 5.

Harley 7315, f. 250r-v, 'Great William concerned'. See p. 92 n. 47.

Lansdowne 852, ff. 14v–16r, 'To give the last amendments'; f. 16r, 'Good people what will you'; f. 16v, 'Six tedious months'; f. 118r, 'Great William concerned'; f. 122v, 'When Church was mother'; f. 277v, 'What fast for horrid murder';

f. 287r, 'Our business is drinking'. See pp. 46, 75, 81, 83, 87–88, 90 n. 22, 96, 98–99, 100 n. 13.

Sloane 1731A, f. 133r, 'Six tedious months'; f. 147r, 'Great William concerned'; f. 164r, 'Hail happy William'. See pp. 83–84, 91 nn. 30 & 44.

Sloane 2717, f. 98r, 'Our government thrifty'. See pp. 48 n. 5, 83, 91 n. 32.

Stowe 305, f. 213v, 'Good people what will you'; ff. 213v–14r, 'Hail happy William'; f. 216v, 'Rejoice ye fops'; f. 279r–v, 'To give the last amendments'. See pp. 48 n. 5, 75, 82, 86–87, 101 n. 22.

Bodleian Library, Oxford

Ballard 29, f. 145v, 'Now love and war'. See p. 44.

Eng. poet. c.9, p. 235, 'When Church was mother'. See p. 100 n. 13.

Eng. poet. e.50, pp. 86–87, 'Great William concerned' (twentieth-century transcript from the 'Fraser ms', p. 186, sold at Sotheby's in 1925).

Eng. poet. e.87, p. 36, 'All in the land of cider'. See p. 45.

Eng. poet. f.13, ff. 69r–71v, 'Whether those hills'; f. 193r, 'In vain my fair you strive' (beginning 'Madam in vain you strive'). See pp. 43–44, 102, 106.

Hearne's Diaries 9 [March–May 1706], pp. 27–28, 'As man in Westminster'. See p. 60 n. 22.

Hearne's Diaries 11 [June–September 1706], pp. 102–04, 'Hail happy William'. See p. 86.

Montagu e.13, f. 104v, 'The great Sir George'.

Rawlinson C.986, f. 15r, 'Here lie the relics' and 'Rejoice ye fops'. See pp. 88, 91 n. 27.

Rawlinson D.361, f. 211v, 'Good people what will you'; ff.212v–13r, 'Hail happy William'. See pp. 75, 87, 91 n. 43.

Rawlinson D.383, f. 55r, 'Good people what will you' (2 stanzas only). See p. 75.

Rawlinson poet. 81, f. 34r, 'Hail happy William'; f. 42v, 'When Church was mother'. See p. 100 n. 13.

Rawlinson poet. 169, f. 9r, 'Hail happy William' and 'What fast for horrid'. See pp. 81, 88, 90 n. 22.

Rawlinson poet. 173, ff. 130v–32r, 'To give the last amendments'. See p. 100 n. 18.

Rawlinson poet. 181, f. 1r, 'Whither ye impious Britons'; f. 10r, 'Great William concerned'; f. 13r, 'Rejoice ye fops'. See pp. 80, 82, 88, 149–51.

Rawlinson poet. 207, ff. 18v–19r, 'The clergy and the laymen'. See p. 80.

Smith 23, p. 103, 'When Church was mother'; p. 113, 'Accept my Lord'; p. 127, 'When Church was mother'. See p. 97.

pr. bk. Firth b.21, f. 61v, 'Accept my Lord'.

Cambridge University Library

Add. 5962, f. 46r, ''Twill puzzle much' (beginning 'The author sure must take great pains'). See pp. 81, 91 n. 25.

Add. 7112, f. 35v, 'Good people what will you'. See p. 85.

Carlisle Archive Centre

Within D LONS/L, 'The great Sir George' (information from Ellis, VII, 628–29; precise reference not traceable).

Essex Record Office, Chelmsford

D/DW Z4, 'The great Sir George'.

Hertfordshire Archives and Local Studies, Hertford

D/EP F35 (= Sarah Cowper's diary), pp. 4–5 (inverted), 'All in the land of cider' (abridged text). See pp. 45, 48 n. 20.
Within D/EP, 'The great Sir George' (information from Ellis, VII, 628–29; precise reference not traceable).

Holkham Hall, Norfolk

686, pp. 204–05, 'Great William concerned'; pp. 289–90, 'Hail happy William'. See pp. 91 n. 44, 92 n. 47.

Leeds University Library

Brotherton Collection Lt 79, f. 131r, 'Here lie the relics'; f. 132r-v, 'Hail happy William'. See pp. 87, 91 n. 43.
Brotherton Collection Lt 81, f. 6v, 'Accept my Lord'.
Brotherton Collection Lt q 11, item 14, 'Hail happy William'. See pp. 86, 91 n. 39.
Brotherton Collection Lt q 38, pp. 191–92, 'Great William concerned'. See p. 92 n. 47.
Brotherton Collection Lt q 40, f. 14r, 'Here lie the relics'; f. 14v, 'Hail happy William'; f. 15r-v, 'To give the last amendments'. See pp. 87, 99.
Brotherton Collection Lt q 55, ff. 1r-2r, 'To give the last amendments'. See p. 98.

Limerick University Library

Moyaliffe Papers P6/2035, 'To give the last amendments'.

Longleat House, Wiltshire

PO/vol. XI, f. 36, 'The great Sir George'.

National Library of Scotland, Edinburgh

2092, f. 18v, 'Good people what will you'. See p. 75.
3807, p. 286, 'The great Sir George'.

Nottingham University Library

Portland Pw V 41, pp. 111–13 and 137–38, 'To give the last amendments' (two copies). See p. 100 n. 17.
Portland Pw V 43, pp. 462–63, 'Accept my Lord'. See p. 100 n. 5.

Portland Pw V 44, pp. 282–86, 'Your primitive players'; pp. 432–33, 'The great Sir George'. See pp. 46, 99 n. 1.

Portland Pw V 48 pp. 186–87, 'Great William concerned'. See p. 92 n. 47.

Portland Pw V 171 verso, 'Here lie the relics'.

Portland Pw V 249, ff. 1r-2r, 'First then we must confess'. See p. 47.

Portland Pw V 856, ff. av-br, 'First then we must confess'. See p. 47.

Trinity College, Dublin

879/1, f. 93r, 'To get false fame'; f. 103v, 'When Church was mother'; 879/3, f. 4r, 'Now love and war'; f. 165v, 'Out of the deep'. See pp. 44, 57–58, 59 n. 6, 100 n. 13.

Worcestershire Archive and Archaeology Service, Worcester

Lechmere Archives 40 (i), p. 3, 'When I your charms'; p. 4, 'A most ungodly work'; p. 10, 'Since in the last sessions' and 'Accept my Lord'; pp. 14–15, 'Must Sylvia then'. See pp. 46–47, 63, 66, 95, 107 n. 1.

Literary manuscripts (American repositories)

Chicago University Library, IL

PR1195.M73, p. 141, 'The great Sir George'.

Folger Shakespeare Library, Washington, DC

M.b.12, p. 304, 'The great Sir George'; part 3, ff. 211r-12v, 'Your primitive players'. See pp. 46, 99 n. 1.

Harvard University Library, Cambridge, MA

Eng 606, f. 38r, 'When Church was mother'; f. 29r, 'The great Sir George'. See p. 100 n. 13.

Eng 834, folder 3, 'Accept my Lord'.

Huntington Library, San Marino, CA

EL 8911, 'Hail happy William'.

Minnesota University Library, Minneapolis, MN

690235f, p. 96, 'Here lie the relics'; pp. 101–02, 'With Job-like patience'; p. 106, 'Cease hypocrites'; p. 106, 'Hail happy William'; p. 107, 'Our government thrifty' (beginning 'The parliament thrifty'); p. 108, 'Great William concerned' (beginning 'King William concern'd'); p. 108, 'When Catesby and Faux'; pp. 131–32, 'Are all those lights'; p. 132, 'Ne're blame the hero'; p. 132, 'Six tedious months'; pp. 141–42, 'To our monarch's return'; p. 161, 'Good people what will you'; p. 181, ''Twill puzzle much' (beginning 'The author sure must take great pains'); p. 182, 'Rejoice ye fops' (beginning 'Rejoice ye sots'); p. 208, 'For missing thee'; p. 209, 'No sooner our hero'; p. 210, 'Now love and war'; pp. 210–11, ''Tis odd indeed' (beginning 'Its odd indeed'); pp. 211–12, 'Dunned by the bells' (beginning 'Dup'd by the bells'). See pp. 41–42, 46, 72–74, 78–89, 90 nn. 8 & 15, 91 nn. 25 & 31, 92 n. 49, 108 n. 6, 140–43.

Princeton University Library, NJ

RTC01 no. 38 (Robert Taylor Collection, Restoration poetry 5), p. 103, 'Here lie the relics'; p. 160, 'Good people what will you'; p. 162, 'Hail happy William'; pp. 182–83, 'What fast for horrid murder'; pp. 292–94, 'To give the last amendments'. See pp. 68, 81, 87, 90 n. 22, 100 n. 17, 101 n. 22.

Yale University Library, New Haven, CT

Osborn b.90, p. 1, 'When Church was mother'. See p. 100 n. 13.
Osborn b.111, p. 36, 'To our monarch's return'; p. 304, ''Twill puzzle much' (beginning 'The author sure must take great pains'). See pp. 46, 81, 91 nn. 25 & 45.
Osborn b.201, p. 101, 179. 'Accept my Lord' (two copies).
Osborn b.204, p. 30, 'To give the last amendments'. See p. 100 n. 17.
Osborn c.111, p. 26, 'To give the last amendments'; p. 59, 'Accept my Lord'; p. 89, 'The great Sir George'. See pp. 99, 100 n. 17.
Osborn c.171, p. 9, 'Here lie the relics'.
Osborn c.189, p. 150, 'To give the last amendments'. See p. 100 n. 18.
Osborn c.233, p. 87, 'To get false fame' (beginning 'To gain dishonour and immense disgrace'); p. 99, 'In vain my fair you strive' (beginning 'Madam in vain you strive') and 'Whilst this bumper'. See pp. 44, 68, 68.
Osborn c.555, p. 358, 'Come beaus virtuosos'.
Osborn c.570/1, p. 3, 'Rejoice ye fops'; p. 52, 'What fast for horrid murder'; c.570/2, p. 131, 'Whither ye impious Britons'. See pp. 80–82, 90 n. 22, 91 n. 44, 149–51.
Osborn fb.207/1, p. 49, 'Here lie the relics'; fb.207/3, p. 9, 'Whither ye impious Britons'; p. 10, 'Good people what will you'; p. 12, 'Hail happy William'. See pp. 80, 85, 87, 91 n. 43, 149–51.
Osborn Poetry Box VII/5, 'Good people what will you'. See p. 75.
Osborn Poetry Box XIII/8c, 'Good people what will you'. See p. 75.

Music manuscripts (British repositories)

British Library, London

Add 31453, ff. 169v–70r, 'Enchanted by your voice'; f. 181r, 'While Galathea you design'. See p. 64.
Add 33234, f. 46r–v, 'All the follies of love'; ff. 129v–32r, 'Haste Charon haste'. See p. 67.

Bodleian Library, Oxford

Mus. d.246, ff. 3v–4v, 'While Galathea you design'. See p. 71 n. 13.

Tenbury 1232, ff. 11r-15v, 'Yes my Aminta'. See pp. 62, 107 n. 1.

Christ Church, Oxford

Mus. 49, pp. 133–40, 'Haste Charon haste'.
Mus. 389, pp. 61–60 (inverted), 'Haste Charon haste'.
Mus. 1141a, f. 47, Mus. 1142a, ff. 34–37, and Mus. 1212(A), ff. 1r-5v (three
    fragmentary autograph scores previously a single whole), 'Bless Albion bless'.
    See pp. 61–62.
Mus. 1212(B), ff. 1r-8r, 'Yes my Aminta' (autograph score). See pp. 61–62.
Mus. 1219(F), ff. 1v-2r, 'To our arms on earth and seas'. See pp. 56, 59.

Durham Cathedral Library

Bamburgh M193/1: 39, 'Oil and vinegar'. See p. 67.

Fitzwilliam Museum, Cambridge

Mu. 120, pp. 103–09, 'Haste Charon haste'; p. 318, 'Oil and vinegar'; p. 321, 'Tom
    making a manteau'. See pp. 65, 67.

York Minster Library

M.12 S, pp. 56–57, 'Come all ye high churchmen'; pp. 117–19, 'Haste Charon haste'
    (chorus only); p. 121, 'As sharper when his coin grows low'; p. 122, 'Thus while
    the eight'. See pp. 65–66.

Music manuscripts (American repositories)

Chicago University Library, IL

446, ff. 3v-5r, 'Haste Charon haste'.

Folger Shakespeare Library, Washington, DC

V.b.197, pp. 3–9, 'Haste Charon haste'.

William Andrews Clark Memorial Library, UCLA, Los Angeles, CA

fo235M4, pp. 10–18, 'Haste Charon haste'.
M1579P98.1720, p. 18, 'Thus while the eight'. See p. 71 n. 18.

APPENDIX D

❖

Printed Witnesses of Poems and Songs Attributable to Henry Hall

As in Appendix C, I employ shortened versions of the first lines of poems and songs, and as elsewhere in this study, I do not cite printings later than 1721. If not otherwise stated, the place of publication can be taken to be London. Full bibliographical details may be found in *ESTC*. I do not generally cite reissues that have the same title as the original printing.

Without music

1689   *The Theatre of Complements* (1689), p. 152, 'From a due dose of claret'.

1694   *Gentleman's Journal; or, The Monthly Miscellany*, January-February 1694, p. 28, 'Out of the deep'; March 1694, p. 64, 'Although for every different dress'; May 1694, p. 131, 'I never did eat'; pp. 140–42, 'All own the young Sylvia'; June 1694, pp. 179–80, 'I love to madness'; July 1694, p. 188, 'As Phoebus did with heat'; p. 206, 'Like two sage sisters'; August 1694, p. 220, 'We neither are Christians'; October 1694, p. 263, 'Too roughly Sir you paint'.

1697   *Wit and Eloquence, or the Accomplish'd Secretary's Vade Mecum* (1697), pp. 155–56, 'I love to madness'; p. 179, 'All own the young Sylvia'.

1698   *Orpheus Britannicus: A Collection of All the Choicest Songs for One, Two and Three Voices, Compos'd by Mr. Henry Purcell* (1698), p. vi, 'Music the chiefest good'.

1700   John Blow, *Amphion Anglicus: A Work of Many Compositions for One, Two, Three and Four Voices* (1700), p. ii, 'A public good'.
        Luctus Britannici, or the Tears of the British Muses for the Death of John Dryden Esq (1700), pp. 16–20, 'Greece had a Homer'.

1702   *Orpheus Britannicus: A Collection of the Choicest Songs for One, Two and Three Voices, Compos'd by Mr. Henry Purcell* [...] *The Second Part* (1702), p. ii, 'Next to the man'.

1703   *POAS*, II (1703), p. 264, 'Good people what will you'; p. 267, 'What fast for horrid murder'; p. 321, 'Here lie the relics'; pp. 322–23, 'Whither ye impious Britons'; pp. 401–02, 'Hail happy William'.

1704   *Diverting Post*, no. 2 (28 October-4 November 1704), p. 2, 'To our arms on earth and seas'; no. 3 (4–11 November 1704), p. 1, 'From the bright mansions'; p. 2, 'Lucinda has the de'l'; no. 7 (2–9 December 1704), pp.

1–2, 'An honest good farmer' (but beginning 'A good honest farmer'); p. 2, 'Since the town is our own'; no. 9 (16 December 1704), p. 2, 'To Phyllis fools'.

Et tu Brute? or, the M — 'd C — l (1704), 'To give the last amendments' (Foxon E479).

Miscellaneous Works Written by His Grace George Late Duke of Buckingham [...] Also State Poems on the Late Times by Mr Dryden [...], I (1704), pp. 84–85, 'Hail happy William'.

The M — 'd C — b: or the L — th consultation. Et tu Brute? [...] *From a correct copy* (1704), 'To give the last amendments' (expanded text, Foxon E480–81).

POAS, III (1704), p. 342, ''Twill puzzle much'; pp. 392–95, 'To give the last amendments'.

1705 Defoe, Daniel, ed., *The Review*, 21 July 1705, p. 239, 'When Church was mother' (first two lines).

Diverting Post, no. 12 (6–13 January 1704, i.e. 1705), p. 2, 'In vain my fair you strive' and 'We heard indeed'; no. 13 (13–20 January 1704, i.e. 1705), p. 2, 'Now love and war'; no. 20 (3–10 March 1705), p. 1, 'The jovial crew' and 'To get false fame'; no. 21 (10–17 March 1705), p. 1, 'Phyllis in vain'; no. 23 (24–31 March 1705), p. 1, 'Once in a reign'; p. 2, 'Hark to the war'.

1706 Defoe, Daniel, *Jure Divino: A Satyr* (1706), p. 262 n (Book XI), 'When Church was mother'.

Deliciae Poeticae; or, Parnassus Display'd (1706), pp. 80–82, 'Haste Charon haste' (reissued as *Mirth Diverts All Care; Being Excellent New Songs Compos'd by the Most Celebrated Wits of the Age* [...], 1709).

Diverting Post, n.s. no. 1 (February 1706), p. 1, 'As man in Westminster'.

'A new song, set by Mr D. Purcell' ('To our arms on earth and seas'). printed on the verso of the single-sheet *A New Ode, Being a Congratulatory Poem on the Glorious Successes of Her Majesty's Arms* [...] *Set to Musick by Mr. Jer. Clark* (1706; ESTC N2304, Foxon N162).

1707 *The Miscellaneous Works of the Right Honourable the Late Earls of Rochester and Roscommon*, II (1707), pp. 84–87, 'Haste Charon haste'.

POAS, IV (1707), p. 17, 'Accept my lord' and 'When Church was mother'; p. 113, 'The great Sir George'.

1708 *Oxford and Cambridge Miscellany Poems* ([1708]), p. 194, 'Enchanted by your voice'; pp. 325–27, 'Come beaus virtuosos'.

1712 Edward Ward, *Miscellaneous Writings in Verse and Prose Both Serious and Comical*, 2nd edn, III (1712), pp. 326–27, 'Good people what will you'.

1714 *Political Merriment, or Truths Told to Some Tune* (1714), pt 2, pp. 45–47, 'All in the land of cider'.

1715 *A New Academy of Complements, or The Lover's Secratary* [sic] (1715), p. 124, 'Dragoons have a care'; pp. 132–32, 'How happy's the mortal'.

A New Collection of Miscellany Poems (1715), pt 1, pp. 29–32, 'All in the land of cider'.

1720 *Wit and Mirth; or, Pills to Purge Melancholy*, VI (1719–20), p. 261, 'All own the young Sylvia'; p. 285, 'I love to madness'.

The Remains of Mr Thomas Brown, Serious and Comical, in Prose and Verse (1720), pp. 73–74, 'Good people what will you' (also issued as *The Works of Mr Thomas Brown*, V, 1721).

A True and Faithful Narrative of Oliver Cromwell's Compact with the Devil for Seven Years (1720) [*ESTC* T135445], pp. 26–28, 'Haste Charon haste'.

1721   *The Grove* (1721), pp. 53–55, 'If rhyme for rhino'; pp. 95–96, 'Lucinda has the de'l'; pp. 98–101, 'All in the land of cider'; p. 126, 'Whilst this bumper'.

A Miscellaneous Collection of Poems, Songs and Epigrams (Dublin, 1721), I, pp. 53–54, 'Lucinda has the de'l'; p. 126, 'Come beaus virtuosos' (beginning 'All ye beaux'); II, p. 226, 'Now love and war'.

With music

1685   *The Theater of Music* [...] *The Second Book* (1685), pp. 47–51, 'Haste Charon haste' (reissued as *The New Treasury of Music*, 1695).

1688   *Comes Amoris; or, The Companion of Love* [...] *The Second Book* (1688), pp. 22–23, 'From a due dose of claret'.

1691   *Vinculum Societatis, or, The Tie of Good Company* [...] *The Third Book* (1691), p. 5, 'In vain I strive'.

1693   *Gentleman's Journal; or, The Monthly Miscellany*, November 1693, pp. 388–90, 'While Galathea you design'.

1694   *Thesaurus Musicus* [...] *The Second Book* (1694), pp. 4–5, 'Enchanted by your voice'; pp. 11–13, 'In vain my fair Sylvia'; p. 14, 'While Galathea you design'.

1695   *Deliciae Musicae* [...] *The Second Book* (1695), pp. 7–9, 'As Phoebus did with heat'.

1699   *Mercurius Musicus; or, The Monthly Collection of New Teaching Songs*, January 1699, pp. 8–9, 'Charming fair Amoret'; August 1699, pp. 171–72, 'While Galathea you design'.

Wit and Mirth; or, Pills to Purge Melancholy (1699), p. 64, 'How happy's the mortal'.

1700   *Mercurius Musicus; or, The Monthly Collection of New Teaching Songs*, March and April, 1700, pp. 14–17, 'Sing what shall we sing'; August 1700, pp. 50–51, 'Should a legion of cares'; p. 59, 'Lucinda has the de'l'.

1702   *Supplement of New Catches to the Second Book of the Pleasant Musical Companion* (1702), no. 10, 'Tom making a manteau'.

1703   *A Collection of the Choicest Songs and Dialogues Composed by the Most Eminent Masters of the Age* (a bespoke collection, 1703), song 105, 'In vain I strive'; song 276, 'While Galathea you design'; and song 310, 'Charming fair Amoret', as listed in Hunter, 5, pp. 14, 17, 18, the latter two songs recorded only in the BL copy G. 151 and the Library of Congress copy M1620.C7 Case, respectively.

1704   *Monthly Mask of Vocal Music*, March 1704 (unpaginated), 'Come take of your liquor'.

1706   *Monthly Mask of Vocal Music*, September 1706 (unpaginated), 'So glorious a victory'; October 1706 (unpaginated), 'As sharper when his coin'.

Wit and Mirth; or, Pills to Purge Melancholy, IV (1706), pp. 30–32, 'Come beaus virtuosos'.

1707   *The Second Book of the Pleasant Musical Companion*, 5th edn (1707), no. 110, 'Tom making a manteau'; no. 113, 'Dragoons have a care'; no. 118, 'Come all ye high churchmen' (reissued as *The Pleasant Musical Companion*, 5th edn, 1709).

      Monthly Mask of Vocal Music, February 1707 (unpaginated), 'Thus while the eight'.

1709   *The Jovial Companions, or Merry Club* ([1709]), item 14, 'Come take of your liquor'; item 31, 'Tom making a manteau'; item 64, 'Thus while the eight'.

1710   [*Collection of catches*] (1710; Hunter 73), 'Tom making a manteau'.

      Monthly Mask of Vocal Music, August 1710 (unpaginated), 'When I your charms'.

1711   *Catches for Flutes, or A Collection of the Best Catches* (1711), 'Tom making a manteau'.

1714   *Wit and Mirth; or, Pills to Purge Melancholy*, V (1714), pp. 94–95, 'Lucinda has the de'l'.

1716   *The Merry Musician; or, A Cure for the Spleen*, pt 1 (1716), pp. 275–76, 'All in the land of cider'.

1719   *Wit and Mirth; or, Pills to Purge Melancholy* (1719–20), III, pp. 124–25, 'How happy's the mortal'; v, 264–66, 'Come beaus virtuosos'.

1720   *The Pleasant Musical Companion*, 6th edn (1720), p. 49, 'Come all ye high churchmen'; p. 80, 'Tom making a manteau'; pp. 82–83, 'Dragoons have a care'; p. 92, 'Oil and vinegar'.

Undated single-sheet songs, with music

British Library, G.304.(78.), 1700?, 'In vain I strive'.

British Library, G.316.m.(18.), 'As sharper when his coin'.

British Library. G.316.o.(5.), 'So glorious a victory'.

British Library, H.1601.(214.), 1710?, 'How happy's the mortal'.

Bodleian Library, Harding Mus. E. 118 (84), c. 1703, 'In vain I strive'.

Bodleian Library, Harding Mus. G.234 (8), c. 1700, 'How happy's the mortal'.

Bodleian Library, Harding Mus. G.411 (9), 'Tom making a manteau', an extract from [*Collection of catches*] (London, 1710; Hunter 73).

Bodleian Library, Harding Mus. G.435 (9), 'When I your charms'.

Hereford Public Library, Pilley Collection, 2314, 'Come take of your liquor', 'So glorious a victory', and 'Thus while the eight'.

BIBLIOGRAPHY

❖

This Bibliography excludes all manuscripts and (with some exceptions) all contemporary printed works containing poems or songs attributable to Henry Hall. These are instead listed in full in Appendices C and D.

Manuscript Sources

Exeter, Exeter Cathedral Library

D&C 3560, Chapter Act Book, Oct 1667-Jun 1677
D&C 3561, Chapter Act Book, Jun 1677-Mar 1685
Vicars Choral, VC 1

Hereford, Hereford Cathedral Library

HCA 3396, Vicars Choral, Visitations. Answers of the Vicars Choral to the questions of the Dean and Chapter at a visitation, 30 Oct 1694
HCA 3934/5 and 3936/3, Dean and Chapter Property, Leases, 1699, 1700
HCA 7002/2/7, Dean's Peculiar Marriage Bonds, 1683–99
HCA 7003/1/3, Act Books of the Vicars Choral, Act Book 'B', 1 Sept 1660–20 Sept 1717
HCA 7003/4/3, William Cooke, 'Biographical Memoirs of the Custos and Vicars Admitted into the College of Hereford from 1660 to 1823', mid-19th century
HCA 7031/3, Chapter Act Books, 20 Jan 1600/01–10 Feb 1712/13
HCA D858/1/2, Baptisms, Marriages and Burials in the Parish of St John the Baptist, 1687–1727
HCA D859/1/1, Registers of Marriages in the Cathedral, 1686–1727

Hereford, Herefordshire Archive Service

BG11/17/5/80 and BG11/17/5/86, Hereford City Records, Miscellaneous Papers, 1651–1847
HD5/2 and HD5/4, Hereford Diocesan Call Books
Q/RD/14/12, Herefordshire County Quarter Sessions Records, Deposited Deeds

Leeds, Leeds University Library, Brotherton Collection

MS Lt q 5, prose memoir of Henry Hall kept with the manuscript collection of Hall's poems

Oxford, Bodleian Library

MS Wood D.19(4)

Printed and Electronic Sources

A Miscellaneous Collection of Poems, Songs and Epigrams, 2 vols (Dublin: [for T. M. Gent], 1721)
A Tryal of Skill; or, A New Session of the Poets (London, 1704)
ASHBEE, ANDREW, ed., *Records of English Court Music*, 9 vols (Snodland, Kent: Andrew Ashbee, 1986–96)

ASHBEE, ANDREW, and others, *A Biographical Dictionary of English Court Musicians, 1485–1714*, 2 vols (Aldershot: Ashgate, 1998)

AYLMER, G. E., 'Duncombe, Sir Charles (bap. 1648, d. 1711), Financier', in *Oxford Dictionary of National Biography*

BALDWIN, OLIVE, and THELMA WILSON, eds, *The Monthly Mask of Vocal Music, 1702–1711: A Facsimile Edition* (Aldershot: Ashgate, 2007)

BARRETT, PHILIP, 'The College of Vicars Choral', in *Hereford Cathedral: A History*, ed. by Gerald Aylmer and John Tiller (London: Hambledon, 2000), pp. 441–60

BEAL, PETER, 'Poems by Sir Philip Sidney: The Ottley Manuscript', *The Library*, 5th series, 33 (1978), 284–95

BEEKS, GRAYDON, 'Rawlings [Rawlins], Thomas (c. 1703–1767), Musician and Music Copyist', *Oxford Dictionary of National Biography*

BLOW, JOHN, *Amphion Anglicus: A Work of Many Compositions for One, Two, Three and Four Voices* (London: printed by William Pearson for the author, 1700)

BODEN, ANTHONY, 'The Three Choirs Festival', in *Hereford Cathedral: A History*, ed. by Gerald Aylmer and John Tiller (London: Hambledon Press, 2000), pp. 461–69

BODEN, ANTHONY, and PAUL HEDLEY, *The Three Choirs Festival: A History*, 2nd edn (Woodbridge: Boydell Press, 2017)

BOND, SHELAGH, ed., *The First Hall Book of the Borough of New Windsor*, Windsor Borough Historical Records Publications, 1 (Windsor: The Royal Borough of New Windsor, 1968)

British Library online manuscripts catalogue <https://searcharchives.bl.uk>

Brotherton Collection Manuscript Verse database <https://library.leeds.ac.uk/special-collections-manuscript-verse>

BUCKINGHAM, GEORGE VILLIERS, DUKE OF, *Miscellaneous Works Written by His Grace George Late Duke of Buckingham*, 2 vols (London, 1704–05)

——*Plays, Poems and Miscellaneous Writings Associated with George Villiers, Second Duke of Buckingham*, ed. by Robert D. Hume and Harold Love, 2 vols (Oxford: Oxford University Press, 2007)

BURKE, JOHN, *A Genealogical and Heraldic History of the Commoners of Great Britain and Ireland*, 4 vols (London: Bentley, 1836–38)

CAMERON, W. J., 'A Late Seventeenth-Century Scriptorium', *Renaissance and Modern Studies*, 7 (1963), 23–52

CAMERON, W. J., ed., *Poems on Affairs of State: Augustan Satirical Verse, 1660–1714*. V: *1688–1697* (New Haven, CT: Yale University Press, 1971)

Catalogue of English Literary Manuscripts, 1450–1700 <https://celm-ms.org.uk>

CHEVILL, ELIZABETH, 'Clergy, Music Societies and the Development of a Musical Tradition: A Study of Music Societies in Hereford, 1690–1760', in *Concert Life in Eighteenth-Century Britain*, ed. by Susan Wollenberg and Simon McVeigh (Aldershot: Ashgate, 2004), pp. 35–54

Clergy of the Church of England Database <https://theclergydatabase.org.uk/>

CONNOR, HENRY, 'Mistress Joyce Jeffreys and her Physician, Dr Bridstock Harford (1607–1695)', *Journal of Medical Biography*, 24 (2014), 545–50

COOPER, BARRY, 'Keyboard Sources in Hereford', *RMA Research Chronicle*, 16 (1980), 135–39

COOPER, THOMPSON, rev. MARY CLAPINSON, 'Parry, William (bap. 1687, d. 1756), Antiquary', in *Oxford Dictionary of National Biography*

CORLEY, T. A. B., 'Saffold, Thomas (bap. 1620?, d. 1691), Astrologer and Nostrum Seller', in *Oxford Dictionary of National Biography*

COWLEY, ABRAHAM, *Poems: Miscellanies, the Mistress, Pindarique Odes, Davideis, Poems Written on Several Occasions*, ed. by A. R. Waller (Cambridge: Cambridge University Press, 1905)

COX, THOMAS, *Magna Britannia Antiqua et Nova: or, a New, Exact, and Comprehensive Survey of the Ancient and Present State of Great-Britain*, 6 vols (London: Caesar Ward and Richard Chandler, 1738)

CRUICKSHANKS, EVELINE, STUART HANDLEY, and D. W. HAYTON, eds, *The House of Commons, 1690–1715*, 5 vols (Cambridge: Cambridge University Press, 2002)

CUNNINGHAM, ROBERT, *Peter Anthony Motteux, 1663–1718: A Biographical and Critical Study* (Oxford: Blackwell, 1933)

DANCHIN, PIERRE, ed., *The Prologues and Epilogues of the Restoration, 1660–1700: A Complete Edition*, 4 vols (Nancy: Presses universitaires de Nancy, 1981–88)

DAVIES, J. D., 'Ottley, Adam (bap. 1655, d. 1723), Bishop of St David's', *Oxford Dictionary of National Biography*

DAY, CYRUS LAWRENCE, and ELEANORE BOSWELL MURRIE, *English Song-Books, 1651–1702: A Bibliography with a First-line Index of Songs* (London: Bibliographical Society, 1940)

——'English Song Books, 1651–1702, and their Publishers', *The Library*, 4th series, 16 (1936), 355–401

DEFOE, DANIEL, *Jure Divino. A Satyr in Twelve Books* (London, 1706)

Deliciae Musicae [...] The Second Book (London: Henry Playford, 1695)

Dictionary of Welsh Biography <https://biography.wales/>

Digital Miscellanies Index <https://dmi.bodleian.ox.ac.uk/>

DUNCUMB, JOHN, *Collections towards the History and Antiquities of the County of Hereford*, 2 vols (Hereford: E. G. Wright and others, 1804–12)

ELLIS, FRANK H., ed., *Poems on Affairs of State: Augustan Satirical Verse, 1660–1714*. VI: *1697–1704* (New Haven, CT: Yale University Press, 1970)

——*Poems on Affairs of State: Augustan Satirical Verse, 1660–1714*. VII: *1704–1714* (New Haven, CT: Yale University Press, 1975)

English Short-Title Catalogue <estc.bl.uk>

EZELL, MARGARET J. M., 'The *Gentleman's Journal* and the Commercialization of Restoration Coterie Literary Practices', *Modern Philology*, 89 (1992), 323–40

——*Social Authorship and the Advent of Print* (Baltimore, MD: John Hopkins University Press, 1999)

FOSTER, JOSEPH, *Alumni Oxonienses: The Members of the University of Oxford, 1500–1714*, 4 vols (Oxford: Parker, 1891–92)

FOWLER, ALASTAIR, ed., *The New Oxford Book of Seventeenth Century Verse* (Oxford: Oxford University Press, 1991)

FOXON, DAVID F., *English Verse, 1701–1750: A Catalogue of Separately Published Poems, with Notes on Contemporary Collected Editions*, 2 vols (London: Cambridge University Press, 1975)

——*Libertine Literature in England, 1660–1745* (New York: University Books, 1965)

GRANGER, JAMES, *A Biographical History of England*, 5th edn, 6 vols (London: Baynes, 1824)

GRIFFIN, DUSTIN, 'The Social World of Authorship, 1660–1714', in *The Cambridge History of English Literature, 1660–1780*, ed. by John Richetti (Cambridge: Cambridge University Press, 2005), pp. 37–60

The Grove: A Collection of Original Poems, Translations, etc. (London: for W. Mears, 1721)

GRUBB, JOHN, *The British Heroes: or, A New Ballad in Honour of St George* (London: John Morphew, 1707)

GUTHRIE, NEIL, *The Material Culture of the Jacobites* (Cambridge: Cambridge University Press, 2013)

GWYN, WILLIAM B., 'Cruel Nero: The Concept of the Tyrant and the Image of Nero in Western Political Thought', *History of Political Thought*, 12 (1991), 421–55

HAGEMAN, ELIZABETH H., and ANDREA SUNUNU, 'New Manuscript Texts of Katherine Philips, the "Matchless Orinda"', *English Manuscript Studies*, 4 (1993), 174–219

HALL, HENRY, *A Dialogue on the Death of Henry Purcell*, ed. by Peter Holman (Richmond: Green Man Press, 2008)

HAMMOND, PAUL, 'Anonymity in Restoration Poetry', in his *The Making of Restoration Poetry* (Cambridge: Brewer, 2006), pp. 49–72

HANHAM, A. A., 'Howe [How], John Grobham [Jack] (1657–1722), Politician', in *Oxford Dictionary of National Biography*

HAVERGAL, F. T., *Monumental Inscriptions in the Cathedral Church of Hereford* (Hereford: Simpkin, Marshall, 1881)

HAWKINS, SIR JOHN, *A General History of the Science and Practice of Music*, 5 vols (London: for T. Payne & Son, 1776)

HEARNE, THOMAS, *Remarks and Collections of Thomas Hearne*, ed. by C. E. Doble and others, 11 vols (Oxford: Oxford Historical Society, 1885–1921)

HERISSONE, REBECCA, *Musical Creativity in Restoration England* (Cambridge: Cambridge University Press, 2013)

HIGHFILL, PHILIP H. JNR, KALMAN A. BURNIM, and EDWARD A. LANGHANS, *A Biographical Dictionary of Actors, Actresses, Musicians, Dancers, Managers, and Other Stage Personnel in London, 1660–1800*, 16 vols (Carbondale: Southern Illinois University Press, 1973–93)

HOPKINS, DAVID, 'Motteux, Peter Anthony [formerly Pierre-Antoine Le Motteux] (1663–1718), Journalist and Translator', in *Oxford Dictionary of National Biography*

HORN, ROBERT D., *Marlborough, a Survey: Panegyrics, Satires, and Biographical Writings, 1688–1788* (New York: Garland, 1975)

HOWARD, ALAN, ed., *Odes on the Death of Henry Purcell*, Purcell Society Edition, Companion Series, 5 (London: Stainer & Bell, 2013)

HUNT, R. W., and others, eds, *A Summary Catalogue of Western Manuscripts in the Bodleian Library at Oxford*, 7 vols (Oxford: Clarendon Press, 1895–1953)

HUNTER, DAVID, *Opera and Song Books Published in England, 1703–1726: A Descriptive Bibliography* (London: Bibliographical Society, 1997)

—— 'The Publishing of Opera and Song Books in England, 1703–1726', *Notes*, 2nd series, 47 (1991), 647–85

HUSBANDS, JOHN, ed., *A Miscellany of Poems by Several Hands* (Oxford, 1731)

ILES, PAUL, 'Music and Liturgy since 1600', in *Hereford Cathedral: A History*, ed. by Gerald Aylmer and John Tiller (London: Hambledon Press, 2000), pp. 398–440

JAGGER, NICHOLAS, 'Kenrick, Daniel (b. 1649/50), Poet and Physician', in *Oxford Dictionary of National Biography*

JONES, E. D., 'The Ottley Papers', *National Library of Wales Journal*, 4 (1945–46), 61–74

KEARNEY, PATRICK J., *A History of Erotic Literature* (London: Macmillan, 1982)

KENRICK, DANIEL, *A New Session of the Poets, Occasion'd by the Death of Mr Dryden* (London, 1700)

—— *A Sermon Preached in the Cathedral-Church of Worcester, at the Lent Assize, April 7th, 1688* (London: David Mallet, 1688)

KNIGHT, CHARLES A., *A Political Biography of Richard Steele* (London: Pickering & Chatto, 2009)

Literary Manuscripts: 17th and 18th Century Poetry from the Brotherton Library, University of Leeds <www.literarymanuscriptsleeds.amdigital.co.uk>

The Literary Works of Matthew Prior, ed. by Bunker H. Wright and Monroe K. Spears, 2nd edn, 2 vols (Oxford: Clarendon Press, 1971)

LORD, GEORGE DEFOREST, and others, eds, *Poems on Affairs of State: Augustan Satirical Verse, 1660–1714*, 7 vols (New Haven, CT: Yale University Press, 1963–75)

LORD, GEORGE DEFOREST, ed., *Poems on Affairs of State: Augustan Satirical Verse, 1660–1714*. 1: *1660–1678* (New Haven, CT: Yale University Press, 1963)

LOVE, HAROLD, *English Clandestine Satire, 1660–1702* (Oxford: Oxford University Press, 2004)

—— *Scribal Publication in Seventeenth-Century England* (Oxford: Clarendon Press, 1993)

LUCKETT, RICHARD, 'The Playfords and the Purcells', in *Music and the Book Trade from the Sixteenth to the Twentieth Century*, ed. by Robin Myers, Michael Harris, and Giles Mandelbrote (New Castle, DE, & London: British Library, 2008), pp. 45–67

MACDONALD, HUGH, *John Dryden: A Bibliography of Early Editions and of Drydeniana* (Oxford: Clarendon Press, 1939)

MAGGS BROS, *Shakespeare and Shakespeareana*, Catalogue no. 434 (London: Maggs Bros, 1923)

MILSOM, JOHN, *Christ Church Library Music Catalogue* <library.chch.ox.ac.uk/music/>

MONOD, PAUL KLÉBER, *Jacobitism and the English People, 1688–1788* (Cambridge: Cambridge University Press, 1989)

NEWSHOLME, DAVID, 'The Life and Works of William Davis (c. 1675/6–1745)', 3 vols (unpublished doctoral thesis, University of York, 2013)

Odes on the Death of Henry Purcell, The Parley of Instruments, dir. by Roy Goodman and Peter Holman (Hyperion Records, CDA66578, 1992)

OGG, DAVID, *England in the Reign of James II and William III* (London: Oxford University Press, 1955)

OGILBY, JOHN, *Aesopic's: A Second Collection of Fables Paraphras'd in Verse* (London: Thomas Roycroft, 1668)

OLDMIXON, JOHN, *Poems on Several Occasions* (London: for R. Parker, 1696)

Oxford Dictionary of National Biography <https://www.oxforddnb.com>

PALEY, RUTH, 'Justice and Sir John Fenwick', *King's Law Journal*, 19 (2015), 507–24

[PARRY, RICHARD], *The History of Kington, by a Member of the Mechanics' Institute of Kington* (Kington: Humphreys, 1845)

PERCY, THOMAS, ed., *Reliques of Ancient English Poetry*, 3rd edn, 3 vols (London: J. Dodsley, 1775)

Perdita Project database <https://web.warwick.ac.uk/english/perdita/html/>

PICKERING, OLIVER, 'Hall, Henry (c. 1656–1707), Musician and Poet', in *Oxford Dictionary of National Biography*

——'Henry Hall of Hereford and Henry Purcell: A Postscript', *The Library*, 7th series, 3 (2002), 194–98

——'Henry Hall of Hereford's Poetical Tributes to Henry Purcell', *The Library*, 6th series, 16 (1994), 18–29

The Poems and Fables of John Dryden, ed. by James Kinsley (London: Oxford University Press, 1962)

The Poems of John Oldham, ed. by Harold F. Brooks (Oxford: Clarendon Press, 1987)

The Poems of Sir George Etherege, ed. by James Thorpe (Princeton, NJ: Princeton University Press, 1963)

PRICE, JOHN, *An Historical Account of the City of Hereford* (London: D. Walker, 1796)

PURCELL, HENRY, *Catches*, ed by Ian Spink, in *The Works of Henry Purcell*, 22A (London: Novello, 2000)

——*Orpheus Britannicus: A Collection of All the Choicest Songs for One, Two and Three Voices, Compos'd by Mr. Henry Purcell* (London: for Henry Playford, 1698)

RAWLINSON, RICHARD, *The History and Antiquities of the City and Cathedral-Church of Hereford* (London: for R. Gosling, 1717)

RAY, JOHN, *A Collection of English Proverbs*, 2nd edn (London: John Hayes, 1678)

Répertoire international des sources musicales <https://rism.info>

ROSE, DIANA JULIA, 'MS Rawlinson Poetical 147: An Annotated Volume of Seventeenth-Century Cambridge Verse' (unpublished doctoral thesis, University of Leicester, 1992)

SADIE, STANLEY, and JOHN TYRRELL, eds, *The New Grove Dictionary of Music and Musicians*, 2nd edn, 29 vols (London: Macmillan, 2001)

SHAW, WATKINS, *The Succession of Organists of the Chapel Royal and the Cathedrals of England and Wales from c. 1538* (Oxford: Clarendon Press, 1991)

SHAWCROSS, JOHN T., 'A Note on Milton's Latin Translator', *Milton Quarterly*, 21 (1987), 65–66

SHOESMITH, RON, '"A Brave and Ancient Priviledg'd Place": The Hereford Vicars Choral College', in *Vicars Choral at English Cathedrals: 'Cantate Domino' — History, Architecture and Archaeology*, ed. by Richard Hall and David Stocker (Oxford: Oxbow, 2005), pp. 44–60

SOWERBY, SCOTT, *Making Toleration: The Repealers and the Glorious Revolution* (Cambridge, MA: Harvard University Press, 2013)

SPINK, IAN, 'Church Music II: From 1660', in *The Seventeenth Century*, ed. by Ian Spink, Blackwell History of Music in Britain, 3 (Oxford: Blackwell, 1992), pp. 97–137

——*Restoration Cathedral Music* (Oxford: Clarendon Press, 1995)

STOW, JOHN, *A Survey of the Cities of London and Westminster* (London: for A. Churchill and others, 1720)

STRICKLAND, AGNES, *Lives of the Queens of England from the Norman Conquest*, 6 vols (London: Bell, 1904)

THOMPSON, ROBERT, 'Playford, John (1621x23–1686/7), Music Publisher', in *Oxford Dictionary of National Biography*

TIGHE, R. R., and J. E. DAVIS, *Annals of Windsor, Being a History of the Castle and Town*, 2 vols (London: Longman, 1858)

TILLEY, MORRIS PALMER, *A Dictionary of the Proverbs in England in the Sixteenth and Seventeenth Centuries* (Ann Arbor: University of Michigan Press, 1950)

TOMLINSON, HOWARD, 'Restoration to Reform, 1660–1832', in *Hereford Cathedral: A History*, ed. by Gerald Aylmer and John Tiller (London: Hambledon, 2000), pp. 109–55

Union First Line Index of English Verse <https://firstlines.folger.edu/>

WALLIS, P. J. and R. V., *Eighteenth Century Medics (Subscriptions, Licences, Apprenticeships)*, 2nd edn (Newcastle upon Tyne: Project for Historical Bibliography, 1988)

WARREN, AMBROSE, *The Tonometer* ([Westminster], 1725)

WILSON, C. ANNE, *Food and Drink in Britain from the Stone Age to Recent Times* (London: Constable, 1973)

WOOD, BRUCE, 'Hall, Henry (i)', in *The New Grove Dictionary of Music and Musicians*, 2nd edn, ed. by Stanley Sadie and John Tyrrell, 29 vols (London: Macmillan, 2001), x

WRIGHT, GILLIAN, *Producing Women's Poetry, 1600–1730: Text and Paratext, Manuscript and Print* (Cambridge: Cambridge University Press, 2013)

Yale University Library online catalogue <https://orbis.library.yale.edu/vwebv/>

ZIMMERMAN, FRANKLIN B., *Henry Purcell, 1659–1695: His Life and Times*, 2nd edn (Philadelphia: University of Pennsylvania Press, 1983)

INDEX

❖

This index excludes references to Hall's own poems and songs,
for which see the Appendices.

Lightning Source UK Ltd.
Milton Keynes UK
UKHW030330200123
415647UK00004B/45